ICONS

WINDOWS ON ETERNITY

ICONS

WINDOWS ON ETERNITY

Theology and Spirituality in Colour

Compiled by Gennadios Limouris

WCC Publications, Geneva

Faith and Order Paper 147

Cover design: Rob Lucas

Cover illustration: Icon of the seventh ecumenical council,
  Russian tradition, 17th century

© 1990 WCC Publications, World Council of Churches,
150 route de Ferney, 1211 Geneva 2, Switzerland

Table of Contents

Introductory Note

GENNADIOS LIMOURIS

This publication, however belatedly, is being issued by the World Council of Churches to commemorate the 1200th anniversary of the Seventh Ecumenical Council in 1987. This Council affirmed the veneration of icons of Christ and the saints as an essential part of the Christian teaching and worship of the ancient Church. Theologians, historians, iconographers, artists, people of God from different traditions have contributed to this volume, and brought together here is a rich and wide variety of ideas and insights. The focus is on the background and theology of the Seventh Ecumenical Council and the meaning of icons for today.

There are areas of continuing controversy, but they are to be expected; they are less important than the value of the common work that has gone into this publication. Behind that is the conviction that we are celebrating a living reality.

Icons present theology, history, art and spirituality in colour, expressions, lines. They are a window on heaven and on eternity. Icons and other forms of art are instruments of prayer and, as such, as important as the preaching of the Word of God. All human beings are called to partake in this new reality. They are called to be "partakers of the divine nature" (2 Pet. 1:4). This is what is meant by the famous patristic adage from St Athanasius of Alexandria, so often quoted to indicate the nature of salvation: "God was made man (anthropos) so that we might be made God."[1] The implications of this new destiny offered to all who have "put on Christ" (Gal. 3:27) concern not only human beings, who are thus reinstated in their royal dignity and office, but also the whole of creation which is re-created in Christ and called to renewal and transfiguration through the deification of humanity. And this is a reality because God is love and the Godhead is a community of persons from all eternity, and we are called to be a communion of truth and love, a plurality of persons in perfect unity, united one with another and all with God through Jesus Christ in the Holy Spirit.

Thus icons, like liturgy, are meant to help us in our worship and prayer. Through the lines, forms, expressions and colours they announce the Good News of the Gospel and open new horizons for Christ's message to penetrate all parts of the world. This is precisely the missionary dimension of icon paintings. They are signs, tools, and they can help us in the ecumenical quest for the unity of the Church.

The book is divided into four sections. The first is the historical part in which we learn of the history and conflicts of the iconoclastic period and the decisions of the Seventh Ecumenical Council viewed from an ecumenical perspective, and of the final triumph of icons and their restoration in the Church. The second is the theological part, and goes into the meaning of icons and their theological significance as understood in the traditions of East and West. The third deals with the icons, spirituality, and the contribution of the iconographers. The last part presents living experiences, interviews and personal stories.

We are deeply grateful to all those who have contributed to this important book.

NOTES

[1] St Athanasius of Alexandria, *Oratio de Incarnatione Verbi* 54, in *PG* 25, 1926.
[2] St Theodore the Studite, *Antirreheticus*, III, 11, 5, in *PG* 99, 420A.

The Doctrine (Horos)
of the Veneration of Icons

As Formulated by the Seventh Ecumenical Council (787)

... We retain, without introducing anything new, all the ecclesiastical traditions, written and not written, which have been established for us. One of these is the representation of painted images being in accord with the story of the biblical preaching, because of the belief in the true and non-illusory Incarnation of God the Word, for our benefit. For things which presuppose each other are mutually revelatory.

Since this is the case, following the royal path and the teaching divinely inspired by our holy Fathers and the Tradition of the catholic church — for we know that it is inspired by the Holy Spirit who lives in it — we decide in all correctness and after a thorough examination, that, just as the holy and vivifying cross, similarly the holy and precious icons painted with colours, made with little stones or with any other matter serving this purpose, should be placed in the holy churches of God, on vessels and sacred vestments, on walls and boards, in houses and on roads, whether these are icons of our Lord God and Saviour, Jesus Christ, or our spotless Sovereign Lady, the holy Mother of God, or the holy angels and holy and venerable men. For each time that we see their representation in an image, each time while gazing upon them we are made to remember the prototypes, we grow to love them more, and we are even more induced to render them veneration of honour *(timetike proskynesis)* by kissing them and by witnessing our veneration, not the true worship *(alethiné latreia)* which, according to our faith, is proper only to the one divine nature, but in the same way as we venerate the image of the precious and vivifying cross, the holy Gospel and other sacred objects which we honour with incense and candles according to the pious custom of our forefathers. For the honour rendered to the image goes to its prototype, and the person who venerates an icon venerates the person represented on it. Indeed, such is the teaching of our holy Fathers and the Tradition of the holy catholic Church which propagated the Gospel from one end of the earth to the other. Thus, we follow Paul, who spoke in Christ, and the entire divine circle of Apostles and all the holy Fathers who upheld the traditions which we follow...

The Triumph of the Icons as Means of Dialogue and Sign of Unity

CHRYSOSTOMOS OF MYRA (Konstantinidis)

The year 1987 marked the 1200th anniversary of the Seventh Ecumenical Council of Nicea (A.D. 787) which was decisive for the restoration of the holy icons in the liturgical life of the Church. The occasion provided the opportunity for a reconsideration of some great moments in Christian history which have left their indelible mark on the uninterrupted Tradition of the Church. It was such moments that ensured the continuation of this Tradition, once for all delivered to the saints, in spite of the quarrels and divisions which threatened to subvert the history and life of the Church.

On 24 September 787 the Seventh Ecumenical Council, convened by the Empress Irene and Patriarch Tarasius, began its work at Nicea where the First Ecumenical Council had met in 325 in order to deal with the problem of Arianism. Nicea II was convened to deal with a new heresy, iconoclasm, which had been poisoning the life of the Church for more than half a century and had produced numerous martyrs, especially among the monks. What was called the quarrel over icons was rather a heroic fight in defence of the faith.

In order to defend the dogmatic legitimacy and liturgical use (including the veneration) of the holy icons, the Second Council of Nicea proclaimed, on 13 October 787, a decree which stated, among other things, "that the honour rendered to an icon is really directed to its prototype and consequently whoever venerates an icon actually venerates the person who is represented by it". The intention of the conciliar decision was to condemn iconoclasm, without laying itself open to its critics. Thus it drew a very precise distinction between the "veneration of worship", which is addressed only to God, and the "veneration of honour", which is rendered to the persons of the saints through their icons. It was in connection with the latter that the Council's decision reinforced the belief of the Church in the intercession of the saints and especially of the holy Virgin Theotokos, who regained the place of honour she had always occupied in the context of the Byzantine liturgy, prayer and piety.

Nicea II was important not only for the East but also for the entire Christian world, since it defended the Christian Tradition, establishing some of its fundamental principles. It should also be stressed that this Council, like all the Councils which were convened during the first period of the life of the Church both in East and West, whether local or ecumenical, was the principal means through which the Church set in motion in an effective and fruitful way the mechanism of dialogue. We usually regard the Councils from the point of view of their final dogmatic decisions and, therefore, see them primarily as meetings which settle the "terms" of the faith and condemn, or anathematize, those who deny them. The fact is, however, that the actual dogmatic results of each synod were reached because of certain presuppositions, or conditions, related to their convocation, which not only allowed but invited discussion between the different parties of the contestants. By providing the opportunity for long discussions of the issues that were raised, each of the Councils was able to accomplish its work in the framework of dialogue and openness. The fruit of such work, understood to have been ultimately due to the guidance of the Holy Spirit, was the formulation of the fundamental truths of the faith which consequently led to the condemnation of the errors and those who continued to promote them.

The historical data relating to Councils in general and to the Seventh Ecumenical Council in particular clearly reveal that the Council in the life of the Church was not just one of the means, but rather the principal means, for establishing the correct understanding of the Church against the heresies of the opponents. Seen in this perspective, the Seventh Ecumenical Council is an ideal model for all dialogues in the Church of Christ, seeking to gather Christians in the mystery of the Eucharist and thus lead them towards that ultimate mystery which is the one undivided Church of God.

In this light we can understand the special importance of the 1200th anniversary for the churches which are now engaged in bilateral and multilateral dialogues, seeking to discover the way towards the unity of the Gospel. This importance lies not only in the doctrine concerning the holy icons, with all its profound theological and spiritual meaning, but also in the fact that the churches are becoming aware that unity can only be achieved if they persist in the endeavour of rediscovering together "the road to Emmaus" of the Tradition, which is transmitted by Christ and finds its definition in the most significant phase of the history of the Church — the period of the Ecumenical Councils of the undivided Christendom.

We therefore have every reason to welcome warmly the publication of this book in honour of the holy icons, which is sponsored by the Faith and Order Commission of the World Council of Churches. It is of tremendous significance that the Christian churches of today are coming to understand more and more the importance of the conciliar period of undivided Christendom, when the Church, gathering strength from the decrees and decisions of its Councils and Synods, defended itself against the heresies and disputes which threatened the maintenance of the uninterrupted apostolic Tradition.

We rejoice in the participation of the World Council of Churches in the commemoration of the Seventh Ecumenical Council of Nicea II by publishing articles and witnesses by theologians, historians and iconographers which underline the importance of this Council and the profound spiritual and theological meaning of icons for today.

The Ecumenical Significance of Icons

EMILIO CASTRO and GENNADIOS LIMOURIS

Gennadios Limouris: In 1987 the Orthodox churches commemorated the 1200th anniversary of the Seventh Ecumenical Council. What does this event mean for the World Council of Churches and the ecumenical movement in general?

Emilio Castro: First, let me express the hope that this important historical event will be an occasion for celebration and commemoration, not only for the Orthodox churches but for all Christian churches. We belong to the same history and we share the same tradition. So while we remember the polemics about the icons in our internal, more limited confessional and denominational traditions, such an occasion as this anniversary gives us a chance to grow in reciprocal knowledge, to be aware of the power of history, to try together to interpret to each other the meaning of that Council, and so go beyond the polemics to a constructive aspect of the veneration of icons.

GL: What do you think this publication on the icon in ecumenical perspective could mean for Christians and churches today?

EC: I hope it will serve an educational purpose. This kind of specialized publication broadens the understanding of all our churches and helps the rank and file of the congregations to understand each other's spirituality. So the important thing about this book is that we will not only have access to a traditional type of spirituality, but also to new sources of spirituality for today. I would like to see this book open the door to a real dialogue about new icons. What is the contribution of artists today to the world of beauty and to the worship life of Christians and of the Church?

GL: What do you think of the statement that "the Church is an icon"?

EC: I understand that the Church could be considered as the historical representation of the family of faith, a foretaste of the Kingdom, an icon of the humanity to come. This is the challenge to the Church: to be that pure icon, to be such a Trinitarian community, such a community grounded in love, that it would be like an icon pointing beyond itself to the Trinity which is the centre of the Church's adoration. I would like to emphasize that the icon in itself has no pretensions. A good icon invites us, or obliges us, to forget it and to see the reality beyond. I think that that is the real sense in which the Church could become an icon of Jesus Christ — an icon of the Kingdom. Only if we do not claim anything for ourselves do we, like John the Baptist, point towards Christ.

4

GL: Together with other gifts and souvenirs in your office, there are icons which you have received on different occasions when visiting Orthodox churches. Do they convey any special meaning to you?

EC: As you say, these are gifts from friends and from churches, and I cherish the fact that they were given as signs and symbols of our common faith, of the common spirituality which we share. If I, as a Methodist, give you a book of sermons by John Wesley, you will read the sermons not only to learn something of John Wesley's insights, but also in remembrance of the bonds of friendship between us. It makes a lot of difference if I can remember that this icon comes from Constantinople and that one from Bucharest. Behind them are love and friendship, and also the spirituality and histories of faithfulness and suffering.

Secondly, these icons bring me into the total life of the universal Church. They remind me that my horizon as a Methodist and Protestant, rich as it is and thankful as I am for it, is not the whole life of the Church. So I am obliged to ponder on a common history, the common richness of Christianity. Finally, of course, these icons are there to point beyond themselves to the reality they want to mediate. They are visible reminders of the Gospel, of the history of God's love in Jesus Christ.

GL: Is an icon a "purely artistic" object for you or has it a liturgical element of worship and prayer?

EC: I cannot make the difference your question presupposes. Of course, if it is a purely artistic object it would not be an icon. An icon should be art in the service of piety, art under the discipline of the content of the message, under the discipline of the subject that cannot be limited in its representation but comes to us through that representation. But I do not like the supposed contradiction between artistic and liturgical elements because beauty also belongs to the worship of God. So I would not use the description "art for art's sake" in referring to the icon, but rather say for God's sake let us offer the best art that we are able to produce.

GL: When I said purely artistic, I meant in the secular sense, because today we find icons everywhere, even in beautiful drawing-rooms. People consider icons artistic. They buy expensive ones, without any spiritual or other considerations.

EC: And that has a value in itself. We are talking about the soul of the believer tuning in to the spirit of God and that could be the main vocation of whatever we call an icon in terms of our conversation. I suspect that real art always points beyond itself to something that is not under the control of the artist. So I hope that even modern art could become an icon for us and function as an icon, if it awakens our soul to the contemplation of the Lord.

GL: Would you say that icons are sacramental?

EC: That could be the right word to use — the icon has a sacramental function even if the Church has never declared the icon sacramental!

GL: What is the significance of icons for ecumenical gatherings and worship in our chapel here at the Ecumenical Centre?

EC: I think the polemics about the icons are the first consideration. I come from Latin America where our Protestant churches have found their own identity, as opposed to the prevailing Roman Catholic Church. Obviously there is a certain rejection of iconic or image representation of the life of Jesus and the Gospel. So it is good that in an ecumenical setting we have something that takes us a little beyond our own tradition. I also think that the Orthodox who come to the Ecumenical Centre and look at our chapel would be pleased to find a couple of icons there, but they would not feel entirely at home because the altar area is totally open. There is a symbolic arch to mark the separation, but there is no way of muting your liturgical prayers which need to be said in the mystery of the altar to preserve that mystery. That is a problem for those of the Orthodox tradition. In most cases, I think, this sort of thing is good because, while in no way denying my tradition, it invites me to open it up to other perspectives, to other possibilities. The first significance is that it reopens polemics in a constructive way.

The second meaning is to learn to respect the differences. I know that at the beginning I also wanted to say: "All right, if that helps my Orthodox friends, why not?" As if it were something that helps some people and not others. This is one step that is necessary in the ecumenical movement — to respect the spirituality of the other in their own symbols before I apply my own spirituality as the standard for all. But then we begin to dialogue and to correct each other, and you Orthodox have been repeatedly telling us that it is not worship of the image. Icon veneration has nothing to do with the prohibition in the Old Testament. This is offering the beauty and the insight of the artist's perception as a means, as a tool, a service to our souls in an attempt to go beyond the icon, to the source of the inspiration for the artist, to the source of all our spiritual life. And that is a necessary correction. And we will tell you, yes, but remember, in this or that place we see superstition, we see people who are worshipping this particular icon and have forgotten that it should be only an entry into the mystery of God. This reciprocal correction has a value in itself.

Finally, I think we are coming to the moment of inspiration through icons. I remember in particular the beautiful presentation that took place at the Sixth Assembly of the World Council in Vancouver of the Icon of the Trinity which was explained, as it was projected on a screen, so that people could understand its tremendous symbolism, its power to point to the mystery of God. In the ecumenical exercise we are reopening polemics, but also learning to respect the differences, correcting each other and growing together in faith.

GL: You mentioned that you come from Latin America. We often see pictures of slums where people are holding small icons in their hands — perhaps people from the Roman Catholic tradition. In those difficult situations, what do you think a small icon in their hands can represent? Does it have some significance for these people?

EC: You should remember that the majority of the people in Latin America come from traditional Roman Catholic piety. Many of those poor people do not have access to books or the printed word. Therefore the icon takes on another dimension, as a didactic instrument. But we must recognize that, as you say, in moments of despair we must be aware of the possibility that the icon may well become a talisman that is believed to possess magical powers. The ecumenical movement and the renewal movements in the Roman Catholic Church are also trying to eliminate this magical use of the icon and go deeper into its spiritual potential. This is part of the correction that is needed, but you point very clearly to the fact that for the poor people in some countries in Latin America, or in the Philippines, the presence of an image that has perhaps been in their home for many years is a kind of psychological and spiritual assurance.

GL: You mentioned the presentation of the Rublev icon of the Trinity in Vancouver. What do you think about this koinonia, this communion of the three angels in an ecclesiological perspective, when we speak about the unity of the Church?

EC: It refers to the prayer of Jesus that "all may be one, as you in me and I in you, that they may be one in us". I mean the unity of the Church is unity in the life of God. It is not a kind of business transaction, it is a growing together into the worshipping of God, and in that sense the icon helps illustrate that beautiful thought in John 17:21.

GL: What is the role of an Ecumenical Council in Church history, in particular today in the search for Church unity?

EC: At one level the Ecumenical Councils are a kind of yardstick to measure how faithful we are to the permanent Tradition of the Church. I know there are churches which do not want to have creeds; they like to have a central affirmation like "Jesus is Lord", and then the text of the Bible, but they agree that they belong to the Tradition of the Church. The Councils are one way of giving content to the Tradition of the Church. We could use them now in an attempt to translate their positive meaning for today, not so much related to the polemics of former times, but to the new missionary situation, to the new confrontations, to the new challenges we are facing today. So the Ecumenical Councils are useful as we search for the unity of the Church. But I would also like to see that, as we discuss the common faith needed in order to accept each other as participants in the one Tradition of the Church, we could define it in terms of the early Councils so that we do not need to rewrite the common core of doctrine. It is easier if we recognize ourselves in that Tradition, and from there we can accept the plurality of expressions of our own cultural identity, and so on. So it is very important that those Councils be brought back to the consciousness of the churches. The main value of those Councils, of course, is that some of them took place in the totally undivided Church even before the internal Orthodox polemics, and others took place before the big Western/Eastern division. So in any case they speak from an early Tradition that we all cherish almost in its totality.

GL: Does that mean that the icon could play a role in the search for visible unity among the churches?

EC: In this sense — like the Icon of the Trinity that we mentioned before and the Icon of Peter and Paul after the Council of Jerusalem — it is a good representation of what we are looking for in this conciliar fellowship. Inasmuch as the icons express the unity that is God's will for his Church, they will be helpful. We should not impose a specific tradition of icons which corresponds to a certain story, province or sector of the Church on all others. While I would respect the local tradition of people in Greece or the Middle East, we need to look for those icons which incorporate that sense of oneness in God and oneness of God's people.

7

GL: That means that we can compare the icons with other expressions of other traditions. Some churches use crosses — in Africa, for example, handmade wooden crosses are used in worship, and also as an expression of this dialogue with God.

EC: Of course! An icon or the historical cross are offered out of our thankfulness to God in order to express our faith that goes beyond the object. So, yes, there are liturgical expressions in some countries which do not belong to my particular Uruguayan culture, but which I need to respect. Music, architecture, colours — inasmuch as they are offerings of our creativity and testimony to God's ultimate creativity — promote the relation of human beings and communities to the source and centre of our very faith. Thus they have a role to play and we should be very thankful for them.

GL: How do you interpret the representation of a saint in an icon?

EC: That is exactly what I meant when I said we need to respect plurality because most of those saints, even if they are remembered in the liturgical calendar of the Orthodox churches, come from a certain period, and are known or respected or recognized in particular places. I would not pretend to be a judge of that. I would say that I receive the testimony of a particular church, and its contribution to the totality, but these icons are more limited in their potential to take me into the mystery of the Trinity and into adoration than those which belong to our common biblical and 1st-century history. So I do recognize that for people in different places the representation of one particular saint is a help for their own spiritual life. But I would make a categorical distinction between the icons which attempt to describe the givenness of the Gospel and point to elements of the Gospel, and those which are addressed more to particular stories and peoples centuries later. Let me take a very well-known name in the Western and the Orthodox world: St Francis of Assisi has become so well known in what he represents — peace, respect for the environment, and so on. An icon of him might function almost at the level of an icon representing some of the Apostles; but there are not too many who have become known and recognized universally.

GL: My question relates to the problem of deification (theosis) and seeing the saints as a model. When I speak of the saints and the communion of saints, these are people emerging from the people of God and not coming from another planet.

EC: Of course. I come from the Methodist, Latin American tradition. It is thanks to the ecumenical movement and the World Council of Churches that I have been awakened to an understanding of Orthodox spirituality. And it is through that that I have come to appreciate the value of icons in helping me to see a little of the final mystery of God. But now you are raising a series of theological issues which are very dear to the Orthodox tradition — and we are struggling with them. But I would still need to find intellectual categories to see if we are talking about the same thing. Theosis, I understand you to say, is the recapitulation of all those things that Paul speaks of in Ephesians and Corinthians. But when you translate the word theosis and use the English word "deification", at that moment we tremble. In fact, it is only a translation but in Greek it does not put fear into me! I see that as the final culmination of God's will. When you talk of deification, then all my Barthianism, the infinite distance between God and human beings, is evoked. So as I say, I am trying to see if the biblical history of the transfiguration should not be the real entry for us to understand this Orthodox theological reflection.

But coming back to the icons, I can see that icons of saints could be a good way of reminding us of the cloud of witnesses of which the Apostle speaks, and of the communion of saints which we confess in the creed. And in that sense they could fulfill a function — they do fulfill a function. But without claiming any authority on the subject, I would say that there is a difference today between an icon of the Trinity, an icon of the holy family, an icon of the Apostles and an icon of St Anthony, and so on.

GL: We are commemorating many events in our history of these 2000 years. Recently we celebrated the fortieth anniversary of the World Council. Where are we now?

EC: All the families of the Christian Church have grown together and greatly influenced each other. Of course, every church believes that it is complete in itself, but every church which has been involved in this process of searching for unity has been learning and receiving inspiration from others. And this book on icons is one illustration of that reciprocal learning. So the Christian scenario today is totally different from the picture in 1948. We have come to know each other, love each other, and trust each other. We have also grown together in doctrinal matters, as the attempt of the convergence document of Lima on baptism, Eucharist and ministry indicates. But of course we are coming to the moment of truth now. That means that the Orthodox should be challenged to be more specific in their demands to other churches for recognition. What is that common tradition which we need to belong to? I think that because of this growing together we are more inside that common tradition than we intellectually recognize. We need to bring our minds to the level of our spirituality!

Protestants of all kinds, including Anglicans, should be obliged to say what their conception is of the Church and the authority in the Church which they demand or offer as a basic component of the reciprocal recognition we are aiming at. And, of course, we cannot at this moment escape from facing together the question of the relation between the universal and the local Church. And that is a vital theological and spiritual challenge before us. So we grow together in mutual knowledge, in reciprocal spirituality, in solidarity and in suffering together. Now we need to confront the real intellectual challenges and to hope and pray that it will not be necessary to wait another forty years before we can celebrate at the one table of the Lord.

The Ecumenicity of the Seventh Ecumenical Council

VLASSIOS I. PHEIDAS

Crisis in conciliarity and canonical criteria of the Council's ecumenicity

The Seventh Ecumenical Council (787) was convened to deal with an ecclesiastical problem which, as it developed, took on serious theological and soteriological dimensions. As we know, the simple question of venerating holy icons came gradually to be linked to Christology, to the mission of the Mother of God in the mystery of divine economy in Christ, to the honouring of saints and relics, to the teaching on the human person, to the content of Christian spirituality, and so on. These serious theological developments were clear right from the start, which was why Patriarch Germanos of Constantinople called for the immediate summoning of an Ecumenical Council. This impinged on the Emperor's prerogative of settling internal ecclesiastical problems. But the sole competent organ for settling such questions was the Ecumenical Council. As such it struck a blow at Leo III's ideas of political authority. "I am a king and a priest," he declared. The Emperor saw his arbitrary initiatives disregarded on the matter of honouring icons, and his ideas on the relationship between the two powers (priesthood and kingship) and their representatives (patriarch and emperor) challenged. It was necessary, in the circumstances, to convene an Ecumenical Council, both to settle the issue of icons and to restore the traditional balance between Church and state.

Leo III's (717-740) refusal to discuss who should wield political authority and therefore to approve the summoning of an Ecumenical Council, made such a convocation practically impossible; but as the situation became even more bitter, other expressions of church conciliarity were brought into play. They took the form of patriarchal Synods, which disapproved of both the theological basis and the politics of the iconoclasts. The decisions taken by these local Synods made up, to some extent, for the absence of an Ecumenical Council, as they decided independently to break off communion with those who would not accept their rulings.

Nevertheless, ratification by an Ecumenical Council was necessary, for it alone could express the conscience of the whole oikoumene, and witness in the Holy Spirit to the authenticity of local church traditions. Of course, the truth of the faith is lived in its fullness — or should be — by each church, but the authentic

---

● This paper was translated from French by the WCC Language Service.

doctrinal formulation of such an experience is the task of the Ecumenical Council, canonically summoned and in complete harmony with the conciliar conscience of the Church.

It is on the basis of these criteria — the canonical summoning of all the local churches of the oikoumene through their administrative heads and the unviolated expression of the conciliar conscience of the Church — that the ecclesiastical conscience promotes the work of every synod. Thus the Council of Hieria (754), convened as ecumenical by the iconoclasts, was condemned as uncanonically summoned and as tainting the conciliar conscience of the Church, both by its workings and by its decisions. This synod placed the Church's awareness of its conscience on another basis, because the fact that it was by the iconoclastic Emperor Constantine V (740-775) was a *denial* of the claims of Leo III, i.e. that the emperor could unilaterally and arbitrarily settle the whole question by decree.

In itself, the Council of Hieria was the first victory of the iconophiles, because the Emperor was obliged in the end to recognize the sole competence of an Ecumenical Council for settling the question, and consequently departed from Leo III's position. Thus the Byzantine emperor recognized the traditional "symphony" of the two powers and moved away from the principle of the subordination of the one to the other which Leo III had dared proclaim. Nonetheless, the uncanonical mode of convoking, constituting and putting into action the Council of Hieria was completely contrary to the Church's canonical tradition. The deviation of the iconoclastic Council of Hieria from these canonical criteria was to become a continual source of discontent.

Thus the decisions of the iconoclastic Council of Hieria were not approved by the papal See and the patriarchal Sees of the East (Alexandria, Antioch, Jerusalem), while church circles in the jurisdiction of Constantinople expressed a strong reaction in the dioceses of the 338 bishops who took part in the Council. The reasons (canonical criteria) for their disapproval were the following:
— all the patriarchal Sees were not invited to or represented at the Council;
— the Emperor imposed his wishes on the Council, thereby limiting the freedom of the bishops; and
— the Council's decisions did not agree with the patristic and, in general, ecclesiastical tradition on the veneration of holy icons.

The Seventh Ecumenical Council marks the return to the centuries-old conciliar tradition of the Church and the condemnation of any deviation from the authentic ecclesial conscience. Patriarch Tarasius of Constantinople accepted his election to the patriarchal See on the explicit understanding that the whole issue of icons should be dealt with by an Ecumenical Council. In the brotherly greetings he sent to the other patriarchs, he sought, beyond the usual things (acceptance of the letter as orthodox, inscriptions of the new patriarch's name in the diptychs and canonical mnemosynon), the participation in a future Council of all the patriarchal Sees through the appointment of canonical representatives. Thus the views of all the local churches would be *canonically* represented. In point of fact, all the patriarchates adhered to the patristic tradition of icons and had publicly refuted the decisions of Hieria. Empress Irene agreed to the ecumenical patriarch's position and took the necessary steps to convoke the Ecumenical Council. In a letter to the pope of Rome she proclaimed the binding power of the Ecumenical Council and her determination — as the political authority — to ensure the liberty of the bishops on the matter of the veneration of icons.

It is noteworthy that questioning the legitimacy and ecumenicity of the Council of Hieria's decisions should have taken place through a systematic listing of the canonical criteria of the conciliar tradition. Such a listing — authentically voicing the conciliar conscience of the Church — had never before been effected with such canonical precision. The Seventh Ecumenical Council condemned the iconoclastic Council of Hieria on the basis of the canonical criteria of the Church's conciliar conscience:

> Having started from a lie, which they have undertaken to defend with all this empty talk of theirs, these accusers of the Christians have also ended up with a lie. For how is this Council "holy", since it did not even take into account what is holy? It is rather cursed, profane and intrusive... Again, how is this Council "great and ecumenical", if those presiding over the rest of the Church neither accepted nor consented to it but rather dismissed it with an anathema?... Their word was truly full of cloudy smoke, darkening the eyes of the foolish... because it was spoken locally as from an obscure quarter and not from the top of the mountain of orthodoxy. Neither was their voice gone out into the whole earth in an apostolic fashion, like that of the six Holy and Ecumenical Councils. Again how could it be the seventh, if it failed to agree with the six Holy and Ecumenical ones which preceded it? For whatever is placed seventh ought to follow after the things which were placed and enumerated before it, since whatever does not participate in those which are enumerated with it cannot be enumerated with them... Thus, this council also having nothing golden or valuable in its dogmas, but being entirely inferior to copper and counterfeit, and full of deadly poison, is not worthy to be enumerated together with the six most reverend Councils which shine forth with the golden victories of the Spirit...[1]

The Pope and the ecumenical character of the Council

Vittorio Peri[2] places a particular emphasis on the interpretative approach of that important conciliar document, for, as he rightly remarked:

> We thus have an interesting list of conditions and characteristics. It can be seen from this list that these are absent from the so-called Council of Hieria. They are thus declared to be indispensable by implication if a Council is to be regarded as ecumenical... Moreover, we find in the list certain items about Ecumenical Councils which the episcopate of the time throughout the world already considered as traditional; the foremost of these being recognition of an accepted canon law drawn up to govern councils of this kind...

As an argument in favour of the papal primacy and the Pope's position vis-à-vis an Ecumenical Council, Peri invokes the pentarchy of patriarchs and the phrase concerning their place in an Ecumenical Council. Through curious associations or disassociations, Peri twists the sense of the phrase, and takes the letter and the spirit of it in such a way as to arrive at the following conclusion:

> The first decisive defect preventing the irregular Council from claiming to be ecumenical and to be so regarded seems, in the thinking of the conciliar Fathers, to be the lack of the personal cooperation of the Roman pontiff at the Council. The pope's actual approval seems to be fundamental and indispensable for the validity of a body like this and of its conclusions. He must work along with it — must be a "collaborator", as the document, using a technical term,[3] affirms. The bishop of

Rome's behaviour and actions emerge clearly from this as parallel to the behaviour and action of the entire conciliar assembly. The ecumenicity of the Council depends on the unanimous agreement[4] of the two parties... Further analysis of the text from a conciliar angle yields no basis for the claim that if a Council is to appear legitimately ecumenical in the eyes of all Christians, the other participating churches and especially the four main patriarchates of the East would be given the secondary role of giving formal approval. The text of Nicea II is explicit about this too: the irregular Council which preceded it could not claim to be truly ecumenical because it lacked the unanimous agreement of the four Eastern patriarchs and of the churches under their aegis... From the context, then, it seems we may say that another condition for ecumenicity is constituted by their supporting presence and identity of views, arising out of the agreement of the four patriarchates which in union with Rome recognize each other as the conciliar[5] representatives of the entire Christian oikoumene. It is however true — or such at least seems to us quite the best available opinion — that the position of the patriarchs in relation to the conciliar body is significantly different in one point from that of the Roman pontiff — namely that of primacy, which is recognized as being properly his: the pope is co-worker — "collaborates" — with the council; the patriarchs "are in agreement" with him. When both conditions are seen to be fulfilled, the Councils and their decisions are in line, even in terms of canon law, with the principles necessary for them to have ecumenical status and authority...[6]

In order to establish this interpretation of papal primacy, Peri is obliged to overlook certain fundamental aspects of the text, which would have led him to quite a different conclusion:

a) He separates the actual text from the introductory rhetorical question: "Again, how is this Council 'great and ecumenical' if those presiding over the rest of the Church neither accepted nor consented to it, but rather dismissed it with an anathema?" This question introduces the time-hallowed and immutable canonical principle of the agreement of the five patriarchs for the recognition of a Council as ecumenical. This renders plausible the otherwise groundless separation between the pope and the patriarchs of the East.

b) Probably by an oversight, he misinterprets the text because the patriarchs of the East, in the text, are three and not four as he states arbitrarily. For the Sees of Alexandria, Antioch and Jerusalem are explicitly mentioned in the text but not the See of Constantinople.

c) The three patriarchal Sees of the East are described in the text as being in relation to Constantinople and not to Rome — as Peri takes the meaning to be. So the insertion of the See of Constantinople among the patriarchal Sees of the East is groundless in the text and, in consequence, it is arbitrary to insert it among the Sees, which the text states must be "in agreement" with the decisions of an Ecumenical Council. On the contrary, together with Rome, Constantinople is placed among the "collaborators" and not simply among those who have to be "in agreement". Moreover, the Greek original of the text does not permit any other interpretation.

d) Peri's distinction between the "collaborators" and "those in agreement" does not convey the true spirit of the text. "Synergos" (collaborator) simply means the need for participation or canonical representation in the Ecumenical Council by the papal See. For historical reasons — the Arab conquest — the three patriarchal Sees of the East (Alexandria, Antioch and Jerusalem) were unable to attend or to send canonical representatives; so the Seventh Ecumenical Council understood the basic canonical principle of the five patriarchal Sees, "the five-headed realm of the Church", on the grounds of a concrete historical reality. Therefore, instead of participation, the simple agreement of the three patriarchal Sees is of necessity accepted by recognizing the ecumenicity of a Council, and upon the explicit understanding that the papal See will participate or be canonically represented at the Council, seeing that it had no similar objective impediment.

e) To take a canonical "kat' oikonomian" solution to ensure the workings of an Ecumenical Council as an ecclesiological principle on which to base papal primacy is to misread the text, seeing that the See of Constantinople is implicitly understood as also being "synergos". Moreover, a solution "kat' oikonomian" in no way abolishes the canonical principle of "kat' akribeian", according to which an Ecumenical Council is made up of all the patriarchal Sees participating and agreeing.

Thus the papal See sent the usual canonical delegation, bearing documents, but the patriarchal Sees of the East, under Arab rule, were unable to acquaint themselves even with the patriarchal documents. The views of these Sees were represented atypically at the Council, but their representation was considered authentic on account of the known official decision of these Sees.

Reception of the Council's ecumenicity and right to inclusion among the Ecumenical Councils

The Seventh Ecumenical Council was, as we have seen, fully aware of its ecumenicity because:

1. It was summoned in strict accordance with the relevant canonical tradition, and all the patriarchal Sees were invited to attend.
2. In it were represented the official views of all the local churches as they had been expressed by diverse means.
3. It was able to act freely, without political or other interference.
4. Grounding in Scripture and Tradition was sought for the experience by all the local churches.
5. The Council's decisions constituted an authentic succession to the preceding six Ecumenical Councils, inasmuch as these decisions reflected true Orthodoxy.
6. The errors of the iconoclastic Council and the need to safeguard the faith from them were made manifest.
7. Through the unhindered expression of the universal Church conscience, the veneration of holy icons was upheld as being in accordance with the traditional means of expressing the Orthodox faith.

1. Difficulties in the reception of the Council's ecumenicity

Judging by the spirit of the whole affair, the "reception" of the Council should have been a simple matter, for the ecclesiastical conscience had expressed itself clearly to maintain the Orthodox tradition of venerating icons in the preceding sixty years of struggle. In actual fact, however, serious difficulties arose concerning reception both in the East and the West. In the West, a poor Latin translation of the Council's rulings was to blame. In the East, there was a certain reluctance to include the Council among the other six Ecumenical Councils, despite the immediate acceptance of its rulings. It was more logical that the West, notably the

Frankish dominions, should refuse this inclusion, as they refused the theological content of the Council. The patriarchates of the East expressed reservations purely on the matter of numbering the Council among the Ecumenical Councils.

In his letter to the patriarchs of the East (867), the Ecumenical Patriarch Photius wrote that the non-recognition of the ecumenicity of the Council by some of the patriarchal Sees of the East was in no way related to doubt about the validity of the Council's theological decisions: "For whatever was ratified by it, as indeed all else, they study and revere, but as regards the Council itself they do not seem to know that it must be acknowledged in the Church."[7] The Patriarch attributes this omission to the insufficient knowledge of the Council acts: "... the acts which it was probably not easy to bring to you because the barbarian and alien race of the Arabs had taken hold of the state. For this reason many of its ordinances, although they are honoured and held in high esteem, are not understood to belong to it, as they say, because they have no such knowledge."[8] Nonetheless, Photius, when presenting the same subject to the Synod of Constantinople (879-880), hints at a subtle distinction in the mode of receiving the theological decisions of the Council: "As for the Church of the Romans, as well as for the thrones of the East, they accept its dogmas in the same way (as the See of Constantinople), but there is perhaps some doubt amongst some as to whether it should be listed together with the other six Holy and Ecumenical Councils and be acclaimed as the Seventh..."[9] The difference in formulation between the two testimonies of Photius is certainly due to the fact that the letter of 867 was restricted to the patriarchal Sees of the East, which fully accepted the theological content of the Council's decisions, whereas the exposition before the Synod of 879-880 referred also to the Church of the West, where the Frankish bishops had repeatedly expressed their theological reservations, as we shall see later.

So there were theological and ecclesiastical problems regarding the reception and inclusion of the Council among the Ecumenical Councils. An official proclamation of the latter required action in that direction of the "ecclesiastical conscience", and Photius was working at it. Reception of the Council and recognition of its ecumenicity had, canonically, to be unanimous; then the heresy of the iconoclasts could be condemned and true Orthodoxy triumph:

> It is necessary, then, that this one also... should be acclaimed together with the six Councils which preceded it as Great and Holy and Ecumenical. For to fail to do this and act accordingly means, first, to do injustice to the Church of Christ, by overlooking such a Council and by breaking up and dissolving to such extent its bond and coherence; and secondly, to allow the iconoclasts to open their mouths more widely, even though they are no less than the other heretics and it is well known that their impiety is hateful, by suggesting that their impiety was not condemned by an Ecumenical Council but rests only upon the judgment of one throne, and therefore to give them an excuse for their atrocities. [10]

Thus the need to proclaim immediately the ecumenicity of the Council and its numbering among the Ecumenical Councils was dictated by the fact that:
1. The Council, convoked canonically as ecumenical and working as such, condemned the iconoclastic heresy ("who are no less than the other heretics"), that is to say, it condemned a heresy analogous to those condemned by the earlier Councils.

2. Not to receive the ecumenicity of the Council would favour the activity of the heretics, who could then maintain "that their impiety was not condemned by an Ecumenical Council, but rests only upon the judgment of one throne".

3. The lack of such a proclamation "does injustice" ("adikeia") to the Church, because, on the one hand, the "bond" ("syndesmos") and "connection" ("synapheia") between the local churches are seriously disrupted through not unanimously recognizing the ecumenicity of the Council and, on the other hand, because only through such a proclamation can the Council's teaching be handed down as an obligatory doctrine to all the faithful of all the local churches "... delivered to the whole pleroma of the churches which are under you".[11]

4. The proclamation of the Council's ecumenicity certifies the continuity and authenticity of the faith of the Church as formulated, and its absolute agreement with the doctrinal decisions of the preceding Ecumenical Councils, whereas the absence of such a proclamation casts doubts on this agreement.

From the above it is evident that the difficulties arising both in the East and the West concerning the reception of the Council were causing grave ecclesiastical and ecclesiological problems.

2. Reactions in the West

In the West the position of the papal See with regard to the veneration of icons was from the start clear-cut and definitive for the evolution of iconoclasm, since from the outset the relevant decree of the iconoclastic Emperor Leo III had been disapproved. The position was further clarified by the Councils of Rome (731) and Lateran (769) as iconoclasm evolved; for oriental monks fleeing from persecution to Rome and the West generally brought with them a supplement of information on the ecclesiastical and theological dimensions of the quarrel. Acting on this information, Pope Hadrian was prepared to comply with Ecumenical Patriarch Tarasius' request, and promptly got together a canonical delegation to participate in the Council. However, he linked its mission to other problems confronting the papal See, such as its jurisdiction in East Illyricum and southern Italy. The lively participation in the Council of the papal delegates and the other bishops of the West gives an indication of the clear conscience of the Western Church concerning the traditional veneration of icons. Thus Pope Hadrian received at once the decisions of the Seventh Ecumenical Council and published its acts in an initial Latin draft for the archbishops of the West.

Nevertheless, reception of the Council's decisions did not come easily in the Frankish dominions. The rough-and-ready Latin translation was vague on certain crucial theological points, and Frankish theology was undermined. Study of the acts, both of the iconoclastic Council of Hieria and of the Seventh Ecumenical Council, by Charlemagne and the bishops of the Frankish dominions was the basis of the teaching of the Roman Church, still fresh from fighting adoptionism, and not yet having fully digested the strong effects of Gothic Arianism. The *Libri Carolini* recorded the hesitations of the Roman magisterium with regard to the decisions of the Seventh Ecumenical Council as formulated in a bad Latin translation. The position of the Council of Frankfurt (794) was more or less against them, while Pope Hadrian was obliged to defend the Council's decisions on icons. In his letter, he stressed that:

1) papal acceptance of the decisions is due to the fact that they are in full harmony with Roman tradition, especially with the teaching of Pope Gregory I, and that not to accept them would cause iconoclasm to flare up again in the East;

2) papal acceptance of the decisions has not yet been officially announced in writing in the East.

Nevertheless, these difficulties were not finally definitive for the reception of the Council in the West, despite continued suspicion in the Frankish state. Of course, the position of the Franks was not completely negative towards the veneration of holy icons, but on account of the poor quality of the Latin translation they were not able to grasp the theological basis of the Council's decisions on icons. For them, icons were necessary to adorn churches, i.e. they accepted an aesthetic criterion, but not the theological criterion of the necessity of preserving, in its entirety, the spirituality of worship through icons. That, at least, was what the *Libri Carolini* insinuated. One could, however, maintain that Charlemagne and the Frankish bishops should not have let themselves be influenced by the arguments against icons put forward by the Council of Hieria, seeing that they were all well acquainted with its decisions — as is evident from the preface to the first book of the *Libri Carolini*.

Pope Hadrian's defence of the Seventh Ecumenical Council, in accordance with Roman tradition, served to check Frankish reservations and paved the way for the final reception of the Council by the Western Church. Though there was no concrete opposition to this, it was not mentioned among them in ecclesiastical acts of the 9th century. Visibly, Church practice in the West was influenced by the fact that, in the East, its ecumenicity was not recognized by the iconoclastic patriarchs of Constantinople on account of the recrudescence of iconoclasm (815-843) and the rehabilitation of the Council of Hieria. It is characteristic that Pope Nicholas I condemned Patriarch Photius of Constantinople by pleading the authenticity of "the six Ecumenical Councils".[12] In presenting the problem to the synod of 879-880, Photius is clear on the Western Church's position: "As for the Church of the Romans as well as for the thrones of the East, they accept its dogmas in the same way (as the See of Constantinople), but there is perhaps some doubt amongst some as to whether it should be enumerated together with the other six Holy and Ecumenical Councils and whether it can be acclaimed as the Seventh."[13]

3. Trouble in the Orient

In the East, the prestige of the Seventh Ecumenical Council was enormous right from the beginning, but the iconoclastic tendencies were not wiped out by the sole application of the Council's rulings. On the basis of the general principles of canonical tradition and because of the importance of the matter, we may suppose that the Ecumenical Patriarch Tarasius promptly recognized the ecumenicity of the Seventh Ecumenical Council. Patriarch Photius of Constantinople did so immediately upon his accession to the patriarchal throne. In his synodical letter to Pope Nicholas I he states categorically:

> Having this mind and confessing without any wavering the faith which has been established in and is preached by the catholic and apostolic Church, I accept the seven Holy and Ecumenical Councils... and also the sacred and great Synod which was summoned at Nicea for the second time to excommunicate and reject the iconoclasts as fighters of Christ and accusers of the Saints... These, then, seven Holy and Ecumenical Councils I accept...[14]

It seems obvious that counting Nicea II as the Seventh Ecumenical Council was, from the start, the firm policy of the iconophile patriarchs of Constantinople. Before the Synod of 879-890, Photius says explicitly: "As for our own church it always calls it and acknowledges it as the Seventh and honours it with the same seniority as the other six Holy Ecumenical Councils..."[15] This testimony shows that Patriarch Tarasius of Constantinople had already numbered the Council among the Ecumenical Councils. A hint of this is given in the preface to the *Libri Carolini*, where there is a special mention of the Byzantine proposal to count the Council among the Ecumenical Councils. However, the resurgence of iconoclasm (815), the rehabilitation of the iconoclastic Council of Hieria (754), and the influence of iconoclastic patriarchs in the See of Constantinople during the second period of iconoclasm (815-843) did not give sufficient respite for the Seventh Ecumenical Council's decisions to become current Church practice. The restoration of the veneration of icons (843) could not be combined with the automatic numbering of the Council among the Ecumenical Councils, because it had previously been declared null and void by the iconoclastic synod held in Saint Sophia (815). A new conciliar decision was necessary to recognize the ecumenicity of the Council of Nicea.

The Ecumenical Patriarch Photius was extremely keen that this pending canonical question be settled. In his letter to the patriarchal Sees of the East, asking them to condemn Pope Nicholas I (867), he characteristically stresses the need to attend to the matter: "Indeed we thought it necessary to add this also to our letter so that the Holy and Ecumenical Seventh Council should be put together and numbered together with the other six Holy and Ecumenical Councils for all the pleroma of the Church which is under us."[16] One can deduce from this that the decisions concerning holy icons had been accepted, but that the inclusion of the Council among the Ecumenical Councils had not yet received the seal of approval:

> For some fame reaches us, that some of the churches under our apostolic throne number the Ecumenical Councils as far as the Sixth, and are ignorant of the Seventh; but whatever was ratified by it, and indeed all else, they study and revere, as for the Council itself they do not happen to know that it should be acknowledged in the Church, although it retains the same authority with the other Councils... It is necessary, then, as we said, that this one also should be acknowledged together with the other six Councils as Great and Holy and Ecumenical.[17]

4. Proclamation of the ecumenicity of the Council

Before the Synod of Constantinople, Patriarch Photius expounded officially, once again, the need for all the patriarchal Sees to proclaim the ecumenicity of the Council of Nicea (787) and its numbering among the Ecumenical Councils, so as to clear up the confusion reigning in the Church. As his main argument, Photius cited the fact that all the patriarchal Sees "accepted and held in high esteem its dogmas", and that the reticence of some concerns only "the enumeration of this one together with the rest of the Holy and Ecumenical Councils". His proposal took on a particular dimension from the fact that, at the Synod of Constantinople there were delegations of all the patriarchal Sees, who could thus voice their official opinion on the matter:

> If it is agreeable to all of you, let us strengthen and ratify not only its dogmas and ordinances as acceptable to all, but also its enumeration together with the six Holy and Ecumenical Councils, regarding it as the Seventh to have taken place and to have been so called after them and as enjoying equal rights of seniority with them. [18]

To this proposal of Patriarch Photius, the papal delegate, Cardinal Presbyter Peter, gave an immediate response, declaring his full agreement with a unanimous synodical (conciliar) proclamation of the ecumenicity of the Council of Nicea and its inclusion among the Ecumenical Councils:

> We want to remind your holiness of the Holy Council which took place at the time of the most holy Pope Hadrian and St Tarasius Patriarch of Constantinople concerning the holy and sacred icons, that, as since ancient times in unanimity with the holy churches everywhere the holy Church of the Romans upheld and accepted its dogmas and ordinances, likewise now it has proved rightly acknowledged that it should be called Seventh and be numbered with the remaining six Holy and Ecumenical Councils. Furthermore whoever does not uphold this, and does not acknowledge the Holy and Ecumenical Council which was summoned at Nicea for the second time to be the Seventh, let him be anathema. [19]

From this declaration it is clear that the papal See, albeit defending in the West the doctrinal decisions of the Seventh Ecumenical Council, did not count it officially among the Ecumenical Councils. It is evident that the papal representatives at the Synod of Constantinople had orders from Pope John VIII to make such a declaration following on previous discussions with Patriarch Photius before the Patriarch submitted his proposal.

An analogous declaration was made before the Synod separately by delegates of the patriarchal Sees of the East after the announcement, by all the members of the Synod, that

> it is necessary that, along with the entire acceptance and union of the Church of the Romans which took place through the mediation of our most holy Patriarch Photius, we too should add our agreement to this matter so that no discordance might be seen to exist amongst us concerning this matter... [20]

This announcement by the members of the Synod makes it clearer still that the Patriarch of Constantinople's proposal aimed at the unanimous reception by the patriarchal Sees of the aforementioned official act of the Patriarch with the intention of numbering the Council of Nicea among the Ecumenical Councils so that, during the Synod's formulation, "no discordance might be seen to exist amongst us concerning this matter". The unanimous decision of the Synod (council) of Constantinople brought to a happy close the issue of the ecumenicity of the Seventh Ecumenical Council, even if in fact the decision was not immediately applied in the West.

The ecumenical character of the Council and the contemporary ecumenical dialogue

The Seventh Ecumenical Council (787) was the last of a chain of Ecumenical Councils within the ancient, undivided Church — that period before the great schism (1054) between the churches of East and West. This Council is of great significance for the ongoing ecumenical dialogue on the restoration of Christian unity. As we have seen, the doctrinal decisions of the Council concerning the veneration of icons caused various reactions in both East and West as soon as its work was over. The cautious stance of the Protestant Reformation towards the veneration of icons was, to some extent, the culmination of trouble in the Western Church, which had never been fully capable of incorporating in its tradition the theology on icons of the Eastern Church. On the contrary, the pre-Chalcedonian churches of the East, which had adopted a somewhat reserved attitude, after the Fourth Ecumenical Council (451), towards the possibility of portraying Christ, on account of their Christological teaching (Severus of Antioch, Philoxenos of Hierapolis, and so on), proceeded to follow a convergent course and incorporated more fully the icon in their divine worship, theology and spirituality, even though they did not participate in the theological debates of the 8th and 9th centuries.

The icon is indissolubly linked to the particularity of confessional theology and to the spirituality of the Christian churches and confessions; a favourable or unfavourable attitude towards them stems from corresponding Christological and consequently ecclesiological presuppositions. That Protestants and Roman Catholics are moving towards a more positive evaluation of the theology and spirituality behind icons is due to the Christocentric research of recent years — as is evident from the ecumenical dialogue of today. It follows that the theology of the icon of the Seventh Ecumenical Council — the common spiritual heritage of the patristic tradition of the undivided Church — can be pinpointed as a characteristic "sign" of the progress towards unity, a bridge towards the common patristic tradition.

Moreover, in the ecumenical dialogue, the Seventh Ecumenical Council is linked to the solution of various ecclesiastical and ecclesiological problems. This includes the numbering of the Council among the Ecumenical Councils of the undivided Church.

The prospects for ecumenical dialogue arising from the conscience of the undivided Church, as expressed in the Seventh Ecumenical Council, may be summarized as follows:

1. The institution of the Ecumenical Council is a necessary function of the synodical (conciliar) conscience of the Church, and not independent of it. Through the inspiration of the Holy Spirit working in it, the whole Church expressed itself, whether through the canonical representation of all the local churches or through the subsequent mobilization of their ecclesial conscience during the process of reception, not only of the doctrinal decisions, but of the actual ecumenicity of the Council.

2. The Council's decisions on matters of the faith should express not only horizontally the official views of all the local churches of the oikoumene, but also, vertically, across the boundaries of time, a continuation of the apostolic tradition of the faith as lived without interruption by the Church. By apostolic tradition is meant Holy Scripture and the patristic tradition as formulated in earlier Ecumenical Councils. Should this not be the case, the Council cannot be numbered among the Ecumenical Councils and its decisions are not acceptable to the ecclesial conscience.

3. Orthodoxy of faith may be present even when there is disagreement as to the ecumenicity of a particular Council, but this presupposes at least the express reception into the life of the Church of the theological content of the decisions of the ambiguous Council. But disagreement always causes a problem for Church unity in faith and charity. While temporary non-recognition of the ecumenicity of the Seventh Ecumenical Council did not lead to a break in communion between the

Sees of Rome and Constantinople, during its approximate half-century, thanks largely to agreement on the veneration of icons, the Ecumenical Patriarch Photius did successfully struggle to obtain from all the patriarchal Sees recognition of the ecumenicity of the Council, placing it among the other Ecumenical Councils, through a unanimous decision taken at the Synod of Constantinople.

4. Reception of the ecumenicity of a Council presupposes, of course, the reception of its doctrinal decisions into the faith and life of the Church, with the possible exception of secondary aspects. This can be seen from Photius's presentation of the arguments for numbering the Seventh Ecumenical Council among the previous ones, which he put forward at the Synod of Constantinople: "As for the Church of the Romans, as well as for the thrones of the East, they accept its dogmas in the same way (as the See of Constantinople), but there is perhaps some doubt amongst some as to whether it should be listed together with the other six Holy and Ecumenical Councils and be acclaimed as the Seventh."[21] However, if they receive only "paraplesios", the doctrines of the Seventh Ecumenical Council, this implies a certain divergence in the mode of understanding or living the "horos" (ruling) of the Council. But this is not considered an obstacle to the proclamation of the Council's ecumenicity and inclusion among the Ecumenical Councils, because it would seem that the divergence concerned only the mode of application and not the theological content of the "horos".

5. Disagreement — in spite of acceptance of the decisions — concerning the recognition of the ecumenicity of a Council, while not necessarily entailing a break in ecclesiastical communion, is harmful to the Church's unity ("adikein es tin ekklisian"), which is why the Synod of Constantinople judged it necessary that "mide en touto eie en emin diaphonia".[22]

The importance of these considerations for contemporary ecumenical dialogue could properly be evaluated from a simple recollection of the existing differences regarding the institution of Ecumenical Councils, their number and their binding power ("authentia") on the various Christian churches and confessions. These important differences will have to be discussed in those bilateral and multilateral dialogues where the number of recognized Ecumenical Councils is as important as their binding power on the Church.

The Seventh Ecumenical Council thus marked a turning point in the historical continuity of the conciliar conscience of the Church and in the authentic proclamation of the uninterrupted continuation of the Apostolic Tradition in the faith, life and spirituality of the Church, and as such served and serves the ecclesial unity of the Christian world in true faith and charity.

NOTES

[1] Mansi XIII, 208-209.
[2] V. Peri, "La Synergie entre le Pape et le Concile oecuménique", in *Irénikon*, 56, 1983, pp.170f.
[3] *Sunergates?* (translator's note)
[4] Greek: *Symphonia* (translator's note)
[5] Text: synodal. *Synodos* = Council in Greek. Patrinacos, *A Dictionary of Greek Orthodoxy*, p.102. (translator's note)
[6] *Ibid.*, pp.172-174.

[7] *PG*, 102, 740.
[8] *PG*, 102, 740.
[9] Mansi XIII, 493.
[10] *PG*, 102, 740-741.
[11] *PG*, 102, 740.
[12] *PL*, 119, 852 and 1053.
[13] Mansi XIII, 493.
[14] *PG*, 102, 592-593.
[15] Mansi XIII, 493.
[16] *PG*, 102, 740.
[17] *PG*, 102, 740-741.
[18] Mansi XIII, 493.
[19] Mansi XIII, 493.
[20] Mansi XIII, 493-496.
[21] Mansi XIII, 493.
[22] Mansi XIII, 493-496.

The Church of Rome
and the Ecclesiastical Problems
Raised by Iconoclasm

VITTORIO PERI

After the challenge of Arianism,[1] the crisis caused by the iconoclastic movement was the most serious and dangerous in Christian history. For about 150 years the crisis prevailed within the whole Christian Church and threatened to change its identity, which was defined in the creed of A.D. 381 ("of the 150 Fathers") as "one, catholic and apostolic".[2] The spread of the doctrine which sought to justify the removal of all images from public liturgical celebrations and private devotion was such as to undermine not only the central dogma of Incarnation, defined by the Ecumenical Councils, but also the structures on which the Church had built its unity and communion for eight centuries.

The iconoclastic doctrine and praxis enjoyed the ideological and political support of the dominating power in Byzantium. The long and difficult resistance to the spread of iconoclasm led to discrimination, persecution and martyrdom — especially of monks, priests and bishops, but also of the ordinary faithful — and was surely no less extensive and violent than that of the first centuries. But it was the first time that such persecution was planned and executed against the whole Catholic Church, under the pretext of defending the orthodox doctrine and freedom of worship and public preaching, by emperors who were supposed to be models of faith.

The common feeling and conception of the ruler presented him as "pontifex imperator". His authority was universally considered sacred and absolute. The defence of the true religion was part of his responsibility.

As far as iconoclasm was concerned, the situation came about through the doctrinal orientation and the practical obedience of the Catholic bishops, mainly those from Byzantium.

Because part of the divine right of the emperor was to establish the law in the only Christian state, the iconoclastic crisis concerned all the churches, even those no longer under the effective power of the ecumenical *Basileus*, such as the patriarchates of Alexandria, Antioch and Jerusalem, situated in Muslim principalities, or the Western patriarchate which extended up to the new Latino-barbaric kingdoms. The suppression of this heresy was considered, especially by the Byzantine church, to be an important victory for the whole Christian Church, celebrated every year in the great feast of Orthodoxy.

23

Written and non-written traditions in the life of the Church

The most insidious feature of the iconoclastic crisis, like that caused by Arianism, was due to the theological strength of the basic statement, which gave it a doctrinal basis. The distrust of icons, born in an intellectually advanced climate and in Christian communities not very disposed, because of old local habits, to pictorial representations in worship and piety, found encouragement in certain circles of Christian spirituality. Apart from the apologists, who strongly upheld the spirituality and transcendence of the only God against the many anthropomorphous and zoomorphous representations of heathen and idolatrous cults, this Christian position found its spokesmen in authors like Eusebius of Caesarea, Epiphanius of Salamis, Philoxenus of Mabbug and, in the West, Augustine of Hippo. It also drew on specific texts of the Bible, such as Exodus 20:4, Wisdom 14:13-20, Isaiah 44:9-20, 2 Corinthians 5:16, and Revelation 13:15. The supporters of the holy images could use the Scriptures only by interpreting their statement in the light of faith and the Tradition lived by the Church. The risks of superstitious and practical idolatry did indeed exist and were not just imagined in popular devotion to the icons, in contexts which were culturally and spiritually backward. As far as the ordinary people were concerned, there was a definite catechetic value in images and pictures of religious and biblical scenes, as long as they fixed in their memory the characters and events of the history of salvation, and made them think of the superior realities of the Spirit. But it was always possible that recalling the divine transcendence through images might become a distraction from this transcendence, or a materialistic or magical conception of it. In 824 Michael II denounced attitudes of this kind in a letter to Mouis I the Pious by saying:

> Many clergymen and laymen, disregarding the Apostles' traditions and the Fathers' definitions, have been the cause of new disadventures. First, they removed the venerable crosses from the holy churches and substituted images, in front of which they put lights and burnt incense, paying them the same honour as the holy symbol on which Christ, our real Lord, allowed himself to be crucified for our salvation. They sing psalms to these images, adore them and ask them for help. Many of them dress the images and make them their children's godfathers at baptisms. Others, wanting to become monks, neglect the religious who used to receive their cut hair, and, instead, use the images, preferring to drop their hair on them. Among the priests and the clergymen, some scratch colours off the icons in order to mix them with the offerings to those wishing to receive Holy Communion. Some others put the Lord's Body in the images' hands and those who want to receive Holy Communion have it from those hands. Some, despising the Church, have used as an altar the shelves on which the icons lay in private houses, and have celebrated the Holy Sacrifice on them. Many practices of this kind, forbidden and opposed to our religion, have been followed in the churches. The men who are learned and wise consider them completely worthless.[3]

Christians in many regions of the empire who were nearer to Arabs and Jews and their manifestations of worship and prayer were able to compare these religious practices with those of other monotheistic religions. This pointed to a higher level of spirituality which could be achieved by even the simplest and most ignorant of the faithful educated in an aniconic cult.

The 338 bishops gathered in 754 at Hieria declared that it was the Seventh Ecumenical Council and formulated a definition of faith *(horos)* in which they expressed the theological reasons for the elimination of icons of Christ, the Mother of God and the saints from Christian worship.[4] These statements seemed particularly valid because of the absence of texts in the Bible, or of precise conciliar definitions authorizing the ancient practice of venerating the holy images. The written traditions seemed rather to support the opposite attitude: they all taught that God had a spiritual, invisible and transcendental nature. Even from this aspect, it was the first time that the churches had been obliged to focus on the decisive role of their liturgical praxis and of their living tradition — present, for the mystery of the Holy Ghost, in the actual conscience of the group of the Church's shepherds and in the sense of the Church possessed by the faithful — in order to determine the orthodoxy of their doctrine of faith. Without the community life of the faithful of all Christian generations, every letter and written word remains ambiguous and dead. In the end, it kills the faith.

Iconoclasm obliged the whole Church to specify more clearly the unanimous patristic teaching about the inspiration of the Bible and its correct interpretation in the light of the revealed truth and in support of the ecclesiastical traditions. It also imposed on the Church the need to consider the serious problem of the relationship between the written and non-written traditions, in order to determine the true faith and the rule of the liturgical and personal prayer of the Christian people.

Church and state

The iconoclastic movement was able to initiate a discussion about the Christian validity of two postulates which till then had been considered fundamental and indisputable. These were about the definition of the exact relationship between the imperial state and the Catholic Church, as it had established itself from the reign of Constantine to that of Justinian. The first presupposition, adopted by the dominating political theology,[5] was that the emperor, who received his absolute power directly from God, had to be not only Christian, but perfectly orthodox, so that his duty was to protect the freedom of the Church by law and force. He had to be able to recognize the right doctrine and defend it against any theoretical or practical challenge from heretics or heathens. The second presupposition considered it natural that the civil world (oikoumene) and the administrative divisions and military and political borders of the only universal empire, the *res publica Romanorum*, should coexist and cover the same territory. This also led to the idea of a necessary parallelism between these divisions, at their different levels, and the ambit of the ecclesiastical jurisdiction of bishops, metropolitans and Catholic patriarchs over their respective churches and groups of churches. Everywhere, a hierarchy reigned in both organizations — state and Church: the importance and dignity of the metropolis and larger cities, in contrast to the smaller towns on the empire's borders. For the official political philosophy considered this empire to be unique, universal and eternal — apart from obviously being Christian; the rights acquired by each church in relation to the others were considered definitive and immutable, they were recognized and defined as traditional in canon law, and were protected by civil law. Thus, each ecclesiastical circumscription had a well-defined geographical and territorial area, in which the bishop had authority over the faithful.

The iconoclastic crisis dramatically revealed the weakness, or at least the serious limitations of these theoretical presuppositions. Changing historical situations meant that not only the bishops but the whole Church discovered there might be emperors who, while claiming to be Christian and orthodox, used the rights which came to them through their titles of "faithful in Christ", "defender of the Church" and "external bishop" to lawfully impose the heresy on the whole Church, starting from the Catholic bishops. Bishops could be chosen and exert their sacred power only with the emperor's approbation, and only by respecting the faithfulness to him required of a subject. They could not oppose the will of the man representing, for the Christian state, the *lex animata*. The repetition, under various emperors, of a situation of this kind could no longer be attributed to the incoherent Christian behaviour of one autocrat or another who abused his absolute power, just as each Christian can be orthodox and a sinner at the same time. This policy against the Catholic Church led to a crisis in the traditional relationship between the political power and the Church's freedom in its apostolic mission. Historical experience had shown that the Christian emperor, who had to be orthodox, might in fact not be so, but went on declaring himself to be orthodox and abusing his sacral prerogatives in order to persecute the true Christians. These true Christians — including the bishops — could not lawfully oppose the emperor without incurring lèse-majesté and breaking the canonical and state laws. So in the best realized Christian state, one could not declare oneself to be Christian and to oppose heresy. The harmony between the two powers — civil and ecclesiastical — was shown to be utopian.

The Church in history

The long crisis of iconoclasm inevitably had repercussions on the churches of the Byzantine imperial state and on those which no longer came inside its historical and military borders, or were existing, as was the case for Rome and other dioceses of the Italian peninsula, in a regime of political half-autonomy from Byzantium. The need for maintaining the same dogma, the same doctrine and the same praxis in the worship of all churches, in a communion of faith with each other, highlighted a new historical situation which had been developing since the first four Ecumenical Councils. While the one Catholic Church was still present in most of the regions which had belonged to the Roman empire, the heir of this empire, the Byzantine state, no longer had any effective power in many of them but only some theoretical claims of principle. Consequently, the real limits of jurisdiction of the different patriarchates and various diocesan churches did not always correspond to those provided for and established by the "ancient rights". Christianity, which had physically disappeared under the migratory push of the new people, had often left only the name of the ancient and venerable diocesan Sees, and existed only in the memory and the manuscripts of ecclesiastical archives; these Sees were always registered, with their rank, in the order *(taxis)* of the churches in the universal state.

Other Christian communities had meanwhile arisen and continued to arise among people who were strangers to the traditional civil organization of the empire. In many cases these Christian groups also had new diocesan seats or ethnic bishops. From the ecclesiastical and political point of view, in the regions of the empire still in the hands of the "barbarians", the fixed immutability of the churches' canonical and territorial order — sanctioned *in perpetuum* in the official acts! — was in effect simply theoretical. The measures taken by Leo III the Isaurian against the Church of Rome which, in the name of the common Tradition, opposed the new theological doctrine on the holy images and rebelled against the imperial injunction to reform the liturgy by eliminating icons from worship and popular piety, affected both ecclesiastical and civil order. They reinforced and underlined the distance, which had already existed for a long time, between the official ideology of the Christian empire — officially accepted by everyone — and its application. The inclusion of the churches of southern Italy in the patriarchate of Constantinople, carried out because of the presence of the Byzantine government in that region, interrupted the traditional jurisdiction constantly exerted on them by the Roman See and recognized by all the churches since the First Ecumenical Council. Even if this modification seemed to be based on the presupposition of only one possible Roman empire, the orthodox and eternal one (and in this case a doctrinal heresy or political apostasy deprived a local church of the rights it had enjoyed till then), it effectively denied it. In fact, it clearly demonstrated that the political and ecclesiastical borders were not immutable at all, both in fact and legally. Moreover, the loss of Palestine and Syria, the fall of Alexandria and the Pentapolis had anticipated this. The new situation already contained all the premises which made it extremely difficult, if not impossible, to appeal to the institution, which had till then offered a way of overcoming the most serious and generalized dogmatic and disciplinary crisis. The supreme ecclesiastical authority, that of the Ecumenical Council, had till then worked by following a formula and a practice which were strictly connected with the imperial political theology.[6] Time was now revealing the insufficiency of this political theology, increasingly unrelated to the conditions in which the Church actually lived.

The reception of the Councils

The main consequence of the Seventh Ecumenical Council, in 787, was the reluctant acceptance of its findings by the most important Christian churches of that period — Constantinople, Rome, the Frankish church — which received it after discussions and delays far greater than those following other similar Councils. Historically, this can be explained by considering the very different cultural and political situations in which the various churches found themselves. Some of them remained inside the empire's borders under the emperor's rule, even if they felt the effects of the different conditions reigning in each region of an enormous state, which included different peoples. Some were under Arab rule in a position of religious subordination to the dominant Islamic religion, and their faithful were subject to clear social and legal discrimination. Others, in the West, were bound to the new Christian national reigns and to their specific particular interests. The Church of Rome enjoyed relative autonomy, including the area of temporal administration, as a Byzantine duchy of Rome, and this lasted till the first half of the 8th century:[7] nevertheless, its existence was delicate and unstable due to its relationship with the Lombard and Frankish reigns and the Byzantine duchies in southern Italy. Acceptance of the conclusions of an Ecumenical Council (even if regularly assented to by the representatives of all the churches) could no longer depend on the organized strength of a universal Christian state, which attributed the value of civil laws to its definition of faith and its sacred canons, and brought them into operation by various administrative measures. This could still happen, in this form, only in the Byzantine empire and only with the emperor's approbation of the Council Fathers' doctrinal and disciplinary deliberations.

As far as the other churches were concerned, acceptance had to take into account the situation in which each church lived, and the attitude of each political authority (Christian or non-Christian) to the results of a Council which had been planned, presided over and directed by the Byzantine emperor. From Constantine onwards, this was one of the main features of an "Ecumenical" Council. The fact that there were two stages to iconoclasm made it far more difficult for all the local churches — in which the full eucharistic communion of faith and morality mysteriously gives life to the only universal Church of Christ — to accept and bring into effect common positions in ecclesiastical life. The various Synods which dealt with the question of the holy images and made laws about it — often with the agreement of bishops and the support of legal Christian kings — often took opposing dogmatic and disciplinary positions.

In 754, at Hieria, near Chalcedon, 338 bishops put the question of the images into a dogmatic context and solved it in favour of the iconoclastic position, according to the will of the Emperor and theologian Constantine V, greeted on that occasion as "equal to the Apostles". Moreover, the Council considered itself a sequel to the six previous Ecumenical Councils and arrogated this title to itself; 33 years later at Nicea, 367 bishops, summoned by Emperors Constantine and Irene, disavowed the previous Council and its definitions, restored the worship of the holy images and claimed the title of Seventh Ecumenical Council, denied to the previous Synod. The fact that Pope Hadrian's legates, who were at Hieria to represent him and his church, signed the acts of 787 did not prevent the bishops of the Frankish church, at the Council of Frankfurt, from condemning the veneration of icons, on the anti-Byzantine line of the author of the *Capitolare de imaginibus* which criticized the dogmatic conclusions of the Second Council of Nicea as heretical. At Easter 815 the iconoclast Emperor Leo V, who had obliged Patriarch Nicephorus to abdicate, wanted another Synod. It was celebrated at Constantinople, in the basilica of St Sophia, and it restored as ecumenical the Council held at Hieria in 754 and its doctrinal and canonical statements, in opposition to Nicea II. During this period the ancient churches, which were free from Byzantine political control — such as that of Jerusalem and, because of its recent rejection of the heretic emperor, that of Rome — maintained their traditional teaching and liturgical and devotional practice as far as the holy images were concerned. But they officially recognized the Council of Nicea of 787 as ecumenical only in 880, during the Council of Constantinople, convened for the union of the churches of Rome and Constantinople after twenty years of polemics. Only from this date on did the ecumenicity of that Council find universal acceptance, and much later there were still objections to it in the Frankish Church.

These events — more than any similar previous ones — made it clear that the ecumenicity of a Council was not granted to the whole Church by the mere will of the bishops who had celebrated it, or by the indispensable legal formalities: imperial sanction of its acts, signatures of the bishops and, above all, of the representatives of the five great patriarchates (Rome, Constantinople, Alexandria, Antioch and Jerusalem). The universal execution of its decrees could not be completely granted any more even by the measures of the state power, taken by the emperor. A Council celebrated as "ecumenical" could no longer affect the life of all the churches, as it used to, with recognized and efficacious "ecumenical" authority. The effective ecumenicity of a Council came to be mainly a process of assimilation by each church of the defined dogmatic orientations and of the canonical dispositions promulgated by the Council Fathers. Only when it becomes part of the liturgical life and the ordinary catechetic teaching of each church does a Council acquire substantial ecumenicity. This process begins immediately after the conclusion of a Council and develops during the following years, contributing to a deepening of the apostolic faith, to which every decision of an Ecumenical Council remains faithful. The resistance of the monks and the faithful to the innovations which the iconoclasts had attempted to introduce into the traditional doctrine and devotion was in many cases so tenacious as to lead to martyrdom. These reactions developed in all the Christian churches, both inside and outside the borders of the Byzantine empire. As during the Arian heresy, when most of the bishops and the representatives of the state, even Christians, were long doubtful about the determination and the defence of the church's dogma, so during the long crisis of iconoclasm the complementary but constitutional role of the people of God in preserving the right faith was clear. The ordinary people's awareness of the faith plays a major role in the recognition and realization of the ecclesiastical ecumenicity of a conciliar doctrine or practice.

The popes and iconoclasm

The iconoclastic crisis lasted for more than a century and became increasingly serious. It emphasized the new difficulties which historical conditions brought about in the life of the Church. It is surprising to see the perspicacity shown by the popes in realizing these difficulties and in denouncing their causes. This is seen in the official letters which Gregory II, Gregory III[8] and Hadrian I[9] wrote to the emperors and patriarchs of Constantinople. They were conscious of the continuity in the traditions of their church and the decisions of the popes who had preceded them. For example, Hadrian I recalls not only the interpretations of his two predecessors who were the first to face the iconoclastic crisis, but also those of Zacharias, Stephen II, Paul[10] and Stephen III.[11] Referring to the practice of their own church as far as the holy images were concerned, they gave a detailed list of Roman places and liturgical rites, and justified both the painting of icons and the acts of veneration, with a theory of the sacred art following the classic one interpreting art as a mimesis of nature. This theory centred on the mystery of Incarnation. Gregory II wrote to Germanus of Constantinople: "If the Lord has not been incarnated, do not give his sacred image a physical shape."[12] Obviously this is an argument *ab absurdo*, which confirms the indisputable truth of the Christian faith. Only if the facts of Jesus' historical life as told in the Gospels were not true (which is absurd) could they not be represented with images, figures and colours; the same could be said for salvation history episodes told in the Old Testament. The Church has always forbidden idols and idol worship because the gods they represent do not exist in reality, and idols are consequently false and deceiving. But human beings and the things created by God do exist, for instance his incarnate Son and his mother. So it is quite appropriate to use words, writings and images to invite all Christians, by using their eyes and minds, to rise from the creatures to the Creator, and from the Incarnate Son to the invisible Father. Christ and the martyrs have been visible, so their features can be reproduced. Rome's basilicas are full of mosaics, frescoes and holy icons, executed according to orders of the popes; the holy images have been venerated liturgically by all the bishops of

Rome in succession. St Gregory the Great, Augustine, and the Greek Fathers Gregory of Nyssa, Basil, John Chrysostom and Athanasius venerated the holy images. Year by year the record of patristic authorities collected by the popes in order to defend the worship of images became richer and richer, and correct interpretations were continuously suggested for those passages in the Holy Scriptures which the iconoclasts quoted in their favour. Tradition is against them. But the most original and "Roman" confutation of the iconoclasts' statement that nothing was written about the holy images in the first six Councils is contained in Pope Gregory II's letter to Emperor Leo III. This passage is one of those "authentic fragments by this pope" which even the most severe critics are disposed to recognize:[13]

> You wrote: "why is there nothing in the six councils about images?" In fact, Emperor, nothing has been said about bread or water, or about eating or not eating, or about drinking or not drinking, because you well know that these things have been handed down from the beginning for men's life. In the same way, images have been handed down. The bishops themselves brought the icons with them; nobody who loved Christ and God set off on a journey without holy images.[14]

The appeal to Tradition, which is always present in the Church's life through the work of the Holy Spirit and which can be seen in lived faith and liturgical practice, gives the right value to the dogmatic and conciliar formulas. In fact, they are an authentic expression of the Tradition and reflect the revealed mystery with absolute faith; nevertheless, they can always be improved, in order to be understood by people of every period. The Nicene Creed of 325, even if immutable as far as the expression of the faith was concerned, was completed in 381 at Constantinople by adding the articles about the Holy Spirit. As Gregory of Nazianzus reminds Cledonius,[15] these articles were not yet included in the Nicene Creed because the theological argument about the Holy Spirit had not come up yet. At the beginning of the 9th century Pope Leo II would teach the Frankish bishop[16] that the symbol of faith, professed by all the churches following the Councils' rules, does not contain explicitly all the truths of faith. The texts of the ecumenical councils can be considered as living and venerable only if the continual and mysterious inspiration of the Holy Spirit can be discerned in them. Otherwise they become a dead letter, whose veneration would be idolatry. Since the first imperial dispositions about iconoclasm, the popes realized that a discussion was being launched about the political theology which had been in force in the imperial church since the age of Constantine. To this Leo III the Isaurian clearly referred in order to be obeyed. He had in fact reminded the pope: "Imperator sum et sacerdos",[17] "pontifex et imperator".[18] Even the pope was not able or did not want to oppose this conception of the "imperator et caput christianorum"[19] by divine investiture. In fact, he continued to recognize the rights and the role of the Christian emperor in the Ecumenical Councils and in the ecclesiastical organization in order to guarantee orthodoxy of faith and the Church's freedom, even when he reproached him for not respecting his duties:

> Where is the emperor, friend of Christ and pious, who, according to custom, has to sit in the Council, give a prize to those who speak well and expel those who are far from the truth, if you, who are the Emperor, behave like a revolutionary and a barbarian?[20]

This theory presupposed that the emperor was by nature the first defender of the faith and morals professed and taught by the bishops of the Catholic Church. His temporal power was absolute and, in the public right of the Church, also superior to the power of the bishops' government. Nevertheless, the emperor had the legal right to invite the bishops to discuss and define the dogmatic proposals, in order to judge their correctness, only if he showed himself to be the perfect Orthodox believer, the "faithful Christian", as his official titles declared. But how would he be regarded if he left the right Catholic doctrine and became a heretic? The iconoclastic crisis showed dramatically the weakness of this theory, as similar crises had done already. When the popes refused to have the imperial instructions about the worship of images put into operation, they knew they would be helped by military forces, which could protect them from the coercion of the political and judicial power of Constantinople. But because of this refusal, they lost ecclesiastical jurisdiction over the lands of the Western patriarchates subjected to the Byzantine Empire. In spite of this, they did not deny the theory of the supreme and sacred imperial power, which was considered legal because it was conveyed by God. But they made a distinction between a true Christian emperor and an emperor who simply held this title. Gregory II says in his second letter to Leo the Isaurian:

> You wrote: "I am an emperor and a priest." This has been demonstrated by deed and word by those who have been emperors before you, because they protected the Church's properties and interests with the bishops, seeking vigorously for the truths of Orthodoxy: Constantine the Great, Theodosius the Great, Valentinian the Great, Justinian the Great and also the great Constantine, father of Justinian of the Sixth Council. These emperors reigned in a way worthy of God: they summoned councils in accordance with the bishops, looked for the truths of dogmas, built and embellished the holy churches. They are priests, because they demonstrated it with their works. [21]

Writing to Constantine and Irene, Pope Hadrian I praised them because they rejected iconoclasm, and invited them to persist with this attitude, following the example of Constantine the Great, Helen and all "the other orthodox emperors", "all the orthodox and absolutely Christian emperors" who preceded them. If they have the same attitude that these men have towards the orthodox faith and the Roman church, their names will spread around the world, with the glorious titles of "new Constantine" and "new Helen" — titles which can be considered as "really pious and given by God". The *imperium* and the power were gifts which the Christian and orthodox emperor was given by that God "in whose hands are all the world's reigns and for whom all the kings reign and all the princes command". And St Peter's protection enables the emperor to subdue all barbarian people. The letter ended with the following wish: "God, who ordered you to reign and reach the height of imperial power, may allow you to enjoy the sceptre of imperial power." [22] But which authority in the Christian empire could decide if an emperor who had received absolute power from God was a true Christian emperor or not? This could certainly not be judged by an Ecumenical Council, which could be convened and presided only by the emperor himself; neither could it be done by the bishops of the empire's dioceses who, as ecclesiastical officers, were not able to oppose the emperor without being charged with insubordination and high treason and consequently removed from their office, confined to a monastery or deported. Not only did the popes assert with energy the difference between a real

Christian emperor and a man who only had this title, but they also emphasized the opportunity of referring to a distinction between the ecclesiastical power and the imperial one, which had already been present in the tradition for a long time and had been recommended by Maximus the Confessor, John of Jerusalem and Theodorus the Studite. The dogmas concern the bishops, not the emperors.

> One is the formation required for the ecclesiastical system and another is the one possessed by the men of the world to deal with the things of the world... Just as the bishop does not have the power to interfere with the palace's matters or propose imperial dignities, so the emperor cannot interfere with the Church's business, propose elections in the clergy, consecrate the symbols of the Holy Mysteries of receiving Communion without a priest... Can you see, Emperor, the differences between the bishops and the emperor?[23]

In the 8th century this principle, which went back to the age of Constantine, could not lead to the surmounting of the "Roman" imperial political theology, which aspired at harmony between the Christian state and the Christian Church, both universal. It was extremely difficult to specify who should defend — and, in case of deviation, authoritatively correct — the harmonious relationship between the two powers. It had not yet been possible to make a clear distinction between the two powers and there was no way of eliminating the reciprocal interference and guaranteeing respect of the harmony commonly recognized in theory. The popes' interventions during the iconoclastic crisis show that Rome was conscious of the problems arising from forbidding the worship of icons. The principle and the organization established by Constantine and followed by his successors came to a crisis. It is significant that Hadrian I, in order to defend the worship of images, recalls a hagiographic legend, which later became very widespread. Constantine, about to convert, had seen in a dream two heavenly persons. When Pope Sylvester, who had hidden on the mountain of Soracte, brought him the images of the Saints Peter and Paul, the Emperor recognized them as the two persons of his dream. The so-called "donation" of Constantine and the theory of the *translatio Imperii* to the Western Holy Roman Empire were affected by a profound theological discussion influenced by politics, which finally came to a crisis due to historical circumstances. The argument about iconoclasm was solved in an Ecumenical Council, according to the canonical tradition of the united church. But the Council of Nicea in 787 was held in particular conditions, which allowed for a better understanding of the necessity of each individual church's participation for a Council to be truly ecumenical. It was not sufficient that it was summoned by the ecumenical emperor or that it was celebrated with this intention by the bishops whom he had gathered in order to discuss the ecclesiastical matters fixed by the agenda of the imperial secretariat of the Council. When the bishops who were present or represented at the Council (among them were, as the law required, those from the five patriarchates) had signed the dogmatic and disciplinary conclusions, these were promulgated as law of the Christian state, and all the empire's citizens had to obey them. The various churches remained inside the frontiers of the only Christian empire and the conciliar decisions were automatically accepted by the patriarchal or regional synods and were applied in daily ecclesiastical life. After the bishops' signature, a control was normally effected, in order to guarantee the faithfulness of the bishops themselves to the mandate received, and to carrying it out. Imperial approval gave validity to the works of a Council. The Council of

Hieria had been summoned as ecumenical by the emperor, it was celebrated as such by many bishops lawfully in office and it was followed by the promulgation of imperial laws about icons, opposing the Church's tradition. It clearly appeared that the real ecumenicity of a Council lay in the acceptance of the doctrine from the Church's side. The historical conditions had changed: Rome, Jerusalem, Antioch and many other Christian churches born among the new people of Europe were no more included in the empire's borders and no more subject to its political influence. Their bishops could refuse — more easily than Byzantine bishops could — the ecumenicity of a Council, convened and celebrated by a heretical emperor. The iconoclastic crisis generated a new consciousness of how important it was for each church to adhere to the common apostolic doctrine, in order for the true ecumenicity of a conciliar teaching to be recognized. The Church of Rome came to this awareness sooner than other churches.

NOTES

[1] M. Simonetti, *La crisi ariana nel IV secolo*, Studia Ephemeridis "Augustinianum", 11, Rome, 1975.

[2] G.L. Dossetti, *Il simbolo di Nicea e di Costantinopoli*, Rome, Edizione Critica, 1967, p.251.

[3] G. Dumeige, *Nicée II*, Histoire des conciles oecuméniques, 4, Paris, 1967, pp.260-261.

[4] *Ibid.*, pp.236-238.

[5] The bibliography on this subject is very rich. An ancient and direct testimony can be found in *Menae patricii cum Thoma referendario. De scientia politica dialogus quae extant in codice Vaticano palimpsesto*, ed. C.M. Mazzucchi, Milan, 1982, pp.36-55 and 82-93.

[6] V. Peri, "Concilium plenum et generale. La prima attestazione dei criteri tradizionali dell'ecumenicità", *Annuarium Historiae Conciliorum*, 15, 1983, pp.41-78.

[7] B. Bavant, "Le duché byzantin de Rome. Origine, durée et extension géographique", *Mélanges de l'Ecole française de Rome. Moyen Age-Temps modernes*, 91, 1979, pp.41-88.

[8] It is certain that Gregory II and Gregory III wrote to the emperors of Byzantium in order to refuse iconoclasm (cf. *Epistula Adriani papae... Constantino et Irenae Augustis*, Mansi, *Sacr. Conciliorum... collectio*, XII, Florentiae 1766, 1061A); for the authenticity and the documentary value of the preserved texts, cf. J. Gouillard, "Aux origines de l'iconoclasme: le témoignage de Grégoire II", in *Travaux et mémoires du Centre de recherche d'histoire et civilisation byzantines*, 3, Paris, 1968, pp.243-307.

[9] Mansi, XII, 1055A-1072C.

[10] L. Duchesne, *Le Liber Pontificalis. Texte, introduction et commentaire*, I, Paris, 1955, p.464: "Fortissimus enim erat orthodoxae fidei defensor; unde sepius suos missos cum apostolicis obsecratoriis atque amonitoriis litteris praefatis Constantino et Leoni Augustis direxit, pro restituendis confirmandisque in pristino venerationis statu sacratissimis imaginibus domini Dei et salvatoris nostri Iesu Christi, sanctaeque eius genetricis atque beatorum apostolorum omniumque sanctorum, prophetarum, martyrum et confessorum."

[11] *Le Liber Pontificalis, op. cit.*, I, pp.476-477: "Haec vero omnia promulgata, continuo et diversa sanctorum Patrum testimonia de sacris imaginibus domini Dei et salvatoris nostri Iesu Christi sanctaeque et gloriosae eius genetricis semper virginis Mariae dominae nostrae et beatorum apostolorum omniumque sanctorum ac prophetarum et martyrum seu confessorum in eodem adlata sunt concilio. Et subtilius cuncta perdagantes, statuerunt magno honoris affectu ab omnibus christianis ipsas sacras venerari imagines, sicuti ab omnibus praedecessoribus huius apostolicae sedis pontificibus et cunctis venerabilibus Patribus usque actenus de earum honoris affectu observatum et cunctis ad memoriam piae conpunctionis est traditum; confundentes atque anathematizantes execrabilem illam synodum quae in Greciae partibus nuper facta est pro deponendis ipsis sacris imaginibus."

[12] Mansi XIII, 96A; PL 89, 508D.

[13] Gouillard, *op. cit.*, pp.274-275.

[14] *Ibid.*, p.305; Mansi XII, 979DE; PL 89, 523C.

[15] Gregory Nazianzus, *Epist. ad Cledonium contra Apollinarem*, II, 1, PG 37, 193C.

[16] V. Peri, "Leone III et il 'Filioque'. Ancora un falso e l'autentico simbolo romano", *Rivista di Storia e Letteratura Religiosa*, 3, 1968, pp.3-32; ID., "Leone III e il 'Filioque'. Echi del caso nell'agiografia greca", *Rivista di Storia della Chiesa in Italia*, 25, 1971, pp.3-58.

[17] Gouillard, *op. cit.*, p.299; Mansi XII, 975D; PL 89, 521C.

[18] Gouillard, *op. cit.*, p.305; Mansi XII, 979E; PL 89, 523CD.

[19] Gouillard, *op. cit.*, pp.277 and 279; Mansi XII, 959B and E; PL 89, 512A and 513A.

[20] Gouillard, *op. cit.*, p.293; Mansi XII, 970AB; PL 89, 518B.

[21] Gouillard, *op. cit.*, p.299; Mansi XII, 975DE; PL 89, 521C.

[22] Mansi XII, 1076C; the passage is in the Latin text of the papal letter, integrated by Anastasius the Librarian.

[23] Gouillard, *op. cit.*, p.301; Mansi XII, 978CD; PL 89, 522AC.

Protestantism and the Seventh Ecumenical Council

Towards a Reformed Theology of the Icon

ALAIN BLANCY

The Council held at Nicea in 787 was the Seventh and final Ecumenical Council. Known as Nicea II, it represented a consensus — something generally received and recognized by all Christendom. We are separated from it by twelve centuries of history — but also by some hundreds of kilometres, for geography frequently tells us something about history. Thus in the Latin West this Council's decision to re-establish the veneration of icons was misunderstood and so had a bad reception almost from the start. Theological misunderstanding was symptomatic of a cultural break which had long been threatening. We find evidence of this in the fatal error by which the Greek *proskynesis* was rendered by the Latin *adoratio* (for which the correct Greek is *latreia*) — a term which, it is generally agreed, must be reserved for God alone.

Charlemagne, the emperor of the West, was to reject out of hand any veneration of images, for this was held to be idolatrous. The two halves of the Christian world were already no longer able to understand each other. So much so that the sequel to the translation error, which perhaps was itself not so accidental as some have liked to think, was the opening up of a more dangerous chasm: there was a profound difference, and subsequently divergence, in the way the faith was understood. We shall come back to this. But it was to be the fate of images to be given a negative rating in the West on the two counts of iconoclasm and idolatry. The former resulted from a failure to understand the true nature and purpose of icons. The latter was due to excessive, undisciplined use of images without any checks or canonical restraints.

Images and the Reformation

The Protestant Reformation, when it came on the scene, was no longer to encounter mistrust or prohibition of images displayed to the faithful; quite the reverse, for images abounded. Initially, of course, they were approved and used as an instructional device, a *liber pauperum*, illustrating the Bible for those who could not read. But, as time went on, since images were left to the free inspiration of artists and lacked the proper context, they came to be a means of gratifying popular piety, and serving the purpose of the ecclesiastical authorities. They were thus no longer on course and this was to make plain the gradual estrangement of

● This paper was translated from French by the WCC Language Service.

East and West during the middle ages. We can see this when we trace the development from Romanesque to Gothic art, itself to yield place to the free currents of the Renaissance.

The Reformation did not challenge or condemn art, but was content to banish it from worship and from the churches. This it did, however, with great vigour. In this it was clearly at odds with the Renaissance. It was to call forth an iconoclasm which it perhaps did not intend to be violent and destructive, but was perforce unable to contain everywhere. As always happens, there was more discrimination in the initial criticism than in the way it was implemented by the public at large. The Reformers' objection was simply to the veneration of images as such, not to all decoration of churches, any more than to the educational element of illustrating the Bible for the illiterate or for plain people. They did not even wish images to be destroyed when these were used for divine services, but simply sought their removal from choir and altar, which were set apart for other ways of representing and communicating the mystery of God.

Quite simply, the second commandment was to be reasserted, in all its distinctiveness from the first. For whereas in the first commandment the idolatry opposed was external, the second attacks the internal idolatry which equates God with one or other of his creatures. God cannot be represented in any shape whatever. Conversely no representation made by human hands, even seen on the analogy of Scripture, could be the object of public worship or private devotion.

But the violence of the iconoclastic outburst at the Reformation was doubtless more closely linked with the importance the middle ages had attributed to a piety of this kind and to the support it was given by the Church's hierarchy. Why was this so? What was the nature of the change? What was its purpose? Did a legitimate elementary devotional need have to be satisfied? Was it to be used to establish a power over the people, a power claiming to have their interests at heart? Was the veneration of images not a phenomenon similar to indulgences, which were based on the idea of purgatory and were the object of such bitter hostility from the young Reformation movement? For veneration went far beyond any educational uses, to which as such objection could hardly be taken — remembering how much Scripture and revelation itself make use of these in the shape of parables, figures, representations, stories and rites in the context of history to explain through meaningful narratives events which have a sacramental value. At all events this is where opinions differ and contrary positions are taken up. Here, it seems, there is not merely a difference of degree to be accounted for, but a difference in kind; not an excess of quantity but a switch of quality, and so a break in continuity. The divergence in material circumstances was bound to develop into a divergence of standpoints.

The Reformation used the traffic in indulgences as a reason for highlighting the hard core of the Gospel, i.e. justification by faith (alone). Any other way to salvation, whether by works or by indulgences, was out of the question — forbidden and to be condemned. And what was true of indulgences applied to images also. They represented another approach to the divine, alongside and indeed outside the Word which, with the sacraments, was the one legitimate means of communication between God and humanity, or Christ and his Church.

Anything with images added was simply a diminution of the sovereign Word of God and so of the authority of Scripture as the sole vehicle for that Word.

Thus the difficulty lay not in images as such — this was very much a secondary factor — but in the role they were thought to play — and were in fact made to play — in the access to salvation, as soon as they ceased any longer to be purely representational, educative or decorative.

The theological criterion

For the Reformation the fundamental principle serving as a criterion for any theological or even ecclesiological judgments centred in the Christological focus given to salvation and faith. This made it impossible to compete with — or add to — the uniqueness of salvation by grace alone and of justification of the sinner through faith alone — a salvation and faith founded on Christ alone, to whom Scripture alone bears authentic witness. Such is the unique character of mediation, and its sole manifestation in Jesus Christ. This focus on what is essential in God's revelation, and on his plan of salvation in Jesus Christ, which is confirmed by the *testimonium internum Spiritus Sancti* — the internal witness of the Holy Spirit in each believer as a member of the Church — ensures his continuous presence in two ways: in the Word of God duly proclaimed and in the faithful administration of the sacraments of baptism and the Lord's Supper. The *viva vox evangelii* in preaching and the confirmation which is its sign and seal in the sacrament are wholly and indeed exclusively adequate to make present and effective the work and person of Christ the Saviour. No image — *eikon* — exists, other than this twofold presence and action through Scripture duly proclaimed and the sacraments duly administered. This ministry of the Word and sacraments, based on the witness of Scripture to Christ and on the institution of the sacraments by him, is at once necessary and sufficient (cf. the Augsburg Confession, Article 7). It is necessary if the meaning and scope of the grace of salvation and the faith which implies justification are to be made real; and it is sufficient to give access to these. Corresponding to exclusive focus on Christ and the Spirit who exclusively bears witness to him — i.e. to the exclusive, complete validity of grace and faith for salvation, and to the uniqueness of the witness of Scripture and the Spirit — there is the uniqueness of the ministry of the Word and sacrament for the upbuilding and preservation of the one Church, the one Body of Christ. *Sola gratia, sola fide* and *sola scriptura* are formulae which necessarily imply and involve not just the "one Church" but also the "one ministry" which correspond to the "one Spirit". And for the Calvinist Reformation, the culmination of this is in the formula *soli deo gloria* — glory given to God who is himself the One God. This being so, what more can images add — at least as an essential? Anything they might add would simply detract from the essential. The Christological focus is at the same time a fullness. Everything else springs from it as a derivative but is not as such part of it. Everything else represents fruits and consequences, but not causes or conditions. "It is finished." There is nothing lacking in the work and person of Christ, Son of God, Mediator and Saviour, to whom the Spirit bears witness in the hearts of believers.

Everything else was to be handled and adjudged by individuals at their own discretion, provided they do not seek to turn such things into criteria, principles, motivating factors or elements that challenge the faith. Should that happen, they must be opposed in the name of the uniqueness of what is necessary and sufficient for salvation.

To put it yet another way: whatever is not Christ, his person and his work, and immediately and continuously appertaining to him, can only either reflect or echo him — it can never represent or replace him. This is true even of the Word and sacraments, and the ministry and the Church. There will always be a gap, a difference, an otherness, between what Christ is and what has its origin in him. There is neither fusion nor confusion between the means of grace and the author of grace. Means are the medium but not the mediation itself, for the mediator is unique, like his mediation — his sacrifice offered once for all. Church and ministry cannot be identified with him, but stand over against him as his opposite numbers and partners in the new covenant which he alone is to establish. Christ communicates himself by the Spirit, through the witness borne to him by Scripture and the Church and made present by the ministry of the Word and sacrament. This circumstance in no way lowers the high status of the ministry or the Church, nor of the Word or the sacraments. On the contrary it sets Head and Body, Bridegroom and Bride in their proper context as complementary opposites in the covenant, and effects the communion and communication between Christ and his Church, between him who sends and those who are sent. Still more: within the ministry we have to distinguish between the minister and his ministry, the subject and the object, the servant and what constitutes service. One is not to be identified with that for which one is the vehicle; the Word and sacrament remain external to one in so far as they are of Christ and are Christ. One serves them by making them audible, perceptible, accessible and operative. Here the same distinction can be drawn within the ministry as holds good for the relation between Christ and his Church.

What does this mean for the problem of images? The only kind of representation is that of the Gospel communicated by preaching and the sacraments. And there is no other access to the grace of salvation than "faith that is not seen" and is without merits or works of justification. Even that faith is not a work of human beings, nor is it the product of human strength or imagination. It is specifically the renunciation of all initiative, of "faith that is seen", it is a surrender to the gift of God itself. Thus one aspect of the means of grace is that (logically) they simply exclude any "middle" — or intermediate term, or medium — and in any event, as has been stressed above, a medium inevitably excludes any actual mediation, both in principle and in practice. It is there only to point towards the *sole* mediation and Mediator, and it makes that its point of reference both subjectively and objectively. Thus by a kind of negative or apophatic theology all representations dissolve, leaving only that — and that One — towards which alone faith strives.

This focus and this ascesis yield a twofold liberation: on the one hand, they bring freedom from the sin of idolatry, which is highlighted by the degree of importance, and by the role, attached to any mediation other than that exclusive to Christ — even, and indeed above all, in the subtlest form of the autonomy of matter and the created world, when these are brought outside the scope of submission to the Creator and of the obligation to give him the glory, and are erected into instruments of redemption by and for themselves, particularly in science and technology. And on the other hand this focus and ascesis bring freedom for inventiveness and creativity in all fields which are not so much

Plate 1: *Baptism of Jesus, mosaic, 15th century, monastery of Daphni, Greece,
copy presented to the WCC by Ecumenical Patriarch Athenagoras in 1967*

Plate 2: *Icon of the resurrection, mosaic, 14th century,*
Chora monastery (now the Kariye museum), Istanbul

Plate 3: *Icon of Pentecost, 1988,*
by Vassiliki Papantoniou, Greece

Plate 4: *Icon of St Paul's vision at Troas (Acts 16:9), 1975,*
by Rallis Kopsidis, St Paul's Church,
Orthodox Centre of the Ecumenical Patriarchate,
Chambésy, Geneva, Switzerland

dependent on salvation as flowing from it, whether ethical, educational, scientific, technical, economic, legal, or political — in a word, pertaining to culture as opposed to the realm of worship. In a nutshell, we are then concerned with consequences, fruits and expressions, either allowable or indeed laid upon us in life by faith — like so many shock waves engendered by the original irruption of revelation and divine redemption in Jesus Christ. They cannot be reckoned as part of a series of which he is one, any more than the interpretation of Scripture can be reckoned among them. They are different in kind. The issue here is rather of witness through service — or service through witness — to what is and remains without confusion the sole, universal source of salvation, whence everything comes and to whom everything returns — the initiator and end of faith.

But how does this tie up with the question of icons, the image controversy? Before answering this question we may at least ask how exactly everything said ties up with the idea of representation, images or icons. What are Scripture and sacrament, or Church and ministry of the Word and sacrament? Are these not related to Christ as representations, images or icons in the full sense of the term, that is, in their sacramentality, if we may be so bold as to use this description? Sharing in his uniqueness, but each unique on its own account, and each with its place in a hierarchy, are they not indeed related sacramentally to him whom — and that which — they express, interpret and make present? The only question, then, is to know what we really mean by "sacramentality" and in turn by representation, image and icon.

Or again, if we take the question a little farther, should we not be making a distinction between two kinds of manifestations or representations — those directly connected with making salvation present and transmitting it, i.e. the means of grace, and their derivatives — secondary witness, reflected brilliance — which are simply images or concrete illustrations and practical applications of the former. And how are the place, rank, function and value of these derivatives to be assessed in relation to the means of grace, and both in relation to that which alone is necessary and sufficient? If the means are instrumental, are the derivatives more in the nature of effects, products or fruits? If, after all, any images are involved, they would be as it were on two levels. But this merely raises a question and does not provide an answer.

What is at stake in icons — the theology of the Incarnation

How then are we to understand what the Reformation was trying to express in relation to the intention of the Second Council of Nicea in 787?

Let us take another look at the circumstances prevailing at the time of the Council. Iconoclasm was perhaps no longer first and foremost a religious, but rather a political question. Religious reform was a pretext by which the political authorities could gain control of the Church. Thus the Council's activity represented a struggle for spiritual liberty and the freedom of the Church. Behind the professed desire to purify the faith there lurked in reality the arrogance of an imperial authority which wanted to take over for its own advantage the worship, or at least the veneration, given to icons, and focus it on the person of the emperor himself. Nevertheless, this reform was regarded by Christians as an innovation quite contrary to a tradition that was already hundreds of years old. It was felt to be an attack on the faith.

39

But above all, outside the purely political context, the theology of icons was affirmed and reinforced at the Council. At the time, the precise point of it was missed in a Western world still close to paganism and struggling against it on the northern frontiers of the Empire. The Council's theology was a theology of the Incarnation and it depended directly on the Christology of Chalcedon which had been defined four centuries previously. The canons of Nicea make it clear, in particular, that representation of the figure of Christ was not merely legitimate but requisite, because of and on the basis of the Incarnation. It was not enough to represent him symbolically by a cross, lamb, or good shepherd, for he had come in person to dwell among human beings. So it was essential to represent him in his own person. Also, as a result of the line taken in the Chalcedonian Christology as to the unity of the two natures, divine and human, in the one person of Christ, there is no objection to thinking of the divine as having human features, nor is there any reason to reject what is human on the plea that at present Christ is glorified and seated at the right hand of the Father. Thus it is clear that the veneration given to the image is in fact due by right to the one represented in it — its prototype. The image acts only as a mirror or an avenue of access to what and whom it represents. Veneration of the icon is subordinate to adoration of the one represented in it, namely Christ. It is perfectly true that other considerations still played a part. But the essential feature is something based on that theology of the Incarnation, the reality and realism of which must not be obfuscated or obscured by recourse to the symbolic. The Incarnation is something other than symbolic and something more than sacramental. It is a personal — or as the Greeks would have said, a hypostatic — union. To be sure, this union is not a fusion, and so the image is not a pattern of the person it represents, but neither is it dissociated from him — it is not something separate from the one represented. True God and true man without separation and without confusion: the Christology of Chalcedon fits the case of the icon perfectly and is expressed in it.

To rule out the possibility or necessity of the icon is to deny or reject the two natures of Christ and their personal union originating with and in the man Jesus. Better still, in representing one who is of the earth we are also representing one who is heavenly — using the visible to represent the invisible — and by giving access to the one we are opening up the approach to the other. The crucified Jesus is the risen Christ and likewise the risen Christ is still marked by the stigmata of the cross.

Thus the underlying question is not that of images but of Christology — not the crass question of icon-worship, but the subtle though essential one of how salvation is revealed. In *ikonodoulia*, the veneration of icons, what is at stake is the very central question of the faith: Christ as God and man, and the other way round. Can we say, then, that it is a vain and barren undertaking, impossible and forbidden, to represent him? Not in the least, if every moment of his existence from before his birth and beyond his death are inseparable, and if humiliation and exaltation, death and resurrection are also for their part indissolubly united. More to the point, if it were not so, it would be all up with our faith and our salvation. The "triumph of Orthodoxy", that is, the final restoration of the veneration of icons in the East in 843, is in fact the victory of faith in Christ the Lord and Saviour. *Mutatis mutandis*, icons and Mariology are comparable. To call Mary mother of God — *Theotokos* — as the Council did, is not to have her and her status primarily in mind but rather Christ and his person, or, more precisely, the true humanity of the Son of God and the true divinity of the son of Mary. This was imagery, yet also a real expression of the dual nature of Christ in one person. Turning it into some kind of Mariolatry created a pernicious and unhappy distortion, which has divided Christians to no purpose. Thus not the icon but the truth of the faith is to be checked in this context.

Conditions for a Reformed theology of icons

a) For a Christology of humiliation, not exaltation

What conclusions can we draw from this for a theology that stems from the Reformation? Once the underlying meaning and real purpose of icons have been established, there is at bottom nothing against such a theology. Icons are not meant to be or do anything other than express what is central to the faith — the person and work of Christ. This too is why there is no icon properly so called in which he would not be present. This is particularly true for the Virgin, who is never represented by herself. In other words, icons would be made acceptable from the strictly Reformed standpoint by a recognition that — even if there is nothing detrimental in the fact that they are artistic masterpieces — they are not a work of human hands but another expression of the one initial and indeed unique, primordial and definitive work of God himself, in the creation and redemption effected in Jesus Christ. Here, the function of icons would not be to raise human beings towards God but much rather to bring God down towards humanity. And for a Reformed theology that would be essential. Human beings can never raise themselves towards God and even if they could, they would not be allowed to do so, for that is the supreme sin; and Christ, as the prototype of every icon, is the one who once for all renounced the desire to claim divinity and be equal to God (Phil. 2:6). Hence it is right that the icon should represent the Son of God in his humiliation, and, by that alone — but nevertheless genuinely — his exaltation to the right hand of God, again in terms of the Christological hymn in Philippians 2:6-11. Even though made by human hands, the icon can convey by the grace of God the hidden presence of him who is represented solely by Jesus Christ, and not just some kind of human piety, endowed though that might be with an aura of mysticism. For a Reformed Christian, an icon will not reflect human enlighten-ment but divine kenosis. It will operate against all human temptations to self-glorification, even by making use of Christ, and against the temptations of the powers that be to claim to represent God. Thus the icon is not an image but anti-image. Because it is less than an image, it is infinitely more. It is thus the opposite of the Turin shroud, that relic which is venerated in Roman Catholic devotion and derives its value from the fact that it is virtually a photographic reproduction of a crucified martyr whose features and wounds had been reputedly imprinted for ever into the fabric. The claim is that the mortal remains of Jesus would thus reveal his transcendence, through the energy released by his flesh as it underwent transfig-uration. What a strange kind of realism — what a curious quest for proof — not just of the portrait of Jesus, but of his divine origin and destiny, the mere radiation of which would explain the (photographic) negative created by the impression on the shroud. Now everything in this photographic idea of Jesus runs counter to what the icon in essence is. The icon is a thousand miles removed from this human

41

appropriation of the person of Jesus. It derives its nature not from Thomas's desire to see and touch the Crucified in the Risen Lord but from the adoration accorded him by that same Thomas — "My Lord and my God!" — who does not ever touch him or physically verify the identity of the vision. The inspiration of the icon comes rather from the Pauline affirmation, "even though we once regarded Christ from a human point of view, we regard him thus no longer". And "if anyone is in Christ he is a new creation; the old has passed away, behold, the new has come" (2 Cor. 5:16-17). This newness which holds good for the Christian does so *a fortiori* for Christ himself. It also applies to the icon, in which the physical likeness is not so important as the spiritual gift that is given expression in it.

What is more, how can one lapse into the worship of images made by human hands when everyone who is in Christ is already made in his image? If he himself is the icon *(eikon)* of God and if everyone who believes in him is made, created and recreated in his image, what can any other form of representation add? Only the spiritual person can judge spiritual things (cf. 1 Cor. 2:11ff.). Only those created in the image of Christ can know him and recognize him as being himself the image of God. What more is required?

It would at all events be a false and illusory move to have recourse to science and technology to test the authenticity of an image of Christ held by a piece of fabric. Orthodoxy certainly does like to speak of an icon "as not made by hands" *(acheiropoietos)*, but to precisely the opposite effect from the Turin shroud which, though allegedly a portrait of Jesus and so not made by human hands, does nevertheless start from the human end to arrive at the divine; while, if I am not mistaken, the Orthodox approach is the other way round, with its view of the icon as divine condescension making itself available for contemplation by assuming in barest outline a human form. The stress is not on the same element nor on the same operative factor. At all events Protestants will for their part continue to be extremely allergic — not to say frankly hostile — to the shroud as a display and demonstration of divinity in humanity. To them what is adduced as proof has the opposite force. And this is where the risk is great that we may see them throw out the baby with the bath-water. Thank God, the icon is not a portrait and is not aiming at a physical likeness; and if it is not to be adored, neither is it there for aesthetic reasons; it is not even an object of contemplation, nor of prayer, as such — all of which uses are feasible with a devotional image where mental and physical virtues are brought into prominence. The icon, on the other hand, has a dynamic which suits the Protestant. It fulfills a function, almost a ministry. It is word made manifest; it is the effective vehicle of a message. It is not only bound to be accompanied by an inscription or description, but it also follows rules which are its grammar and makes corresponding sense. It is discourse even more than it is image. Because it is only two-dimensional and dismisses or rejects the third dimension that we find in all statuary, it is at once text and context, that which is written and that which is read, sign and meaning, plain word and parable. In a wholly different sense a dimension of depth opens up in it for the believer. Its well-known reversal of perspective simply expresses the transformation or conversion of vision occurring in it. This dynamic is essentially to be associated with the Protestant understanding of Word and sacraments, and especially of the Eucharist, of which the Reformation was to say, in line with the Church Fathers, that it was the only real image or "icon" of Christ. Icons can neither be defined nor understood, nor are they accessible apart from their purpose and the fulfilment of their mission. As the Word exists only when proclaimed and the sacrament when administered, so that the Gospel can be made present and effective through them, so too the icon is there only to fulfill its purpose — to call forth and produce the communication and communion of believers with their Lord. This it does just by being itself, that is, by the realization of the purpose for which it was made.

Protestants nevertheless continue to be hesitant and stop on the threshold when it comes to using icons in their faith, devotion, theology and church. History really has turned custom into a tradition. Past polemics with a Western world which was regarded as iconoclastic have not been overcome, and there may yet be other good reasons for continuing a struggle which ought only to be a rearguard action.

For Roman Catholicism after Vatican II has carried out a revolutionary purging of its liturgy and current forms of devotion. It has focused again on that which is essential, and alone necessary and sufficient. The ecumenical dialogue has something to do with this and is deriving great advantage from it. The Reformed concentration on Christology has become the Roman Catholic "hierarchy of truths". Christ and the Spirit are sufficient witnesses to themselves as present and active in the Church and in the world. The Word and the sacrament are sufficient to transmit salvation through the ministry that serves them.

b) Between identity and difference

But there is more to it than that: the gap and the difference between the Christ of history and the Jesus who is present. This has been emphasized by the quotation from 2 Corinthians 5:16f. To the Reformed tradition, which here is distinct from the Lutheran, the Christ who is present also includes the Christ in glory. As such, his appearance is neither accessible nor capable of transmission. The Reformed Protestant is somewhat torn between the earthly Christ who was, and the Christ in glory who is to come — obsessed more than in any other Christian tradition by the tension of time and history. Is it so impossible to give essential unity to what time separates in history? I think not — on the one condition that the means must be kept available for overcoming the tension and the fragmentation while still respecting time and history. These means are the Word and the Spirit. It is a Word which gives meaning to each link in the passage of time and a Spirit which makes this Word present here and now. Free from confusion with any external likeness or analogy or similarity, the Word and the Spirit are the presence and work of Christ. They are successors of the earthly Christ and they anticipate the heavenly Christ. We might alternatively say that it matters less to the Reformed Christian to affirm the identity than to note the difference. It is Christ himself who makes the difference, and is thus the same — himself. He presents and represents himself with features which differ and which also make the difference what it is. In the icon what is at stake is the dynamic which leads us from flat, static identity to a difference that is fruitful and full of promise. What matters is to realize what Christ desired, the transformation and transfiguration of the world and its recreation in the image of its Creator and Redeemer. Here imagination holds the reins — not servile imitation. This is how the Church operated in the first days of its existence. Faithfulness is not servility. The Apostle Paul, following Peter and like him, was able to interpret the Gospel of reconciliation in terms of the coming together of Jews and Greeks, which was not a stated part of the original programme. This creativity is an iconic pattern. So we have to trace out the patterns, or rather reproductions of the one pattern, with a regard for times and places, so that they may really be icons of Christ the Lord and Saviour and of his grace, which calls faith into being. Here the icon has a future that matters to all of us. It is the icon or image of Christ in the least of his brothers and sisters (according to Matt. 25:31-45); it is the icon of love which opens up every liturgy for diakonia. It is the icon of the Word and sacrament, opening us up towards our neighbour, and the icon of theology which opens us up towards ethics. It is likewise those for whom and to whom Christ gives himself, and who are "changed into his likeness *(eikona!)* from one degree of glory to another; for this comes from the Lord who is the Spirit" and who sets us free (2 Cor. 3:19).

c) The icon: word or image?

There is however yet another difficulty for the Reformed Christian in relation to the icon. It arises from the fact that the relation of image to Word is the opposite of what holds good for the icon, where the Word comes to the aid of the image as its legend. For the Reformed Christian, the opposite holds good. The image merely comes to the aid of the Word, which is primary and dominant. Even the Eucharist is still the Word, the Word signified — the visible sign, signature and seal, all of which still depend on the Word. The Word is in the key position.

Things are of course less simple in practice, since now the Word itself has some of the characteristics of sign, form and hence icon.

This is precisely where modern science, linguistics and especially semiotics are a great help. They lessen the gap and the difference said to exist between image and word, icon and text. But they also show that the word is increasingly making way for a polysemic world of signs of which it is just one specific example. Modes of discourse are multiplying, but they converge in their role of communication. The modern world tends to replace the privileged language of the word, i.e. of discourse, by that of the image, the picture, that is, of representation. It was thought for a time that this meant a switch back from hearing to seeing, from time to space, from sequence to contemporaneity, from duration to the instant, from history to presentness, from an indirect to an immediate relation: that is, a decisive switch from the age of Gutenberg to that of Marconi. Might it be just as much a return from the word to the icon? Matters are not so simple. For the image in turn becomes language — a mode of discourse — particularly when it is in serial form — it integrates the world of communication and in turn becomes discourse when it takes on the sequential appearance of a film.

It could well be that common interests would establish unexpected alliances between those who defend the icon and those who champion the Word — the Orthodox and the Reformed Christians. For what the world offers as a revolution in communication — the switch from word to image, from "message" to "massage" (or "medium", following McLuhan's formula) — may be less a conversion than a perversion. For it represents the most basic regression of the mind towards that which fascinates, and of reason to that which makes it captive. The power of the image is so totalitarian. It subjects and subjugates the subject! For neither rejoinder nor response is possible to the power of the image, which is monolithic and reduces the world to a show, in which the individual is a passive spectator. It robs of responsibility and so of liberty and substitutes an imaginary, manipulated world for the real one which is God's creation. The integrity of the world and of humanity is at stake. This change can evoke equally scepticism and nihilism or totalitarianism and possessiveness. And because of the media there is in fact no difference between an image or picture which thrusts a face at us and propaganda which pushes us towards a particular standpoint. Just as images have form and colour, so too discourse creates sound and noise. The screen is shattered by the insidious, outsize impact of the medium, which gives the subject a force very different from that of an actual presence or a dialogue between partners.

Against this captivity of humanity and the world — this perversion of creation and mockery of the creature who is made in the image of the Creator, this wrong done to his will to save, this twofold negation of his grace and of the faith that corresponds to it — a holy alliance or covenant between word and icon proves to be urgently needed, to defend what lies behind the divine Incarnation and the work of salvation, and to liberate the personal relation — which it calls into being and sustains — between the Creator and his renewed creatures. Where God makes a covenant and communicates by his Word and shows his face in a Father-Son relationship, how can we permit the establishment of something which disfigures both God and humanity? How can we allow disregard of the one and subjugation of the other? It is therefore important for icon and word, word and icon to display their character of reciprocal relationship within the setting of the covenant between God and humanity — a character established and made effective by Jesus Christ in his person. If the one partner is discredited the other too is diminished. If we lessen the role of humanity as a creation in the image of God, we tarnish the glory of its Creator. In these circumstances icon and Word have the same part to play. They belong to the same category, for they are in a mutual two-way relationship. There, reciprocity is a *conditio sine qua non*.

Conclusion

Thus while Protestantism and Orthodoxy issue from two different ambiances and relate to two different traditions, they can live in communion on the basis of the same values, and subscribe to the same theology, whether this is expressed more through word or through icon.

Social and Political Consequences of the Iconoclastic Crisis

TODOR SABEV

Iconoclasm shook the Byzantine empire and the undivided Church at the time of the Ecumenical Councils to a degree comparable only to the Arian and Monophysite struggles of previous centuries. It brought about a movement whose scope, radical views, ambitions and aims have been compared with the 16th-century Reformation.

The age of iconoclasm can be divided into three distinct phases: (1) its emergence and development under Emperors Leo III (717-740) and Constantine V (740-775), and the iconoclastic Council of 754; (2) the Seventh Ecumenical Council in Nicea, 787, when it was arrested; and (3) its revival (815-842) and final extinction (up to 867).

Iconoclasm as an imperial policy was proclaimed with Leo's exhortation to the people in 726 and the first imperial decree of 730.[1] It intensified, and led to the violent persecution of the monastic clergy during the rule of Constantine V. The Second Ecumenical Council of Nicea restored the iconophile doctrine and peace in the Church. Military reversals then led Leo V to resurrect the iconoclastic policies, but in 843 icons were definitively restored and their veneration was solemnly proclaimed as part of Orthodox belief. Throughout this period, religious, social and political factors — all inter-related — played a significant role in shaping the iconoclastic movement and its development.

Religious, socio-economic and political factors

The reign of Leo III "the Isaurian" marked a positive phase of the empire, which had been disrupted by twenty years of revolution and invasion. Administrative, military, economic and social reorganization helped consolidate the concerns in Asia Minor and the imperial power around the capital. A major victory was won against the Arabs in 740. Constantine V had noteworthy success in northern Syria and the Balkans, and thus became enormously popular.[2] Difficulties in socio-economic life, however, had repercussions on the internal situation and foreign policy, and also influenced Church-state relationships in an age of feudalism, with its tendency to Caesaro-papism.[3]

For many centuries the veneration of icons had been one of the chief expressions of Christian piety. Nevertheless, since the beginning of the 4th century many hierarchs, theologians and common people had considered Christianity a purely spiritual religion which practised the cult of icons.[4] During the first phase of iconoclasm this spirit prevailed in several regions of the Christian East, especially in Armenia and neighbouring areas. In Asia Minor the controversy was strong, and even before 720 some hierarchs, such as Bishop Constantine of Nacolia (in Phrygia), Metropolitan Thomas of Claudioupolis, and Metropolitan Theodore of Ephesus, visited Patriarch Germanus I (715-729) and asked him to take steps against the worship of images. The Patriarch refused and in some letters defended the Orthodox tradition of the veneration of icons, but he did not prevent the bishops from opposing it.[5]

A certain misinterpretation and misuse of image worship also contributed to the confusion and controversy.[6] In the eastern borderlands of the empire antagonism to the veneration of religious images was influenced by Monophysites and Paulicians, proselytizing Jews and neighbouring Muslims with their horror of idolatry.[7] Another factor in favour of iconoclasm was the emperor's conception of his role as God's vice-regent on earth. The government was determined to preserve unity in the faith and the integrity of the multinational empire.[8] This concerned especially the eastern and western regions of the empire.

Military and civil reforms called for a full state treasury. In 727-728 Leo III made a double levy of the regular taxes and ten years later he raised an additional tax to rebuild the walls of Constantinople. The realization of his plans led him to risk violating Church property and revenue. This was consonant both with the interest of the army, a part of the state administration and the majority of poor citizens, especially peasants. The Emperor's projects, however, were linked to a process of secularization, confiscation of property and interference in the internal life of the privileged Church and powerful monasteries. Moreover these projects touched upon holy traditions, spirituality, worship and Orthodox theology. Therefore, the plans of the iconoclastic emperors met with Church opposition, especially by the monastic clergy and numerous monasteries. Iconoclasm became an integral part of the social and political programmes of Emperors Leo III and Constantine V.[9]

The immunity of the Church from taxation on its ever-increasing lands reduced the revenue of the state. The popularity of monasticism with its tens of thousands of monks[10] meant fewer soldiers and labourers in the fields. The monasteries were considered dangerous centres of unrest; many depended on the "miraculous icons" they possessed to attract a great number of pilgrims, with their donations in money and in kind. And it was only the vast properties of the Church which escaped state taxation: a considerable segment of the population (about 100,000) were outside the control of state administration. On the other hand, by the control of education and the influence they had over popular opinion, monks and nuns held real power in the state. Monasteries and icons were therefore considered by iconoclastic emperors as obstacles to the implementation of their social reforms and the realization of their political ambitions.[11]

The many privileges of the monasteries began to attract people who did not have a real vocation for monastic life or Christian spirituality. All these turned the state authorities against monasticism and provided arguments for bringing the Church under control and confiscating monastic property.[12]

The critical attitude of the Roman See at the end of the 720s/the beginning of the 730s towards Leo's first steps and taxation met with the Emperor's firm action against the Church in the West. Leo III increased the capitation tax of Sicily and

Calabria by a third and transferred the patrimonies of the apostles Peter and Paul (amounting to three and half talents of gold) to the imperial treasury in Constantinople. New-born males were to be registered for taxation.[13] The churches of Sicily and Calabria and the dioceses of Eastern Illyricum (Dacia and Macedonia), and probably of Crete, were transferred from Roman jurisdiction to that of Constantinople.[14] Socio-economic and political issues were clearly as crucial as religious and canonical considerations.

Theophanes[15] and Theodore the Studite[16] testified that, at the end of the 8th century and the beginning of the 9th, the municipal tax in Constantinople was repealed and some import and export duties were reduced, but these measures created great confusion and ruined the finances. In order to remedy the impoverishment of the state treasury, Emperor Nicephorus I (802-811) reimposed the old taxes. In 810 the finances were reorganized in such a way that Church lands and Church tenants had to pay their share.[17] The gradual increase in taxation in rural areas, which began under Constantine's reign, sharpened the social struggle and created political unrest.[18] The civil war in 821-823 began as a social-revolutionary movement, organized by Thomas the Slav, who proclaimed himself champion of the iconodules.[19]

Seeing himself as both "emperor and priest",[20] Leo III aimed at assuming full control over ecclesiastical matters and gave new strength to iconoclastic Caesaro-papism. He contended that "the Lord, having entrusted the realm to the emperors, has likewise commanded them to tend Christ's faithful flock, after the example of Peter, the chief of the Apostles". Here we find not only the final deduction from the Justinian "harmony" between Church and state, but a "new theocratic logic" and "iconoclastic attempt to destroy the independence of the Church, and simply to fit into the theocratic framework".[21] This resolute Caesaro-papism of all the iconoclastic emperors involved not only active intervention in the internal life of the Church, such as the nomination and deposition of patriarchs and bishops, the creation of new dioceses for adherents of the iconoclastic doctrines and so on, but also aimed at the complete submission of the Church. It therefore became a source of tension and division. The Church, and particularly the monasteries, met the challenge of iconoclastic Caesaro-papism with courage and determination. A large number of Orthodox believers continued to follow its spiritual guidance.[22]

Division among Christians

During the whole period of iconoclasm there were clearly distinguishable groups of iconophiles (image lovers), and of iconoclasts to which belonged hierarchs, priests and monastic communities. Such a deep controversy within the Church adversely affected religious life and ethics, and caused social chaos and political discord as well. The forced removal and replacement of many patriarchs, metropolitans and bishops, together with their followers and supporters, was another factor leading to tension which had social and political repercussions. Some of these clergymen were educated laymen, trained in the civil service, who had reached high positions in the imperial court, were ready to make a compromise with state authority and able to influence public opinion outside the Church and through Church institutions.[23]

The iconoclastic Council at Hieria near Constantinople in 754 condemned the worship of images as heretical and prepared the way for imperial persecution.[24]

For three decades the iconodules still had to reckon with the theological rationale of the Council of 754, without being entirely capable of dealing with it.[25] The iconoclastic Council of 815 confirmed the decisions of Hieria.[26] The situation was troubled in Church and society throughout the entire Byzantine empire, and to a certain extent influenced relationships with other patriarchates in the Christian East.[27]

Many ordinary believers, of course, were unable to argue theologically.[28] Very often, their belonging to one camp or the other was motivated by social and political factors, and by the influence of Church leaders or state authorities. The popularity of victorious statesmen and disappointment with certain emperors also played an important role. Faithfulness to Orthodoxy as a blessing and seeking ways to further the welfare of Church and society was a guiding principle for both iconophiles and iconoclasts, particularly during the glorious reign of Constantine Copronymus, and at the beginning of the 9th century when the Byzantine empire faced a series of wars, invasions and revolts.[29] Several times iconoclastic actions provoked riots and grave conflict in Church and state.[30] The misuse of icons and the distortion of veneration of religious images (e.g. something close to idol worship, the reverence of the material substance of icons, etc.)[31] also provoked disputes in Church and society.

Radical political expression of conflict and hostility

Shortly after the first decree against icons was published (in 730) a revolt broke out in Greece itself. Though this was a rather unique event of its kind, opposition to iconoclasm bore the potential of a political movement. The uprising in Greece, the measures taken in Italy to drive out imperial officers, and the severe condemnation of violent and heretical expressions of iconoclasm were clear signs of such powerful support for Orthodoxy.[32] The revolutionary atmosphere and insurrection of the beginning of the 820s should also be attributed to these events.

The army was loyal to the iconoclastic emperors. In Asia Minor, which was the main source of recruits, there were several groups opposed to religious images. If Asia Minor had become the bastion of iconoclasm, military units would have considered it their duty to support and develop the iconoclastic movement.

However, the monasteries, under the spiritual leadership and courageous stand of Theodore the Studite, organized a major ecclesiastico-political movement against the "iconoclastic party". Encountering monastic resistance, the emperors and military chiefs confiscated monasteries and transformed them into military barracks.[33]

By passionately pursuing different aims and often with deeply divergent interests, the imperial army and the monastic communities greatly contributed to social and political division.[34]

For more than a century iconophiles were hunted down, humiliated, exiled, and persecuted. Many representatives of the clergy followed the example of Christians of the early Church: they witnessed to Jesus Christ in truth and selflessness. Some of them (e.g. St Stephan)[35] were murdered for not repudiating the Orthodox doctrine. Monks were forced to march through the hippodrome, humiliated before the mob, compelled to renounce celibacy and terrorized into marriage or flight from monasteries. A large number escaped to southern Italy, Cyprus, Syria, Palestine and the northern shores of the Black Sea. All this created a mixture of reactions: frustration and fanaticism, sympathy, and determination to side with those who suffered.[36]

During the iconoclastic period several emperors were more concerned with gaining and keeping power than with the welfare of the state. They did not hesitate to eliminate obstacles in their path. Personal morality, social ethics and Church canons were often neglected. The power struggle led to conspiracy, energetic counter-measures and "purge of enemies". All this had lasting repercussions on the political life of large segments of society.[37]

The iconoclastic crisis and its repercussions on financial measures, as well as ecclesiastical jurisdiction over Illyricum and southern Italy, alienated Rome from Constantinople.[38] The new boundaries between the two ecclesiastical centres slowly became "walls of separation". The Church in the West refused to accept iconoclasm and in 731 a local council in Rome condemned iconoclastic doctrines.[39] The intransigence of Constantine V contributed to the political rapprochement between Rome and the Frankish king. This shattered the ancient imperial Church and the total empire — the oikoumene. It challenged the universalism of both the Church and the Byzantine empire. Divisive elements added further tension and in the 60s and 70s of the following century a crisis situation was reached which anticipated the final schism between East and West (1054).[40]

On the road to flexibility and unity: the positive role of the Seventh Ecumenical Council

Under the reign of Leo IV (775-780) "the adherents of Orthodox piety gradually acquired confidence again".[41] The obstacles were removed and conditions were now favourable[42] for the opening of the Seventh Ecumenical Council (28 September 787), in which a considerable number of abbots and monks participated. A theologically moderate and sound conciliar definition made a precise distinction between "adoration" and "veneration" of icons,[43] and peace and unity were restored. The twenty-two disciplinary canons also contributed to healing wounds and improving situations created by iconoclasm, including issues of church property (canon 12), simoniacal abuses, etc.[44]

Unfortunately iconoclasm revived with renewed strength at the beginning of the 9th century. Its supporters were chiefly in Byzantine government and military circles. On Palm Sunday 815, thousands of monks went in procession through the capital city, carrying icons. A bloody persecution began again, marking the second period of iconoclasm. In the following decades, however, socio-economic and political difficulties contributed to the failure of the iconoclastic policy. In 842 the movement collapsed and a new era of Orthodoxy began.

On the first Sunday of Lent 843, the reinstatement of icons was solemnly proclaimed, and this memorable Sunday has since been celebrated as the historical "triumph of Orthodoxy".[45] It should also have been a turning point in reconciliation, reunited efforts and common witness of the undivided Church of the Christian East and West. New circumstances, however, prevented Rome from associating with the "triumph of Orthodoxy".

The legacy of the Second Council of Nicea towards full unity

This event of 843 ended a particular quarrel which had drained all the energies of the Church, especially in the East, for a whole century. A lasting peace was inaugurated, which was no longer to be troubled by the question of the veneration of icons until the Reformation. However, even the restoration of icon veneration by the Seventh Ecumenical Council failed to bridge the differences between East and West, particularly regarding papal patrimonies, the rights of jurisdiction, Church authority of Rome and Constantinople, and the use of the title "Ecumenical Patriarch".[46] The confusion and controversy caused by the *Libri Carolini* concerning the decisions and spirit of Orthodoxy of the Seventh Ecumenical Council, the coronation of Charlemagne by Pope Leo III, the disputes over jurisdiction in Bulgaria and Patriarch Photius's accusation concerning "innovations" in the Western Church, further alienated East and West, with fatal repercussions for both Church and society and economic and political relationships.

The 1200th anniversary of the Second Ecumenical Council of Nicea reminds all local churches associated with the traditions of the Christian East and West of the legacy of the undivided Church, and should strengthen the efforts towards full conciliar fellowship and visible unity in freedom and diversity.

NOTES

[1] See Theophanes, *Chronographia*, ed. C. de Boor, Vols 1-2, Lipsiae, 1883, p.404.

[2] See in detail George Ostrogorsky, *History of the Byzantine State*, transl. Joan Hussey, Oxford, 1956, pp.138ff.; C.W. Previte-Orton, *The Shorter Cambridge Medieval History*, Vol. I, Cambridge University Press, pp.245f.

[3] Cf. *ibid.*; in detail D. Angelov, *History of Byzantium*, 2nd ed., Vol. I, Sofia, 1959, pp.205ff.,259ff. (in Bulgarian).

[4] Cf. N.H. Baynes, "The Icons before Iconoclasm", in *Byzantine Studies and Other Essays*, London, 1955, pp.226-239.

[5] Cf. correspondence of Patriarch Germanus on this subject in Migne, *Patrologia Graeca (PG)*, pp. 98, 147ff.

[6] Cf. Alexander Schmemann, *The Historical Road of Eastern Orthodoxy*, Crestwood, NY, St Vladimir's Seminary Press, 1977, p.204; Previte-Orton, *op. cit.*, p.247.

[7] *Ibid.*; A.A. Vasiliev, *Histoire de l'Empire Byzantin*, translated from the Russian by Brodin and A. Bourguine, Vol. I, Paris, 1932, pp.338ff.

[8] Schmemann, *op. cit.*, pp.210,224.

[9] See "La fête de l'Orthodoxie au Phanar", homily of Metropolitan Konstantinos of Derkon, in *Episkepsis*, No. 374, 15 March 1987, p.3.

[10] Cf. I.D. Andreiev, *Germanus and Tarasius, Patriarchs of Constantinople*, S. Possad, 1907, p.79 (in Russian).

[11] Previte-Orton, *op. cit.*, p.247; Schmemann, *op. cit.*, pp.210ff.

[12] *Ibid.*; Fr Dölger, *Regesten der Kaiserurkunden des Oströmischen Reiches von 565-1453*, Munich-Berlin, 1924, Nos 324,327,333,337; cf. also homily of Metropolitan Konstantinos, *op. cit.*, p.3.

[13] Dölger, *op. cit.*, No. 300.

[14] *Ibid.*, No. 301.

[15] *Op. cit.*, p.475.

[16] *Ep. I, 6*, in *PG*, 99,929ff.

[17] Previte-Orton, *op. cit.*, p.251.

[18] *A History of Byzantium in Three Volumes*, Vol. II, Moscow, 1967, p.60 (in Russian).

[19] Angelov, *op. cit.*, pp.292-295; Ostrogorsky, *op. cit.*, pp.181-182.

[20] J.D. Mansi, *Sacrorum conciliorum nova et ammissima collectio*, Vol. 12, col. 975.

[21] Schmemann, *op. cit.*, pp.212,214.

[22] Cf. *ibid.* See in detail *The Cambridge Medieval History*, Vol. IV, part I, ed. J.U. Hussey, London, 1927, pp.71ff.; Ostrogorsky, *op. cit.*, pp.144ff.,152ff.,179ff.

[23] *Ibid.*; Previte-Orton, *op. cit.*, pp.245ff.; cf. *A History of Byzantium in Three Volumes*, *op. cit.*, p.61.

[24] Cf. *ibid.*; Mansi, *op. cit.*, Vol. 13, cols 323f.,327,346,354,355.

[25] See *The Cambridge Medieval History*, *op. cit.*, pp.75f.

[26] See the "Synodal Acta", in G. Ostrogorsky, *Studien zur Geschichte des Byzantinischen Bilderstreites*, Breslau, 1929, pp.48-51; cf. *idem*, *History...*, *op. cit.*, pp.179f.

[27] See "Text of Memorandum of Patriarchs of Alexandria, Antioch and Jerusalem", in *PG*, 95,345-386.

[28] Cf. Schmemann, *op. cit.*, p.205.

[29] *Ibid.*, pp.202ff.; Previte-Orton, *op. cit.*, pp.247ff.

[30] *Ibid.*

[31] *Ibid.*

[32] *Ibid.; A History of Byzantium in Three Volumes*, *op. cit.*, pp.63,71.

[33] Cf. *ibid.;* Dölger, *op. cit.*, Nos 324,327,333,337.

[34] Cf. *ibid.*

[35] See "Vita S. Stephani junioris", in *PG*, 100,1069-1186.

[36] Cf. Ostrogorsky, *op. cit.*, pp.148ff.

[37] *Ibid.*, see in detail, pp.148ff.,178ff. Angelov, *op. cit.*, pp.259-298, and related bibliography.

[38] Theophanes, *op. cit.*, p.410; Dölger, *op. cit.*, No. 301.

[39] Ph. Jaffé and G. Wattenbach, *Regesta Pontificum Romanorum ab condita Ecclesia ad annum post Christum natum 1198*, Vols 1-2, Leipzig, 1885, 1888, post. 2233.

[40] *Ibid.*, see posts 2448,2449; cf. also in *PG*, 96,1215ff.; Mansi, *op. cit.*, Vol. 12, cols 1055-1075,1127-1146; cf. J. Bury, *The Imperial Administrative System in the Ninth Century*, London, 1911, pp.94,141; *A History of Byzantium in Three Volumes*, *op. cit.*, pp.54,58,63.

[41] Theophanes, *op. cit*, p.455.

[42] Cf. *ibid.*, pp.461f.

[43] Mansi, *op. cit.*, Vol. 13, cols 373-379.

[44] Fr Kempf, Hans-Georg Beck, Eugen Ewig, Josef Andreas Jungmann, *The Church in the Age of Feudalism*, in the series *History of the Church*, eds H. Jedin and John Dolan, Vol. III, London, Burns & Oates, 1980, p.36.

[45] *Ibid.*, pp.36-47; Schmemann, *op. cit.*, pp.208-209.

[46] Cf. Ostrogorsky, *op. cit.*, p.163.

St John Damascene's Teaching about the Holy Icons

GEORGE D. DRAGAS

John Damascene (c.652-c.750) was a monk at the famous monastery of St Savvas in Palestine, which was under Arab rule when in 726 Emperor of Byzantium Leo Isaurus (717-740) began the first round of state opposition against the use of icons in the Church.[1] The first reactions to this imperial iconoclastic policy came swiftly from the top men of the Church of that time — Patriarch Germanus of Constantinople (715-729), who suffered martyrdom, and Pope Gregory II of Rome (714-731), while the other patriarchs of Alexandria, Antioch and Jerusalem were also against the imperial policy but could not do very much about it, since they were in territories occupied by Arab Muslims.[2]

It was the Damascene, however, an extremely able theologian, who provided the first extensive refutation of the iconoclastic positions and put forward a coherent Orthodox reply. He did this by means of three *Apologetic Discourses to those who Defame the Holy Icons,*[3] which have become classical expositions of the Orthodox view on this matter. They were extensively used by the Seventh Ecumenical Council which marked the restoration of the use of icons in the Church and the triumph of the Orthodox position. The 1200th anniversary of the summoning of this great Ecumenical Council provides us with the opportunity to try and summarize their doctrine and reappraise their significance for today.

The comparative study of the contents of these discourses reveals that they share a common pattern of argument and that for the most part they repeat almost identically the same basic points. This essay will therefore give a close analysis of the first discourse in its entirety, and only summarize the other two discourses, concentrating on material in them which is not found in the first. Having done this, we shall conclude with a systematic restatement and appraisal of the basic theses.

I. The basic arguments of the first discourse

1. Iconoclasm, the Church's Tradition and the truth of God

The opening paragraphs of the first discourse clearly show that for John Damascene iconoclasm had such far-reaching ecclesiological implications that it constituted a direct attack against the Church.

> Like a sea storm it attacked the Church which God built upon the foundation of the Apostles and the Prophets, Christ his Son being the chief cornerstone, reaching

> its peak with recurring waves; it shook and troubled the Church by the malicious
> impulse of evil spirits and attempted to divide the robe of Christ which was woven
> from above, and to cut to pieces his Body, which is the Word of God, and the
> Tradition of the Church, which has been established from above.[4]

Such was indeed the case, because iconoclasm went against "the preservation of
the ecclesiastical legislation" which cannot be changed, because it is connected
with the salvation of human beings.[5] Furthermore, iconoclasm relied on the
erroneous assumption that the Church can fall and needs to be restored, inasmuch
as it could fall and had actually fallen into idolatry by using icons in much the
same way as the pagans had used idols.

John is convinced about the Church's infallibility. It is wrong, he says, to
suppose that the Church has fallen from perfection even slightly. Wrong also is the
call for a return or restoration of the Church to the right path, because it is not
measured by anything else but by its own ancient Tradition, which is handed down
from generation to generation.[6]

The threat of iconoclasm to the unity of the Church, by defying the Church's
established Tradition, is ultimately seen by John Damascene as a problem
concerning the truth in general and the truth of our knowledge of God in particular.
It is to this end, then, i.e. to the defence of the truth, that the Damascene directed
his work.[7]

2. The truth about God: the invisible God who became visible by assuming a visible form

The truth about God, says John Damascene, is given to us by revelation. In the
Old Testament we learn that God is unique and invisible and therefore no images
of him are admissible.[8] In the New Testament this unique invisible God is revealed
in Jesus Christ, his Incarnate Son, who is identified with his Word.

In Jesus Christ the unique God is revealed in three persons[9] and his invisible,
uncreated Godhead has been irrevocably united with our visible and creaturely
humanity. Christians, therefore, venerate (lit. prostrate before) and worship the
One God in the Trinity of the Father, the Son and the Holy Spirit, in and through
the mystery of the Incarnation.

The human nature which God united to the person of the Son has become a
permanent truth about God, which cannot be bypassed. Consequently, Christians
can no longer venerate and worship God independently of the humanity of Christ,
i.e. the mystery of the Incarnation. It is precisely in acknowledging this truth, says
John Damascene, that "I dare to draw an icon (image) of the invisible God not as
invisible, but as having become visible for us through his partaking of our flesh
and blood". He goes on: "I do not draw an icon of the invisible Godhead, but I
paint an icon of the flesh of God which was seen. If it is impossible to draw an icon
of a soul, how much more impossible is it to do this of God who gives to the soul
its immateriality?"[10]

3. Why Christian icons do not contradict the Old Testament prohibition of images of God

All this is quite clear, but there is still a crucial question which requires a more
precise answer. Is it not true that Deuteronomy 6:13 and Exodus 20:4 explicitly
prohibit images of God? If this is so, then how can Christians draw icons of God

without suggesting that the Incarnation introduced a contradiction to an earlier divine precept?

In replying to this, John Damascene argues that a careful reading of the Scriptures, which goes beyond the letter to the spirit, persuades us that the above question/objection is based on an erroneous understanding of these verses. Other verses, he says, such as Deuteronomy 4:12,15-17,19; 5:8; 12:3, and Exodus 34:17, demonstrate the real aim of God's prohibition of images (icons), namely, "that no created thing should be worshipped instead of the Creator, nor should the veneration of worship be rendered to anything else except to the Creator".[11] Consequently, the making of images was prohibited for the Hebrews, "because of idolatry and because it is impossible to make an image of God who is immeasurable, uncircumscribed and invisible".[12]

In view of all this, argues John Damascene, we are to distinguish between God's commandment to the Jews against idolatry and God's revelation in Jesus Christ, through which we have come to acquire the habit of distinguishing between "what is uncircumscribable and undepictable" and "what is visible and depictable". Inasmuch as God's form has not been seen (Deut. 4:12 and Acts 17:29), God as God cannot be depicted. When, however, "you consider that the incorporeal has become a man for you, then, you can draw a depiction of the human form which is God's own and not a mere man's". The following passage summarizes in a superb way the thought of the Damascene.

4. Icons do not depict the invisible God but the form which he took in the Incarnation

> When the invisible One becomes visible in the flesh, then, you can depict in icons the likeness of the One who was seen. Or again, when the One who is incorporeal, formless, immeasurable, without magnitude, without finitude in the superiority of his own nature and existing in the form of God, is contracted, by taking up the form of the servant, into measurability and magnitude and puts on himself the characteristic feature of a body, then, you can draw on a panel and exhibit him who condescended to be seen. Draw his ineffable condescension, the birth from a virgin, the baptism in the Jordan, the transfiguration of Thabor, the passions which became the cause of impassibility, the death, the miracles, the symbols of the divine nature, which were acted out by Divine activity (energy) through the activity of the flesh, namely, the saving cross, the burial, the resurrection, the ascension into heaven. Write them all in word and in colours, without fear and without constraint.[13]

5. The veneration of icons is one of honour, not of worship

Our saint also points out that both the depiction and the veneration of icons present no problem if one considers that Scripture witnesses to different kinds of veneration, e.g. that of Abraham before the sons of Hamor or Emmor (Gen. 23:7, cf. Acts 7:16), or that of Jacob before his brother Esau and before Joseph's staff (Gen. 33:3), or those of Joshua son of Nun and Daniel before the Angel of God. None of these venerations, says John, amounted to an offering of worship. They were all "venerations on account of honour" offered to those who are superior in authority (or office), which are clearly distinguishable from the veneration of worship which is offered only to God.[14]

John Damascene will explain this distinction more elaborately further on but not before he has explained the nuances of meaning of the term "icon". This is because the variety of icons suggests a variety of venerations.

6. The general nuances of meaning and types of icons

"An icon is a likeness which exhibits the characteristics of a prototype from which it differs in some particular respect."[15] In other words, an icon is a likeness with a difference! A variety of types of icons belongs to this general meaning, and John Damascene provides several examples:

1. The first type of icon is the Son of God who is acknowledged to be "the living, natural and undifferentiated icon of the invisible God, bearing in himself the whole Father and being identical with him in all respects, with the only exception that he is naturally caused by the Father".[16]

2. Then there are the icons and examples of the things which God is going to bring about, i.e. "the predestinations" of his pre-eternal will, as Dionysius the Areopagite calls them, which are the forms of his perception.[17]

3. Other icons are certain visible things which indicate other invisible ones. Such are Scripture's descriptive language about God and angels, or the icons within creation which are like dim lights of God's Light. Such, indeed, are the Trinitarian icons of the "sun-like rays" or of the "running spring" or "overflowing river", or that of "wind, the speech and the spirit" which is in us, or "the rose tree, the rose flower and the sweet fragrance" which St Gregory Nazianzus (the Theologian) mentions.[18]

4. Again there are icons which indicate in a hidden way future events. Such, for example, are the Ark of the Covenant, or the Rod of Aaron, or the Jar with the Manna, all of which are icons of the Holy Virgin, the Bearer of God; such are also, the Brazen Snake, which is an icon of him who through the cross abolished the bite of that other snake which led to all evils, or the sea, or the water, or the cloud, all of which are connected with ancient Israelite history and have been seen as icons of the Spirit acting at baptism.[19]

5. Another type of icon is that which depicts events commending a miracle or an honour, or a dishonour, or a virtue, or a vice, which instructs oncoming generations.[20]

This type comprises two kinds of icons: (v.1) "those consisting of discourse written in books" — such as the Law which God engraved on Tablets, or the lives of Godly people which were written down by the will of God — and (v.2) "those perceived by the senses" — such as the Jar of Manna, or Aaron's Rod, which were kept in the Ark as memorials.[21]

Each of the above icons, says John, obviously has its own logic and purpose and has been ordained by God, so that every opposition to it is rendered irreligious. It is this purpose which actually governs the veneration which is rendered to each type of icon.[22]

7. The various kinds of veneration

Generally speaking "veneration" is a symbol of submission and rendering of honour to someone,[23] but John speaks of three kinds of veneration.

Firstly, there is the veneration of worship which is offered to God alone who is venerable by nature. Second, there is the veneration which is offered to God's friends and servants on account of God who is naturally venerable. Finally, there is the veneration which is mutually offered by one human being to another on account of honour.

As an example of the third type John mentions Abraham's veneration of the sons of Emmor (Gen. 23:7). In connection with the second type, he mentions: the Angel who was venerated by Joshua and Daniel, God's places, God's footstool which was venerated by David (Ps. 131:7), or the Tent in the wilderness which was venerated by the whole people of Israel, or the Temple in Jerusalem which is venerated by the Jews, or the leaders who were ordained in their office by God — such as Esau and Pharaoh who were venerated by Jacob (Gen. 33:3, 47:7), or Joseph who was venerated by his brothers (47:7).

Having thus explained the meaning and various kinds of veneration, John concludes that one should either oppose all kinds of veneration, or accept them with their proper reasonableness and manner.[24]

8. The Law does not prohibit but commands the making of icons

St John picks up again the argument against the making of icons based on the prohibition of the Old Testament Law and attempts to refute it on the basis of the Old Testament itself. He argues that if the Law is not to be regarded as contradictory, then its prohibition of images should not be set against its commands which relate to the making of images, but the proper meaning of both instances should be brought out.

Several commands relating to the making of images are to be found in the Law and are connected with the making of carved images of the Cherubim (Ex. 25:18), the Ark, the Jar, the Mercy-seat — all of which are hand-made — and indeed the very Tabernacle itself which is an icon, i.e. a shadow and example, of heavenly realities. The meaning of this, says John, is that, since God as indescribable cannot be represented through an icon of himself or through an icon of somebody else, lest creation is rendered veneration of worship as if it were God, God ordered the icon of the Cherubim to be made in such a way that it represents servants standing before him and overshadowing the Mercy-seat, i.e. the icon of the divine mysteries. These divine mysteries, i.e. the Ark, the Jar, the Mercy-seat and, indeed, the whole Tabernacle, all of them made of dishonourable or "valueless" matter (as the iconoclasts contended) were icons, a shadow, or a copy, of heavenly realities, put up for the service of the priests, as Hebrews 8:5 clearly states. In fact, says John Damascene, the whole Law was an icon or foreshadowing as Hebrews 10:1 clearly suggests. In view of all this one cannot reasonably claim that the Law prohibits the drawing of icons.[25]

9. The Incarnation, icons of God and the Christian attitude to matter[26]

St John goes on to explain that the ecclesiastical tradition of making icons of God stems from the Incarnation. Whereas before the Incarnation God was incorporeal and formless, now that he has appeared in the flesh and lived among human beings it is possible for what is visible of him to be depicted. The visible aspect is the matter which now belongs to God in a personal way. In rendering veneration to this matter, Christians actually venerate their Creator who became matter for them, condescending to dwell in matter and, through matter, to work out their salvation. Far from being revered as God, this matter is and will be ceaselessly revered as the instrument through which human beings are saved. Of course it is understood here that, though in one sense this matter is not God, i.e. in the sense that it is a creature which came into being out of nothing, in another sense it is God, as constituting God's body, i.e. in the sense that it irrevocably became the same with that which anointed it (the Godhead) on account of the personal union without, however, becoming uncreated, since it retained the "terms" (boundaries) of its own nature, that is, it remained flesh, ensouled with a rational and mindful soul.

Apart from this matter, which has been personally united with God, there is other matter to which reverence and veneration is also rendered, because it has also been an instrument in the Incarnate God's saving activity and, as such, is truly imbued with divine energy and grace. Such matter is the thrice-flourishing and thrice-blessed wood of the cross, the venerable and holy mountain of Golgotha, or the life-bearing and life-giving stone of the holy Sepulchre which is the source of our resurrection or the blank-ink and the all-holy book of the Gospels, or the life-giving Table which supplies us with the bread of life, the gold and the silver out of which we construct crosses, patens and chalices and, above all these, the Body and Blood of our Lord. If one is not prepared to forego the rendering of reverence and veneration to all these, says the Damascene, then one should also keep the ecclesiastical tradition and veneration of the icons of God and of God's friends who are sanctified in name and are, therefore, overshadowed by the grace of the Holy Spirit.

Again one should not regard matter to be dishonourable or valueless, lest one is identified with the Manicheans. Dishonourable and valueless is only sin which does not have God as its cause, but constitutes a human invention derived from a self-determined deviation and tendency of the will from what is natural to what is unnatural. Nor should one dishonour, or disallow the use of, icons on the basis of the Law, because they have been made of matter. This is clear from the cases of Beseleel, son of Or, and Eliab, son of Achisamach, who were appointed by God to prepare the various materials for the Old Tabernacle (Ex. 31:1-6) and from God's command to the Israelites to offer material things for the construction of the same Tabernacle (Ex. 35:7-11).

The Law cannot contradict itself, by prohibiting and commanding the construction of icons. Besides, the Law cannot be taken at its face value, because, in this case, one would also have to keep the sabbath, the circumcision, etc. Keeping, however, the Law in a Jewish way incurs losing the benefit of Christ and falling away from the grace of the Gospel (Gal. 5:2-4). It also incurs a return to the position of ancient Israel who could not see God, and a departure from the Christian stance according to which the glory of the Lord is mirrored in the uncovered persons of the Christians.

10. Icons as reminders which sanctify the sense of sight by God's energy

Another point explained by John Damascene is the function and effect of icons on the human beings who use them. They are "reminders" of the sanctifying energy of God, through which the senses of the human beings are sanctified. As reminders of God's grace icons sanctify in particular the sense of sight — "the first of the senses" in the saint's understanding — just as the letters of the Bible, as similar reminders, sanctify the sense of hearing. In the words of John Damascene: "What discourse is to hearing, that the icon is to sight."

This function and effect of icons are clearly seen when one considers that the Old Testament icons, the Tablets of the Law, the Rod, the Golden Jar containing the Manna, were reminders to the people of Israel of the saving events which had taken place and served as prefigurations of the future grace. "Who", says John, "could deny that these were icons, i.e. heralds preaching from afar?" They were all placed before the countenance of the people, so that, seeing them, they would offer veneration and worship to God who worked through them. They were not "gods" but icons, serving as reminders of God's energy.[27]

Similar, says the Damascene, was the case of the twelve stones which were taken from the Jordan (Josh. 4:8,21) to remind the sons of the Israelites how God had led the people through the Jordan. And he concludes:

> How then could we avoid depicting in icons the saving sufferings and miracles of Christ our God, so that, when my son asks me "what is this?", I may explain to him that God the Logos became man and that through him not only Israel passed through the Jordan, but the whole human nature returned to the ancient blessedness? or that through him the human nature was lifted from the lowest parts of the earth to the places above every principality and has sat on the very throne of the Father?[28]

11. Why not only the icons of Christ and his Mother but also those of all the saints are acceptable

To accept the icons of Christ and his Holy Mother and object to the icons of the saints means, according to John Damascene, to reject the honour and glory of the saints. This is contrary to the teaching of the Scriptures which clearly state that "God glorifies those who glorify him" (2 Kings 2:30, Gal. 4:7 and Rom. 8:17), or assimilate to himself those who are his own (1 John 3:2). This means that as the flesh of Christ was glorified and deified by virtue of its union with the person of the Son of God, similarly the saints, who are united with him, become glorified and deified.

To stress this point further, our saint quotes from the 40th Oration of St Gregory Nazianzus which explains Psalm 82:1 ("God has stood in the midst of the gods"):

> The Saints were filled with the Holy Spirit when they were alive and even after the end of their life on earth the grace of the Holy Spirit continues to remain in their souls and in their bodies which are laid in the tombs, as well as in their likenesses and holy icons, not of course, in any essential way, but by grace and energy.[29]

This point, which is typical of Orthodox belief, reveals that nothing that belongs to the nature of the saints, whether spiritual or material, is ever deprived of the sanctifying energy of the Holy Spirit, which remains with it until the end of the present time, when this power will raise it to that perfect integrity which is promised by the Resurrection of Christ.

If the ancient Temple of Solomon, says the Damascene, was decorated with the icons of Cherubim, Seraphim, palm trees, snakes, lions and little springs, how much more appropriate it should be for the walls of the house of the Lord to be decorated with the forms and icons of the saints, especially if we consider that the icons of Christ and of the saints are filled with the Holy Spirit? In ancient times the Temple and the people were cleansed and sanctified through animal blood, but now it is the Blood of Christ, the first-fruit of the martyrs, and the blood of the saints on which the Church is built.[30]

Christ, says St John Damascene, is King and Lord and the saints are his army. As such the saints cannot be separated from the Lord. They are God's inheritance, co-heirs with Christ, partakers of the divine glory and kingdom, the friends of Christ (John 15:5). In view of this it is unbecoming to strip them of the glory which the Church gave them. So, then, the Damascene can draw the conclusion:

> I venerate the icon of Christ as the icon of the Incarnate God, of our Lady the Theotokos as the Mother of the Son of God, and of the saints as the friends of God who shed their blood in fighting against sin, imitating Christ who first shed his Blood for them, by shedding their blood for him. By recording their achievements and sufferings by means of icons, we are sanctified and are prompted to imitate them zealously. In honouring their icons, we honour them because, as St Basil says, "the honour of the icon passes to the prototype". [31]

If we raise temples in the name of the saints, then we should be also able to honour them. In the Old Testament not only were temples not raised in the name of human beings, but also the death of the righteous was mourned rather than celebrated, and if one were to touch a corpse one would become unclean or impure according to the Law of Moses. Now, however, "we no longer lament but rather celebrate the memory of the saints' death". If we keep these memories and celebrate them with pomp and jubilation, then we should also be consistent and accept their icons. To celebrate the death of the saints and to make their icons as memorials is the result of Christ's work (economy) which John describes in a superb way: [32]

> Since God the Logos became flesh, i.e. since he became like us in all respects without sin, and irrevocably deified the flesh through the mutual and unconfused coinherence, i.e. of his Godhead and his flesh, we too have become truly sanctified; and since the Son of God and God, who is impassible in his Godhead, has died in his assumed (humanity) and paid off our debt, having shed for us a secured and wondrous ransom — for the Son's Blood is appealing and reverent to the Father — we have been truly set free; and since he descended into Hades and preached deliverance to the saints, who as prisoners had been bound there since the beginning of this age, and, having bound up the mighty one, rose again through the superiority of his power, rendering incorruptible the flesh which he took from us, we have become truly incorruptible. Since then we have been born through water and Spirit we have been truly adopted and have become truly inheritors of God, Paul calls the faithful "saints". Hence, we do not lament but celebrate the death of the saints. Hence we are no longer under a Law, but under grace, being justified through faith and knowing only the true God. [33]

The deeper problem, then, which John Damascene detects in the rejection of the icons of the saints is exactly the same as that which lies behind the rejection of the icons of Christ and his Mother. It is ultimately the rejection of the Gospel of the Incarnation in its real implications for humanity, i.e. the rejection of the grace of God under which we stand. As such it implies a return to the Old Testament law which, however, is completely unacceptable to Christians who hold that "the Law was good, as shining in a dark place until the day dawned and the illuminator shone into their hearts" (2 Pet. 1:19), or "the living water of the knowledge of God covered up the seas of the nations". [34]

It is interesting to observe that in this connection our saint quotes such verses as 2 Corinthians 5:17, Galatians 2:14 and 5:3 in order to argue about the unacceptability of a return to "the old" from "the new", to Judaism from Christianity.[35] Interesting also is the way in which our saint at this point makes a contrast between Jacob's saving vision of God (Gen. 21:30), which, he says, was an immaterial prefiguration of what was to come, and his own vision of the God who appeared in the flesh, which sets the memory on fire. The conclusion to which all this leads is the acceptability of depicting the saints through icons. In his own words: "If the shadow of the Apostles, their handkerchiefs and aprons, expelled sicknesses and turned demons away (Acts 19:12), how should the shadow and icon of the saints be not glorified? You should either cancel out the veneration of all matter, or you should cease innovating and 'removing eternal boundaries which your fathers laid down' (Prov. 22:28)."[36]

12. The Church's Tradition confirms the use of icons

In the final chapters of his first *Apologetic Discourse* (23-27), John Damascene argues for the traditional foundations of the use of icons by the Christians.

1. He first turns to the well-known distinction, drawn by St Basil the Great, between "written" and "unwritten" "ecclesiastical ordinances", citing the relevant extract from the latter's treatise *On the Holy Spirit* (ch. 66).[37] He illustrates the "unwritten ordinances" by referring to the places of Golgotha and the Holy Sepulchre, the triple immersion at baptism, the turning to the East at the time of prayer and the manner of celebrating the Eucharist, all of which are connected with veneration and worship, and urges upon his readers Apostle Paul's command that all the traditions which were handed down by the Apostles, whether in word or in writing, should be observed by Christians, including, of course, the tradition relating to holy icons.[38]

2. Then he replies to the objections of his opponents. The pagan abuses of icons (idols), he says, have nothing in common with the pious use of Christian icons, just as pagan incantations have nothing to do with Christian exorcisms. The former invoke the presence of demons, the latter cast the demons away.[39] He also argues that to recall the divine and wondrous Epiphanius's explicit rejection of icons and the blessed Athanasius' prohibition of reliqueries, in order to produce a "traditional argument" for the rejection of icons, is utterly futile, because such an argument fails both to make explicit reference to particular context and historical circumstance and to establish a patristic consensus. In other words, "to cite an instance out of context is totally insufficient for overturning a tradition of the whole Church which extends from the earth's one end to the other".[40] Actually the point which John Damascene makes here is still applicable today, because the careful research of contemporary scholars into the Christian tradition of icons in the early centuries has not rendered any traditional evidence in support of iconoclasm.[41]

3. Finally, having argued once more that the use of icons in the Church does not contradict the norm of Holy Scripture, when the latter is understood in the Spirit,[42] the saint produces a whole array of citations from the Fathers followed by his own expository comments in support of the tradition of icons in the Church. By doing this he provides a remarkable demonstration of the inner coherence and consistency of the living tradition of the Church, which establishes not only the orthodoxy of the construction and liturgical veneration of icons in the Church, but also the remarkable richness of the Church's patristic wisdom.[43]

II. The argument of the second discourse

1. The holy icons and the truth of God

The second discourse, which was written to clarify the first, begins with the truth about God which human beings gradually lost after their Fall and which is considered to be the central issue in the iconoclastic controversy.[44] The devil, the initiator of the Fall, who, according to John Damascene, has always been at work misleading humanity about the truth of God, leading them now to deceptive self-deification, or atheism, and now to idolatry, or heresy (whether theological, which asserts monotheism against the Trinity or tritheism against the unity of God, or Christological, which separates the two natures of the one Christ by introducing two persons), is once more at work through the iconoclastic movement which represents his new devices.[45] He cannot suffer seeing the saving wonders of Christ and the victorious struggles of the saints depicted through icons and used both against his falsehood and for the glorification of God. Thus he stirs up opposition to the icons as being, allegedly, idolatrous and irreligious, while he misleads the simple by distorting the patristic true usage of icons.[46] All this is nothing but a direct attack upon the truth.

The truth is, says the Damascene, that Christians do not accept any icons of God as God, or of human beings who are believed to be gods, but of God as Incarnate who was seen on earth in the flesh and conversed with human beings. Icons of the Incarnate God are aids to the human mind which cannot be detached from corporeal things.[47] To reject the icons of the likeness of the Incarnate Lord is to prevent people from gazing at the Lord's Incarnate condescension and power and even to refuse to acknowledge the glory which God gives to the saints. But this is not the tradition of the catholic Church, received from the Apostles, Fathers and Councils of the Church and kept to this day. To reject this tradition is to change the Gospel and, therefore, to come under the apostolic anathema (Gal. 1:8).[48]

2. The tradition of the icons and the Bible

As regards the biblical arguments of the iconoclasts, St John once again refutes them by expounding their true intention and coordinating them with the wider biblical teaching. The Old Testament prohibitions of images of God (e.g. Ex. 20:4, Ps. 97:7), as it can be clearly seen in Exodus[49] and Deuteronomy,[50] were due to the prevailing idolatry of that time which obscured the truth of God's invisibility.[51] Besides, one should set against these prohibitions the Old Testament commandments which prescribe images (Ex. 26:31, 37:6-7)[52] and especially the fact that, although he spoke in many and various ways to the Israelites of old through the prophets, God has in these last days spoken to us through his Son (Heb. 1:1). The Scriptures, then, do not stand in opposition to icons when they are read intelligently and with a discerning mind. On the contrary, says the Damascene, such is the power and truth given to us in the Scriptures, especially in the Gospels, that we cannot help embracing and loving them, or kissing them with our eyes, our lips and our hearts — something that we could not do with any other Scriptures, e.g. those of the Manicheans, the Gnostics, or the other heretics.[53]

In concluding his biblical argumentation St John makes the following statement:

> It is really and truly for the glory of God and his saints, the promotion of virtue, the avoidance of evil and the salvation of the souls, that icons are accepted with due

honour, as images, remembrances, likenesses and books for the illiterate. They are embraced with the eyes, the lips and the heart, are venerated and loved as likenesses of God Incarnate, of his Mother and of the communion of the saints who shared the sufferings and the glory of Christ, conquered and overthrew the devil, his angels and his deceit.[54]

It is clear that ultimately for the Damascene the decisive argument for the use of icons is the Gospel of the Incarnation of God and especially its far-reaching and saving implications. As he goes on to explain, it is because in Christ the divine nature has assumed our nature and thereby a life-bearing and saving remedy has been given to us, so that our nature has been glorified and led to incorruption, that the death of the saints is celebrated, churches are built in their honour and their icons are painted.[55]

3. The state-sponsored iconoclasm is an unlawful interference

Such are the foundations of the Church's practice and no one, not even the emperor, can interfere with them. This is the topic which St John develops next, as he goes on to defend the independence of the Church from the state as far its traditions and faith are concerned. The unacceptability of state interference in church affairs is expounded on the basis of a series of biblical examples, which include the cases of King David (1 Chron. 28:3), of Saul and Samuel (1 Sam. 15:27f.), of Jezebel and Elijah, of Herod and John the Baptist (Acts 12:23) and of the Scribes and Pharisees and the Lord (Matt. 22:17ff.). The words of Christ (Matt. 22:17f.) and of St Paul (Rom. 13:7) are central to John's argument which concludes with the following statement:

> We will obey you, O emperor, in those matters which pertain to our daily lives: payments, taxes, tributes; these are your due and we will give them to you. But as far as the government of the Church is concerned, we have our pastors, who have preached the word to us; we have those who interpret the ordinances of the Church. We will not remove the age-long landmarks which our fathers have set (Prov. 22:28), but we keep the Tradition we have received. For if we begin to erode the foundations of the Church even a little, in no time at all the whole edifice will fall to the ground.[56]

4. Icons and the proper attitude to matter

John Damascene argues next against the iconoclasts' negative attitude to matter. Christians hold, in opposition to the Manicheans, that matter is good and appropriate for the worship of God. This is clearly stated in Genesis 2:31 and demonstrated by the use of matter in the Old Testament for the worship of God (Ex. 35:4-10),[57] especially for the construction of the Cherubim and the Meeting-Tent, and also for the construction and decoration of Solomon's temple, all of which clearly were icons. Christians, says the Damascene, follow this tradition. In using matter

> they do not venerate matter, but the Creator of matter, who became matter for them, allowed himself to dwell in matter and worked out their salvation by means of matter. For the Logos became flesh and dwelt amongst us (John 1:14), and it is obvious to everyone that the flesh is material and creaturely. They, therefore, revere, blush before and venerate the matter through which their salvation has been achieved. They revere it not as God, but as being imbued with divine energy and

grace. Is not the thrice-flourishing and thrice-blessed wood of the cross made of matter? Or is it not of matter that the sacred and holy mountain, the place of Golgotha, consists? Or is it not of matter that the life-bearing stone, the holy sepulchre, the source of our resurrection also consists? Or is it not of matter that the ink and the leather covers of the Gospels are made? Or is it not of matter that the life-giving Table, which supplies us with the Bread of life, is constructed? Or is it not the case that the gold and the silver from which both holy crosses and patens are made, also consist of matter? Or is it not the case that our Lord's Body and Blood, which are above all else, also consist of matter? Thus one should either abandon the respect and veneration of all these, or one should submit to the ecclesiastical tradition and the veneration of the icons of God and of God's friends who are honoured as saints and are, therefore, overshadowed by the grace of the Holy Spirit.[58]

5. Icons and the Apostolic Tradition

Not to accept this Tradition in the name, as it were, of the Old Testament means to fall from the grace of Christ into the condition of the law; and to reject the icons of the saints, who are the Lord's army, is to reject the Lord, who is their King. Yet the temple with its animal and plant decorations has now passed away and has been replaced by the churches which are consecrated by the Blood of Christ and his saints and are adorned with their holy icons.[59] The Church's ordinance has been handed down by the Apostles, not only through their writings but also through unwritten traditions, which include the veneration of holy places, the holy cross and the holy icons.[60] No emperor can interfere with this tradition and no demonic pagan abuse or ancient Hebrew practice can suffice to overturn the tradition of the icons, because the latter is based on the God who truly became Incarnate and his servants and friends through whom the demons are cast out.[61] The alleged condemnation of icons by St Epiphanius is a spurious one since no father of the Church fights the others who have also received the same Spirit.[62] John Damascene explains that if everything that has been connected with the redemptive and saving passion of Christ is regarded as venerable (e.g. the Cross, the lance, the reed, the sponge, etc.), then how could one refuse to venerate the icons of the Saviour and of his servants?[63]

6. Conclusions to the second discourse

With this teaching St John reaches the final part of his treatise which draws out his main insights and conclusions. First of all he stresses the fact that both the testimonies of the Scripture and of the Fathers are unanimous in confirming that the use of icons in the Church is an ancient tradition and no recent innovation. From the beginning God revealed himself through icons. Not only did he make man to be an icon of himself but also showed icons of himself, rather than his essence, to his prophets and saints. The Burning Bush was such an icon, prefiguring the Theotokos who was to bear the Incarnate Son of God. If that icon was holy, how much more holy must be the icons of the Theotokos herself and of the Incarnate God himself?[64] The Old Testament icons, centred around the earthly Temple, or the heavens as God's throne, were means of his presence and indwelling in the world.[65] Furthermore they were based on the pattern shown by God to Moses on the mountain (Ex. 25:40) — something which is confirmed by the testimony of the Epistle to the Hebrews (cf. especially Heb. 8:4-9,13; 9:2-5,24 and 10:1).[66] All of them were a shadowy prefiguration of the icon which was to come, i.e. of the icon of the Christian manner of worship, which is, in turn, an icon of the future goods, i.e. of the Jerusalem which is above and which is immaterial and not made with hands (cf. Heb. 13:14 and 11:10). Thus we reach the final sentence of this discourse which makes much clearer John Damascene's teaching about the icons of the Old Testament and of the New Testament: "All that took place under the Law, and all that takes place under our own manner of worship, are for the sake of the heavenly Jerusalem which is to come and which has been designed and made by God to whom belongs the glory in the ages, Amen."[67] The Old Testament icons were prefigurations of the New Testament ones which have actually replaced them. The New Testament icons, in their turn, are prefigurations of the eternal and irreplaceable icons of the heavenly Jerusalem which is to come.

III. The third discourse

There are two basic parts to this third discourse which seems to be a sort of systematization of the previous two discourses. The first part, consisting of chapters 1-13, deals with three main topics, firstly with the truth of God and the unity of the Church which iconoclasm attacks, secondly with the refutation of the iconoclastic argument based on the Old Testament explicit prohibitions of images of God, and thirdly with the justification of icons on the basis of the incarnational perspective of the New Testament. The second part deals with two main topics, firstly with the meaning and types of icons and secondly with the meaning and types of veneration.

1. Iconoclasm as an attack against the truth and the Church

As in the previous two discourses, St John begins by talking about the truth of God and man's Fall from it through the devil's deceit, thus making it absolutely clear that the whole debate about icons impinges upon the very heart of the truth as Christianity perceives it. Once more the truth is expounded in terms of the One God in the Trinity of the Father, the Son and the Holy Spirit and also in terms of the two natures, Godhood and manhood, and the one person (hypostasis) of Christ. Reference is also made to the nature of evil which is specified as an unnatural act. Iconoclasm, then, is introduced as a new but totally unjustifiable plot of the devil against the unity of the Church,[68] based on the allegation that icons depict God in his Godhead, even though it is clear that in the Church's mind icons in no way depict the undepictable and invisible nature of God, but his depictable Incarnation, "by way of a mirror, or a sort of puzzle, which befits the density of the body" and which is necessary for the mind which is attached to corporeal realities.[69] The fact is that icons are opposed by the devil, because, as presentations of the glory of Christ and of the achievements of the saints, they are means of sanctification and salvation handed down and hallowed in the Church by Apostles, Fathers and Synods.[70]

2. Icons and the Old Testament prohibitions of images (idols) of God

To the basic argument of the iconoclasts that icons are idols and, as such, are explicitly condemned in the Bible (Ex. 20:24) and in the Fathers, John replies as in the previous discourses that one should really perceive the true sense of the biblical statements, paying attention to their proper context; but he also adds a rather extensive comment about the necessity of recognizing the different phases of revelation.[71] In the Old Testament phase, he explains, icons were prohibited because God's invisibility and immateriality were not clearly perceived and because the Israelites were prone to worshipping idols as gods (Ex. 32:1ff.).[72] In a rich and powerful chapter John articulates the biblical doctrine of God bringing together the Old Testament prohibitions of images (idols), which stressed God's unity, and the New Testament revelation of God in and through the Incarnate Son, which opens up the mystery of the Holy Trinity. In doing this he adds the following statements concerning the veneration of the flesh of the Incarnate God and the depiction of it through icons:

> ... I do not venerate the creation apart from the Creator, but I venerate the Creator who was created for me, and who has come down to the level of the creation without suffering any depreciation or deflation, in order to glorify my own nature and render it communicant of the divine nature. I simultaneously venerate the royal purple of the body together with the King and God, not as a garment, nor as a fourth person; God forbid; but as coming to be on a par with God and like that which anointed it in an irrevocable way. For the nature of the flesh was not turned into Godhead, but as the Logos became flesh without mutation, likewise the flesh also became Logos, not losing whatever it is, but rather becoming identified with the Logos according to the one Person (according to the hypostasis). Therefore I dare to depict in icons the invisible God, who for our sake partook of flesh and blood. I do not depict the invisible Godhead, but I depict the flesh of God which was seen; for if it is impossible to depict a soul how much more impossible it would be to depict the One who made the soul immaterial?[73]

3. Icons and the incarnational perspective of the New Testament

In this light John re-examines the Old Testament prohibitions of images of God found in Exodus (20:4, 34:13,14,17) and Deuteronomy (4:14,15-17,19; 5:7-9) coordinating them with the New Testament teaching (2 Cor. 3:6, Rom. 1:25, Acts 17:29), and searches for their hidden meaning and purpose, which is none other than the worship of the Creator alone.[74] But his main point is that this Old Testament pedagogy has now been superseded by the revelation of God through his Incarnation.

Thus "... when you see the incorporeal becoming man", you are no longer bound by the statement of Deuteronomy 4:15 ("whose form you have never seen"), "and therefore you can make the figure of the human form". In other words,

> when the invisible becomes visible in the flesh, then you can depict the likeness of the One who was seen... or when he who is in the form of God puts on the form of the servant... then you can draw on a panel the One who condescended to be seen, his ineffable condescension, his birth from the Virgin, his baptism in the Jordan, his transfiguration on Thabor, his passion which procured impassibility, his miracles which are symbols of his divine nature and energy and were constituted through the operation of the flesh, the saving burial of the Saviour, the ascension into heaven...[75]

It is clear that the New Testament revelation of God in a human form does not contradict the Old Testament teaching on the invisibility of God's form. Thus the depiction of God's human form — the form assumed by the Saviour — is not unacceptable, especially when one considers that images of creaturely things associated with God's presence and energy were actually permitted and even ordered in the Old Testament.[76] In this light not only the icons of the human form of the Incarnate God, but also those of his followers whose sanctity and example became known in the Church, are allowed.[77] Such icons are connected with or belong to the persons they depict and whatever else. They are reminders of our duty to render to those they depict what is their due.[78] Furthermore St John emphasizes the importance of the bodily form of the human nature which visibly represents, as it were, the whole nature, visible and invisible. Similarly the depiction of the bodily form of Christ through an icon visibly represents his complete humanity which was irrevocably united with his invisible Godhead.[79] The denial of the one incurs the denial of the other because their unity is severed by the first denial. This in the case of the icons is the work of the devil who wants Christians to deny Christ.[80]

4. The meaning and types of icons

The definition of an icon which is here provided is identical with the one in the first discourse, though in this case it is made clearer through the presentation of greater variety of terms and of examples. In the last analysis an icon is a likeness with a difference.[81] Here, however, we are also told what an icon is for. It is designed to manifest or point to what is hidden. Thus in the case of a human being an icon depicting its body actually points to its invisible soul which dwells in it.[82] As for the types of icons John mentions six, i.e. the five of the first discourse[83] and another one which is placed third. Thus we have (1) a natural icon (e.g. the Son in relation to the Father),[84] (2) an icon which is identical with God's pre-eternal will or predestinations,[85] (3) an icon by imitation (e.g. man in relation to God),[86] (4) an icon as a corporeal form or type of another incorporeal thing,[87] (5) an icon of future things,[88] (6) an icon as a memorial of events, miracles, virtues, i.e. actions, which includes either words or things seen by the senses.[89] There are also two further points that the Damascene adds in this connection.

Firstly he distinguishes between things which are depictable and things which are undepictable, counting among the first all the material bodies and among the second, angels, souls and demons. The latter, he says, are very often depicted corporeally, but their icons denote an incorporeal and a sort of intelligent sight — they are corporeal forms seen through an immaterial vision of the mind, as for example, the Cherubim. Only the divine nature is completely and utterly undepictable, even though the Scriptures do provide some sort of "types" of God which were granted to the prophets as aids to our weakness. But even these types are perceived by the mind and not by the bodily senses. Furthermore God's nature is utterly incorporeal, whereas those of angels, human beings and demons are corporeal when compared to God's and incorporeal when compared to material bodies.[90]

Secondly, there is the point about God being the first icon-painter! God made the first icon by giving birth to his only-begotten Son and God; but he also made man after his own icon and likeness. Indeed on this basis God himself appeared to the saints of the Old Testament — Adam, Jacob, Moses, Isaiah and Daniel — in the form of a man (according to Heb. 11:13). This did not mean that the saints actually saw the nature of God, but that they saw only "the type and the icon of his

Son who was to become Incarnate. If these saints saw and venerated God in the type and the icon which was to come, i.e. the type and the icon of the Incarnate Son of God, our Lord Jesus Christ, and even in the icons of God's messengers, then how could any one deny to Christians the right to venerate the icons of Christ and of his friends?" The Incarnation of God is the key to understanding these icons and their veneration.[91] But what exactly is meant by veneration?

5. The meaning and types of veneration

In the first discourse the Damascene distinguished on one occasion between two types of veneration, "one of honour" and "one of worship",[92] and on another occasion between three types of veneration, "that of worship" (offered to God alone), "that of veneration" (offered to God's friends and servants on account of God who is venerable) and "that of honour" (offered by one human being to another).[93] Here his teaching is far more elaborate. First of all he distinguishes between five manners of veneration: (1) "that of worship" which is offered only to God,[94] (2) "that of a response to a miracle or to a strong desire" which is also rendered only to God,[95] (3) "that of thanksgiving for goods received",[96] (4) "that of need or hope for receiving benefits",[97] and (5) "that of repentance and confession" which is of a triple nature: (a) "that of gratitude", (b) "that of one who is hired or employed" and, finally, (c) "that of servitude".[98]

6. Who are venerated in the Scriptures and in what manners is veneration offered to creatures?

Finally St John Damascene outlines seven cases of veneration rendered to creatures on the basis of the scriptural evidence.

1. There is first of all the veneration which is rendered to those in whom God rests, i.e. to Mary the Theotokos and to all the saints. These are the people who, by their own free choice and by God's indwelling and cooperation, have become assimilated to God to the extent that they are called gods, not being such by nature but by grace. St John provides a whole array of verses to illustrate this case (Lev. 19:2, 31:12; 2 Cor. 6:16; Matt. 10:1; John 14:12; 1 Kings 2:30; Rom. 8:17 and Ps. 18:1) and explains that the saints are imbued with the divine power as the iron is imbued with fire when it is placed in the furnace and comes to be regarded as fire. They are venerated as those who have been glorified by God, or who were made by God terrible to their adversaries and benefactors to those who come to them with faith, not as being gods and benefactors by nature, but as God's servants and ministers who, on account of their love for God, have come to acquire a special boldness. The saints mediate before God for those who come to them and to him with faith so that their requests may be granted according to their faith. The Apostles are a perfect example of this, for not only they themselves but also their aprons and handkerchiefs granted healings to the believers who turned to them for help (Acts 19:12).[99]

2. There is also the veneration rendered to those created things through which and in which God worked out our salvation, either before or after the Lord's manifestation and Incarnate dispensation. These include holy places and holy things, like the mountain of Sinai, Nazareth, Bethlehem, and Golgotha, Mount Sion, the Mount of Olives, Siloam, Gethsemane, etc.; or like the wood of the cross, the nails, the sponge, the reed, the sacred and saving lance, the garment, the

robe, the sheets, the swaddling clothes, etc. These are revered and venerated, says St John, not on account of their extraordinary nature, but because they became vessels of the divine energy through and in which God in his good pleasure wrought our salvation. Not only places and things but also angels and human beings who became "places" of God's indwelling and saving energy are equally revered and venerated. Such were the holy Theotokos and the holy Apostles to whom the following verses from the Psalms are applicable: Psalms 25:8, 131:7, 98:9, and 103:4. [100]

3. Another type of veneration is rendered to those things which are dedicated to God, such as the books of the Gospels, or the other sacred books, or even the vessels which are used in the divine liturgy, i.e. patens, chalices, censers, lamps, tables, etc. [101]

4. A fourth type of veneration is rendered to the icons seen by the prophets, or the icons which prefigure things which are to come, such as the Rod of Aaron, the Jar and the Table which prefigured the Virgin Mary, or the Tent with the Cherubim and the other sacred contents. To these we must add the type of the precious cross and the icons of the bodily character of God, of his Mother and of his followers who belong to him. [102]

5. The fifth type of veneration is that which Christians render to one another on account of their sharing in God or of their being in God's image. By doing this they humble themselves to one another and fulfill the law of love. [103]

6. The sixth type of veneration is that which is rendered to principalities and powers. [104]

7. The last one is the veneration which is rendered to masters by servants or to benefactors by those who received from their beneficence. [105]

All these seven types of veneration, says the Damascene, indicate that veneration is a symbol of fear, desire, honour, submission and humility. None of them, however, can be identified with that veneration which is rendered to God as God and which is due to be rendered to him by all. [106]

In the two final chapters of this treatise St John makes a plea to Christians to remain steadfast in keeping the tradition of the Church relating to icons. His plea is so rich in nuances that it deserves to be presented here as the highlight of his entire exposition.

> See how much power and what sort of divine energy is granted to those who come to the icons of the saints with faith and a pure conscience. Therefore, brethren, let us stand on the rock of the faith and the tradition of the Church, not removing the boundaries which our holy Fathers have set, nor giving ground to those who wish to innovate and to demolish the structure of the holy catholic and apostolic Church of God. If permission is granted to whatever one wishes, then little by little the whole body of the Church will be dissolved. No, my brethren, no, Christ-loving children of the Church, you should not put your mother to shame by removing her beauty. Accept her who pleads her case through me. Learn what God says of her: "You are all fair, sitting beside me and there is no stain in you" (Song of Songs 4:7). Let us venerate and worship only the Maker and Creator, who is venerable God by nature. But let us also venerate the holy Theotokos, not as God, but as the Mother of God according to the flesh. Furthermore let us venerate the saints, as the select friends of God and as those who possess boldness before him. For if human beings are urged by the Apostle (Tit. 3:1 and Rom. 13:7, and cf. Matt. 22:21) to venerate kings, who are often corrupt, irreligious and sinful and also those who are ordained by them as

rulers and who are often violent, how much more ought you to venerate the King of kings, who alone rules by nature, and his servants and friends, who have ruled over the passions and have been appointed rulers of the entire earth? "For you shall enthrone them, says David, as rulers over the whole of the earth" (Ps. 44:19), those, that is, who have received authority against demons and diseases and to be co-rulers with Christ in a kingdom which is incorruptible and indestructible, whose shadow alone was sufficient for casting out diseases and demons. Are we, then, to regard the icon which truly portrays the prototype as weaker and less honourable than shadow?

Brethren, Christian means faith, and he who comes in faith will gain much. On the contrary, he who wavers resembles the waves of the sea, hit by the wind and broken, and will not receive anything. But all the saints were able to be pleasing to God through their faith. We ought, therefore, to accept the tradition of the Church in uprightness of heart and not in many thoughts. God did make man to be upright, but they pursued many thoughts. We should not allow ourselves to learn a new faith, as if the tradition of the Fathers is in dispute. For the divine Apostle warns: "If anyone preaches to you another Gospel than the one which you received, let him be anathema" (Gal. 1:9). We venerate, then, the icons, not offering the veneration to their material but to those who are depicted by them. "For the honour given to the icon passes on to the prototype," according to St Basil. You, therefore, the most sacred flock of Christ, the people who bear the name of Christ, the holy nation, the body of the Church, may Christ fill with the joy of his resurrection and make worthy to follow the traces of the saints, the shepherds and teachers of the Church, so that you may come to enjoy his glory in the radiance of the saints. May you reach this glory through his grace and eternally glorify him together with his Father who is without beginning, to whom belongs the glory in the ages of the ages, Amen. [107]

Epilogue

The above teaching clearly shows the pattern of Orthodox thinking concerning the holy icons. Icons are connected with God's revelation, both in the Old Testament and in the New Testament. They do not convey God's essence but God's acts in the forms which they assume. They are biblical and traditional means of presenting this revelation and communicating the divine grace which is embedded in it. They ultimately rest upon the great event of God's Incarnation in Jesus Christ with all its far-reaching implications for God's revelation and gift of salvation. It is from this crucial, central and decisive event of Christ that St John Damascene, like the Orthodox Fathers of the Church who preceded him, looks back to the Old Testament history of salvation and forward to the New Testament saving economy. In both instances he finds a rich variety of icons which are means of revelation and sanctification and which are connected with the practice of the human being's return to God and appropriation of his saving and sanctifying grace. As such they are monuments and aids to faith without which the grace of God cannot be appropriated by human beings. Their value to faith is particularly inestimable today when the "image" has been not only fully appropriated by modern culture as a powerful means of communication but has reached a point of inflation because of its non-religious and secular content. The holy icons are powerful representations of that content in human experience which is centred upon God's eternal and saving act. As such they are windows into that ultimate reality which alone satisfies the deepest and truest desires and aspirations of the human existence.

NOTES

[1] This iconoclastic (= icon-breaking) policy, as it came to be called, was to last for over a century and went through two major phases (726-780 and 815-842). It was officially sanctioned by two iconoclastic Councils in 754 and in 815, which were condemned by two Orthodox Councils, the Seventh Ecumenical Council in 787 and the Council of 843 under the reign of Theodora, when St Methodios the Confessor was Patriarch of Constantinople (843-847). This dispute, which shook the Greco-Roman Empire, centred in Byzantium and its neighbours, provided the occasion for the production of a great deal of theological literature, some of which acquired official status in the Church and became universally acclaimed. Such were especially the *Apologetic Discourses* of St John Damascene and of St Theodore the Studite (759-826).

[2] Cf. E.J. Martin, *A History of the Iconoclastic Controversy,* London, SPCK, 1930, and P.J. Alexander, *The Patriarch Nicephorus of Constantinople* (Ecclesiastical policy and image worship in the Byzantine Empire), Oxford, Clarendon Press, 1958. Also M.V. Anastos, "Iconoclasm and Imperial Rule, 717-842", in *Cambridge Mediaeval History*, Vol.IV, Part 1, Cambridge, 1967, pp.61-104, and Stephen Gero, *Byzantine Iconoclasm during the Reign of Leo III* (CSCO Vol. 41, Subsidia 41), Louvain, 1973 and *Byzantine Iconoclasm during the Reign of Constantine V* (CSCO 384 Subsidia 52), Louvain, 1977. Cf. also Patrick Henry, *Schools of Thought in the Christian Tradition* (the formulators of icon doctrine), Philadelphia, Fortress Press, 1984.

[3] See note 1.

[4] Ch.1, *PG* 94:1232A.

[5] Ch.2, 1233AB.

[6] *Ibid.*

[7] Ch.3, 1233CD.

[8] Deut. 6:4,13, Ex. 20:3, Ps. 96:7, Jer. 10:17.

[9] In the Greek Orthodox patristic tradition, which St John follows, the three-personal understanding of the One God is the supreme dogma, which differentiates the Christian perception of God from Jewish monotheism and pagan polytheism. This dogma is closely interconnected with the other cardinal Christian dogma of the incarnate saving economy of the second person of the Holy Trinity, the eternal Son and Logos of God.

[10] Ch.4, 1236C.

[11] Chs. 5-6, 1236D-1237B.

[12] Ch.7, 1237C.

[13] Ch.8, 1240AB.

[14] *Ibid.*, 1240B.

[15] Ch.9, 1240C.

[16] *Ibid.*

[17] Ch.10, 1240D-1241A.

[18] Ch.11,1241A-Ca.

[19] Ch.12, 1241CB.

[20] Ch.13, 1241D.

[21] *Ibid.*, 1244A.

[22] *Ibid.*

[23] *Ibid.* Ch.14.

[24] Ch.14, 1244B.

[25] Ch.15, 1244C-1245A.

[26] Ch.16, 1245A-1248B.

[27] Ch.17, 1248CD.

[28] Ch.18, 1249A.

[29] Ch.19, 1249BCD.

[30] Ch.20, 1249D-1252B.

[31] Ch.21, 1252CD.

[32] *Ibid.*, 1253ABCD.

[33] *Ibid.*, 1253ABC.

[34] *Ibid.*, 1253C.

[35] *Ibid.*, 1253D.

[36] Ch.22,1256A.

[37] Ch.23, 1256B.

[38] *Ibid.*, 1256C.

[39] Ch.24, 1256D-1257A.

[40] Ch.25, 1257C.

[41] Cf. Norman H. Baynes, "The Icons before Iconoclasm", in *Byzantine Studies and Other Essays,* London, Althon Press, 1955, pp.226-239. Also Sister Charles Murray, "Art and the Early Church", in *The Journal of Theological Studies,* 28, 1977, pp.303-345, and C. von Schönborn, *L'icône du Christ* (fondements théologiques élaborés entre le Ier et le IIe concile de Nicée (325-787), Paradosis xxiv, Fribourg, Suisse, Ed. universitaires, 1976.

[42] Ch.26, 1257C-1260A.

[43] *Ibid.*, 1260Bff. The same applies to the other two discourses. Cf. also cls. 1313ff. and 1360ff.

[44] Second Discourse, Ch.1, 1284BC.
[45] *Ibid.*, Chs. 2-3, 1285ABC.
[46] Ch.4, 1285C-1288A.
[47] Ch.5, 1288AB, and cf. Ch. 11a, 1293D-1295A.
[48] Ch.6, 1288BC.
[49] Ex. 32:1ff. Cf. the N.T. comment on this in Rom. 1:23,25.
[50] Deut. 4:12,9,15-17,19; 5:7,15 and cf. Acts 17:29.
[51] Chs.7-8, 1288D-1292C.
[52] Ch.9, 1292C-1293A.
[53] Ch.10, 1293ABC.
[54] *Ibid.*
[55] Ch.11, 1293D-1295A.
[56] Ch.12, 1295AB.
[57] Ch.13, 1298-1300A.
[58] Ch.14, 1300ABCD.
[59] Ch.15, 1301ABC.
[60] Ch.16, 1301C-1304A.
[61] Ch.17, 1304BC.
[62] Ch.18, 1304C-1305A.
[63] Ch.19, 1305AB.
[64] Ch.20, 1305B-1305ABC.
[65] Ch.21, 1308C.
[66] Ch.22, 1308C-1309B.
[67] Ch.23, 1309C.
[68] Third Discourse, Ch.1, 1317-1324A.
[69] Ch.2, 1320BC.
[70] Ch.3, 1320C-1321A.
[71] Ch.4, 1321A-1324A.
[72] Ch.5, 1324AB.
[73] Ch.6, 1325AB.
[74] Ch.7, 1325B-1328B.
[75] Ch.8, 1328B-1329A.
[76] Ch.9, 1329B-1332A.
[77] Ch.10, 1332BC.
[78] Ch.11, 1332D-1333A.
[79] Ch.12, 1333D-1336A.
[80] Ch.13, 1336BCD.
[81] Ch.16, 1337AB.
[82] Ch.17, 1337BC.
[83] Cf. Part II (6) of the present essay, and Chs. 9-13 of the First Discourse, i.e. cols. 1240C-1244A.
[84] Ch.18, 1337C-1340B.
[85] Ch.19, 1340C.
[86] Ch.20, 1340C-1341A.
[87] Ch.21, 1341AB.
[88] Ch.22, 1341C.
[89] Ch.23, 1341C-1344A.
[90] Ch.24-25, 1344B-1345A.
[91] Ch.26, 1345B-1348C.
[92] Cf. Part II (5), i.e. Ch.8, col.1240B of the First Discourse.
[93] Cf. Part II (7), i.e. Ch.14, col.1244.
[94] Ch.28, 1348D-1349A.
[95] Ch.29, 1349AB.
[96] Ch.30, 1349BC.
[97] Ch.31, 1349C.
[98] Ch.32, 1349D-1352A.
[99] Ch.33, 1352A-1353A.
[100] Ch.34, 1353ABC.
[101] Ch.35, 1353CD.
[102] Ch.36. 1353D-1356A.
[103] Ch.37, 1356B.
[104] Ch.38, 1356B.
[105] Ch.39, 1356B.
[106] Ch.40, 1356C.
[107] Chs.41-42, 1356C-1360A.

Law and Grace
in Cranach's Painting

IRMGARD KINDT-SIEGWALT

In a religious painting that has become famous (Plate 10), Lukas Cranach depicts a truth on which Martin Luther shed fresh light in his exhaustive study of St Paul's Epistle to the Romans, namely that, by the standard of God's righteousness, man (Adam) cannot pass the test. He fulfills none of the commandments that God has given him to live by. His thinking and acting lead to death rather than life, his lot ends in absolute remoteness from God. In Christ, however, God himself takes up the cause of man. Faith in Christ's death on the cross and Resurrection for our sake changes man's heart and creates the new man who lives from the righteousness of God (Rom. 1:17 and 3:21-28). Cranach takes this contrast, this two-fold prospect of the old and the new life, of the old and the new covenant, as the main theme of his "Law and Grace". Hence the painting really becomes a diptych with a parallelism of corresponding elements of form and substance. There is an Adam side (left) representing the fate of the old covenant and a Christ side (right) representing the new covenant.

The painting is guided by essential Bible quotations given at the bottom edge but not themselves (in scrolls) in the picture story. The Tree of Life from Paradise constitutes the vertical central axis of the painting, rising out of a hedge that delimits horizontally the whole picture event. The branches of the Tree of Life reach up in both halves of the picture to the sky, to the cloudland of God whose angels announce his revelation design. That this met with no success on Adam's side is evident from the dead branches, whereas the leafy branches on Christ's side of the picture indicate the fulfilment of God's will. The border of the picture on Adam's side gives a powerful expression of the very jaws of hell and the stony ground carries the naked Adam, pursued by grinning Death and Devil, straight to it. Imploringly, Adam lifts up his hands to heaven. "Who will set me free?" Scholars and sages at the right-hand edge of this part of the picture, holding the tables of the Ten Commandments, are unable to exonerate him. The cause of Adam's inexorable fate is visible in the background, where he is being tempted by Eve with the apple which, according to the serpent, will make him like God. Will he also be able to live without God, who is seated on a throne in

---

● The painting discussed in this paper was done by Lukas Cranach the Elder, c.1535, and is in the Germanisches Nationalmuseum, Nuremberg, Federal Republic of Germany. The text was translated from German by Maurice Chapman.

heaven behind and above him with outspread arms? The left side of the picture gives a clear answer to this question. He will finally meet the God of life within his condemnation to death. For Luther and Cranach this is as it was for St Paul — the inevitable consequence to which disobedience of the God-given law leads Adam. The painter just states this fact. He does not evoke fear and trembling as was often the intention of medieval painters. Cranach is much more interested in the event corresponding to this disobedience on Christ's side of the painting. There the place corresponding to the Tree of Knowledge in Paradise is taken by the bronze serpent set on a pole in the desert (Num. 21:8-9; John 3:14).

This story is a typological pointer in the Old Testament to the coming forgiveness in Christ in the New. Whoever realizes his or her sin and perceives God's mercy in this serpent is saved from death. What is merely suggested in the blue distance of the Old Testament (Cranach depicts Mount Sinai and the Israelites' tents in the wilderness) takes place before all eyes in the mission of Christ. The whole of salvation history, i.e. the history of God's action of grace towards man, is recorded on Christ's side of the picture. Mary and the shepherds are shown as humble listeners to the angels' message of the Saviour of the world, who hovers above the earth as a child holding a cross.

But more important than this receptiveness is the content of the message of salvation: the son of God suffering and dying on the cross for our sake. Cranach sets Christ crucified clearly before our eyes. From his right side flows the precious blood poured out for the sins of the world. God's Holy Spirit enables man in his heart to believe in this message from God in so far as he is properly instructed. We see John the Baptist in the role of a teacher in conversation with Adam standing on the left side of the cross. John is pointing to Christ crucified and the Lamb offering himself to God. The blood of Christ reaches Adam's heart, and in believing recognition of Christ's saving death Adam folds his hands. He expresses his adoration and gratefulness for God's grace.

And then we see that the grave could not hold this dead man, that the stone of the tomb is rolled away and the burial chamber open. Christ is standing as victor with both feet on the serpent lying on the ground that tried to bring death. "O death, where is thy victory? O death, where is thy sting?" (1 Cor. 15:55).

Whereas the dark area of hell on the left side reaches nearly up to God's heaven, Cranach has painted the rock tomb on Christ's side of the picture in bright colours as a sign of the life transcending death of the one who has reconciled man to God and has been raised to heaven. The ascension is also suggested. The risen Christ is no longer visible in earthly terms and instead the painter draws our attention once more to the picture of Christ crucified in the centre of the painting. This is the message Luther has discovered anew: the crucified Lord who alone is able to justify man. We cannot do anything more or less than Adam does: fold our hands and give thanks to God for his gift of justification by grace.

Unlike the Reformation iconoclasts, Luther was firmly of the opinion that pictorial representation can aid the proclamation of the gospel. In the same way as Christ himself used visual images in his parables, pictures can provide object-lessons of the great items of faith, the message of salvation for the sinner through faith alone. They must of course be suited to this teaching function and merely suggest — without attempting to represent — the secrets of God which are beyond human powers of expression and indescribable.

Cranach has tried to do justice in forms and colours to this task and to this request of Luther's. The Bible quotations on the borders are brief reminders to us that God himself is speaking to us.

The Reformation
and the Theology of Images

GEORG KRETSCHMAR

I

Reformation is not a new way of doing theology. Throughout the Western middle ages, especially the later years, people longed for a renewal of the Church at all levels, on the model of the early Church. In the 16th century such hopes intensified. They repeatedly assumed revolutionary and then counter-revolutionary features and, though at least to some extent they must be considered to have been disappointed ultimately, they produced very varied types of renewed Church. At all events in the second half of the 16th century, all religious sections regarded themselves as reformed, some in accordance with the Confession of Augsburg; others "reformed according to the Word of God", that is, actually, according to the insights of the Swiss Reformation; others again — the later Anglicans — appealed especially to the model of the patristic age; and many appealed to the reforming decrees of the Council of Trent.

The differences can be succinctly but significantly demonstrated in the attitudes adopted to the representational arts in the widest sense, which also reveal the many intermediate shades of opinion between the groups. Even now the mediaeval cathedrals of Europe bear witness to those divisions. In France and Switzerland many churches still bear traces of the image-breaking in the 16th century, and also, in France, of the Revolution of 1789. In Protestant Germany, especially north Germany, and Scandinavia, the Gothic cathedrals still stand often with at least part of their old artistic decoration. Many Catholic churches were renovated in the 17th and 18th centuries in the Baroque and Rococo styles — the old driving forces of artistic abundance since the late middle ages had free scope again. In England we often find both unbroken Gothic tradition and traces of an outburst of iconoclasm; Scotland followed the Swiss line or, more precisely, Calvin. Reformation itself had in fact been experienced in correspondingly very different ways. In Paris it was accounted one of the decisive events that on 3 June 1528 a statue of the Virgin Mary — with the child Jesus, on the wall of a house — was found to have had the head chopped off. Naturally it was at once assumed that the culprit was a Lutheran. The City, the University, and the king himself, sought to atone for the outrage by huge penitential processions. Early in 1528 the Luther of history had attacked in passionate protest certain specific reformed measures in Wittenburg with the argument that revolutionizing church services from above, removing images from the churches, constituted coercion of consciences and furthermore was meaningless and external, for God wanted our innermost heart, our total selves — wanted faith. Only from that deep level in the worshipping community, he maintained, could a true reformation of the Church develop. He called for faith of that kind, certainly not for penitential processions. The alterations themselves were stopped by the authorities. Such varied modes of behaviour are, of course, connected with differing convictions, and this again points back to theology and preaching.

II

To understand this conflict we must go further back. The mediaeval West was accustomed to many sacred images in the churches and statues in the streets and squares of the towns. The later middle ages saw a blossoming of sacred art and piety. As regards Germany, it has been said that people had probably never been as pious as they were on the eve of the Reformation. In fact, however, this applies to the whole of Central and Western Europe. Yet the West never developed a theology of icons; at that time in fact it was a stranger to anything of the kind.

Even as early as in Charlemagne's time, the Franks had shown little understanding of the iconoclastic controversy in the East. The Synod of Frankfurt in 796 had deliberately opposed both iconoclasts and iconodules. The peoples of the West could not follow the distinction drawn by the Second Council of Nicea between the worship due to God alone, and a veneration in specified forms which (it was said) should be given both to the saints and to icons; especially as the type of image which the Fathers of Nicea II actually had before their eyes, "icons", was not commonly found in the West. Nor was the attempt of the popes of the period to mediate between East and West particularly successful. The theology of the classical age of scholasticism then made the writings of the Greeks their own and took over from them the thesis that veneration of the sacred image is directed to the prototype, Christ himself. In the later middle ages, however, such ideas are no longer in evidence. As to canon law, in the Crusades it was acknowledged that there were seven Ecumenical Councils of the ancient Church, but the Seventh was the very one that played no part at all. Even at the Council for union with the Eastern Churches in Florence 1439-1445, the Roman church in 1442 imposed on the Copts only the recognition of six holy and universal Synods: no mention is made of sacred images.

In fact they existed, and so did statues. While in earlier days they chiefly consisted of representations of particular events in the story of salvation, similar to the Orthodox festival icons, in the later middle ages there are also devotional pictures, often of Christ on the cross, and of the Madonna suffering with her Son and protecting us. These are not intended to teach, like the earlier type, but to stimulate private meditation. Pilgrimages began to be made to holy images. In spirituality, therefore, there were certainly analogies to Orthodoxy, but there was no recognized theology of images and consequently no theologically established justification for these new forms of piety. There were two possible ways of overcoming this discrepancy between theology and devotion: either by criticism of the devotion or by a new theology legitimizing such practices. We may note straight away that even the 16th century in the West produced no theology of sacred images as a basis for their veneration.

This again is connected with the particular images which were now being produced in such abundance: they were always the work of a particular artist, and so even as sacred images they were in the first place human works, an expression of the artistic genius of a gifted person who was usually known by name. There were certainly analogies to this in the East; I refer to the icons of Andrei Rublev (died c.1430) in Russia, or to those of Cretan artists of the 16th century. These, too, are pictures intended for meditation. They remain, however, within the framework of a particular tradition of worship, namely that of Orthodoxy.

It must be added that in the middle ages too there was repeated criticism of images, with roots quite different from 8th-century Eastern iconoclasm. We find the ascetic warning against splendour and wealth, as in Bernard of Clairvaux and his Cistercians and also later in the mendicant orders. In many towns it was in fact friars of those orders who were the agents of the gospel preaching of the 1520s with which the reforming upheaval began.

Those towns generally were the home of the new forms of piety. The devotional picture corresponds to the emergence of the individual, intent on saving one's soul. To be a donor of sacred images was one of the good works by which pious families or fraternities and municipal bodies, or on occasion princes, sought to gain God's favour, and above all his mercy at the Last Judgment. It must be said quite plainly that only as a result of this kind of piety in the rich cities was the economic basis created for the blossoming of painting in the later Middle Ages.

III

The preaching of the early evangelical movement was directed against that very kind of piety whenever those practising it no longer looked for salvation from God through the crucified and risen Christ but sought to effect it for themselves by their own powers, using every possibility offered by the Church to obtain grace for money or works. Preaching that God gives himself in Christ through the Gospel and desires man's heart, not his bustling activity, could certainly link up with mediaeval Passion mysticism and the criticism of trusting to wealth and power. It was critical of the Church in the sense that even the whole ecclesiastical apparatus could come to look like an illusory means of taking out an insurance policy on salvation. Where such preaching found credence, the flourishing piety industry was undermined, as was also the art of painting sacred pictures, whether the protest was aimed directly and expressly against images in church or not.

In fact, however, the connection is even closer. In many cities the pious donors of pictures themselves became just as pious iconoclasts. And that affected not only the donors but also the artists themselves. None whose conscience was touched and who was convinced by that preaching could go on working as before. Iconoclasm was not the work of individual fanatical demagogues, but the expression of a deep revolution in piety.

This should be borne in mind when we inquire into the theological arguments that were advanced for image-breaking. Between the beginnings in Wittenberg in 1522 to the fully accomplished work of Calvin in Geneva there was a long road.

The initiator of the movement was Andreas Bodenstein, known from his birthplace as Karlstadt (c. 1480-1541) — Luther's senior colleague in the

Wittenberg theological faculty, a Thomist, and archdeacon of the All Saints foundation. Since 1517 his study of Augustine and mystical writings had led him into new paths; in the indulgence controversy he sided with Luther, and in 1521-22 in association with others he made an attempt to translate his theological views into concrete form, and so reform the Wittenberg church on the basis of the love of God and Holy Scripture, while rejecting the academic theology he had previously pursued.

What this in practice meant was a mass without the sacrifice of the mass, the removal of images from the churches, and a system of provision for the poor intended to ensure that among Christians there need no longer be any who were beggars. As we have noted, the linking of criticism of images and a pious concern for the poor already had a tradition behind it. For Karlstadt, images were in contradiction to the first commandment that we must worship God alone; on the altar above all they are intolerable, and so it is "good, necessary, praiseworthy and godly" to remove them. They are not even to be used as a "Bible for the laity", which is how Pope Gregory the Great had described the use of images. To hold a carved or painted crucifix before the eyes of the dying is wrong, for at most that can remind them "of Christ's fleshly suffering, which is of no avail". "Those who praise images teach Christ's wounds but not Christ's power, without which no one is saved." This is an argument which distantly recalls the 8th-century iconoclasts, but here it is not a question of the correct application of Christological dogma, but of the inwardness of the relationship with God. Spirit and world diverge to such an extent that all external means become useless as instruments for mediating faith. If to have any dealings with images from the world of God's saving action is idolatry and seduces the heart to cling to something which in fact does not save, then indeed images must be "rejected".

When John Calvin (1509-1564) came to Geneva in 1535, there had been no images there for a long time. He worked out his theology, therefore, not in confrontation with forms of devotion which he had before his eyes, but with earlier experiences of his own and with books. Controversial literature in the meantime, however, had grown into a mountain of books. In 1540 the decisions of the Councils of 754 and 787 were published, and in 1549 the arguments of Frankish theology of the Carolingian age became available *(Libri Carolini)*. The Geneva reformer had to tackle this, especially as he had a high opinion of valid church tradition. If the Second Council of Nicea had really been ecumenical, it would have been necessary to follow it. Consequently, Calvin contests the legitimacy of the 787 synod on the plane of canon law, using the arguments of Carolingian theology, but as regards the substance of the case he expressly stands by the decision of the iconoclasts, for of course he considered the destruction of images to be right, which the Franks had denied. In fact, however, he could really have done nothing other than reject the 754 conciliar text too; at least its teaching on veneration of the holy cross, and its line of argument with a particularly pointed, realistic doctrine of the Eucharist were after all unacceptable for him. Furthermore, Calvin takes as a premise the discovery that according to the text of the Old Testament commandments of the decalogue can be numbered differently from the division previously customary in the West, but corresponding to that given in the catechism of the Orthodox church, with the prohibition of images as a distinct second commandment.

Calvin's working over of tradition, however, is always for the purposes of his own specific inquiry: what is God's revelation? It is axiomatic that God reveals himself only in his Word, and that Word is oral or written language. On that basis it is impossible to include images in God's way of revelation to man; there is no proclamation-image. "The prohibition of proclamation or revelation by means of an image of God also sets a clear limit to the use of images not affected by that veto... Historical and narrative pictures permissible in themselves for instruction and encouragement, together with portraits and statues useful merely as decoration, may in no way ever claim to be intended to proclaim the gospel. The former are useful in church teaching, the others at least not harmful in private use provided they are not intended or supposed to make up for the task of preaching" (Margarete Stirm). Certainly in the background here stands the conviction expressed by the Geneva Catechism of 1537: "the spirit has no resemblance to the body". The argument has deeper roots, however. The way Calvin actually deals with the 8th-century Councils of the iconoclast controversy shows he did not really get to grips with the questions at issue in the Byzantine theology of that age. For that matter he probably never saw an icon in his life. One can say, however, that in his *Institutio* of 1559, Calvin built up the most precise and radical position opposed to the icon theology of the 787 Council of Nicea.

With him, theology and practical piety once more coincide. This conception was handed on by the Genevan reformer to the churches of the Reformed confessional family.

IV

There were, of course, protests against the image-breaking in many towns of south-west Germany and Switzerland, and later in France, especially where the Huguenots had the upper hand. Theologically, the traditionalist opponents of such reformations appealed to church custom and to Christ's Incarnation. These could hardly shake Calvin's position, however, for his opponents themselves did not dispute the existence of church abuses that had to be rejected — the question was in fact how to decide what was an abuse and what was not. Nor, of course, had the Genevan ever denied that the incarnate Son of God can be represented in an image. What he had denied was the right to suggest in any way that such representational images could mediate an encounter with God. In fact, however, the texts of the traditionalists were extremely reserved here. The Augsburg Interim imposed by Emperor Charles V on the Protestants in 1548, concerned conditions in Germany, not in Switzerland. It is nevertheless remarkable that in it images are referred to only incidentally: "The altars, vestments, church vessels, banners, likewise cross, candles, statues and pictures, shall be kept in the churches, yet in such a way that they serve only as reminders and no divine honour is paid to these things. And there should be no superstitious flocking of people to the statues and pictures of the saints"; so for instance pilgrimages to images are excluded. The Council of Trent, too, which dealt with the subject of sacred images only in its last session on 3-4 December 1563 and drafted its decree quite specifically with Calvin and France in mind, speaks almost apologetically; for while it expressly refers to the Seventh Ecumenical Council, it does reject any idea that something divine inheres in the sacred images or that one may request anything from them or put one's trust in them which, it says, had been the heathen's practice. Otherwise, too, it gives very much its own interpretation of the 8th-century conciliar decree. "It cannot be said merely to reproduce the Nicea decree and most certainly not to adopt the Greek theology of icons," writes Hubert Jedin, the great specialist on the history of the Council of Trent. "In the appended reforming injunction, again addressed to the bishops, the didactic and educational purpose of images which had always been taken into account in the West is brought to the fore: they call to mind God's benefits and wonderful deeds, especially when they depict biblical subjects and encourage imitation of the saints." Between the theology of sacred images and practical piety there continued to be some tension, but it is noticeable that the abundant late mediaeval production of sacred images did not simply continue here, at least not in Germany.

V

And so we come to the Wittenberg Reformation itself, as distinct from Karlstadt's attempts in 1522, and to Martin Luther. His Ninety-Five Theses of 1517 and his early devotional writings had initiated the evangelical movement.

For him, of course, it was intolerable that a Christian should set his heart on images and not on Christ. Superstitious practices are to be rejected, blasphemous representations must certainly be removed — and for him many a picture that until then had seemed pious was now blasphemy, for instance scenes in which the Madonna or a saint appeared to have taken the place of Christ as Saviour. However, Luther was very much less inclined than the Swiss reformers to expect the superstitious abuse of images; rather he was more afraid of donors placing false trust in their own merits. Images themselves are neither good nor bad, it all depends on how they are used. Here, too, Christian freedom is to be preserved in responsibility before God.

The change-over to actual systematized reformation within the Wittenberg sphere of influence did not come until the years after the devastation — less of places than of consciences — which was the legacy of the great German Peasants War of 1525. In 1529 and 1530 the "Protestants", that is the princes and cities which had newly organized the ecclesiastical system in their territories, had to defend their reformation before — and against — the emperor and the majority of the Diet. In the Lutheran sphere of influence, however, images had not been destroyed, generally speaking at least. Certainly here, too, the Word had been made the focal point, and God's Word for the congregations was of course primarily preaching and Holy Writ; but inseparable from proclamation of the Gospel through preaching is God's action in all his means of grace, namely, in addition to preaching, the sacraments of holy baptism and Holy Communion, and also absolution in confession. How are images connected with such actual proclamation of the Gospel?

The answer must have two thrusts: apologetically against iconoclasts and positively in regard to the incorporation of images into the transmission of the Gospel. Against opponents of images such as Karlstadt, Luther did not appeal to the Incarnation but to creation: God has created man with body and soul. We cannot help making for ourselves images of God and Christ, if not on walls, then in our hearts. "Whether I will or no, when I hear Christ there takes shape in my heart the figure of a man hanging on the cross, just as my face is naturally figured in the water when I look into it" ("Against the Celestial Prophets", 1524/25 against Karlstadt). That is no sin. God himself consents to it and acts in us through external means of grace, the spoken word and the sacraments. That is precisely the way by which he reaches our hearts. We have no right to tear apart spirit and world.

Luther does not stop at defence. He thinks in images, understands images and can therefore deal candidly with those actually in the mediaeval churches. In his sermons he constantly has recourse to examples. He particularly liked representations of Christ's descent into hell, the theme of the classical Orthodox Easter icon, the "Anastasis" (= resurrection) (cf. mosaic, St Mark's, Venice): "Hence it is customary to paint it so on the walls, showing how Christ goes down, cowled and with a banner in his hand, comes to the gate of hell and strikes the devil and drives him away, storms hell and brings out his own, just as they also made a play for children on Easter night. And I am glad that it is represented like that, acted out, sung or narrated for simple people. And these things should be left as they are, so that people will not trouble too much about lofty clever ideas as to exactly how it may have happened, because of course it did not take place in a bodily way... For paintings of that kind show very well the force and utility of this article of the creed, why it happened, why it is preached and believed, how Christ has destroyed the power of hell and stripped the devil of all his power. If I have that, I have the true kernel and understanding of it and should not ask further or ponder how it happened or is possible... And that is undoubtedly how it has come down to us from the ancient Fathers; that is how they spoke and sang about it, just as the old hymns still tell us and as we sing on Easter Day: 'He broke hell and bound the hateful devil in it'" (16.4.1533). This is the old Western tradition of images as the Bible of the laity, yet with a new emphasis, for the biblical story is of course not only narrated to those who cannot read it themselves, but is explained to the Christian who must understand the saving significance of the article of the Western Apostles' Creed. As against Karlstadt, the picture does by contrast actually point to the power of the cross and the Resurrection.

Hence Luther also valued illustrated editions of the Bible. The pictures should help the reader to understand. In this case, however, it is no longer a matter of existing images, but involves new commissions to artists. In fact Luther had occasionally made suggestions for altar paintings. In one place he considered a representation of the institution of the Lord's Supper; once he suggested a text from Psalm 111 as a legend, to help the congregation to praise and thanksgiving. In that case the image has no longer the function of explaining Scripture, but of holding up before the eyes of the people of God at divine worship what the reason for all celebration is, Christ's institution as it is made known in the liturgical action, thus leading the congregation to devout participation. Furthermore, under his supervision paintings on doctrinal subjects were produced, though certainly of the iconographically new type, to portray the way of salvation for humanity — Adam — fleeing from God's wrath to the cross of Christ. Such a representation can only be understood as an image intended for devout meditation.

For such endeavours it was essential that the reformer should find artists who accepted his ideas. This was achieved above all through his personal friendship with one of the great painters in Germany, Lukas Cranach (1472-1553), burgomaster of Wittenberg. Cranach's workshop and school produced not only polemical propaganda pictures — which Luther employed on a very massive scale, but were not in themselves, of course, in dispute (after all, who would be seduced into the veneration of images by a satirical drawing, a cartoon as we would say today?) — but also biblical illustrations and panel paintings for churches. Precisely in his case, however, it is evident that the themes he dealt with had changed since his pre-Reformation period. He had no reason to be ashamed of his beautiful Madonnas, and they stayed where they were. Now, however, something different was needed, pictures which would help to teach Christendom the correct understanding of salvation. As well as Cranach, mention should also be made of Albrecht Dürer (1471-1528) in Nuremberg, who expressly reflected on the functions of the artist in the new situation, quite in the spirit of the Wittenberg Reformation.

The fact that so far reference has been made only to the attitude adopted by one man, Martin Luther, is simply because neither the catechisms nor other authoritative doctrinal documents of the Lutheran church — unlike those of the Reformed or the Council of Trent — dealt expressly with this topic. But neither, of course, do they contain any explicit teaching about Holy Scripture, which certainly ranked higher for the Reformation than sacred images.

Church practice varied. There was substitution of images by scriptural verses, for example on the altar, but this did not become prevalent. There were new altarpieces, in the case of newly-built churches, for example; there were also doctrinal pictures. As well as the Cranach type already mentioned, these were chiefly sacrament pictures. Since God through the means of grace, preaching, baptism, Lord's Supper, absolution, brings people into the community of the Church and saves them, the great events of sacred history and also of Church history are readily brought into relation with church services. From the Triune God, from the crucified Christ, from the mission of the apostles by the risen Christ to the whole world, flows that which takes place today in the Church; there is preaching, baptism, the sacrament of the altar is dispensed, absolution is given. Even the submission of the Confession of Augsburg to Emperor Charles V in 1530 was intended to establish correct divine worship, and consequently it, too, could be painted in that way. It is particularly striking that as officiants in these liturgical actions the Wittenberg reformers are sometimes brought into the pictures — and this was really, when all is said, a new form of saint's image, even though that could have been hotly contested by those reponsible for them at that time. Yet from the doctrinal standpoint it would have been quite correct. For Luther's lack of anxiety regarding possible abuse of images proved in fact to be entirely well-founded, or, rather, was confirmed by the subsequent course of history, as was his other assumption that with the end of trust in one's own good works to propitiate God, the system of pious benefactions would wither away. In the long run, however, the material basis for a new flowering of the fine arts in the Protestant territories was thus lost. People like to say that the word supplanted the image. That is not untrue, but then surely injustice is done to the love of pictures, which God can use, even if he is certainly not dependent on them. Music, which was now to flourish in Protestant worship, is perhaps nearer to the word than to the image, but neither does it need private patrons, for it lives instead in the service of the courts and the churches.

Perhaps, however, one may say that theology and piety in the Lutheran domain no longer stood in mutual tension, comparable in this respect to Calvin's Church, though in content very different.

VI

In the Reformation period there was a wide range of attitudes to sacred images, and Church teaching and historical experience do not apparently always perfectly match. At all events, probably the most significant master of religious iconography of the 17th century, Rembrandt van Rijn (1606-1669), lived in fact in Calvinist Holland. It is impossible to speak of a fully elaborated theology of images in any of the Western religious factions, apart from the iconoclasts, but a clear denominational profile is apparent which remains characteristic to this day. Reformed churches have no sacred images; among Lutherans they are possible and usual but are not ceremonially venerated; in the Roman Catholic Church veneration is shown to them, now expressed in the new 1983 code of Canon Law as follows: "The custom of placing in churches holy images for veneration by the faithful is to be maintained; they are, however, to be moderate in number and set up in a suitable way so that no shock is caused to the Christian people and no occasion is given for less appropriate veneration" (can. 1188). The restrictive expressions of the 16th century are definitely maintained, practice differs from region to region and from local church to local church, and also depends on the change of liturgical forms. Since the free-standing altar has become customary in Lutheran churches too, there is naturally no altar-piece any more, only the cross on the altar. On the other hand stained glass windows have much greater importance now than they had in the 16th century. They can radiate a power which no beholder can resist, and they are then certainly more than mere illustrations. But, all in all, we would need nowadays to say more, and to say different things, about the power and seductive force of images; and this lends new urgency to the discussion about the place of sacred images in the Church.

The Orthodox theology of icons was in fact unknown down to our own century, or familiar only to specialists. From accounts of journeys to Russia and Greece of the 16th and 17th centuries, we gather how unfamiliar the behaviour of the Orthodox with their icons seemed to Westerners, and particularly of course to Protestants. That changed after the first world war. People in the West learnt to see Orthodox worship in a new light and to realize that it gives even a church under the cross the strength to remain faithful. Emigrants from Russia, and Greek (also Bulgarian and Romanian) theologians, brought the Eastern theology of icons to the West. Icons became the fashion among art historians and connoisseurs. Theological discussion by the churches about sacred images has, however, only just begun.

For Lutherans it could very well take the Seventh Ecumenical Council as its starting-point. The Confession of Augsburg itself, in 1530, attempted in the article on the veneration of saints (21) to develop a concept of veneration, or *cultus*, which is appropriate to the saints, but sharply distinct from the adoration and invocation of the Triune God, and accordingly includes no invocation of the saints. The guiding idea for this is one of the key-words also with the Byzantine Fathers of the Council of 787: memory *(mneme-memoria)*. Furthermore we see that the conciliar decree itself does not put the icons in place of the proclamation of the Gospel but subordinates them to it: "One way — of transmitting Christian tradition — is also the making of pictorial representations agreeable to the history of the preaching of the Gospel and confirming the truth... about the Incarnation of the Word of God". And finally the icon itself is an unmistakable pointer to the saving event, because it bears an inscription and therefore refers back to the believer's knowledge of God's saving action, and to that extent to the written or oral transmission of the gospel message, and remains linked to this. No Orthodox icon of Mary leaves us in any doubt that it is not just a scene of a mother and son that is represented, but God's Son on his mother's lap or at her side as a pointer to God's way of saving the world.

These are merely suggestions; many questions remain to be cleared up. discussion still has to begin.

BIBLIOGRAPHY

Günter Howe ed., *Das Gottesbild im Abendland,* mit Beiträgen von Wolfgang Schöne, Johannes Kollwitz und Hans Frhr. von Campenhausen, Witten-Berlin, 1957.

Hubert Jedin, *Geschichte des Konzils von Trient IV/2,* Freiburg-Basel-Wien, 1975.

Margarete Stirm, *Die Bilderfrage in der Reformation,* Gütersloh, 1977.

Hans-Dieter Altendorf & Peter Jezler, *Bilderstreit. Kulturwandel in Zwinglis Reformation,* Zurich, 1984.

Gertrud Schiller, *Ikonographie der christlichen Kunst IV/1,* Gütersloh, 1976.

François Boespflug & Nicolas Lossky eds, *Nicée II 787-1987,* Paris, 1987.

Christoph Dohmen & Thomas Sternberg eds, *... kein Bildnis machen. Kunst und Theologie im Gespräch,* Würzburg, 1987.

Theological Presuppositions of the Image Controversy

CHRISTOPH SCHÖNBORN O.P.

In the famous *Libri Carolini* (circa 792) the author, a theologian of Charlemagne's court, pitilessly attacks the Council of Nicea held in 787 for having solemnly approved the veneration of the holy icons. One of his arguments is that a Council should deal with *res necessarias et fidelibus profuturas* (necessary matters of advantage to the faithful), but *res vero ambiguas aut certe inutiles* (uncertain or undoubtedly useless matters) must be passed over in silence[1] as unworthy of the attention of a Council. The lack of understanding of most Westerners for the problem of icons in the East could hardly be more clearly typified. The *Libri Carolini* are certainly a polemical work with a very definite political background, but they also express fairly exactly the attitude that has prevailed in the West in regard to the question of religious art:[2] the question of images has not been felt to be a problem of faith. Why, then, devote an entire Council to it, moreover one intended to be ecumenical? For Charlemagne's theologians, who were not at all hostile to religious art, the images question was envisaged within the framework that St Gregory the Great had assigned to it: *in Basilica sanctorum imagines non ad adorandum sed ad memoriam rerum gestarum et venustatem parietum habere permittimus* (in the basilica we permit images of the saints, not for worship but as reminders of past events and as adornment of the walls) say the *Libri Carolini*,[3] echoing the teaching of St Gregory, who admits that images are useful and emphasizes their didactic value.

Why was it that the question of images could assume such importance in the Christian East, when the West regarded it as a merely secondary matter?[4] What, for the Byzantines, was at stake in the icons controversy?

Sicily for centuries acted as a link between Byzantium and Rome, East and West. And actually in Catania traces of that role are to be found. In 730 the bishop, St James, a Basilian monk, died a martyr of the iconoclast persecution. In 787 Bishop Theodore attended the Second Council of Nicea which re-established the veneration of images. Even from these few facts we may infer that the bishops of Catania had remained attached to the veneration of images. During the iconoclast period two other bishops are mentioned in the roll of bishops of Catania, and both are counted as saints: Sabinus (15 October 760) and Leo II the

---

● This paper was translated from Italian by the WCC Language Service.

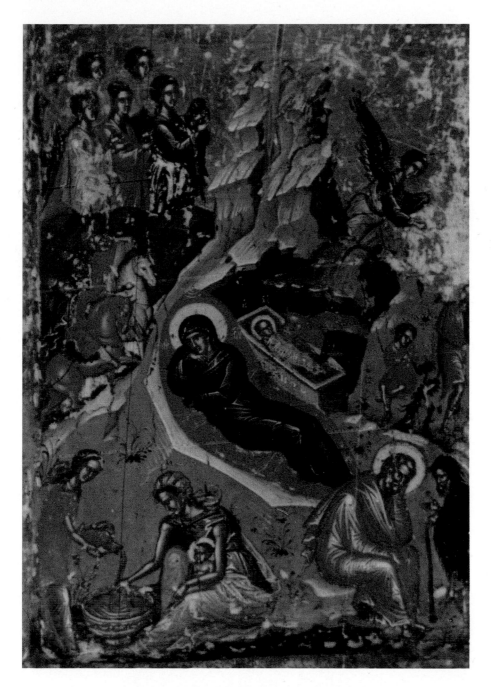

Plate 5: *Icon of the nativity, 16th century,
monastery of Meteoras, Greece*

Plate 6: *Icon of the prophet Elias, first half of the 13th century, monastery of St John the Labadistos, Kalopanaghiotis, Cyprus*

Plate 7: *Icon of St Sergius the Radonez, 15th century,*
St Sergius Lavra, Zagorsk, USSR

Plate 8: *Icon of the Holy Trinity, 15th century, Andrei Rublev,
Hermitage National Museum, Leningrad, USSR*

Wonder-worker, a Benedictine (c. 778).[5] We do not know what their attitude was in regard to the imperial iconoclasm of Byzantium, but the fact that they are regarded as saints leads us to suppose that they too, like Bishops James and Theodore, were attached to the iconophile tradition. Furthermore, we know that the iconoclast emperors had trouble with Sicily and took repressive measures in regard to that province.[6]

The difficult question of the origins of the iconoclast movement[7]

There has been a lot of discussion about the motives of this violent movement which appeared quite suddenly in 726. We must be on our guard against any attempt to explain it by a single cause. History is always a complex fabric, the weave of which is not "explained" when a single thread is picked out. Probably I differ from many historians in taking seriously what the protagonists say about the motives that impelled them. If we read the documents of the period, one fact stands out: Emperor Leo III, the undoubted initiator of the iconoclast movement,[8] declared that he wished to carry out a *religious* reform. Leo wanted to purify the Church, to rid it of idols, that is, of religious images and their veneration. All the evidence agrees in declaring this to be the motive that impelled the Emperor to unleash iconoclasm. Now it is an odd characteristic of historiography that it almost always looks for *unavowed* motives supposed to be hidden behind those that are expressed. It will be said, for example, that *in reality* the Emperor had political, economic, military or some other kind of motives and that the religious motive was merely a pious pretext. I do not agree with that method, common as it is nowadays, because of the claim it makes to understand history better than its protagonists. It claims a superior viewpoint from which it can judge the course of history by revealing the "true" motives which are supposed to have remained as it were "repressed" in the unavowable unconscious of the people of that period.

Instead of that almost "psychoanalytical"[9] attitude of the historian, I am increasingly conscious of the need for a different approach to history, less suspicious, less critical even. To put it very simply, what our sources say must be taken seriously; witnesses must be believed. First and foremost we must start from the hypothesis that they are telling the truth or at least that they regard what they are saying to be the truth.

Why this excursus on historical method? Because the phenomenon we are studying is so surprising, so foreign to our ways of thinking and to our mentality, that we need to forget these and put them aside if we are to understand in the slightest what happened in the iconoclastic period. Of course, after the event it is possible to find economic reasons which may have favoured the spread of iconoclasm (although none of the theories put forward in this sense has been convincing).[10] There were obviously political reasons, too: the Isaurian emperors (Leo III and Constantine V) wished to restore the empire to its ancient splendour, to renew the work of Constantine the Great. But this is just where we can see clearly that this political motive was neither the sole nor the most important motive. In order to restore the empire, the Isaurians in fact considered they were called to a *religious reform*. This religious reform was their chief concern, to such an extent that they sometimes sacrificed political calculation to it.

Iconoclasm: a religious reform

Biblical history taught Christian kings the sad lot they prepared for their peoples if they allowed themselves to be led astray into idolatry. Leo III could not have chosen a more symbolic gesture to signify his intentions than what he did in 726 in ordering the destruction of the famous image of Christ above the Khalke (Bronze) gate of the imperial palace in Constantinople. That image was, as it were, the symbol of the special protection that Christ gave to the most pious *basileus* (king) and through him to the empire. Leo had that image replaced by the symbol of the cross. This double gesture shows us Leo III's intentions: to free the empire from the sin of idolatry and to place it once more under the victorious symbol of Christ, the sign under which the great Constantine had triumphed: *in hoc signo vinces!* Apparently Leo III had expressed his own intention in the following words: "Uzziah, king of the Jews, after eight hundred years removed the bronze serpent from the temple and I after eight hundred years have had the idols removed from the Church."[11] In the Emperor's ideology, Christian people were regarded as the new people of God, and he liked to turn to the Old Testament for parallels both in the conduct of the kings of Israel and in the attitude of the chosen people.[12] What more expressive than this parallel between king Uzziah (actually king Hezekiah), who ordered the destruction in the temple at Jerusalem of the bronze serpent which Moses had made in the desert and which the Israelites had continued to venerate by making it a cult-object, and Emperor Leo ordering the destruction of the image of Christ above the portal of his palace, to put an end to an ancient custom which he considered idolatrous, that of venerating the images of Christ with a cult?

To rid the empire of idolatry! We must try to understand the strength and driving force of such a slogan to understand the power that the iconoclast movement must have had in Byzantium. Leo III — and so, too, his son Constantine V after him — saw himself as that priest-king, that new Moses who was to purify the people of God, of whom God in such an extraordinary way had made him the shepherd. There were so many signs that spoke in favour of a reform of that kind. The empire was threatened by the irresistible advance of Islam. Was the strength of this religion that had suddenly erupted from the depths of the Arabian desert not perhaps due to its purity? Was the decadence of the empire not perhaps a divine punishment for the slow slide into pagan idolatry? And then in 717 the Arab fleet, as though by a miracle, ran aground before the holy city of God: Constantinople was liberated! And what was the meaning of that other portent, the great earthquake of 726? The emperor discerned in it a sign of divine anger at the cult of images.[13] An impressive series of military successes came as confirmation that God was blessing the work of reform. Finally, the empire seemed to be rousing itself; the glorious days of Constantine the Great were returning! The movement rapidly established itself and then Constantine V sought to give it its final consecration: an Ecumenical Council was solemnly to crown the religious reform initiated by his father Leo III. Constantine V had a liking for theological questions, as the great Justinian had had. He drew up a series of "questions"[14] for study by the bishops, who were then meeting in a Council, to give a definition of the true and exact teaching of the Church. The Council met in Constantinople from 2 February to 8 August 754; 338 bishops took part. Apparently the pressure from the Emperor on the Council's decisions was no greater than in other Councils. There does not appear to have been any opposition to the long "definition" *(horos)* which those bishops voted and the Emperor promulgated. [15]

This fact requires explanation. How could such a large number of bishops, clearly without much opposition, endorse the Emperor's iconoclast reform? Various explanations suggest themselves. Since 726 the emperors and their patriarchs had had time to establish a large number of bishops favourable to their policy. But why did that policy meet with such a favourable response? First of all because the idea of religious reform must have appealed to many churchmen. Furthermore, vast and intense theological activity had been undertaken to collect patristic testimonies favourable to the rejection of religious images. Had not very ancient texts been found rejecting the veneration of icons? St Epiphanius, Eusebius of Caesarea and many others! And, after all, who could fail to be moved by the simple scriptural argument: "You shall not make for yourself a graven image, or *any* likeness..." (Ex. 20:4). What further need was there to argue if the decalogue itself forbade, absolutely beyond appeal, not only any cult of images but even the mere making of images of any living being? And Islam was there to remind Christians of the force of unconditional obedience to that commandment. All this was more than sufficient to convince a bishop that the iconoclast reform was well-founded. Constantine V had also taken a further step. In his "questions" he had pursued the inquiry to the point of a very subtle theological argument. As though he wished to justify the initial act of iconoclasm, the destruction of the figure of Christ of the Khalke on the orders of his father, he raised the dogmatic question: is an image of Christ compatible with the Orthodox faith? His argument, very succinctly, was as follows. Christ is *one;* he is one person in two natures, God and man. If one wants to make an image of Christ, what is to be depicted? His divinity? That is impossible because it is "uncircumscribed", infinite. His humanity, then? But that would mean separating it from the divinity and consequently dividing Christ. The rejection of images is no longer grounded in Old Testament law but receives a Christological justification. "We ask you", the Emperor writes, "how it is possible to depict our Lord Jesus Christ, that is to say represent him, who is one only person *(prôsopon)* of two natures, immaterial and material, through their union without confusion?" [16] The Emperor cleverly suggests here a dilemma which the synod of 338 bishops in 754 was to make more explicit: the iconodules must choose between two ways, both heretical and long since condemned: either to say that the icon represents only Christ's humanity, which is the heresy of Nestorianism, for they are separating the human element from the divine in Christ; or to claim to depict Christ, God and man, which is the monophysite heresy, because they confuse the incomprehensible divinity with the humanity of Christ. [17] That poses a radical dilemma, and the only escape from it is to recognize that the mystery of Christ cannot be captured in human art. In Byzantium there was no better method of discrediting an adversary than by convicting him of kinship with the great Christological heresies.

We can now try to sum up the findings of our inquiry. Iconoclasm was primarily a movement of religious reform. That was what gave it impetus and provided its surprising energy. For almost a century it held the stage in Byzantium. Two Councils (in 754 and 815) were devoted entirely to it; the hierarchy to a large extent supported it. Yet the iconoclast movement was not victorious. The iconodules prevailed during a first period of a quarter of a century (between 787 and 813), and after a second phase of iconoclasm, less active than the first, the movement was finally defeated in 843. It is easy to say after the event that the end was inevitable, but all the same it is by no means obvious. Why was iconoclasm not victorious in the Byzantine church?

The reasons for defeat

Many Protestant historians — who have moreover often rendered great services to research on our problem — make no secret of their regret at the defeat of the iconoclast movement. For them it meant a relapse of the Greek church into Hellenization, into scarcely veiled paganism, from which the iconoclast reform had been intended to lift it. For the iconodules, on the other hand, the year 843 marks the "triumph of Orthodoxy" and the event is celebrated annually under this title on the first Sunday in Lent. Slide into paganism or victory of Orthodoxy: what is the real significance of the defeat of the movement initiated by Emperor Leo III?

Here once more we must be on our guard against "monocausal" explanations. Political reasons certainly played a part, although the iconodule emperors, and empresses above all, had much less success on this level than the iconoclast emperors. There was, however, another factor which to my mind is too little emphasized: the tensions, not to say internal contradictions, of the iconoclast movement. The idea of that reform was clear, its attraction undoubtedly strong, but how was it to be realized? In practice, iconoclasm proved to be a movement full of inconsistencies. Is it possible, for example, not to sense a contradiction in the fact that the emperor had the icons of Christ destroyed but continued to require the traditional mark of respect to his own image everywhere in the empire? What was the extent of the prohibition of images by the law of Moses? Did it apply to the representation of human beings? But in that case how was it possible to permit, as the Isaurians did, secular art with its hunting scenes and horse races? Islam was more consistent by forbidding any representation of animals. Why exclude religious while allowing secular images? That in itself went against the letter of the Decalogue. Another question was even more delicate: what justification was there for purely and simply equating images of Christ, the Virgin, the saints, with the idols of the pagan divinities? Is it possible to place them unequivocally on the same level? And finally, the most difficult question: from when was the "fall" of the Church, the loss of its original purity, to be dated? This last question displays a dilemma common to all "reforms". If there has been a break in authentic tradition, it must be possible to say when the break occurred. But the iconoclasts were not really agreed on this point. Leo III seems to have considered the malady to be very ancient indeed, for he had come "after eight hundred years" to cure the Church. The bishops of the 754 Council, on the other hand, seem to have regarded it as a recent illness, since for them the six Ecumenical Councils were normative. The "fall" must therefore have happened after 681, the year of the Sixth Ecumenical Council. That could not have been the opinion of the bishops at the 754 Council, who knew that the evil they were combating had existed very much longer. In the 4th century, Eusebius and St Epiphanius had fought it in vain. When then had the "fall" occurred? The question remains insoluble to this day.

Some historians, mainly Protestant, have supposed that the early Church was fundamentally hostile to any religious art and that this "evil" had gradually infiltrated the Church and finally flooded it. The iconoclasts started from a similar view of things. However, it seems that this interpretation is not in accord with the facts; the archaeological findings for some time past have contradicted this idea of an early Church hostile to art, in which only adoration "in spirit and in truth" counted, without images, even less without veneration of images. In fact, while the Church was hostile to everything linked with idolatry, it seems that it was quite neutral in regard to the use of symbols and also, very soon, religious figures. We are thinking above all of sepulchral art. [18] Discoveries relating to Jewish art of the period have contributed to transforming the outlook. Iconoclasm can no longer be regarded as a return to the early Church. To conclude these remarks with a final inconsistency of the iconoclast reform: was it possible to reject en bloc *all* that the centuries of Christianity had produced as religious art, and if a selection was to be made, where was one to stop? The moderate iconoclasts rejected only some forms of the cult of icons, whereas other more radical ones rejected not only images but also the veneration of relics and of the saints, and even invocation of the Mother of God.

The failure of iconoclasm was due largely to the inconsistency of the movement. While it was clear that the aim was a reform of the Church, the means to achieve it were not clear. Uncertainty went hand in hand with violence. The often bloody persecution of the iconodules contradicted the initial good intentions.

The theological bases of Christian art

We started with the thesis that iconoclasm was primarily a movement of religious reform. That thesis is confirmed by a curious fact: in all the vast literature on the image controversy we find *no* trace of any discussion of aesthetic questions. What a contrast with, for example, the Renaissance! The *whole* discussion unfolds on the religious plane. The history of art ought to take account of this fact.

Discussion was initiated by Leo III. A debate developed and for the first time an attempt was made to account expressly for the *positive* reasons for Christian art. St Germanus of Constantinople, who was patriarch when iconoclasm broke out, was the first to oppose Leo. I cannot recapitulate here the positive arguments contributed by the great debate on religious images. I shall limit myself to two remarks.

From the start what was at stake in the debate was clearly perceived by Patriarch Germanus. According to the chronicler Theophanes, Germanus wished to dissuade Leo III from abolishing the holy icons: "Lord, may such an evil never be accomplished under your rule. For anyone who does anything of the sort is the forerunner of Antichrist and the destroyer of the divine economy according to the flesh." [19] "The economy according to the flesh" means God's saving plan accomplished by means of the *Incarnation* of the Word of God. To reject the icon is to reject the Incarnation; this is the principal argument of the defenders of images. Are they jumping to a conclusion? Here we approach a reply to the question raised at the beginning: why is the question of icons so important for the Eastern Church?

Let us try to imagine the effect that Leo III's action could have had: imperial officials come and destroy the image of Christ in front of the whole population of Constantinople. The iconophiles will say: one who destroys the image of Christ, attacks Christ himself, because to see his image is to see Christ himself. From the moment that "the Word was made flesh" (John 1:14), from the moment this Jesus of Nazareth is none other than the Son of God made man, to see his human face is to see himself, to see him, the Word made flesh. That face is the human face of

God, and to destroy the image which makes us see that face is to reject the ineffable mystery of that face. And here is the solution to the dilemma formulated by Constantine V and by the Council of 754: it is sufficient to see, with a loving gaze, eye to eye, the image of that face, to realize that the icon does not represent either the human *nature* or the divine nature, but the divino-human *person* of Christ. *The image makes it possible to meet that person.* The question of icons is so important because the Mystery which these images represent is the most important thing there is: the human Face of God. To cite once more, but in the contrary sense, the phrase of the *Libri Carolini,* there is nothing more *necessaria et fidelibus profutura.* [20]

NOTES

[1] *Libri Carolini* (here = *L.C.*), ed. H. Bastgen, Hannovarae-Lipsiae, 1924, p.125, linn.5-14; cf. H.J. Sieben, *Die Konzilsidee der Alten Kirche,* Paderborn, 1979, p.333.

[2] Cf. S. Gero, "The Libri Carolini and the Image Controversy", in *The Greek Orthodox Theological Review,* 18, 1973, pp.7-34.

[3] *L.C.* III,16: p.138, 2-4.

[4] On the attitude of the Latin Church, cf. the new study by F. Boespflug, *Dieu dans l'art*, Paris, 1984.

[5] Cf. R. van Doren, "Catane", in *Dictionnaire d'histoire et de géographie ecclésiastique* XI, 1949, 1492-1495: 1493.

[6] Cf. C. Emereau, "Iconoclasme", in *Dictionnaire de théologie catholique* VII, 1, 1927, pp.575-595.

[7] I summarize here what I dealt with more fully in an article, "Der byzantinische Bilderstreit — ein Testfall für das Verhältnis von Kirche und Kunst?", in *Internat. Kathol. Zeitschrift Communio,* 11, 1982, pp.518-526 (also in the French edition of this review).

[8] S. Gero, *Byzantine Iconoclasm during the Reign of Leo III*, Louvain, 1973 (*CSCO* 346 — Subsidia 41), p.131.

[9] This attitude is well studied by A. Besançon, *Psychoanalyse et expérience du moi*, Paris, 1973.

[10] On the lines of an analysis of Marxist tendency: H. Bredekamp, *Kunst als Medium sozialer Konflikte. Bilderkämpfe von der Spätantike bis zur Hussiten-Revolution,* Frankfurt, 1975.

[11] Mansi XII, 966 RCD.

[12] Cf. P. Brown, "A Dark-Age Crisis: Aspects of the Iconoclastic Controversy", in *The English Historical Review,* 88, 1973, pp.1-34; cf. also the studies of E. von Ivanka and H. Hunger.

[13] Theophanes, *ad ann.* 6218: ed. C. de Boor, I, Leipzig, 1883, p.404. It was the famous eruption on the island of Santorini, Greece.

[14] The text of these inquiries is accessible in the "reader": *Textus byzantinos ad Iconomachiam pertinentes in usum academicum edidit,* H. Hennephof, Leiden, 1969, pp.52-57.

[15] On this Council cf. S. Gero, *Byzantine Iconoclasm during the Reign of Constantine V,* Louvain, 1977 (*CSCO* 384 — Subsidia 52), pp.53-110.

[16] *PG* 100, 232A (=H. Hennephof, *op. cit.,* 52).

[17] Mansi XIII, 241E and 244D (=H. Hennephof, *op. cit.,* 65).

[18] Mention should be made here of the important study by Sir C. Murray, "Art and the Early Church", in *The Journal of Theological Studies*, N.S. 28, 1977, pp.302-345.

[19] Theophanes, *ad ann.* 6217: ed. C. de Boor, the quotation is on p.404.

[20] For greater details I refer to my study, *L'Icône du Christ. Fondements théologiques élaborés entre le Ier et le IIe Concile de Nicée (325-787),* Fribourg, 1976, and to the German revised and corrected edition, *Die Christus-Ikone. Eine theologische Hinführung,* Schaffhausen, 1984.

The Microcosm and Macrocosm of the Icon: Theology, Spirituality and Worship in Colour

GENNADIOS LIMOURIS

Art and theology in relation to liturgy

Art is deeply rooted in the teaching and Tradition of the Church. Liturgy cannot exist without art. All kinds of experiences, movements, representations have an artistic aspect. The best example is iconography: it can be analyzed and understood theologically only if we take into consideration the "incarnation" of art in the subject matter, colours, lines, expressions, etc.

God, in one sense, is the very first artist. In the creation stories we see the Divine Artist at work, creating the world and humanity, breathing on them beauty and harmony. Following the example of the Creator, the faithful make their own simple efforts in art, which are based on sacramental and spiritual experiences within the Church of Christ.

Art and theology should be analyzed together, and three questions can be asked: (1) What is the legitimate role of art in the Church? (2) How can the missionary and eschatological function of art be determined in a theological context in relation to deification within the Church? (3) And finally, what is the role of icons in the life of the faithful in relation to worship?

The legitimate role of art in the Church

The role of art in the Church was questioned by early monachism. A certain kind of religious consciousness constantly questions its legitimacy, echoing the prophets of Israel. Monachism is an expression of such religious consciousness. It is easy to consider early monachism as monophysitism because art's specific importance for the Church was underlined. What are the limitations of the use of art in the life of the Church? Should we accept it as it is or modify it by adapting it to the folly of the cross, of denying oneself and losing one's life by one's own will in order to follow Christ? It would be unjust to reduce this phenomenon of early monachism to an escape from the world, understanding it as merely negative. The world, which the early monks wanted to renounce, was full of purely human works of Greco-Roman art. The first monks did not understand this and rejected the pagan values of art, seeking another aesthetic. They looked for another world with its own criteria for values. They were inspired by an ideal of beauty — *philokalia* — and at times the aesthetic momentum was to penetrate this spiritual world created by them.

For the development of liturgical aesthetics Fr Alexander Schmemann suggested a schema which sheds light on the question. At the beginning there was a conflict between the first monks and the Christians. The latter were concerned about aesthetics, but the monks preached asceticism, e.g. they preferred psalms instead of singing in their worship services. Later, monachism accepted the aesthetic preoccupation and from that time on assumed a kind of monopoly in Church art. It is interesting to continue in this line and see how the secular faithful took the initiative during the Renaissance and especially in the period of Enlightenment. But strongly imbued by the "secularized" and desacralized aesthetics, this movement calls for a new ecclesial synthesis.

In order to define art, one should analyze its religious value which can be seen in three ways:

1. The spirit of creation, well presented also by the Russian philosopher Nicolas Berdyaev, is one of the fundamental aspects of God's image in the human being.[1] For Berdyaev, for example, the creative instinct was an immediate data, an initial institution, which needed no demonstration, but freely determined the "ego".[2] However, Berdyaev did not recognize the need for asceticism in creative thinking.

In his concept of human destiny requiring utmost freedom for its destiny, Berdyaev arrived at a kind of voluntary subjectivism seeing in the "objectivation" an attitude harmful to humankind. It is true that art should create something different from everyday reality or technology and in a different way. Indeed, art should transpose reality and present it at the level of the spirit. But this effort is a reaction to the real objective which cannot be denied and which should not be destroyed or profaned. This is the first form of asceticism: asceticism in its relation to realism which should be respected on the one hand, and transformed without distortion on the other.

2. Another element of any definition of art is *beauty* ("kallos" in Greek). What is beauty? Pontius Pilate asked Christ: what is truth? Was it prudence or scepticism on his part, or a kind of premonition as he stands before the incarnate Logos and the truth of salvation? Supreme beauty is an attribute of God; beauty places us before a mystery. Beauty is more than art. Art seeks beauty, but attains it only relatively. Beauty is greater than art and is present in reality independently of its representatation. On the other hand, an artist can create aesthetic forms which reveal the content of beauty, but will never attain the ultimate content of beauty since it comes from above, is greater than the human person though present in him or her.

We encounter here a new form of asceticism: the artist should indeed be led by inspiration (i.e. at the highest level, pray) knowing that it comes from above and is a free gift. The artist should be subordinate to the beauty and should represent it to all as an objective value, having had the privilege and responsibility of creating it.

3. Finally, art can never be determined without perceiving the beauty of the work. Having been creative, the artist contemplates his creation in the image of what God did on the seventh day. This is the significance of the sabbath: contemplation, eucharist ("everything is good"), communion-koinonia. I do not mean that an artist can never declare himself/herself satisfied or pleased with himself/herself. On the other hand, there is a certain communion with the artist when the work of art is contemplated and assimilated. This presupposes yet

another form of asceticism: indeed the artist should not despise the people of God but should be in solidarity with all, performing a certain service, a diakonia, to all, a necessary and important function.

In this perspective, it is clear that art in the Genesis stories has a religious function. The human being needs to express the vision of beauty which God has given the world by forming it. He or she expresses this need either through an artistic creation if that is his personal vocation, or through appreciation of a piece of art. The human being, who is also a contemplative being, who prays and communicates while conveying the beauty, expresses his personal mystery. But if art is a means of being in communion with God the Creator, with the cosmos and among people, we should remember that communion is the first aim of the Church. Of course, we need to distinguish between "utility" and "function". To affirm the ecclesial function of art means to affirm that art should express the nature and destination of the Church, or the ferment given by the Saviour to the Church which is both missionary and eschatological. This is clear from the fact that the Church is based upon two fundamental sacraments: baptism, "... go therefore and make disciples of all nations, baptizing them..." (Matt. 28:19), and the Eucharist, "as often as you eat this bread and drink the cup, you proclaim the Lord's death until he comes" (1 Cor. 11:26).

Missionary functions and eschatological nature of Church art

The Church is missionary not only because it has missionary stations in remote places; it is missionary in its being. In other words, mission does not mean only the *bene esse* of the Church, but belongs to its *esse*. In this world the Church needs to be always vigilant, constantly reformed in order to preserve its pentecostal origin. In addition, the Church is not a refuge from salvation, but the community of those who have a vocation to save the world with Christ and in Christ. The essential tools of mission are preaching and the Eucharist. However, language and speech are not the only means of human expression and ecclesial preaching; art is also a necessary and very effective tool. We understand the truth in its logical form through reason, but also through beauty, sensing the aesthetic with our eyes and ears. Church art should express the revelation, preach it in a more intuitive way than the Word, but in the same sense and in connection with it. For Church art and preaching of the Word have the same missionary vocation.

Church art should also express the eschatological nature of the Church. Art in itself has an eschatological character since it transposes the reality given at the level of the Spirit and tries to go beyond the limits of time and space. Art is a search for the immortal and absolute, which is never satisfied: its eschatological character is based upon its religious function. This becomes quite evident in iconography with its eschatological truth of the human body glorified after the death trial, with the required absence of the perspective, or perhaps with a reverse perspective: the prohibition of statues (bas-reliefs or haut-reliefs) is dictated by the concern for eschatological truth free of worldly dimensions. This liberation, this sobriety not only in the art of technology but also in the application of Church art, is necessary because of the eschatological nature of the Church.

It is important not to create the impression of a final installation in this judged or condemned world, called to salvation through an effort of conversion. Church art should never give the impression that the Church is a prisoner of the world; it should discover its royal sovereignty, the glorious liberty of God's children. If we want to adapt Freud's terminology, the sublimation of Christian art is paradox; it goes through judgment and conversion; it is under the sign of the cross because only the way of the cross leads to the glory of the Resurrection.

It is evident that in today's ambiguous and secularized world, Church art is affected by an imitation of the contemporary world. But the Church is a renewing ferment in itself. Thus it should purify its specific art whose principal lines of development we have just traced. Therefore, it is important that Church art be a kind of shock art, both missionary and eschatological, according to the very being of the Church.

Art and worship

> The uncircumscribable Logos of the Father was circumscribed by becoming incarnate, and by transforming the darkened image to the original, united it with the divine beauty. [3]

Art, iconography and icons, in the tradition of the Orient in particular, are especially interesting not only in themselves but also for the whole understanding of this content of art. Matter and form, that is, content and style, are here in such relationship that the one interprets the other and both together interpret the real sense of Orthodox iconography in relation to the West, sometimes in similar tones, sometimes completely differently. The research into this form, therefore, is very important; lack of knowledge about it during the past centuries has led to misinterpretation and neglect by many. Consequently, there is a lack of emphasis in contemporary Orthodox worship on the primarily liturgical significance of this art. Worship is thus deprived of a fundamental element, which contributes to the expression of its strong power and incomparable spiritual superiority — as indicated by its long tradition.

Knowledge of the reasons dictating the particular form which Orthodox art and iconography utilized is necessary precisely because otherwise this form of art is often compared with the religious art of the West and, as a result, the Byzantine form is sometimes condemned as being erroneous, primitive, unnatural, and so on. Western art is admired for rendering the power of naturalism, for presenting real physiognomies and environment, while Byzantine art is criticized for its weakness in rendering natural reality, natural beauty, grace and variety. But it is precisely here that the value of Byzantine art lies, and it is this which concerns its entire particular form.

The real content of Orthodox art is the "new creation" in Christ. The high theology of this new creation in Christ and the actual life-experience in worship comprised the entire interest of this art. The common world, the world of decay, was wholly unrelated to it. The "darkened or unclean image" of the world and of humankind was renewed by the "over-abundant" grace (Rom. 8:21). In order, therefore, for the art to be able to express this work of grace which the Church proclaims, it was necessary that even its form be analogous. For this reason, the iconographies which tried to express the holiness of the persons could not have been mere portraits, that is, pictures which direct us to natural people. Rather, they had to have a particular morphological conception so that the onlooker was uplifted from the transience of this world and endowed with the idea of the reborn creation, the transfigurated creation of the eternal world, of the Kingdom of God.

Therefore, a basic and fundamental presupposition of the form was the idea of a "new" humankind and world in Christ. The Scriptures, the Fathers of the Church and the Ecumenical Councils formulated and developed this idea during Church history and Tradition and presented it to the Church. The art was obligated from the beginning to follow, to "formulate" or to "fashion"[4] this idea, this fundamental belief of the Church. Thus, the art form was subordinated to the authority of the Church[5] but was inter-related with theology; it became the Church's property and only the technical part became the concern of iconographers.[6] The Seventh Ecumenical Council decided that "the invention of the painters is the icon's creation, but the distinguished institution and tradition belongs to the catholic church. For to the painter belongs the art only while the order of fundamentals belongs to the holy Fathers."[7] By contrast, in the West, from the Council of Frankfurt (794) no dogmatic-theological or liturgical significance was attributed to art; it was regarded simply as an element "for the decoration of the churches".[8] This is why it was left free in the hands, and the subjective ideas and concepts of irresponsible artists.

Therefore, Orthodox art, directed and guarded by the Church, gave the appropriate form to its Creed. According to the Church, Christ was not to be represented as a human person. If Christ were pictured as an ordinary mature man (as is done in the West), it would infer the idea of this one nature, the human only; this would be a kind of Nestorianism and as such dangerous to Orthodoxy. Christ, however, is God-man, double in nature. Now, art had to find some form, some iconographic type which would lead the onlooker to think that in the person represented "the whole fullness of the divinity dwells bodily" (Col. 2:9).

Moreover, according to Theodore Studites, "if we say that Christ is the power of God and the wisdom of God, by the same manner His representation must be said to be the power and the wisdom of God".[9] This presupposition directed the inspiration of the Orthodox iconographers to that morphologically ideal type, by which — as far as is possible for art — they represented the *Person* of the Lord Jesus Christ, of God the Logos, while granting that His natures are united without confusion and change. The humanly "beautiful" Christs of Western art or those purely human types influenced by them are dogmatically unacceptable for us, as Kalokyris affirms, since they denote the idea of only the human nature of the Lord.[10] The Seventh Ecumenical Council stated that the Church, even though it may depict the Lord through art in His human form, does not separate in the representation Christ's flesh from His divinity, since it is united in Him and is "co-divine and of equal honour".[11] Christ is therefore represented in Orthodox art as God-man (Theanthropos), the divinity being alluded to in the representation of His Holy Body (which is always referred to in the hypostatic union of the two natures); this again is indicated by the hymn-writer who, filled with adoration (from the idea of divinity that such an icon denotes), writes the following: "... with what eyes shall we creatures of earth see thy image? The image which the armies of angels cannot see without fear as it shines in divine light."[12] Of course, Christ as God, as "the uncircumscribable Logos of the Father" is even for art "unrepresentable". Moreover, "no one has seen God"

(John 1:18). But once the Son "and Saviour Jesus Christ" (Tit. 2:13) "who is God over all" (Rom. 9:5) "was willingly incarnated, being unincarnate, and became what he was not for us",[13] that is, He "partook of our nature",[14] by utter condescension, He *became circumscribable* and therefore necessarily representable. With the reception of the flesh "He also received all of its attributes" in which, of course, the circumscribable is founded.[15] Theodore Studites noted also: "the unformed received form, and the one of no quantity has become equal to quantity".[16] Since, therefore, "the invisible one made himself visible"[17] through the Incarnation and thus "we have seen with our eyes" (1 John 1:12)[18], we became, consequently, capable of "inscribing the form of His resemblance".[19] For this reason, since then, "the Church is redecorated in the bodily icon of Christ which is as a beauty beyond this world",[20] and through it its iconography seeks "representation of the incarnation of the Lord of all, of His sufferings"[21] and of the other events of His life.

These dogmatic presuppositions of the form of iconography — which the West never took into account — are certainly extended to the person of the Mother of God, the Theotokos, and to the saints.

The saints and martyrs lived the "new" life in Christ, they struggled in the present life and achieved the "incorruptible crown" of the heavenly life. Each one of them became a type of the regeneration in Christ, an icon which Christ "reformed to the original by uniting it with the divine beauty".[22] Their represented figures, therefore, could not have been the material and corruptible (those before grace), but those of "holiness", that is, those of heavenly "glory", with which they were clothed.[23] Here again, therefore, Orthodox iconography moves from the belief of the Church that "one is the glory of the heavenly (bodies) and another of the earthly" (1 Cor. 15:40). The saints and martyrs are regarded as "heavenly", citizens of heaven. And because "as the heavenly one is, so also are they who are heavenly" (1 Cor. 15:48), the saints are represented with such a schematic composition in order to dismiss one directly from the forms of daily life, that is, the forms of corruption and to inspire the blessed reality beyond this world, where the light of the incorruptible and heavenly God shines. The physiognomies of the saints, therefore, as they are rendered in the wall-paintings and in the portable icons of the Church, became a continual commentary to the faithful that "the corruptible must be clothed in incorruptibility and the mortal in immortality" (1 Cor. 15:53)[24]. In other words, iconography attempts here to give, in some manner, an idea of the spiritual bodies which will follow the resurrection of the dead, to express the "other glory of the heavenly and incorruptible bodies" (1 Cor. 15:40,48).[25]

But what is the main role and place of an icon in particular in the life of the Orthodox church? This question is so complex for Western people and needs special and particular analysis. A theological and liturgical analysis needs to take into consideration the decisions of the Seventh Ecumenical Council which formulated all the prerogatives of the icons within the Tradition.

In spite of this very important role and relation by their "nuptial communion" between art and theology, iconography and icons in particular, which are celebrated with the 1200th anniversary of the Seventh Ecumenical Council, are exactly the expressions of this liturgical inter-relation and function within the life of the Church.

Iconography as art of depth

Totally characteristic of the content of an Orthodox icon is its depth. It is evident that a spiritual, liturgical and theological art should have sought to express depth and profundity in the representations of its themes. It is for this reason precisely that it neither impresses nor captures those who habitually limit themselves to the surface of things.

It is not possible for one with the presuppositions of an extrinsic impressionistic art to examine and judge iconography, which by its very nature is expressionistic. This is why this art began to be understood among limited circles in Europe and in other continents when expressionistic art succeeded impressionistic art. [26] People began to realize that the essence of art is not limited to the brilliant colours and the impressions which the eye receives, but in addition there is the "inner perfection", the artistic "expression" of a profound life-experience which possesses the genuine artist. Thus, for example, the Germans realized little by little the significance of the expressionism of their medieval art which had been set aside by the art of the Renaissance. Also the Orientalists understood the expressive value of the closed forms of Egyptian art. The historians of primitive and ancient cultures also understood now the importance, for example, of Minoan expressionism. A good example of this is the large eye of the so-called *Parisienne*. [27] Thus, finally, the artistic circles began to understand Byzantine art with its intense features (e.g. the large eyes, the large noses, such as those of the Mother of God), the bright contours, the frontal postures of the saints, etc. — which express its depth, that is the content of Christian dogma and spirituality. The large eyes and other characteristics animated, beyond measure, and interpreted the entire intensive physical life of the persons presented. The frontal attitude of the saints denotes the direct communion between these sacred personages and the faithful.

Being, therefore, an expressionistic art of profound significance, Orthodox iconography is not directed only to the sentiment, but also, and primarily, to the spirit. It does not seek to make a momentary and passing impression but to produce a permanent and continuous impact on the soul.

It is instructive to recall Pseudo-Dionysius the Areopagite (5th century), according to whom the Church should be regarded as a type and an image of the heavenly Church. [28] According to this understanding, all things in the Church allude to the heavenly world, and so it follows that even the painting must not only represent forms of the daily life, but should express the spiritual and transcendental world. This idea became, from the early centuries, a fundamental principle of Christian art. From this point of view, even Greek philosophy, especially the neo-Platonic, created a favourable climate for better understanding of such a Christian ideal in art. Plotinus, for example, in his "Enneads" had spoken about the vision of the world "through inner eyes", by which the profound essence of things becomes understood, such as "the deiform splendour of virtue", a thing which does not occur in the mere external impressions achieved through the bodily eyes. According to Plotinus, knowledge should not be analytical and partial, but whole and direct, achieved through the vision of the true nucleus of things. This nucleus, of course, is not related to the temporary and transient, or to the natural reality directly observable by the senses. [29]

Therefore Orthodox iconography avoided the representation of the sacred forms according to their natural appearance and sought, through a truly marvellous abstraction, to express the *spiritual reality* which constitutes the highest truth. For this reason, iconography did not use certain models of humankind, with which to represent its sacred personages by copying them systematically. One should not think that Orthodox art, during its long history, ignored the natural reality, that is, the so-called realistic element. Of course, as an art essentially spiritual and concerned with the expression of the spiritual world, it insisted — particularly during its formative centuries — on making its true character understood. However, this element of realism was not used as in the West, nor even as it is perhaps understood today (being taught so by the Renaissance) but rather for a definite purpose and only after it was subordinated and assimilated to the whole vigorous spiritual power of Byzantine art. Whereas in the Western art the element of realism constituted an end in itself, and was sought as an artistic ideal,[30] in Orthodox art it served another purpose, namely *the necessity to subordinate the material element to the spiritual*, our lower nature to our higher — something which is manifest and expressed by the complete subordination of the realistic element to the higher spirituality achieved in the creations of this art. Moreover, the manifest subordination of the material to the spiritual in these icons brings out a beauty of high quality which the first elements come to possess from the second, the beauty which the material element "puts on" when it is dominated by the life-giving and life-transforming power of the spirit of Christ.[31] Christ "being formed in likeness to us, deified what He received".[32] And it is such deification, this *theosis* of the human nature, that is made perceptible by this form of icons or iconography in general.

Theosis — transformation into the divine likeness

The aim of the Christian life which Orthodox spirituality describes as the acquisition of the Holy Spirit of God can also be defined in terms of deification (theosis). The Church Fathers, as for example St Basil the Great, described man (anthropos) as a nature creature who has received the order to become a god; and St Athanasius said that "God became man that man might become God". "In my Kingdom", said Christ, "I shall be God with you as gods."[33] Such, according to the teaching of the Orthodox church, is the final goal to which every Christian must aim: to become god, in order to attain theosis, "deification" or "divinization". For Orthodoxy humankind's salvation and redemption mean its deification.

Behind the doctrine of deification there lies the idea of man made according to the image and likeness of God, the Holy Trinity. "That they may all be one," Christ prayed at the Last Supper, "even as thou, Father, art in me, and I in thee, that they may also be in us" (John 17:21). Just as the three persons of the Holy Trinity "dwell" in one another in an unceasing koinonia of love, so man, made in the image of the Trinity, is called to "dwell" in the Trinitarian God.

The idea of deification must always be understood in the light of the distinction between God's essence and his energies. Union with God means union with the divine energies, not the divine essence: the Orthodox church, while speaking of deification and union, rejects all forms of pantheism.

Closely related to this is another point of equal importance. The mystical union between God and man is a true union, yet in this union Creator and creature do not become fused into one single being. Unlike the Eastern religions which teach that man is swallowed up in the deity, Orthodox mystical theology has always insisted that man, however closely linked to God, retains his full personal integrity. Man (anthropos), when deified, remains distinct (though not separate) from God. The Mystery of the Trinity is a mystery of unity in *diversity* and those who express the Trinity in themselves do not sacrifice their personal characteristics. Therefore, man does not become God *by nature*, but is merely a "created god", a god *by grace* or *by status*.

Deification is something that involves the body. Since man is a unity of body and soul and since the Incarnate Christ has saved and redeemed the whole man, it follows that "man's body is deified at the same time as his soul", as St Maximus the Confessor affirms.[34] In that divine likeness which man is called to realize in himself, the body has its place; "Your body is a temple of the Holy Spirit", wrote St Paul (1 Cor. 6:19). The full deification of the body must wait, however, until the Last Day, for in this present life the glory of the saints is as a rule an inward splendour, a splendour of the soul alone; but then the righteous rise from the dead and are clothed with a spiritual body, and their sanctity will be outwardly manifest. "At the day of Resurrection the glory of the Holy Spirit *comes out from within*, decking and covering the bodies of the Saints — the glory which they had before, but was hidden within their souls." Because the Orthodox are convinced that the body is sanctified and transfigured together with the soul, they have an immense reverence for the relics of the saints. This reverence for relics is not the fruit of ignorance or superstition, but springs from a highly developed theology of the body.

Theosis presupposes life also in the Church, life in the sacraments. Theosis according to the likeness of the Trinity involves a common life, but only within the fellowship of the Church can its own life of coherence be properly realized. Church and sacraments are the means appointed by God whereby one may acquire the sanctifying spirit and be transformed into the divine likeness. And one of the supports for this in the daily spiritual life is the icon, this mystery of the "narrow gate" leading into spirituality.

The icon — the "narrow gate"?

"*Icons* again! They're *always* on about icons!" Let us face facts: people do sometimes want to know why. There is no point, of course, in resurrecting a stale quarrel savouring unpleasantly of the iconoclasm of centuries ago; but neither is it a good thing to allow a situation to get worse for lack of clarity. It is high time we looked more searchingly and pragmatically at the role of the icon in the liturgical and theological life of the Church.

For many people today with a Western European background of religion and art, icons seem to be odd paintings; they have often been dismissed as insignificant; the lack of "realism" in icons has been a major problem for Western people. Only slowly has interest penetrated through to the more ancient traditions and works of Christian icon painting. Layers of mental and spiritual misunderstanding had to be shed, as well as layers of dirt and overpainting on the icons themselves, before the true glory and wonder of the great tradition of icon painting could be revealed. The work of scholars, restorers of icons, people of prayer, has opened up the doors of perception,[35] and now we can enter into the secret of the holy icon with a sense of wonder and awe. This entry into the mystic world of the icons can at the same time be an entry into our own interior spiritual life, a passing through the "narrow gate" that leads to life.

Images were prohibited in the law of the Old Testament because they endangered the worship of the one God, who is Spirit. In the East, the sense of the infinite was expressed in the geometrical forms of ornamental art. Among Muslims, the notion of the radical transcendence of God was to be reinforced by non-representational art, by arabesques, and by polygonal decorative art.

Towards the beginning of the Christian era, however, Judaism itself adopted a less rigorous attitude.[36] Compared with the human creature, whose image had been obscured until its likeness to God turned into dissimilarity, only the angelic world remained pure — so pure that its portrayal was even commanded by God (Ex. 25:18-22; 1 Kings 6:23-32). This divine command is extremely significant. It meant that the heavenly world of spirits could be depicted in art, for it possesses human form: the Covenant had ordained the Old Testament's bequest to us of the sculptured icon of the cherubim.

Christ delivers us from idolatry, not negatively by the suppression of all images, but positively by revealing the true human form of God. If Christ's divinity defies representation in any form and if the humanity on its own, separated from the divine, loses all significance, the Fathers of the Seventh Ecumenical Council in their wisdom proclaim that "his (i.e. Christ's) humanity is itself the image of the divinity. Whoever has seen me, has seen the Father." The iconographic function of the visible is affirmed, i.e. its role as image of the invisible.

The icon has its biblical foundation in the creation of humanity in the divine image, which demonstrates a certain conformity between the divine and the human and explains the union of the two natures in Christ. God is able to see himself in the human and be reflected in the human as in a mirror, for humanity is in his image and God speaks our human language. He also has human form. Moreover, the best icon (i.e. "likeness") of God is the human being. During the liturgy, the priest censes the whole church and its members for the same reason he censes the icons; the church salutes the image of God in human beings.

The icon — light of the glory of God

The procedures and principles of a transfigurative art, the art of the icon, were defined by the undivided Church, in particular by the teaching of the Seventh Ecumenical Council.

The first point to be made is that the whole church, with its architecture, its frescoes, its mosaics, constitutes one huge macrocosm of an icon which is to space what the unfolding of the liturgy is to time: "heaven on earth", the manifestation of the divine humanity in which the "flesh" destined for death is transformed into something spiritual.

The icon, therefore, is not purely decorative, nor merely an illustration, as many say, of the Scriptures. It is an integral part of the liturgy and, as one great iconographer and theologian, Leonid Ouspensky, has written, "a means of knowing God and becoming one with him". It permits us to know God in beauty.

For God, indeed, has not only made himself heard but also made himself visible. He gave himself a face, and the icon par excellence is that of the cross.

"Since the Invisible One clothed himself in flesh and appeared visibly, let the likeness of Him who manifested Himself be depicted."[37] The Incarnation is the foundation for the icon and the icon points to the Incarnation. If it is possible for human art to give an idea of the transfigured world, this possibility rests on the fact that the matter used in human art has been sanctified by the Incarnation. "I do not worship matter but the One who created it and who, for my sake, Himself became matter... and by matter saved me," says St John of Damascus. [38] To depict Christ in the mystery of the Incarnation is also to depict the members of his body the Church: the icon depicts not only God becoming human but also humanity becoming God.

The icon, therefore, presents a personal presence. It points to humanity's true face, its face for eternity. The icon simply has to resemble the model; it cannot dispense with this resemblance. While rejecting the subjective impression of the model, however, the icon does not seek a "photographic" objectivity. Its bond is to communicate with the macrocosm and, finally, communion. But here the resemblance finds expression in the encounter of two persons, Christ and the iconographer in the communion of the Church. It is always the same Christ but to each one, on each unique occasion, He reveals himself in a unique way. Thus there are one single holy face faithfully kept in remembrance by the Church, the bride, and as many holy faces as there are iconographers. The reason is that the human face of God is inexhaustible and, as Pseudo-Dionysius the Areopagite has stressed, always keeps for us its inaccessible character as the face of all faces and the face of the Inaccessible One. "Whoever has seen me, has seen the Father" (John 24:9). The Seventh Ecumenical Council forbade any direct depiction of the Father, principle of the Trinity and source of the divinity. In Christ, transcendence makes itself available without ever ceasing to be in the beyond. [39]

What is true of the face of Christ becomes true of the face of a human being filled with the Holy Spirit. The art of the icon thus transcends the opposition — highlighted by the French writer André Malraux — between the arts of the non-Christian East witnessing to an impersonal eternity, and the arts of the modern West dominated by individual sensuality and anxiety. It is in the inexhaustible depths of the face that the art of the icon expresses eternity, which is not fusion but communion, genuine koinonia.

The Orthodox philosopher and theologian Olivier Clément compares the image of Christ with images in other religions — in particular with the image of the Buddha — and even the image of a Christian saint with that of a Buddhist. The Christian face reaches fulfilment in communion. It is enclosed in the microcosm of humanity, whereas the Buddhist face is suppressed in an inwardness where there is no longer the self or the other but an indescribable nothingness. The face, the "prosopon", is in both cases "haloed". But the Christian face is in the light, like iron in the fire, a light which glows and turns the microcosm outwards towards a universe full of hope, towards the macrocosm of humanity. The Buddhist face, on the contrary, expands to become one with the luminous sphere of which the halo is the cross-section. The Christian face is thus, at one and the same time, inwardness *and* outwardness; and the Buddhist face, with its eyes closed in self-recollection, is plunged in the void of silence and interrogation. [40]

Moreover, by a concrete symbolism in which expressiveness defeats all the seductions of allegory, the icon gives us a foretaste of humanity's deification — theosis — and the sanctification of the universe, in other words, a foretaste of the truth of created beings and things. The symbolism is always in the service of the human person; in manifesting the human person, it becomes part of the fullness of communion.

But this light in the icon comes from no precise source for, as the Revelation of St John says, the new Jerusalem "has no need of sun or moon to shine upon it, for the glory of God is its light". This light is always everywhere without casting any shadow, or rather, it is always interior, everything is illuminated from within. It is the very heart of the icon that iconographers designate as "light" *(phôs)*, a symbol of God as the "all in all".

The perspective is often reversed. The lines, instead of converging on a "vanishing point", symbolizing a "fallen" space which separates and imprisons, expand in the light, "from glory to glory". Coming to us from the infinite, almost invariably facing towards us (even a profile would signify absence), the saints make this deified space accessible to us.

Within this setting, the face is depicted with as great a personal likeness as possible, but at peace, integrated, irradiated by the Spirit. Delicate and pure lips and reduced interiorized ears, everything converges upwards towards the larger than life-size eyes, full of gravity and tenderness (as St Macarius the Egyptian says, the sanctified human being becomes "all eyes"!) and towards the broad forehead of wisdom.

For Orthodoxy, however, the theology of light is not merely metaphorical, not just a literary device designed to disguise some abstract truth. As V. Lossky says, neither is it, strictly speaking, a doctrine, an intellectualist system which tends to substitute abstract concepts for the realities of experience.[41] Its negative "apophatic" character finds expression in paradoxical oppositions, in continuity with the theological practice of the Church Fathers who affirmed the basic dogmas of Christianity by confronting our minds with antinomies such as unity *and* trinity in the doctrine of the Trinity, duality *and* unity in the case of Christology. In fact, *just as* dogmas of Nicea and Chalcedon require of us an ineffable distinction between the nature and the person in order to safeguard the mysterious reality (the real mystery) of the Trinity and of Christ, truly divine *and* truly human, *so too* the doctrine of the real distinction between the essence and the energies, which is required of our minds by the antinomy of the unknowability *and* the knowability of God, who is incommunicable *and* communicable, transcendent *and* immanent, has no other purpose than to defend the reality of the divine grace, to leave the door open to the mystic experience outside of which there is no spiritual life in the true sense of the word. For the spiritual life requires that the Christian dogmas be not only confessed but also received by ordinary Christians. Within this universe of discourse, we can have no further difficulty in accepting the hard saying of St Simeon the New Theologian by which the name of Christian is denied to those who have not already had experience of the divine light already in this life.

The notion of the Light is inherent in Orthodox spirituality. The two go together inseparably. We may know nothing, for example, of St Gregory Palamas of Salonika (14th century) or of his role in the doctrinal history of the Eastern Church, but we shall never be able to understand Eastern spirituality if we disregard the theological foundation which found its definitive form in him.

The religious art of Byzantium was long unappreciated in the West as was the equally artistic merit of the Russian icons, as V. Lossky says.[42] It took a long time before we learned to appreciate the Western "primitives" out of the same tradition.

Will it be the same story for the doctrinal and spiritual tradition of Eastern Christianity? If we learn to appreciate this tradition, then doctrinal features which were points of discord in the past will perhaps become fruitful sources of a future spiritual renewal[43] in the movement of Christians and churches towards the hoped-for unity of the Church of Jesus Christ.

The art of the icon, therefore, is in no way limited to a "style" nor is it even something peculiar to the Christian East. The vision of this art of the icon was shared by the Christian art of the West, not only down to Romanesque art but even down to the Italian *Trecento*. It did not itself become stereotyped. While it remained faithful to the same deep inspiration, embodied in the "canons" which stipulate the significance of episodes and the identity of personalities, this inspiration was precisely that of the divine-humanity, which is why, more than once, it embraced and even inspired the explorations of Renaissance humanism. We too often forget that it was from Macedonian art and Serbia that the affirmation of the human in the beautiful reached Italy and in the 13th century inspired there a "transfigured renaissance", a divine humanism, which quickly disintegrated in the succeeding centuries. The movement lasted longer in the Byzantine world, culminating in the first frescoes of Mistra in the Peloponnese, and still more in Constantinople with the tenderness and dynamism of the Karie monastery. Then came the last invasions, which destroyed the Byzantine civilization, internalized and, so to speak, eclipsed Orthodoxy. This was followed by the far-reaching divisions of Christianity. The present encounter of West and East will perhaps permit a new flowering of "divine humanism".

Clearly, the depiction of the uncreated light which transfigures a face on an icon obviously cannot only be symbolic. But the intrinsic originality of this art is seen in what the symbol does for the human face, and in how it expresses the fullness of the individual life. The symbolism of the icon is thus based on the experience of Orthodox mysticism: the huge eyes with their quiet tenderness, the ears abridged as if internalized, the pure and delicate lips, the wisdom of the enlarged forehead — all this bespeaks an integrated being, at peace, enlightened by grace, in a harmonious equilibrium.

The saints are almost always depicted full face on the icons. They welcome the one who looks at them and lead him or her into prayer, for they *are* themselves prayer and this the icon shows. Their postures, their garments, the atmosphere surrounding them — all is infused and ordered by light and peace.

The light of the icon symbolizes the divine light. This light does not come from any one precise source, since the "heavenly Jerusalem" has no need of sun and moon, being illuminated by the divine glory (Rev. 21:23). It shines everywhere, in everything, without casting any shadow. It suggests God himself making himself light for us. It is this basis of the icon, therefore, that the iconographers call "light". The perspective is often reversed. The lines do not converge on a "vanishing point", symbol of a "fallen" space which separates and imprisons, but expands in the light "from glory to glory". Thus, the icon is not only instructive, but also has the quality of a mystery. The divine grace reposes in the icon and this is the most important point, the most mysterious aspect of the theology of the icon: the "resemblance" — likeness — to the prototype and the "name" of the prototype constitute the objective holiness of the image. "The icon is sanctified by the name of God and by the name of the friends of God, i.e. the saints, and this is why it receives the grace of the Holy Spirit."[44] The icon forms an integral part of the liturgy; and it is essential in the celebration of a festival that the icon be exhibited in the centre of the nave.

Liturgical art, and especially the icon, which is moreover inseparable from the Word and from the Church's worship, has a sacramental status. We can speak of the icon as a sacrament only if we abandon a sacramental conception which fragments, parcels up and "thingifies" the sacramental reality, and turn instead to the mystery of the Church, the unique and sufficient sacrament of the salvation imparted by the love of the Holy Trinity in the redemptive work of the incarnate Word and of the Holy Spirit.[45] But then the icon appears as a gift of the sacramental fullness without which Orthodoxy would be seriously impoverished and which is one of the most creative facets of witness both within divided Christendom and in the secularized world by which it is encompassed.

In the Church's living experience however — which is primordial and pre-theological — the icon is a sacrament of the divine humanity of Christ (i.e. a mode of Christ's presence and communion with it). "Since God has now been seen in the flesh and been received among us human beings," writes St John of Damascus, "I represent what is visible in God."[46] In this way, St John of Damascus affirms the Christological and "incarnational" foundation of the icon. This is the starting point for a theology of the icon. With its Christological basis, however, this theology of the icon must be no less interiorized and balanced than that Christological basis itself. St Basil helps us to understand this when he affirms in his well-known dictum: "The honour shown to the Image passes to the Prototype."[47] The literary and historical context of this dictum, of course, is the Trinitarian and pneumatological controversy in which St Basil found himself engaged. It was by a secondary but profoundly legitimate and even essential theological extension that this dictum came to be used in the iconoclastic conflict and was eventually given the seal of official approval by the dogmatic definition of the Council of Nicea II.[48]

St John of Damascus, moreover, as Fr Christoph Schönborn has demonstrated, distinguishes the different sorts of images: first, the most perfect, the Son himself, perfect image of the Father; then that of the human being, humanity as created in the image of God and called to resemble God; finally, icons in the strict sense.[49] A contemporary iconographer shows us clearly the painted icon's resemblance to the prototype, which is precisely that of the growing correspondence between the icons we venerate and the inmost likeness which is in the heart of each single human being:

> The divine image and likeness implanted in humanity at creation are, so to speak, the condition invented by the Creator who permits Himself to be revealed in the human image by a tangible means accessible to contemplation. This image and likeness of God, given to humanity at the very moment of its creation, is already a sort of archetypal icon, an image given by God which cannot be consumed even in the Fall of humanity, but must be continually renewed, revived, purified and, by the effect of God's grace and by human asceticism, so to speak, must be ceaselessly painted in the depths of the soul. By ascetism and by sanctification, the image of God is inscribed in the depths of the human heart, and this uninterrupted and indispensable constructive effort is the fundamental condition of the life of human-ity, a sort of persistent imprinting of Christ's image on the very foundations of the soul. In his Incarnation, Christ appeared as the restorer of the divine image in

humanity; indeed, he is more than its restorer; he is the total and perfect execution and achievement of the image of God, the Icon of all icons, the Source of every sacred image, the Image not made by human hand, the living Jerusalem.[50]

On the basis of this correspondence between the painted icon and the image of God in the human heart, we can return to the question of the sacramental character of the icon, i.e. its capacity and its function, on the one hand, to convey and transmit to humanity the sanctifying presence of Christ and of his friends the saints, and on the other hand to lift up to God the prayers of the Church and of the individual Christian. This is the icon as microcosm with, in various degrees and for various reasons, a sacramental value and function. In its sacramental character, therefore, the icon functions in three modes: in its development, in its permanence, and in its mediation. It is these three modes of sacramentality, too, which constitute the icon so that it can simultaneously function in its macrocosm, at all times and in all places.

Every icon, therefore, both in the theological consciousness and in the spirituality of Orthodoxy, is ontologically "miraculous", charged with the life-giving energy of the Spirit of Christ. Here too, the current doctrine of the Church concerning the "objective" sanctity of sacraments *(ex opere operato)* and the transparency of the ministrants of the sacraments to the grace of God *(ex opere operandis)* is fully applicable to the icon, as a place of the divine presence and an instrument of God's grace. While every icon, in virtue of its sacramental nature, is "miraculous", in certain icons the presence of God is manifested more tangibly, and the prayers of the Church can accumulate in them and be "capitalized" with greater density. The grace of God does not scorn to establish and manifest itself in the most beautiful product of human art and prayer.[51]

An identical movement of revelation makes of the icon a "visual gospel", the pictorial gloss of the Gospel. To the declaration of the iconoclasts that "the art of images has no basis in the economy of salvation", the *horos* of the Seventh Ecumenical Council replies: "The more Christians contemplate the icons and the more they remember the One who is represented and try to imitate him, the more they show respect and veneration, without any adoration in the strict sense of worship, which is due to God alone." "Woe betide anyone who would worship images!"

Movement — time — space

The icon represents live matter laid hold of by glory. Beneath the living immobility of bodies, the dynamism of the Spirit rises like a secret sap invigorating all the limbs, diffusing first the palms of the hands and then finally the face, the supreme place of spiritual concentration. The bodies stretch or bend obediently so as to match exactly the lines leading to the spiritual centre of the icon. Their senses are in all respects like our own, yet different, for the saints no longer belong to themselves but to the Spirit moving within them. Surprised at what they hear, the ears seem vibrant with the voice of God; the delicate lips are quickened by contemplation and on them words of praise tremble; the eyes, abnormally dilated, are wide open "to the light which makes them gods".

In his incarnate Word, God became a face turned towards humanity. The human figures depicted full face in the icons expose themselves to the intimacy of direct "eye to eye" inspection, their faces offering the largest possible space for communion. Even a profile representation would signify absence. "When you enter your room, bow to the icon and catch the glance of God!" say the Fathers of the Church. To meet with God is thus possible in these crossroads of contemplation and prayer and here we can find ourselves present at a new Pentecost.

The icon, like the liturgy, transcends *time* and is located at a perpetual "today" — today, the first of the days remaining to us to live for eternity. The icon makes itself the faithful contemporary of the mystery it represents.

The figures represented are also clothed "in classic style", though without further precision. The icon freely depicts, simultaneously, scenes widely spaced in chronological time, placing side by side saints from different periods and widely distant places. It shows the disciples and Christ ascending Tabor on one side *and* coming down on the other side, *and* witnessing the Transfiguration at the summit. The same is true of those nativity scenes that show Emmanuel asleep in the dark cavern while at the same time servants are washing him. A "supra-logical" vision irradiated by faith in the God for whom one day is as a thousand years and a thousand years as one day.

"Behold the earth of Him who is un-earthly, the boundary of the unbounded, the space of Him whom all space cannot contain." These words can be read inscribed on the panel of the first porch at the church of the Chora Monastery in Constantinople. Every church is thus designated as the awesome place where God dwells. In the icon "He who cannot be confined allows Himself to be confined; He who is nowhere in visible things allows Himself to be seen." Under the thrust of the presence of God, the cosmos is transformed: the rocks are stretched upwards by geometric degrees; trees, rivers and monuments join in the pictorial movement, in total submission to the spirit. Uplifted by the Spirit, matter recovers the malleability of its beginnings, as readily worked as the clay under the potter's fingers, soaring up, tier upon tier in balanced movements which seem to defy the laws of gravity. In order to become the *contemporary* of the believer contemplating it, the icon disengages itself from specific localities and from time. For how could walls possibly restrict him whom the world itself cannot hold? Here we have to recall the whole biblical view of the "name" as an evocation of a personal presence. The icon "names" by the forms and colours it employs; it is the representation of a name, hence it makes present a prototype whose holiness is communion. Like the name, it is the medium for an encounter, whereby we are made partakers in the holiness of the One whom we encounter.[52]

Flight from the present world

The icon's summons to contemplation is not unconnected with the unusual kind of humanity offered to us in it. This is one of the deepest dimensions of the icon. The humanity represented in the icon is a humanity associated with heavenly glory. It is a humanity which bears the marks of the hieratical, the priestly: with attitudes and gestures unchanging, unassailable by suffering and death. The eyes are wide open on to another universe. As St John of Damascus said, there is something impressive in this — something also to impress our contemporaries who have acquired an expertness in diagnosing the signs of the ills of our time, something above all to attract our young people who are so interested in other worlds.

In contemplating the icon, the beholder is meant to be led beyond the forms to the frontiers of the undepictable: not by the suppression or the disregard of forms, but by going beyond them, that is, by that long journey which does not arbitrarily violate the visual function by some intellectual trick but turns our beings from the visible to the invisible, by an authentically mystical path that leads us into the night of the senses. Flight from the world is *not* the chief mark of contemplation.

Contemplation, then, is not simply flight from space and time. When the place of prayer no longer contains any other sign, the question forces itself upon us: how can the world around us — the world of space and time, those two characteristics of the incarnation — how can that world become the place where we meet with God, the very substance of the prayer of believers?

Encounter of the East with the West

This is where we wish to put the question of the encounter with the East. The West has become desiccated by its undue use of rationalism and didacticism. In this respect, the icon with its poetry and its experiential character can teach us in the West a salutary lesson. The modern devotees of the icon have taken this lesson to heart. On the other hand, it would be a pity if there were to be a loss of the Western genius for filling space by imposing form on it, and for realism in representation in learning the same lesson. With all its many qualities, the icon has not yet sufficiently proved its capacity to produce from its present store more than certain lessons of the past. It has not yet achieved in the West the sacralization of the contemporary world. What is new, what is urgent, what seizes up the whole religious world is industry and the machine. We must therefore encourage the few painters of icons who state the problem in these terms.

Any icon indicative of indifference to this appropriation of time and space would seem to us suspect. The neo-romanticism of youth today might well feel at home with it and delude us into thinking that everything is fine, but it would only be an excuse for evading the work of building up the world by contenting ourselves with mere dreams of doing so.

The icon — presence of Christ

What the painter seeks to represent in the icon is not human nature but the deified human person. Not by the earthly portrait, which is a sign of absence, a reminder of someone departed, but the transfigured person, namely a *presence* in a new world, the "present-ness" of those who remain living in the light of God. The icon has no independent existence; it is only coloured wood and dust. Its whole value is derived exclusively from the fact that it leads to him whom it represents. It is the image of the invisible because Christ made himself visible for us in the Incarnation, and his Incarnation justifies the icon. That is quite fundamental.

> If it were the icon of the invisible God we imagined we were creating, we should be quite mistaken. For that is impossible, since he is bodiless, faceless, invisible and infinite. But that would *not* be what we were creating and we should be making no mistake in depicting the image of the God who was incarnate, who revealed himself on earth in the flesh, who moved among us and assumed the nature, the three-dimensional substance, the form and the colours of our flesh and blood.[53]

Human substance, saved from then on, can express the mystery of deified bodies, since God became human so that humans can become God.

109

The icon, then, is Christ's *presence* in our midst. This is why the icon is consecrated: the image becomes the equivalent of a sacrament whereby the persons depicted are personally present. Consecration removes the icon from the realm of the artist's studio, even of the religious artist's studio, in order to turn it into a medium for the divine presence. The role the icon plays for the believer is that of *anamnesis*, i.e. a living memorial of a special moment in the life in Christ. The icon sends us somewhere beyond itself: the artist is effaced behind the Tradition; the work of art becomes a place of the presence.[54] The more humble the icon is, i.e. the more authentic in theology and contemplation, the less of an obstacle it becomes and the more of a springboard.

The icon thus remains a gamble with the impossible. "To whom then will you liken God or with what likeness compare with Him?" (Isa. 40:18). How difficult it is to meet this challenge is clear from history; but it is also clear from history that the prayer of the Church has been the master of history, a seed of life sown to guide humans from this earth to the eternal God.

No idolizing of the icon!

The icon is not an object to be worshipped because it is not an idol. An idol differs from an icon in that the icon is a likeness of a true thing and its original, whereas the idol is an image of a false and non-existent thing and is not to the likeness of an original, just as were the idols of the non-existent gods of the Greeks. We call those images which embody the whole figure statues, carved or sculptured figures in general. A natural picture or image differs in respect of its hypostasis from that which caused it, that is from the one who produced or begot it, seeing that Father and Son are two hypostases; it does not, however, differ with respect to and in respect of its nature, seeing that they are but one as far as regards the nature of humanity. An artistic painting, on the contrary, in respect of its essence differs from the original because the original is an animate and living human being, whereas his picture or icon is an inanimate and lifeless matter. That is why the Seventh Ecumenical Council said:

> An icon is not like the original with respect to and in respect of essence, but with respect to hypostasis or, more explicitly speaking, in point of imitation of the hypostasis, it is one with the original. For the hypostasis of the icon and that of the original one is the same, as is proved by the fact that the original can be seen in the icon, while, on the other hand, the icon subsists in the original, precisely as does a shadow in the body it portrays and cannot possibly be separated therefrom; and as is further proved by the fact that it is the hypostasis and not the nature that is depicted or portrayed in the picture. And it is further proved by the fact that in every icon there is inscribed not the name of the nature of the hypostasis or, for instance, such words as "this is the picture of a human being" simply, but the name of the hypostasis or, for instance, words stating that it is a picture of Christ or of John and so on.[55]

Since the Incarnation, the same law holds good between the essence and the types of its manifestation. Religion is the relation of human beings to God and is revealed in the nature of our inner Christ. This relationship was depicted and represented to us by the means of sensible signs and types in the sacraments. In these are harmoniously correlated what is "supersensible" and what is "sensible", the sign and the signified, the being and the phenomenon. Liturgical life consists in distinguishing what is sensible in the mystery from the idea residing therein, and not confounding both, not mistaking that which is sensible for that which is spiritual, the sign for that which is signified, nor separating or saying that which is sensible, the type, the sign as superfluous, or the religious type alone. All visible signs convey and conceal within them the invisible grace of the operating Holy Spirit. In saying all this, we do not deny the possible hidden abuses and absolutization of forms; for abuse leads to ritualism, obscurantism, and superficial attachment to the exterior forms, leading to a superstitious religiosity.

St Basil of Caesarea was the first to point out the importance of icons for penetrating into the mysteries of our faith. [56] Certainly in saying this, he had in mind the old tradition of icons transmitted to him. Asterius of Amaseia, in his eulogy of the Saint Euphemia, describes the pictures seen in her small chapel. [57] Most of the early writings nevertheless distinguish clearly between the prototype and the depicting of the person or event in question, reminding one of an impact resulting from the prayerful contemplation of icons. The more one stands in prayer before an icon, the more one is uplifted to the original. There is no question of worshipping the icons or adoring them since adoration befits only the divine nature; in fact, the honour rendered to the icon, as has already been said, passes to the prototype, and whoever adores the image adores the substance of what is painted. [58]

Thanks to the three famous Discourses of John of Damascus on the defence of icons (pronounced between 726 and 733), we can establish the conscience of the Church with regard to the use and place of icons, thus avoiding extreme views. Without forgetting the invisibility and the absolute immaterialness of God, John of Damascus underlines that certainly, if it is inconceivable to represent the soul, how much more so is it to represent God who has given us this immaterial soul. Nevertheless I dare represent the invisible God, not as invisible, but as being manifested visibly to us thanks to his participation in flesh and blood. I do not in any way represent the invisible divinity, but I represent the visible flesh of God. Further he is reconciling the apparent prohibition of images in the Old Testament with similar cases where God sometimes became visible through theophanies or angelophanies; but the climax is that, while ancient Israel did not see God, we are privileged to see the Incarnate Son of the Father. [59] Elsewhere he clearly exposes the pedagogy of icons. Often we are illiterate and thus the Fathers have painted the icons representing the most significant facts from the earthly life of our Lord, of the Theotokos, the angels, etc. [60]

We constantly ask for their intercessions: prophets, patriarchs, saints, Apostles, martyrs, confessors and all the pious who are asleep in the Lord. This is a living tradition, clearly defended by the Councils. It is implied, of course, that we are addressing our prayers not as if they were gods or divine persons, but simply as to brothers and sisters; they are asked to intercede before the throne of God for our sins and for the Church militant (statements of Theodosius during the Seventh Ecumenical Council). Parallel to the veneration of saints is the honouring of their relics.

Now such veneration can be understood from another point of view too. Each church building, in order to be consecrated, needs relics of saints. Such a practice seeks to show the unity of faith and the fact that the place of worship with the parish as an ecclesiastical community is not an independent body, which appeared suddenly, but is founded on the same faith and holiness of the communion of saints. This explains why each newly built church is dedicated to a name from the ecclesiastical calendar or from the feast of our Lord or of the Virgin Mary. Already in earlier times heretical groups had appeared to reject the cult of saints and the accompanying religious service in their honour. The Church, seeing the danger of splitting the unity, has condemned such dangerous tendencies. The local Synod of Gangra (Paphlagonia in Asia Minor, about AD 340), in its synodical letter, dealing with the case of Eustathius and his heretical followers, condemns them precisely for having rejected the veneration of saints and the use of relics. [61]

Undoubtedly, this link with the saints enables the Church, in spite of historical vicissitudes and upheavals, to maintain its unity with them, always being re-minded of their faith and thus strengthened. This visible manifestation guarantees among the faithful the existing continuity of their invisible presence in our eucharistic worship and encourages the pursuit of the same attitude among those who are alive.

The icon — facing both the visible and the invisible

The icon claims to be the image of the invisible and even a presence of the invisible. There is an element of surprise in such a claim. It comes as a surprise more perhaps to people today than to people in the past. How is the icon to be understood in its deepest dimensions?

Initially, we can define the image as a simple conveyor of information, even if the sacred image by its symbolic character also has a transcendent dimension. In fact, the image describes a personality (or an event); it recalls the person it depicts and thereby becomes a bond between the person represented and the person confronted with the icon.

All this, however, is still within the order of the intelligible. With the icon, however, this order is left behind. The intelligible is only the outward aspect of the icon, whereas its essence is to be the bond of a presence. Although this presence is not the same as the reality of the subject, it cannot for all that be reduced to a simple memorial. But how is the icon to be explained theologically as the bond of a presence? In seeking to answer this question, we shall come to understand the difference between the icon and every other image, and also its place in the Tradition, its role in the liturgical life, as these have been defined in the course of history.

The history of the icon, moreover, as well as the iconoclastic crisis, was marked by the "final triumph of Orthodoxy". We shall confine ourselves to theological arguments which dominate the discussion and the conflict. For the debate is indeed a theological one. Far from being a secondary question or a matter of devotional practice, iconoclasm was a recapitulation of all previous heresies. It was an attack on the very heart of the Christian faith, the meaning of the Incarnation and therefore the very mystery of God the Creator. The reason why the struggle between the iconoclasts and the defenders of icons was pushed even to martyrdom was because in defending or condemning the cult of icons, people were defending or denying the Christian faith itself. [62]

No icon, not even the humblest, is content simply to depict a scene or a personage. It also includes a theological background. Using its own media of form and colour, the image represents in this way what the Scriptures teach in words.

While theology with its arguments lends depth to a doctrine, the image offers, as it were, a vision of this same truth. The image remains within the realm of representational figures even when it transfigures concrete reality to emphasize its theological significance. From the very beginning, icons already included these two elements: the theological aspect has always been inseparable from the concrete representation. This rule will govern every appraisal of iconography.

But the theological event also has another function over and above that of the panegyric. While the latter remains principally within the domain of language and form, making the icon into a *laudatio* or praise of the saint, the theological element keeps fundamentally to the subject represented, whose mystery it reflects, and thereby lifts Byzantine art to its ultimate in spiritualization.

This theological aspect can dominate the entire composition, as can be seen from the 12th century in the "Annunciation" icon of Oustiony, in which the figure of the Immanuel is imprinted in red on the Virgin's breast. Later on, especially in Russia from the 16th century, the theological aspect actually becomes the theme of the representation: the icon henceforth is no longer the hypostatic presence of the prototype but a theological treatise.

This can be illustrated from the development of the icon of the Holy Trinity. In the Byzantine world it was known as the "philoxeneia", i.e. "hospitality" (that of Abraham welcoming the three strangers). This very ancient theme is found from the 4th century onwards on a mosaic of St Mary the Great, depicting the episode narrated in Genesis (18:1-15). The Greek Fathers consistently interpreted this episode as a visit of the Holy Trinity to Abraham. The attention shown to these three heavenly personages is in keeping with this theophanic character. But the details — the articles placed on the table, Abraham and Sarah fussing over their guests, the servant preparing the meal — give a rather historical atmosphere to the whole conception. This form was imitated down to the 15th and 16th centuries and, with Andrei Rublev, the doctrinal aspect dominated and defined the entire composition. The details are reduced to the bare essentials: the three heavenly persons in silent meditation; the table now an altar with nothing on it except the eucharistic chalice. Some of the accessories — the rock, the oak tree, the dwelling — are transformed into symbols; an invisible geometric pattern (chiefly the circle) creates a unity which enables us to guess the painter's intention, namely, to represent the Holy Trinity in its movement of love and as source of salvation for humankind. This conception does not lessen the historical value of the scene but superimposes on it a theological interpretation. In this way, therefore, an icon seeks to pass on the message of the eucharistic reality in the mystery of the Incarnation by the power of the Holy Spirit, or rather, by the whole work of the Holy Trinity. A dynamic icon of Trinitarian action acquires a sacramentary form, the form of its own sacrament of the Kingdom.

The icon as image and participation in the divine

In his analysis of the different types of images, St John of Damascus applies the neo-Platonic categories of Pseudo-Dionysius the Areopagite. The image, for him, is a participation in the model, in the prototype. It is not purely poetical but ontological; participation is an ontological resemblance. By its very nature, participation in the order of the creature is never adequate but always deficient. St John of Damascus, for example, defines the image as "a resemblance which defines the prototype but at the same time differs from it in some respects".[63] The degree of resemblance depends on the degree of participation in the prototype. Starting from the consubstantial image which is the Word, St John of Damascus ends up with the icon, the reflection of invisible realities in matter.

In its perfect form, he says, the image exists only in the Holy Trinity: this image is the eternal Word begotten of the Father and possessing as such the fullness of the divine nature. All that the Father possesses is also the Son's.[64] The Word is a perfect participation, a perfect likeness, without defect.

Its nature is the same as that of the prototype. The next level in this hierarchy is the image God himself has of the things he has created: the world as it exists in "the pre-eternal counsels of God". Here St John of Damascus adopts the term employed by Dionysius the Areopagite, who speaks of "predeterminations". Before they existed, from all eternity, things are presented in the thought of God as a model, an image.

Images of the third kind are visible things as representations of things invisible, "formless so that, in giving them bodily forms, we may have a veiled knowledge of them";[65] the reason being that humanity cannot rise to the contemplation of things invisible without the mediation of visible things. So it is that Scripture is adapted to the inadequacy of the human mind to awaken our desire for God. Nature likewise reveals the mysteries of the faith: the mystery of the Trinity is reflected in the sun, its light and its rays, and to resemble God humanity has received the intelligence, the word and the breath of life.

The fourth type of image is close to the third type: future things which can be prefigured by a thing or an event in the present: the burning bush, for example, evokes the Mother of God, the water and the cloud evoke the Spirit who baptizes.

The fifth class of image is that of things past, made in order to preserve the memory of a person or an event. These images are expressed in lines of words or in drawings on pictures, for all to contemplate. "Thanks to them, we avoid what is evil and aspire to what is good."[66] It is here that St John of Damascus mentions icons: "Today we also paint images (icons) of persons of outstanding goodness, so that we may be reminded of them, and imitate them, and also out of love for such persons."[67] That is as far as St John of Damascus goes in his analysis of the image. Within this hierarchy ranging from the perfect resemblance of the substantial identity between the Father and the Son to material things, the icon occupies the humblest place. Here the analogy is the least perfect. St John of Damascus does not distinguish the reciprocal image, the only one capable of participating in the substance of the prototype, and the artificial image which participates solely by resemblance. For St John of Damascus, the conception of the image is based rather on ontological participation.

These ambiguities are explained, doubtless, by the fact that St John of Damascus had to contend with the fundamental objection of the iconoclasts, namely, that matter itself is evil, incapable of representing spiritual realities. To rehabilitate matter, he sticks to the neo-Platonist categories of Pseudo-Dionysius the Areopagite. For example, he gives ontological participation a new aspect by making Christology his basis:

> I will never cease venerating the matter whereby salvation came to me. But I do not venerate it as I venerate God. How could God possibly be what came into existence from nothing? Even if the body of God is God, having become by hypostatic union changeless, that which gives unction while remaining what it is by

nature, animated flesh of a reasonable soul, created and not created? But I also venerate the rest of that matter through which salvation reached me, as being filled with divine energy and grace. Do not despise matter! It is not something shameful, for nothing that God made is shameful![68]

This passage brings out clearly the richness of the character of the image, even if it is placed last in the hierarchy. The basic principle of this conception remains the incarnation of the Word. In the union of the Word with human nature, the body of Christ became holy, filled with grace. John even calls it *homotheos* (equal to God). And in his body, all matter has been sanctified. It seems that in the thought of St John of Damascus there was the notion of a diffuse communication of the holiness of Christ's body to other forms of matter, an ontological participation between the body of Christ and its effigy. Thus the icon can become a mediator of grace.

At first sight, these two analyses and views of the image — one deriving in spirit and method more from Aristotelianism, the other following the pattern of the neo-Platonism of Pseudo-Dionysius the Areopagite — seem opposed. But in the end they support each other. The analysis of a sign starts from the simplest form and rises to the symbol with its epiphanic character. The analysis of the icon starts with the consubstantial image in the Godhead and descends to the most material of its forms. The latter conception is undoubtedly the richer of the two; it presupposes the Revelation and is more customary in the Byzantine world. What is common to both, however, is the essential feature of the icon: a presence of the ineffable springing forth from matter.

The invisible through the visible

Since God is the creator of all creation (cosmos), there is no sharp distinction between the sacred and the profane, between the physical and the metaphysical. Whatever was edifying was adopted. John of Damascus wrote: "Let us search the wisdom of the profane. Perhaps we can find something useful from there, and we may profit by finding therein something edifying for our souls."[69] The Fathers felt no need to divide history and art into secular and holy. According to the historical Socrates "the good, wherever it is, belongs to one Truth"[70] and this is confirmed by Basil of Caesarea.[71] The Fathers viewed history as a continuous linear process with no disruption in the divine economy. They did not raise the question, "What has Jerusalem to do with Athens?" The God of history before Anno Domini is the same as He of the Christian era. They emphasized the continuity of Christian culture with the Greek past and the new culture. The epiphany of the Logos was simply the apex of a long process in the plans and historical involvement of God who is never absent from His world. He manifests His presence differently according to new situations and with appropriate means.

The Orthodox liturgy puts material elements into the service of invisible communion with God. They are related to worship not only by the fact of their making perceivable that which is mystically enacted by it, but also by their representing Christ's public ministry. These representations, according to St Nilus the Ascetic (5th century), are not made only "in order that even those who do not know letters may through the vision of iconography receive into their memories knowledge of the courageous exploits of those who have genuinely served the true

115

God, and be aroused to emulation", but also in order that they may be used as necessary commentaries of the fundamental themes of worship. [72] The icon is always understood as a non-naturalistic presentation of sacred persons; that is to say, an attempt to render the divine through art, mainly for Christ, and for the spiritualized and deified saints, as they appear in human form. Since "the honour is given to the prototype" and not to the icon itself, this is actually a visual help and guide. The believer must be assisted by the form of the icon to apprehend its prototype and the sacredness of the person presented, so that through it his mind may be guided to the knowledge of God[73] — a phrase incorporated in the formula of the Seventh Ecumenical Council. [74] This is "the verification of truth through the icons". [75] It is from this point of view that the Church saw the iconoclastic opposition to icons in the 8th century, and it is with this same intention that it restored them.

The purpose of iconography is to assist Christians in their pursuit of holiness in their present temporal lives. The Christian has to be reminded in every possible way that, in one's journey towards perfection, he or she is accompanied and sustained by one's "first-born brother", Christ, and the martyrs of the faith. Painting renders an immense service. The primary concern of the early Church remained the beauty of the spiritual world, which it tried to interpret. Its transcendental content was, and is, not physical beauty. Classical beauty and aesthetic harmony had become a divinity in pre-Christian times. Plato recommended to artists that "the ugly should not be depicted in the images of living things nor in structures of any other created things, but these artists must be sought who are intelligently capable of tracing the things which are by nature beautiful and graceful. [76] Christian art, on the contrary, as John Chrysostom states, is not independent; it is in the service of God like a faithful maid: "Each vessel, animal and plant is good not because of its form or its colour, but because of the service it renders."[77] In this sense iconography does not copy nature nor does it seek form or colour as an end, but as a means to a higher end. Not only in the case of icons does the material serve the spiritual, but in many other ways also and, not least among them, in the way of using human gestures.

For example, our body becomes the temple of the Holy Spirit when the water touches it in baptism; or again the physical action of bowing in repentance is required because it demonstrates our inner feelings of contrition and penitence. With our hands we make the sign of the cross in order to remind ourselves of the mystery of our redemption. Symbolic gestures are well known in the Bible. Thus David danced before the Ark of the Covenant; Solomon, kneeling and with his hands raised, invoked God's blessing on the Temple of Jerusalem. The material was always put to the service of the spiritual.

So the starting point of the use of all that is material is that by means of it we show forth our relationship with the realities of the world. For a Christian nothing is unimportant or unworthy. Water, oil, incense, candles, fire, flowers are interpreters of our devotion. Our human wholeness is radically unsatisfied by a kind of religious rationalism, which would try to approach the Eternal more with the mind than with the spirit, the heart and the whole man, and would largely exclude the body. But we are also opposed to a blind formalism in ritual which overemphasizes the importance of the material. In the liturgy the whole material order is invited to enter into the sphere of Christ's glory, and to share in the transformation and deliverance from corruption that it offers. In this way the cosmic dimension of Christ's redemptive work is emphasized.

The whole truth of Christology was at stake during the iconoclastic dispute. The importance of the Seventh Ecumenical Council, therefore, must be seen in this light. Consequently, the icon, as an essential channel of God's revelation, cannot be separated from being a sacred object of liturgical veneration. In these two aspects the Church holds the icon on the same high level of dignity as it does Holy Scripture.[78] Icons, in general, are visible portraits of a deified humanity, of men and women who have recovered the capacity to show forth the divine which had been obscured by sin and who now share in the festival of the new heaven and the new earth. The controversy had nothing to do with the aesthetic aspect of illustrations, even the sacred ones. It was neither a dispute about art's place in presenting the invisible by this or that artistic form. Art itself had to be redeemed which, in historical terms, was brought about in early Christianity. If art was to live and grow, it had to deny itself and plunge, as though into the baptismal font, into the pure element of faith.

The Council's Fathers, after abrogating the false definition of the pseudo-Synod of iconoclastic tendency held in Blachernae, issued a definition as follows:

> We define the rule with all accuracy and diligence, in a manner not unlike that befitting the shape of the precious and vivifying cross, that the general and holy icons painted be placed in the holy churches of God upon sacred vessels and vestments, walls and panels, houses and streets, both of our Lord and of the Theotokos. For the more frequently and often they are continually seen in pictorial representations, the more those beholding are reminded and led to visualize anew the memory of the originals which they represent and for whom moreover they also beget a yearning in the soul of the persons beholding the icons.[79]

By adopting the icons in its worship, the Church did not intend to introduce any "adoration" of icons in the narrow sense of the term. Certain expressions in fact are misleading, and one has to remember the original meaning of the verb "proskynesis" or veneration. In the ancient Greek the verb "kyno" (in the compound verb "pros-kyno", meaning to adore) means to embrace and kiss. The preposition "pros" indicates an intensification of the meaning "embrace and kiss" and implies longing and yearning. Hence, in order to express the full meaning of the original Greek in English, we should have to employ some such phrase as "to embrace and kiss longingly". That is why this Council said: "in all respects to accept and recognize the venerable icons, and to adore them, or, more explicitly speaking, to embrace and kiss them". "Adoration" or its equivalent "worship" (= *latreia*) is rendered only to God. The honour paid to the icon "goes rather to the one pictured or represented by it", as John of Damascus said. Therefore, the icon is honoured conjointly with the one who is pictured in a single act of adoration. For we venerate the person represented in the picture by paying him worshipping adoration.

The beauty of an icon is the beauty of the esteemed person's acquired likeness with God. Its value lies not in its being beautiful in an aethetic sense (= *aisthesis*), but in the fact that it depicts beauty transfigured. The Incarnation is the alpha and omega of icons, the justification being that because God became man, he took a body which was composed of the matter of creation; therefore matter became sanctified or capable of santification. The icon is the local outcome of this. We see, as through a window, into the Kingdom of God where all speculation and debate cease; it is a holy presence which brings us down to our knees as we worship. The Fall brought ugliness and disfigurement into the world and the hymn of the feast makes this point very eloquently:

> Mother of God! The undescribable Word of the Father was made flesh through Thee, and therefore became describable. Penetrating with His divine beauty the impure image of man, He restored it to its pristine state. As we confess the salvation, we depict it in deed and word.[80]

Icons are not venerated on account of the material, but on account of the likeness which they possess to the ones depicted by them. Hence the Council said that when the wood, forming the shape of the Cross in crucifixes, becomes decomposed, it is to be burned. This Council underlines that what the Bible reveals by means of words, the iconographer represents through the icons. Therefore, iconographers ought to familiarize themselves first with the Bible and then paint their icons in accordance with the spirit of the Gospel.

The spiritual microcosm and macrocosm of the icon

The true content of the icon, however, is a real spiritual orientation of the Christian life and, in particular, of Christian prayer. It is the microcosm in which the Christian is manifested and distinguished by his persistence in prayer in the topsy-turvy world around him. The icon thus shows us this microcosmic attitude we are to adopt in our prayers — on the one hand, towards God, and on the other hand, towards the world around us. This is how the spiritual microcosm is opened up towards the macrocosm of the universe. For prayer is conversing with God and it also has dimensions which are universal. This is why, for prayer, an absence of passions is needed; we must be deaf and unresponsive to the external stimuli of the world, a world divided, secularized, dualistic, stricken on one side by ideologies and philosophies and on the other by church divisions, with churches living in expectancy but moving towards a unity which is so difficult not only to achieve but even to envisage.

With the aid of colours, forms and lines, with the aid of symbolic realism, a unique pictorial language, the spiritual world of humanity as transformed into the Temple of God is revealed to us. The inner order and peace to which the Holy Fathers of the Church bear witness are conveyed in the microcosm of the icon by the outward peace and harmony. The whole body of the saint, all its details, even his/her dress and everything around him/her, is unified, restored to a supreme harmony in the macrocosm. We have here a visible manifestation of the triumph over the division and chaos which reigns in humanity and in the world.

But the purpose of the icon is not to stimulate or magnify in us a natural human feeling. It is not something "touching" or sentimental. As Ouspensky says, its purpose is to orient all our feelings, as well as our minds and all other dimensions of our human nature, towards transfiguration, by stripping them of all exaltation which could only be unhealthy and harmful.

At the same time, however, the icon helps us to decipher every human face as an icon. For every human face is an icon. Beneath all the masks, all the ashes, every human being, however ravaged he or she may be by his or her destiny, by the destiny of history and of civilization, carries within him or her the pearl of great price, this hidden face. During the liturgies in an Orthodox church, when the priest censes the people, he censes every individual Christian, and in every individual Christian he censes the possibility, the opportunity, of the icon, in some sense or other, the chance of the ultimate beauty, of true beauty.

This beauty, moreover, is commended in the faces of the saints and can be recognized, among many others, in St John, St Paul, St Nicholas, St Seraphim of Sarov. These faces, rich in beauty, in true beauty, represent the transfigured microcosm of these friends of God, as St John of Damascus was fond of saying. And these friends of God become our friends. We are not alone; no one is alone in his or her solitude. We freeze to death in our solitude; whereas the Church was meant to be this huge "society of friends" with certain people in it who are all friendship and nothing but friendship. Their friendship, moreover, is a totally selfless friendship in our world, a world in which friendship is constantly being secularized, sexualized or politicized, and in which there is this longing for genuine unselfish friendship.

The icon, then, is the Christ, the God who became a face. Then it is also the faces of all the friends of God who are our friends and who insist on including us in their circle. And already, the icon represents the Kingdom of God; anticipating the Kingdom of God, starting from the one place where we see this already anticipated: here on earth in the human face! The Kingdom of God is anticipated, either starting from the beauty of the world, though this is an ambiguous beauty, or starting from certain faces, certain old faces, fashioned by a long life, faces which have not been plunged into resentment or bitterness or the fear of death, faces of those who do not flinch as they approach death, faces that know precisely where they are, and have found again the mind of a child.

Conclusion

"Lord, will you at this time restore the kingdom to Israel?" This was the question put to Jesus before his ascension. "It is not for us", he replied, "to know the times or seasons which the Father has fixed by his own authority. But you shall receive power when the Holy Sprit has come upon you; and you shall be my witnesses in Jerusalem and in all Judea and Samaria and to the end of the earth" (Acts 1:6-8).

The Church at Pentecost accomplishes its mission of bearing witness to Christ. But the task of bearing witness in the world still remains unfinished. Throughout the fluctuations and vicissitudes of history, the Church of Christ, by the grace of the Spirit which quickens it, is and remains the community which witnesses to its faith in the risen Christ in expectation of the complete consummation of the will of the Father, even though we are not permitted to know "the times and the seasons".

Already in the apostolic age, the first Council of Jerusalem (Acts 15) marked a decisive step in the history of the Church. Other Ecumenical Councils or local Synods marked other equally significant steps, based on the Tradition of the Church and the canons of the Fathers of the Church. These Councils, moreover, have also been witnesses to Christ, to the unity of his Church, to the reality of the life in the power of the Spirit, witnesses for their contemporaries but also for the centuries to come, cementing the continuity of a universal Tradition from apostolic times down to the final consummation by God. The Seventh Ecumenical Council has its place in this historical, canonical and theological context.

In our contemporary world, the witness of the Church becomes more than ever an urgent necessity. After past centuries of division, struggle, indifference, and even enmity, the "ferment" of the nations and peoples of the world poses with renewed intensity the problem of the unity of the Church. Although the Assemblies of the World Council of Churches, the Second Vatican Council and even the great and holy Pan-Orthodox Council in preparation, are none of them assemblies of all the divided Christians, each of them has or will have a universal significance.

Such meetings, however, will have a truly ecumenical significance only in so far as within each confession and communion there is a sharpened self-awareness, for the earnest of the future unity cannot be merely a hurried compromise. Quite the contrary! It is in deepening still further their respective traditions and faith that the divided Christian churches rediscover Christ and the true faith of his Church which is his Body, in a dialogue which can only be sincere and honest if it is marked by repentance (metanoia) and a return to the common roots of the Tradition of the undivided Church of Christ. In today's world, in which the assimilation of ideas happens more easily than ever before, it is in the deepest self-searching that our thoughts and hopes should be turned towards unity. Filled with distress at the unstable conditions produced after two appalling wars and fearful of the danger of a further and even worse disaster today, those of the younger generation are looking for a safe haven in the renewed Church, for a dialogue and an answer to their existential concerns, in which they will thus be able to find the peace, the justice and the tranquillity of soul for which they are searching.

Let us hope that the churches will respond to this appeal and without hesitation set aside their pride, their meticulous speculative theological discussions and the secondary reasons which have caused their divisions, and do all in their power, without detracting from the fundamental principles of their existence, to unite together in one immense moral force for the glory of God.

Already having unity, we are pained that it is so little apparent. Let us not forget that God wants us to be active and strong in the faith as we forge that unity. It is up to us, therefore, to see to it that the gifts of grace given to us bear fruit.

Seeing the icon of Christ, John of Damascus could exclaim: "I saw the human power of God and my soul was saved!"[81]

NOTES

[1] E. Porret, *La philosophie chrétienne en Russie*, Neuchâtel; Nicolas Berdiaeff, *Etre et Penseur*, Cahiers de Philosophie, 1944, p.119ff.

[2] N. Berdiaeff, *L'esprit de Dostoievski*, Paris, SCEL, 1932, p.98; *Der Sinn des Schaffens, Versuch einer Rechtfertigung des Menschen*, Tübingen, Mohr-Verlag, 1927, p.89ff.

[3] Orthodox Sunday hymn (Kontakion).

[4] Regarding this "morphosis" in the ecclesiastical sense and the recent movement to promote it, see E. Theodorou, *The Liturgical Instruction and Education*, Athens, 1958, p.11ff; *The Instructive Value of the Triodion in Use*, Athens, 1958, p.69ff; cf. also C. Kalokyris, *Orthodox Iconography*, Brookline, MA, Holy Cross Orthodox Press, 1965, p.43ff.

[5] Cf. also A. Grabar (Skira), *La Peinture byzantine*, Geneva, 1953, p.34; H. Schrade, *Ikonographie der christlichen Kunst I. Die Auferstehung Christi*, Berlin-Leipzig, 1932, p.43ff.

[6] See also *Encyclopédie populaire des connaissances liturgiques*, Paris, Bloud et Gay, 1947, p.213ff.

[7] Mansi, *Sacr. Cons. nova et ampl. collectio*, XIII, p.252.

[8] See Ch.J. Héfélé, *Histoire des Conciles*, Vol. III/3, Paris, 1907-1910, p.1067ff. But which Western picture of the Lord imposes the idea that the whole fullness of divinity dwells bodily in the represented Christ?

[9] Theodore Studites, in *PG*, 99, 361.

[10] Kalokyris, *op. cit.*, p.46.

[11] Mansi, *op. cit.*, XIII, p.344; cf. Theodore Studites, in *PG*, 99, 409C: "The unmixable were mingled; in the uninscribable, the inscribed"; see also for the "co-divine and co-honourable body of Christ" in the *Synodical Letter for Orthodoxy of the Seventh Ecumenical Council*, in *Triodion*, ed. Apostoliki Diaconia of the Church of Greece, Athens, 1960, p.147.

[12] *The Hymn Book (Menaion)* of 16 August (in the psalm "Lord I cry unto Thee").

[13] *Triodion*, *op. cit*, p.137.

[14] *The Hymn Book (Menaion)* of 25 December, ed. Venice, 1890, p.197.

[15] *Triodion*, p.134: "Being in Thy divine nature undescribable Lord, in these last days thou made it possible to be circumscribed by becoming incarnate."

[16] Theodore Studites, in *PG.*, 99, 413C.

[17] E. Schwarz, *Acta Concil. Oecum. Concil. Univers. Chalcedonese*, I, 1, p.13.

[18] Cf. Kalokyris, *op. cit,*, p.48.

[19] *Triodion*, *op. cit.*, p.134. Cf. also the Hymn: "He who is above unobserved by the Cherubim is seen by representation of those to whom He was assimilated" (*The Hymn Book (Menaion)* of 16 August); cf. Ch. Androutsos, *Dogmatics*, Athens, 1930, pp.39-92 (in Greek); see also John of Damascus, *First Oration about Icons*, in *PG*, 94, 1240: "... therefore a living image natural and unchangeable of the invisible God is the Son, bearing in himself the whole Father and possessing in everything identity with Him"; cf. also Theodotos, bishop of Ancyra (5th century), M. Juagie, in *Patrologia Orientalis*, XIX, 3, II *Homélies Mariales Byzantines*, Paris, 1925, p.212ff.

[20] *Triodion*, *op. cit.*, p.134.

[21] *Ibid.*, p.142.

[22] *Ibid.*, p.137.

[23] Cf. the often repeated phrase in the dismissal hymns of the Orthodox church regarding the saints.

[24] 1 Cor. 15:53: "As we have borne the image of the earthly, we shall also bear the image of the heavenly."

[25] Cf. also Philippians 3:21: "... who will change our lowly body to be like his glorious body..."

[26] Mauchair, *L'impressionnisme, son histoire, son esthétique, ses maîtres*, Paris, 1903, p.16ff; cf. also R. Hammann, *Der Impressionismus in Leben und Kunst*, 1907.

[27] See N. Platon, *Führer durch das Archäologische Museum von Heraklion*, Heraklion, 1958, Illustration XII; cf. C. Kalokyris, "New Advances in Christian and Byzantine Archaeology", in *Theologia*, 31, 1960, Athens (in Greek).

[28] Pseudo-Dionysius the Areopagite, in *PG.*, 3, 369sq.

[29] Plotinus, *Plotini Opera*, ed. A. Kirchhoc, Vols I-II, Lipsiae MDC CLVI, Vol. I, pp.11,9.

[30] Cf. I.M. Panayiotopoulos, in *The Great Greek Encyclopedia*, Vol. 21, p.263.

[31] In relation to the "formation" of Christ in us, as St Paul writes, "... until Christ be formed in you", in Gal. 4:19.

[32] *The Hymn Book (Menaion)* of 24 December, p.183; cf. P.N. Trembelas, *Selection of Orthodox Hymns*, Athens, 1949, p.135 (in Greek); cf. also *The Akathistos Hymn*: "by whom — the Theotokos — we are deified", in *The Book of Hours (Horologion)*, ed. Saliveros, p.531.

[33] Hymn for Maundy Thursday.

[34] Maximus the Confessor, *Gnostic Centuries*, 11, 88, in *PG*, 90, 1168A.

[35] See J. Baggley, *Doors of Perception — Icons and Their Spiritual Significance*, London, Oxford, Mowbray, 1987, p.l.

[36] Cf. Catacombe de la Vigna. See also A. Grabar, *L'empereur dans l'art byzantin*, Paris, Belles Lettres, 1936; *Les voies de la création en iconographie chrétienne*, Paris, Flammarion, 1979; *Le premier art chrétien (200-395)*, N.R.F., Paris, Gallimard, 1966; K. Papaïoannou, *La peinture byzantine et russe*, Lausanne, Rencontre, 1965.

[37] St John of Damascus, *Defence of the Holy Icons*, in *PG*, 94, 1239.

[38] *Ibid.*, 1245.

[39] See the excellent recent publication of T.F. Torrance, *The Trinitarian Faith*, Edinburgh, T. & T. Clark, 1988, p.193ff.

[40] Cf. Olivier Clément, *Questions sur l'Homme*, Paris, Stock, 1976, pp.193-195.

[41] Cf. V. Lossky, "La théologie de la lumière chez Saint Grégoire Palamas de Thessalonique", in *Dieu Vivant I* (1945), p.117.

[42] Cf. *ibid.*, p.118.

[43] Cf. Yves Congar O.P., "La déification dans la tradition spirituelle de l'Orient", in *La vie spirituelle 118*, 1 May 1935, p.107.

[44] St John of Damascus, *op. cit.*, *PG*, 94, 1300; cf. Clément, *op. cit.*, p.195. We must remember here the whole biblical concept of the "name" as evocation of a personal presence. The icon "names" by the use of form and colours; it is a represented name; this is why it makes present to us a prototype whose holiness is communion. Like the name, it is the means of an encounter which enables us to partake of the holiness of the one we encounter.

[45] Cf. B. Bobrinskoy, "L'icône, sacrement du Royaume", in *Service orthodoxe de presse* (supplément), No. 112, November 1986, p.2.

[46] St John of Damascus, *Imag.* 1,16.

[47] St Basil, *Treatise on the Holy Spirit* 18,45, in *PG*, 32, 149C; see also in *Sources chrétiennes*, Vol. 17, 1946, p.194; cf. Funk, Abhandlungen II,25.

[48] It should be noted here, therefore, that not only is it found in the *Treatise on the Holy Spirit*, but right at the heart of the most important arguments where St Basil defines, in what is probably a quite unique way in the whole of patristic literature, the "way" (tropos) or particular mode of the action of the Holy Spirit in the undivided Trinitarian economy of salvation. What St Basil is saying is that the Spirit is at one and the same time the *locus* or *place* of Trinitarian worship by the creature and also the *place* of the latter's sanctification by the divine Trinity. It is in the "space" of the Spirit, therefore, that we contemplate the Son and, through him, the Father: "When, under the influence of an illuminating power (that of the Spirit) we fix our gaze on the beauty of the image of the Invisible God and through this ascend to the entrancing spectacle of the Archetype, the Spirit of knowledge is inseparable from this, in itself conferring the power to see the image on those who love to contemplate the truth" (St Basil, *Treatise on the Holy Spirit, op. cit.*, 18,47). St Basil also says: "It is impossible for us to see the Image of the Invisible God except in the illumination of the Spirit" (*ibid.*, 26,64). This pneumatological (Trinitarian) dimension or condition of the vision of Christ, the perfect image of the Father, is fundamental for the theology of the icon. Without it, the appeal of the icon-lovers to St Basil's classic dictum becomes insipid, and the relationship of the image to the prototype becomes external, illustrative and notional.

[49] Cf. St John of Damascus, *Defence of the Holy Icons, op. cit.*, 1,9-13 as cited by C. Schönborn, *L'icône du Christ, fondements théologiques*, Paris, 1976 and 1986, pp.191-193; cf. Bobrinskoy, *op. cit.*, p.5.

[50] G. Kroug, *Carnets d'un peintre d'icônes*, Paris, 1983, pp.35-36 (in French); Russian ed., Paris 1978, pp.15-18.

[51] Cf. Bobrinskoy, *op. cit.*, p.8.

[52] O. Clément, *L'Eglise orthodoxe*, Paris, PUF, 1965, p.107.

[53] St John of Damascus, *Defence of the Holy Icons, op. cit.*, col.1239.

[54] The iconographer does not sign the icon. He remains anonymous. Often we owe our knowledge of a number of celebrated names of iconographers solely to the tradition of the churches which have preserved these names for us.

[55] Seventh Ecumenical Council, *Act 6*.

[56] St Basil of Caesarea, *Letter* 360, in *PG*, 32, 1100.

[57] Asterius of Amaseia, in *PG*, 40, 333-37.

[58] Mansi, *Cons. Collect., op. cit.*, XIII, 380.

[59] St John of Damascus, *Discourse* I, 14, 16, in *PG*, 94, 1236, 1328.

[60] *Ibid., De Fide Orthodoxa* 4,6, in *PG*, 94, 1172.

[61] Synod of Gangra, *Canon 20*.

[62] Cf. V. Soloviev, *La grande controverse et la politique chrétienne Orient et Occident*, Paris, Aubier-Montaigne, 1953, pp.72-73.

[63] This is how canon 82 of the Quinisext or Trullan Synod (*in Trullo*) is to be understood. Only the icon can express the incarnate character of the Christian faith; the Symbol (Creed) retains its place as long as it fulfills its function.

[64] Cf. Colossians 1:15: "He is the image of the invisible God" and also Epistle to the Hebrews 1:3: "He reflects the glory of God and bears the very stamp of his nature."

[65] Christoph Schönborn, *L'icône du Christ*, Fribourg, Switzerland, Editions universitaires, 1976, pp.191-193.

[66] St John of Damascus, *Defence of the Holy Icons*, in *PG*, 94, 1243-1244.

[67] *Ibid.*, col. 1245.

[68] *Ibid.*, 1245.

[69] *Ibid.*, in *PG*, 88, 384.

[70] *Ibid.*, in *PG*, 94, 524, 532.

[71] St Basil of Caesarea, in *PG*, 31, 564, 589.

[72] St Nilus, in *PG*, 79, 577.

[73] St Basil, *De Spirit. Sanct.*, in *PG*, 38, 149,

[74] See Mansi, *Cons. Collect., op. cit*, XIII, 32.

[75] *Synodicon of Orthodoxy*, in *Triodion, op. cit.*

[76] Cf. Plato, *Politeia* 401 b.

[77] St John Chrysostom, *Hom. IV on 1 Tim*, in *PG* 51, 253.

[78] Cf. *Acts of the Seventh Ecumenical Council*.

[79] *Ibid, Act 7.*

[80] Hymn for the First Sunday of Lent.

[81] St John of Damascus, *Defence of the Holy Icons*, in *PG*, 94, 1256.

The Role and Importance of Icons

A Roman Catholic Perspective

ELEUTERIO FORTINO

For the Catholic church in the West "image" has always been used with reference both to coloured forms of art (frescoes, icons, mosaics) and to sculpture (bas-reliefs as well as fully rounded sculptures). This is clear not only from publications on the relationship between art and worship[1] but also from such documentation on art as has come down to us. This conception is to be found as early as the period of the catacombs. In the catacombs we find both frescoes and bas-reliefs on sarcophagi. Examples of the former include the Good Shepherd in the catacombs of St Calisto; the Orante in the catacombs of St Priscilla; the Last Supper in the catacombs of St Calisto; and the "Breaking of Bread" in the catacombs of St Priscilla. Examples of the latter include the sarcophagi with the figures of the Good Shepherd; the resurrection of Lazarus; and the story of Jonah, etc. The Christian Lateran Museum also has the well-known statue of the Good Shepherd.[2]

The Second Vatican Council, in the Dogmatic Constitution on the Church, explicitly instructs all Catholics "that those early decrees regarding the worship of images of Christ, the Blessed Virgin and the Saints, be religiously observed" (*Lumen Gentium* 67). Reference is made to the Second Council of Nicea and the Council of Trent. This suggests a definite continuity throughout the centuries in the attitude of the Catholic church to this matter, which is theological, liturgical and pastoral. It is thus clear that our present practice is the result of a doctrinal, artistic and cultural evolution, as historical details will bear out.

The use of the image is established in the Church

What began as symbolic art in the catacombs developed progressively, taking on diverse forms and styles at different times and in different places. In this slow process there were two problems, one sociological-political, the other purely theological. The first was the issue of the freedom or otherwise of the Church to express itself publicly. It was only after the edict of Constantine (A.D. 313) that Christian art developed fully. The second problem was much more delicate. Christians were diffident about artistic representations, because of an ever-present risk of idolatry, and this had to be overcome. The Old Testament prohibition against making images and worshipping them (Ex. 20:4ff.) was bound to exercise a controlling influence and in fact it helped the Christian conscience to clarify the difference between the use of images in worship and the adoration due to God alone. The mosaic in the church of Saint Pudenziana in Rome (4th century), which shows Christ on the throne with the symbols of the four evangelists (the angel, the lion, the ox and the eagle) and the Apostles Peter and Paul, clearly reveals the place of images in the Christian approach at that time. It embodies a theology of the image. The classical distinction between *douleia* (veneration of images) and *latreia* (adoration of God) was already substantially present even though, over the centuries, especially in what came to be called "popular religiosity", it was not always observed and there was often resistance against the use of images in worship. The *horos* of the Second Council of Nicea (787) was responding to a practice firmly rooted in the Church of Rome. The Council affirms: "We define with all accuracy and diligence that, as with the precious and life-giving cross, venerable and holy images whether painted, or in mosaic, or in any other appropriate material, must be manifested in the holy churches of God, in sacred furnishings and vestments, on the walls, on tables, and in houses and streets."[3]

Rome constantly defended this fundamental position, both during the iconoclastic struggles in the East and in the face of anti-icon insurgency in the West.[4] The concept of the image in the conciliar definition is quite comprehensive and covers both paintings and sculpture. What came to be called in the West "sacred art" developed in these two directions.

Thus, in the West, too, the attitude to icons was strictly linked to the theological climate of the time. The Christological theme soon became dominant. The figure of Christ, increasingly central as the Pantokrator or in other forms, was a reaction against the permanent temptation to Arianism. The Council of Nicea (325) had its influence in the years that followed. The churches in Rome contain a rich anthology of Nicene theology. From the time of the Council of Ephesus (431) the Mariological theme developed, and the basilica of St Mary the Great in Rome was constructed in response to this development. It was probably during the reign of Sixtus III that the extraordinary series of mosaics of the Theotokos were created and they are still there today.[5] The prodigious development of patristic writing provided various new themes and what became most evident was the parallelism between the Old Testament and the New. Although the artistic character of the place of worship is always dependent on liturgy, in the West a pedagogical-catechetical preoccupation dominated the use of images, although it was not exclusive of other related aspects. The words of St Gregory the Great are typical: "In fact what Scripture is for readers, the image is to the eyes of the uninstructed, since in it the unlettered see that which they must imitate. In the image they read what they know not how to read" (Ep. 11,13).

This is, however, the case, in one form or another in the whole Christian world; it is only a question of emphasis and priorities. The Council of Constantinople "In-Trullo" (691) issued a particularly significant instruction on this (can. 82), referring to the symbolic presentation of Christ as a lamb, prefiguring Christ. The Council determined as follows:

> Venerating the ancient prefigurations and shadows as symbols and announcements of the truth, in the tradition of the Church, we prefer the grace and truth that we have received in the fulfilment of the law. That is why, in order that we may put what is pefect before people's eyes — even in painting — we ordain that henceforth in icons, in place of the former lamb, the human face of Christ, or God, the lamb who takes away the sins of the world be seen; thereby we will understand the depth of the humility of the Word Incarnate and we will be led to remember His life in the

flesh, His passion, His death, the cause of our salvation, and of the redemption of the world that stems from them.[6]

The realism in the figure of Christ which the Council required, the anamnetic function of the image of Christ, the salvific meaning of His passion, were intended to give a deeper understanding of the value of the actual Incarnation. This was to happen also in the West where sacred art would be increasingly characterized by realism, both in painting and in sculpture.

Over the centuries there were diverse developments at different times and in different places. Images reflect the evolution in religious sentiment. Different styles developed: the Romanesque with its various schools (Spain, Languedoc, Provence, Burgundy, the countries of the North); the Gothic with its brilliant statuary and iconographic and ornamental sculpture (England and Northern Europe). Between the end of the 13th century and the middle of the 14th, new trends developed under the influence of the Franciscan movement.

Direct interpretation of the Gospel, moving and sincere, succeeded dogmatic theology. In Italy, with Giotto, Duccio and the painters of the basilica of Assisi, religious art sought to represent the sufferings of Christ or to illustrate the life of St Francis of Assisi. A new age was coming.[7] Emotional expression began to prevail. Side by side with work in tempera, the technique of oil painting emerged, pictures painted on wooden triptychs and poliptychs like the Mystic Lamb by Jan and Hubert van Eyck (1420-1432). Christian art assumed picturesque and dramatic expressions. It began to express the mysticism, the disquiet, the anguish and the pessimism of the time. "The simple and grandiose religious art of the 13th century had become a lush forest and festive exuberance ended up concealing the central thought. A reaction was inevitable on the part of the Renaissance and the Catholic Reformation of the Council of Trent."[8] The return to Greco-Roman sources, which we call Renaissance and which began in Florence, was to have great influence on Christian art.

A new vision of people in a three-dimensional world of space was the basis for the whole movement. Naturalism emerged. The doctrine of proportion became the rational basis for beauty. This conception was what united the "fathers of the Renaissance", Brunelleschi for architecture, Masaccio for painting, Donatello and Ghiberti for sculpture. Raphael, Leonardo da Vinci and Michelangelo expressed a beauty and a new vigour which at times have nonetheless been perceived as a kind of revival of paganism.

The Catholic Reformation promoted a new, disciplined art. At the Council of Trent the Catholic Church responded to the controversy which arose at this time about the use of images in worship. The Council's decree was in line with the previous tradition:

> The images of Christ, of the Virgin Mother of God, and of other saints must be kept and preserved in churches; proper honour and devotion should be paid to them, not because there is any divinity or power in them for which they must be venerated, or because one should ask something of them or put faith in the images, as once the pagans did, putting their hope in idols, but because the honour given to them is to be referred to the prototype which they represent; through images, therefore, we adore Christ and venerate the saints whose likeness they manifest. Thus it has been ordained by decrees of Councils — especially the Second Council of Nicea — against the opponents of icons.[9]

The subsequent Catholic Reformation is marked by the Baroque style with its pompous and exuberant forms. Art now devised forms for particular devotion (Bernini, Guido Reni, Rubens, Van Dyck, etc.). It was put at the service of dogma. Art became apologetic and didactic, always more decorative and illustrative. Typical examples are the "Triumphs of the Eucharist" by Rubens.

In all this process of evolution of the image in direct or indirect relation to worship, the icon has always had a place. Although the technique and the theology of the icon underwent a very particular development in the Byzantine world, the icon had a distinct presence also in the West. Certainly, contact with the East had spread this particular form of artistic and cultic expression. In countries like Italy, which have had direct contact with Byzantium, icons are especially abundant.

The Second Vatican Council and sacred art

The Second Vatican Council, the major ecclesial event of this century for the Roman Catholic Church, added its own voice on sacred art and the cult of images.[10] The Council's statements reflect the present attitude of the Catholic church to cultic images. The Constitution on the Sacred Liturgy devotes a chapter to it. The Council affirms first that "religious art and its highest point, sacred art" are to be considered among the most noble activities of the human spirit. The distinction between *religious art*, which takes inspiration from religion, and *sacred art*, which is in direct relationship with worship, helps to situate better the whole issue. Although they have a common inspiration, their function and hence their characteristics are different.

> By their very nature both of the latter are related to God's boundless beauty, for this is the reality which these human efforts are trying to express in some way. To the extent that these works aim exclusively at turning men's thoughts to God persuasively and devoutly, they are dedicated to God and to the cause of his great honour and glory (*Sacrosanctum Concilium*, 122).

This is made more precise as regards sacred art, when the Constitution speaks of the necessary formation in "the spirit of sacred art and of the sacred liturgy" of the artists themselves, because they are "concerned with works destined for use in Catholic *worship* and for the *edification, devotion,* and *religious instruction* of the faithful" (*S.C.* 127). Here is expressed the entire understanding of the Catholic church on sacred art generally, an understanding that applies to images. Inasmuch as sacred art belongs to sacred worship, it must have proper dignity, decorum and beauty, on the principle that the images used for worship must be "signs and symbols of supernatural realities". This is a key requirement for sacred art since it implies its fundamental orientation. These images must evoke a "different world" and must in some way reveal it. Even the most ordinary images must bear signs of the future world.

Sacred art must introduce us to the realm of the redeemed, the transfigured, the sanctified. This requirement does not imply that there should be one style for all times and in all places. The Church has always "welcomed those changes in materials, style, or ornamentation which progress in technical art has brought with the passage of time" (*S.C.* 122). That does not, of course, mean that such developments have always been successful. That depends on many factors, not only technical but also cultural, religious, and spiritual. Moreover, these do not always coincide in any given epoch or for every artist; philosophical and cultural factors will also affect sacred art.

The Council also refers explicitly to "sacred images" and the right ordering thereof: "The practice of placing sacred images in churches so that they may be venerated by the faithful is to be firmly maintained. Nevertheless, there should be a limited number of them and their location should reflect the right order. Otherwise they may create confusion among Christians and encourage the wrong sense of devotion" (*S.C.* 125). This brief statement (a) authoritatively confirms the legitimacy of venerating sacred images; (b) asks for order in their use in a way that implies a theological rationale; this also postulates a certain moderation in the number of images because too many would not allow what lies behind them to be clearly shown; and, (c) recalls the permanent risk there is in this area of engendering false devotions. Knowledge of religious practices shows that this concern is not without foundation.

The Dogmatic Constitution on the Church gives a brief but serious exhortation, asking Catholics that "those decrees issued in earlier times regarding the veneration of images of Christ, the Blessed Virgin, and the saints, be religiously observed" (*Lumen Gentium* 67). The reference to the Second Council of Nicea and to Trent is not simply disciplinary, but has to do with the theological motivations in their deliberations and their pastoral orientation.

But the reference to those Councils does not signify an exclusively retrospective vision of art. On 23 June 1973, Paul VI inaugurated a permanent collection of modern religious art housed in sixty rooms in the Vatican Museum. It comprises more than 500 works by some 260 modern artists. In his address in the Sixtine Chapel to the artists who had offered their works, the Pope put the question: "Is there such a thing as contemporary religious art?" Having analyzed the question, he concluded: "Let us be frank: in our secularized and arid world, at times tarnished by obscene and blasphemous profanations, it does still exist, indeed there is a prodigious capacity — and this is the marvel of it — to go beyond the authentically human and express the religious, the divine, the Christian."[11]

The re-emergence of the icon

In our day the icon has re-emerged in the West. It is one of the most typical forms of Christian art and in different forms, styles and usages it has always been present in the West, as part of the diversified role of images in worship. In fact, several important shrines have grown up around icons. But the contemporary development is quite new because of its extent and diversification. "It is certain that, on our side, icons are in fashion, in exhibitions, auctions, private collections; but there does not seem to be any serious movement towards reintroducing them into worship. They are not part of worship, especially in the ugly modern churches. But the icon is something that continues to develop."[12] Today's interest in icons is cultural, religious and ecumenical. A visit to a church, especially one more recently built, a quick look through a Catholic library or in a shop of religious objects, will reveal the presence of the icon in the West. An increasing number of publications have been brought out on them; they may have expensive four-colour reproductions or be altogether less professional, but they illustrate icons that bear all the marks of theology, technique, aesthetics and history. Christoph Schönborn's study has shown the theological bases[13] of the icon during the phases of its historical development, the Christology implied and the incarnational background to iconography. These are necessary elements if the current re-emergence of the icon in the West is to be a genuine movement. Egon Sendler,[14] basing himself on cultural and theological presuppositions, describes the aesthetics and technique necessary for understanding their message better. The interpretation of the icon is delicate and complex and involves not only theological principles but also philosophical presuppositions, such as the influence of Platonism in theological thought.[15] The translation of works by Orthodox writers has helped Westerners in their understanding of various aspects of this matter which would otherwise be unintelligible to them because of their different cultural background.[16] The phenomenon of revival of interest in icons is indeed evident, but perhaps all the reasons for it are not yet clear. However, some reasons can be identified and some questions asked. Constantin Kalokyris, of the University of Salonika, at the second congress of Orthodox theological schools, has drawn attention to a converging development in modern art:

> The answer is that modern art has found one of its most characteristic elements in the art of Orthodoxy. Modern art has rightly suppressed the third dimension, the scientific perspective. It represents objects according to an axiological ordering, it avoids anatomical truth, and basically uses an expressionist style of illustration, exactly in the manner of Orthodox art... and this is why Byzantine painting is now in fashion.[17]

A more adequate reason, at least regarding the religious aspect, is probably to be found in the ecumenical movement. Contact with the East has in many ways been very fruitful. It reawakens the memory, reminds us of our common past, stimulates change and establishes points of convergence. A significant factor in this regard is the fact that in interconfessional places of worship more and more often one will find an icon displayed.

Given this revival of the icon in the West, which is a positive phenomenon in many ways, certain questions can be raised.

1. First of all, does a given icon bear the same meaning in the West as in the East? Even though there is no doubt that it manifests the same mystery and illustrates one shared dogma, the perception of it will be different in East and West. In fact, if the icon expresses a particular religious orientation, determined by the philosophical and theological vision of the cultural context from which it comes, in order for it to have some effect elsewhere it is not enough for it to be simply transported from its place of origin to its new home. If the icon is removed from its liturgical context — and that includes liturgical milieu, local conditions, iconographic and hymnodic context — it will be a work in isolation; it will be more or less beautiful as the case may be, but as an illustrative work it will have changed quite basically.

2. Second, does the re-emergence of the use of the icon indicate a real return to an authentic dimension of tradition, or is it just a manifestation of the general desire for simplicity in places of worship, so that they are more linear and more bare? If this is the case it would be evidence of a latent modern iconoclasm and of a serious decline in the understanding of the significance of the image.

3. Finally, we may ask whether what is happening is not superficial. Sendler speaks of our "infatuation that involves suspect elements". Though this may be

verifiable in some cases, it cannot be a generalization, yet one has to acknowledge today a certain lack of authentic creativity. The only thing that seems to be happening is that ancient icons are being displayed and reproductions of them are being published. This could mean either that the movement has no roots or that we are now only at the beginning of it. The icon presupposes a harmonious complex of elements (theological, aesthetic, technical and liturgical); it presupposes its own cultural world. Otherwise it remains a mute and blind image.

Concluding observations

> At the inter-ecclesial historic congress which took place at Bari (1969), I felt a deep sadness because, in the dialogue between the churches, the importance of Christian art for this dialogue was never alluded to. [18]

The re-emergence of the icon in the West is helping the development of religious and cultural dialogue. What has come about is a greater mutual understanding. And that indicates ever more clearly that the Christian message of the icon is identical for Orthodoxy and Catholicism in a way that goes beyond proper legitimate theological expressions. This is shown by the continued use of the icon throughout the centuries — in the Roman Catholic Church in various regions — and their present diffusion in new areas. Even though in the West the icon is part of a wide variety of images used for worship (pictorial work, mosaics, sculptures), it nonetheless has its place in the West. Even though it may not have the same liturgical function, it is not foreign to Western liturgy. Even if it is not seen in exactly the same theological perspective, it is not a perspective that is contradictory to the conception of sacred art to be found in the West. One can also legitimately apply to this case what the Second Vatican Council said in the Decree on Ecumenism (n.17) about the legitimacy of different theological formulations:

> In the investigation of revealed truth, East and West have used different methods and approaches in understanding and proclaiming divine things. It is hardly surprising then if sometimes one tradition has come nearer than the other to an apt appreciation of certain aspects of a revealed mystery, or has expressed them in a clearer manner. As a result these various theological formulations are often to be considered complementary rather than conflicting.

NOTES

[1] André Grabar, *Le premier art chrétien (200-395)*, Paris, 1966.

[2] Friedrich Gerke, *Le sorgenti dell'arte cristiana*, Milan, Il Saggiatore-Mondadori, 1969.

[3] Denzinger-Schoenmetzer, *Enchiridion Symbolorum, Definitionum et Declarationum de rebus fidei et morum*, Herder, 1967, pp.600-603.

[4] Emmanuel Lanne, "Rome et les images saintes", in *Irénikon*, n.2, 1986, pp.163-188.

[5] Paolo Verzone, *Da Bisanzio a Carlomagno*, Milan, Il Saggiatore-Mondadori, 1968, p.41.

[6] Periclès-Pierre Joannou, *Discipline générale antique (IIe-IXe s.)*, Rome, Grottaferrata, 1962, pp.218-220.

[7] L. Brehier, "L'arte cristiana nel Medio Evo", in *Enciclopedia della Chiesa*, ed. René Aigrain, Vol. II, Ed. Paoline, 1966, 1195.

[8] *Ibid.*, p.1198.

[9] Denzinger-Schoenmetzer, *op. cit.*, pp.1821-1825.

[10] Giambattista Rapisarda, "Le immagini sacre nelle indicazioni del Vaticano II e della riforma liturgica", in *Culto delle immagini e crisi iconoclasta*, Atti del Convegno di Studi, Catania, 16-17 maggio 1984, Palermo, 1986, pp.153-173.

[11] *AAS* LXV, 1973, pp.391 ff.

[12] Tommaso Federici, "Le icone 'universo simbolico' ci accostano al divino da contemplare e da raggiungere", in *L'Osservatore Romano*, 8 June 1986, p.3.

[13] Christoph Schönborn o.p., *L'icône du Christ, fondements théologiques élaborés entre le Ier et le IIe Concile de Nicée (325-787)*.

[14] Egon Sendler, *L'icône, image de l'invisible. Eléments de théologie, esthétique et technique*, Paris, 1981.

[15] Jean Daniélou, *Platonisme et théologie mystique*, Paris, Aubier, 1944; Dionigi Aeropagita, *Tutte le opere*, Milan, Rusconi, 1981.

[16] L. Ouspensky, *Essai sur la théologie de l'icône*, Paris, 1960; P. Evdokimov, *Théologie de la beauté*, Paris, 1970. In Italy there has also been a translation of the classic manual by the artist monks of Mount Athos: Dionisio Da Furna', *Ermeneutica della Pittura*, Naples, Fiorentino Editore, 1971.

[17] Constantin D. Kalokyris, "La peinture théologique de l'Orthodoxie et le mouvement oecuménique", in *Procès-Verbaux du Deuxième congrès de théologie orthodoxe d'Athènes, 19-29 août 1976*, Athens, 1978, p.563.

[18] *Ibid.*, p.561. This issue of complementary diversity is regarded sympathetically in the Catholic world also. On this cf. Franciso Javier Martinez Medina, "Los iconos orientales y las imagines de Occidente: Valoración y discusión", in *Phase*, n.143, 1984, pp.437-450.

Theology in Colour:
the Icon of Christ's Nativity

NICOLAS OZOLINE

The Seventh Council on "preaching images"

Why do the Orthodox like to speak of "theology in colour"[1] and what does it mean?

For an Orthodox Christian "theology" means the knowledge and teaching of the Church about God and, more widely, about the salvation of humanity and the whole creation.

But what about colour? Does it merely mean red, white, yellow and blue? Certainly not! Colour stands here for all the elements composing an image — be it painted, carved, or put together out of small pieces of glass, like mosaics. Whenever we use the expression "theology in colour", we speak about theology expressed through images, meaning "icon theology".

Those who authorize and encourage us to use all these expressions are the defenders of the holy icons, the Fathers of the Seventh Ecumenical Council (787). Against the iconoclasts, the Council declared firmly: "We preach the Gospel in two ways, by words and by images." Now everyone knows that by words one can preach not only the Gospel, but also heresy. The same may be said about images.

There are images of Christ, the Mother of God, feast days and the saints that do not at all correspond to Church teaching about them. Such images are not only to be found in Italian Renaissance or Baroque art. Unfortunately, quite a number of them are still used in Orthodox churches, and we are so used to them that we often do not even notice them.

An Orthodox icon is an image that shows in its own way the true faith and teaching of the Church. In its own way, because the icon is always more than just an illustration of a sacred text — be it a liturgical hymn or holy Scripture itself; there may even be an apparent contradiction in it, as for instance the representation of St Paul in the icon of Pentecost. Of course, St Paul was not there, but since the icon of Pentecost shows among other things the apostolicity of the Church, St Paul is depicted facing St Peter because no one could imagine apostolicity or even the ministry of St Peter without the complementary ministry of St Paul.

We preach by words and by images, the Fathers say. Preaching is part of our liturgical services, so "preaching images" would obviously have to be "liturgical images". In fact, liturgy appears to be the main key to a correct understanding of icons. Liturgy is always prayer, and an icon is a "liturgical image" because it is used in prayer. Since the essential task of icons is not to illustrate and certainly not merely to decorate, but to function in prayer, nothing alien to or inconsistent with the spirit of prayer, which is "the peace of God that passes all understanding" (Phil. 4:7), may be expressed by an icon. The liturgical function also implies that the icon never exists for its own sake. In a way, it is accepted only inasmuch as it points and leads to the prototype. While praying, our attention must not be captured by the image we see. Consequently, there is need for a certain transparency, achieved by a clear composition, simple forms and harmonious colours as well as faithfulness to the traditional features of the saints.

A first look at the icon

The icon of the birth of our Lord is undoubtedly one of the richest feast icons of the Church in figurative elements and theological content. Even at first glance, we see the different approach to this feast from the familiar manger scenes, which reduce the mystery of God's Incarnation to a touching family event.

For those who are not familiar with the language of Orthodox icons, the complexity and the number of persons portrayed may at first seem rather puzzling. In this case, it is because the icon does not merely represent the Nativity, but also shows the significance of this event according to the teaching of the Church. When we contemplate the icon, we must see it as members of the Church and with the eyes of the Church in the light of the Holy Spirit. Then the Lord may say to us: "But blessed are your eyes, for they see, and your ears, for they hear. Truly, I say to you, many prophets and righteous men longed to see what you see, and did not see it" (Matt. 13:16-17). To those who belong to Christ's mystical Body, the icon — like the whole of the liturgy — gives spiritual insights; they have a glimpse of the new earth and the new heaven. The liturgical triumph over the limitations of time and space in the fallen creation may lead — as in the Nativity icon — to the combination of different scenes and the portrayal of the same persons more than once in one composition. This may seem unusual at first, but if we remember that every icon is an integral part of the liturgy of the feast, from which it cannot be separated, then we shall "perceive with our eyes... and understand with our heart" (Matt. 13:15).

The earliest representations

The earliest representations of the Nativity are to be found in the sarcophagus sculpture of the first half of the 4th century. Like the catacomb frescoes, this art is very much inspired by the typology of Christian initiation, emphasizing biblical prophecy and its fulfilment in Christ, in the Church, and in the life of each catechumen that "all this took place to fulfill what the Lord had spoken by the prophet" (Matt. 1:22). Therefore these sculptures share the rather lapidary language of the catacomb frescoes, summing up simply and eloquently the main events and issues of salvation.

The earliest works show "the babe wrapped in swaddling clothes and lying in a manger" (Luke 2:12). In some cases the Divine Child is lying on a piece of cloth laid over the manger like an altar cloth. The earliest known example of the Nativity, dating from 320/325, belongs to this type. This resemblance of the manger to a Christian altar, which lasted throughout the Byzantine era, is certainly not accidental. Several early Church Fathers such as St Athanasius, St Ambrosius,

St Augustine, St John Chrysostom and others, speak about Christ becoming the bread of life in His Incarnation. Thus, the manger represented as a Christian altar reminds us of the sacramental dimension of Christ's humanity: "I am the living bread which came down from heaven; if any one eats of this bread, he will live for ever; and the bread which I shall give for the life of the world is my flesh" (John 6:51). Close to the manger stand the ox and the ass. Although the Gospels do not mention these animals, they are always present in illustrations of Christ's nativity, and from the earliest sarcophagi we find them right beside the Child. This is an obvious reference to the prophecy of Habakkuk 3:2: "Between the beasts thou shalt be known" and especially Isaiah 1:3: "The ox knows its owner and the ass its master's crib; but Israel does not know, my people does not understand", which foreshadow the words of St John the Theologian: "He came to his own home, and his own people received him not" (John 1:11). St Gregory of Nyssa gives another explanation: "The ox is tied down by the law and the ass carries the burden of idolatry", thus making the first representative of Jewry and the second of paganism, both being freed from their yoke by the Son of God lying between them. This earliest iconography of the Nativity representing the child in the manger with the ox and the ass includes, as the last permanent element, one or more shepherds. They can be easily recognized by their peasant clothes and their staffs. The shepherds' role is to witness and proclaim the good tidings "of great joy which will come to all people" which the angel had told them: "And when they saw it they made known the saying which had been told them concerning this child" (Luke 2:17).

It is interesting to note that the sarcophagi often show the birth of Christ in an open stable, with only a roof and two pillars supporting it. These come out of the Western part of the Roman Empire and Western tradition has always preserved the stable in the scene of Christ's birth.

It may surprise some that the shepherds are always shown as a part of the central scene, whereas the Mother of God is sometimes not there or sitting far off in a corner, frequently not even looking in the direction of the newborn Son, while Joseph does not appear at all. What is this Christmas scene without the "holy family"? To understand what was really important to our forefathers in the faith when they produced and contemplated on the first images of the Nativity in the beginning of the 4th century, we must remember what the manger as an altar, the two animals knowing their master and the witnessing shepherds stand for. They all have one purpose — to make clear, as simply as possible, that the Child lying there in the crib is God Himself Incarnate, the fulfilment of the law and the prophets. This iconography has no narrative, pictorial or even historical concern; it points to a certainty of the Orthodox faith, so bitterly challenged by the Arian heresy — the dogma of Nicea, asserting the godhead of the Son as "of one essence" with the Father.

The absence of the Mother of God does not mean that she is not important. The first scene of the Christmas cycle ever represented is the adoration of the Magi, the wise men from the East, who had seen the star of the newborn King of the Jews and came to worship him (Matt. 2:1-2). In this representation — which appears in Christian art independently from the manger scene and can be found already in catacomb frescoes from the time of Constantine — Christ's Mother takes part fully in the veneration. The meaning of this image is obvious from the

Plate 9: *Icon of St Herman of Alaska, contemporary,
Valamo monastery, Finland*

Plate 10: *"Law and Grace"*, c. 1535, Lukas Cranach,
Germanisches Nationalmuseum, Nürnberg, Federal Republic of Germany

Plate 11: *The burning bush, 1970, children's painting, France*

Plate 12: *Stone cross or khatchkar,*
12th century,
Holy See of Etchmiadzin, Armenia, USSR

gospel and the liturgical texts. What is important is to see again that in early Christian art each idea connected to a given event tends to find its own expression. Each of these scenes, taken independently, is a seal of the salvation in Christ.

The icon

One of the illustrations in this book (Plate 5) shows the icon of the Nativity. This subject was worked on again by the Church at times when the particularly deep theological understanding of the icon coincided with outstanding artistic abilities (as, for instance, in the 6th and 11th centuries in Byzantium and the 14th and 15th centuries in Russia). The image is the result of profound reflection and inspired insight. To understand it we shall first look at the whole composition, then move from scene to scene, and finally see how they have been put together.

If we eliminate for the moment the lower part of the image showing two different scenes, we obtain an almost literal illustration of what we know as the *kontakion* (hymn) of the feast. It is as if St Romanos, the Melodist, was contemplating an icon while writing the first verse of his hymn to the Nativity. The analogy is striking and so accurate that the *kontakion* may be used as a guideline for "reading" the icon:

a) The Virgin today gives birth to Him who is above all being, and the earth offers a cave to Him whom no man can approach.

b) Angels with shepherds give glory.

c) And Magi journey guided by a star.

a') For unto us is born a young Child, the pre-eternal God.

It is clear that (a) and (a') belong together — St Romanos is just closing the circle of his observations by returning to the central scene where he began his "icon in words", thus emphasizing that the very centre of the event as well as of the composition is "a young Child, the pre-eternal God". Hence, we obtain three groups:

a) Virgin, Child, and cave (with ox and ass);

b) angels and shepherds;

c) the Magi and the star;

the first group being the most important and therefore central one. This is confirmed by pictorial evidence: our attention is immediately drawn to the Mother of God resting on her large red childbed. She is the "focus" of the representation, although the Divine Child remains the true centre, whereas the cave serves as the key to a formal understanding of the whole composition.

The "cave of Bethlehem" as the place of Christ's birth is mentioned as early as the 2nd century by St Justin the Philosopher, as well as by the apocryphal Gospels of St James and St Matthew; and in the 4th century it had already become an important place of pilgrimage with a splendid basilica attached to it. This cave is always painted in dark colours, indicating the shadow of death which ruled over humankind before the light "that shines in the darkness" (John 1:4-5) came into the world abasing Himself even to us, He who "fell from on high into the dark depths of the earth" (Canticles 6 and 7 of Christmas Matins). In this sense Christ's Incarnation has already been compared to His descent into hell by St Ireneus of Lyons, and the cave of the Nativity may be seen as a foreshadowing of the cave of the life-giving tomb. Very early on the cave of

135

Bethlehem begins to grow and by means of the reversed perspective soon becomes a real mountain. We shall come back to the pictorial effect of this later. The scriptural reference to this development is in the Prophet Daniel during the vespers of the Nativity: "Just as you saw that a stone was cut from a mountain by no human hand…" (Dan. 2:45). Christ, the "stone cut off without hands", the fulfilment of all prophecies, is represented with his Virgin Mother in a mountain — her Old Testament prefiguration. "Of old, Habakkuk the Prophet was counted worthy to behold ineffably the figure and symbol of Christ's birth, and he foretold in song the renewal of mankind for a young babe, even the Word, has now come forth from the Mountain that is the Virgin" (Hymn of Matins = Irmos, second canon, canticle 4).

We have said *in* the mountain, because according to our understanding both Christ and his Mother are situated in the cave. In Orthodox iconography, events taking place inside a building are never represented as being "locked up" in closed rooms; "rooms" are suggested by an architectural background while the event itself is treated as an "open air" scene (for example, the Annunciation, the Descent of the Holy Spirit, the Dormition, etc.). Naturally, the same is true of non-architectural interiors like caves and grottos.

The question may seem rather secondary but it reminds us of two points. First that, in some cases at least, the language of the icon has become foreign to us because we are accustomed to looking at it just as we look at any picture, with its fore- and backgrounds separated in time and space. And secondly, as far as the theological meaning is concerned, the fact that the Mother and Child are both placed in the cave strongly underlines their unity, thus indicating the true humanhood that the Babe received from His Mother. The reality of the Lord's human nature is further emphasized by the obvious fatigue of the Mother lying on the bed. We must not forget that the oldest preserved Nativity representations of this type date back to the time of St Romanos and Justinian when the great theological issue was the danger of Monophysitism. This reclining posture is the main reason why the relation between the Virgin and the cave is not suggested in a more obvious way. In other icons with caves, such as of Elias, St John, Lazarus and the angel at the tomb, the figure is sitting or standing and thus can more easily be placed within the framework of a cave. This is confirmed by the fact that in the few cases where the Mother of God is shown seated, she is almost always definitely inside the cave, as for instance in the mosaics of Hosios Lukas and the Palatina in Palermo. If this had to be applied to the case of the Mother of God lying down, either the cave would become too big and cease to be a mountain, or the Virgin would be too small, which would upset the harmony of the composition, and be incompatible with the dogmatic position of the Theotokos in the mystery of Incarnation. Finally, in fresco composition, where for obvious reasons the artist can handle space problems more freely, even the Theotokos may be shown lying inside the cave.

Above the grotto we see the "angels that give glory with the shepherds" (Luke 2:8,15). The angelic host is represented on both sides of the upper part of the mountain, uniting heaven and earth. While most of the angels look upwards singing, "Glory to God in the highest!" (Luke 2:14) the Angel of the Lord, who is sometimes depicted slightly larger than the others, looks down upon the amazed shepherd, indicating by the gesture of his hand that he is speaking to him to announce good tidings of great joy.

On the opposite side of the cave the three wise men, who followed the star now shining above the cave, approach to worship the Divine Child. The star is itself a prefiguration of Christ according to the prophecy of Balaam, read during the vespers of Nativity (Num. 24). "There shall come a Star out of Jacob and a sceptre shall rise out of Israel..." And in the fourth canticle of Matins the church sings: "O Master who has risen a Star out of Jacob, Thou hast filled with joy the watchers of the stars, who interpreted wisely the words of Balaam, the soothsayer of old. As the first fruits of the Gentiles were they led unto Thee..." The wise men represent humanity still ignoring biblical revelation and some liturgical texts call them Persians, while others insist they adored the stars, thus referring to the Zoroastrian religion of the Sassanid Empire. The long journey of the very learned Magi ends in a poor cave, where a babe is offered royal gifts, showing that the ultimate sense of human knowledge is the contemplation and worship of the Living God, born unto us a young child. The three men are of different age and each of them brings his own gift, "gold as to the King of ages, frankincense as to the God of all, and myrrh to the Immortal, as the one three days dead". Sometimes the Magi are shown still travelling on horseback, pointing up to the star, whereas in the icon here they are no longer searching for the star but are already contemplating the Sun of Righteousness. "The pure Virgin spoke in wonder as she heard the Magi standing together before the cave, and she said to them, whom do ye seek? For I see that ye have come from a far country. Ye have the appearance but not the thoughts of Persians; strange has your journey been, and stranger your arrival. Ye have come with zeal to worship Him who, journeying as a stranger from on high, has strangely, in ways known to Himself, come to dwell in me, granting the world mercy" (Vespers of the Forefeast).

Beneath the wise men, on the left, "aged Joseph" sits on a rock meditating and plagued by doubts about the Virgin's motherhood (Matt. 1:18-20). It is significant that the righteous Joseph is not mentioned at all in the liturgical texts of the Nativity, which dwell at length on the three wise men, the shepherds, the angels, the manger and, of course, both Mother and Child. During the celebration of the two main feast days, Christmas and the following day, we hear about him only from the Gospel reading, while the hymnography which developed all the other elements of the story keeps silent about him. The reason is obvious: Joseph is not the father of the newborn child. Iconography underlines that he is not considered a main person in this event by clearly separating him from the central group; he is shown isolating himself by his doubts. This idea of isolation and non-communion with what has happened is frequently emphasized by representing Joseph ostensibly turning away from the central group. From the time he first appears in the Nativity scene, his position always expresses the attitude described by a *stichera* of the forefeast "... what is this doing, O Mary, that I see in thee? I fail to understand and am amazed and my mind is struck with dismay... Instead of honour, thou has brought me shame, instead of gladness sorrow, instead of praise reproof... what is this that I now see?"

We are here at the very antipodes of the Nestorianizing tendency showing human nature adoring its own procreation. Joseph — and with him all humankind — is confronted with the "fearful mystery" of God's Incarnation through a virgin.

137

Actually there is not confrontation but rather invitation to join the praise and glorification offered by heaven and earth, invitation to communion. Without this communion, isolated human rationality that has turned its back on Revelation cannot accept the "victory over the order of nature", and the "strange marvel" of the Virgin Theotokos will remain "unto the Jews a stumbling block and unto the Greeks foolishness". In short, the pose of Joseph indicates what is "beyond words or reason", the virgin birth of Christ and, indirectly, the fatherhood of the Holy Spirit.

From the late 14th century on, many icons show an old and bent shepherd standing before Joseph. As one can see from Byzantine miniatures and mosaics of the 10th and 11th centuries (for example, Menologion of Basil II, the Vatican Library and Katholikon of Hosios Lukas), this shepherd originally stood alone or together with others on the left side of the grotto, listening to the good tidings of the angels. He is easily recognized by his profile, position, age, dress and staff. The only difference from his later appearance before Joseph is that he looks up to heaven from where the angel speaks. I cannot help but feel that the reason for his transfer was more a concern for the symmetry of the composition than the generally invoked theological argument of the role of the tempter. Some iconographers of the Paleologian period, inclined to narrative detail, personifications and allegories, might have found it difficult to balance the two midwives from the bathing scene on the right side by the single person of Joseph on the left, and therefore might have looked for a second person to balance the left bottom corner of the composition. But once transferred into the company of Joseph, he almost inevitably had to share in his doubts and finally saw himself condemned to become the personification of them since on later icons he will grow small horns or a short tail. Authorities on icon theology have dwelt on the meaning of the presence here of the devil and his role of tempter, but one question should be asked: is it really such a major contribution to have a presentation of the devil in the Nativity icon, and are future generations of icon painters obliged to follow this rather late development? My answer to both questions would be in the negative. For centuries the meditative attitude of Joseph, emphasized by the fact that he has his back to the event, was clearly understood to suggest the fatherhood of the Holy Spirit and Joseph's scruples mentioned in the Gospels (Matt. 1:19). To justify the introduction of the tempter by referring to apocryphal writings is not convincing, since as a rule such references should be eliminated whenever possible or at least reduced to a strict minimum. And finally, there is no point in introducing one more figure in an already rather crowded composition.

In the opposite bottom corner of the icon we find the bathing scene. It is often said that this representation of the Child's bath is inspired by the apocryphal gospels. This is not true: as far as is known, there is no mention of the Child's bath either in the apocrypha or in the writing of any Church Father from the first millenium. The only hint in literature from the pre-iconoclastic period is to be found in the travelogue of Bishop Arnulf, a late 7th-century pilgrim to Palestine, who relates that close to the Nativity cave in Bethlehem he was shown a stone water-basin which was believed to be the one in which the Divine Child had been washed after His birth. We owe the earliest literary description of the bathing scene to St Symeon the Metaphrastes, a Byzantine author of the 10th century, while the earliest preserved representation of Christ's Nativity with the bathing scene is a Syrian marble plate from the 5th century. Obviously, Symeon was inspired by iconography and not vice-versa. The origin of this scene is in Roman biographical imagery. On sarcophagus reliefs from imperial times, for instance, biographical cycles summarize in typological scenes the lives of Roman citizens. They all begin with the scene of the birth, followed by the bath of the newborn Child. In late antiquity the scene of the bath was borrowed from pagan biographical cycles which were at that time well-known to illustrate the true human nature of Christ who, like any other baby, needed to be washed after His birth. Thus we see that the two scenes at the bottom of the icon are complementary to each other and have a clear Christological meaning: the doubts of Joseph stress the incomprehensible mystery of the pre-existing Logos, coming down from heaven, incarnate of the Holy Spirit and the Virgin Theotokos, whereas the bathing scene insists on the reality of His human nature, since the Babe's body that "suffers" washing is the flesh in which God will suffer and die on the cross. For us the fact that the scene of the Newborn's bath has been borrowed from old biographical cycles is important in two respects: firstly, it explains the ease with which this motive was transferred from Christ's Nativity, or even directly from antique prototypes, to the representation of the birth of the Mother of God, of St John the Baptist, and others, losing in that case its Christological connotation; and second, we realize that the unusual case of Christ being represented twice in one icon (in the manger and in the bathing scene) has its origin in narrative cycles where such repetitions are necessary to the patterns of the image.

As we have seen, the icon of Christ's Nativity consists of five juxtaposed scenes. The relation of these scenes has to be understood in the light of what was said at the beginning about overcoming the limitations of time and space during liturgical celebration. When we worship we leave linear time and in a new multi-dimensional way move freely through ages, periods and events, often using the most unexpected shortcuts. By singing one *stichera* (hymn) after another, we move from one moment and aspect of the feast to another (for instance from a New Testament fulfilment to its Old Testament prefiguration and back again), and yet although they belong to different depths and layers of time they are all *simultaneously present* while we liturgically *commemorate,* that is *actualize,* the whole event. The constant repetition only emphasizes this fact. In the same way these five scenes, which did not all coincide in time and space, are brought together to be contemplated [in a synthetic view of liturgical insight], combining veneration of the event with the teaching of its meaning. The possibility of not simply juxtaposing different scenes which may or may not follow each other, or filling different compartments of a decorated surface (the method largely prevailing in pre-iconoclastic times), but rather uniting them in a composed image could be achieved only by the use of reversed and manifold perspective. Here, this means, when the cave had grown into a mountain. The effect of this was to prevent the introduction of "false depth", which equals separation in time and space, into the composition. Although there obviously is space, this space is organized so that the background is no further off than the foreground ("background figures" are represented on the same scale as those in the foreground), and the various scenes can be placed at different heights and depths of the cave-mountain without mingling and still be *simultaneously present*. This means that linear time is abolished and the only reality is the present tense of the celebration. As St Romanos, the Melodist, put it so clearly:

> *Today* the Virgin gives birth to Him who is above all being...
> *Now* is born a young Child, the pre-eternal God.

NOTE

[1] See Prince E. Trubetskoy, "Theology in colour" (Umozrenie v kraskakh), Crestwood, NY, St Vladimir's Seminary Press, 1981.

Christian Iconography:
an Anglican Contribution

ANTHONY C. BRIDGE

Since the Church of England provides a broad roof, under which people of different traditions and theological options can live and worship together, it is not surprising that it shelters people with different views on the place of iconography in Christian faith and worship, expression and communication. As to the icon in the narrower sense of a particular kind of pictorial representation of people and events in Christian history and mythology and its place in faith and worship, once again there is no unanimity amongst Anglicans. What follows must therefore be read as the opinion of one member of the Church of England and not necessarily that of the majority; though I think that it is true to say that, on the broader front of the arts in general, the majority, even if they have little or no interest in doctrinal aspects of Christian iconography, nevertheless do highly prize the immensely rich heritage of their church in art and architecture, stained glass, wall painting and sculpture, much of which puts its roots down into the parent stock of Byzantine art and iconography. Indeed, very large sums of money are regularly spent on maintaining this cultural heritage, and great care is taken to ensure that it is not spoiled or destroyed by hasty changes to church buildings or their furnishings, changes which may be thought expedient for evangelistic or pastoral reasons by the clergy or people in charge of them for the time being.

The refusal to allow such changes often causes resentment. "Is not the evangelistic task of the Church more important than the conservation of ancient buildings and old works of art?" is a question often asked by angry and frustrated Christians, and in the absence of any accepted doctrine of the place and function of works of art in the service of God, it is difficult not to sympathize with those who ask it. Yet it is based on a very widespread misunderstanding — a misunderstanding at least as widely held in the secular world as it is in the Church — of the nature of works of art. For while they are widely regarded as being amongst the highest products of the human spirit, and while an interest in the arts is regarded as an ennobling thing, it is almost universally agreed that such an interest should take second place to the business of earning a living, paying one's bills, educating one's children, and running a car.

Only when these essential duties have been satisfactorily discharged may someone spend time and money on the arts, if she or he does not want to be accused of gross irresponsibility. Thus, while paying lip service to the value of the arts, in fact they are downgraded to the rank of inessentials — optional extras for the leisured and the cultured. People can get on very well without them. That is the prevailing attitude to the arts both in secular society and — alas! — in the Church.

Prevailing it may be, but it is not only mistaken, it is demonstrably mistaken. For one of the fundamental postulates of evolutionary theory is that no species of animal develops and indulges in a vastly time-consuming activity, unless that activity does something either for survival or for the betterment of the species, and no one can deny that, down the ages, human beings have spent countless billions of hours producing works of art of one kind or another.

In fact, you could make a case for the proposition that one would be better defined as *homo artificiosus* than as *homo sapiens*, for where one has only too often failed to be wise, one has never stopped producing artefacts. Ever since the human being came down from the Darwinian tree-tops and took a slightly different road from that followed by the other great apes, the passage down the brutal paths of history has been marked by a glittering trail of works of art. Human beings have made pots and painted them, blown down reeds and pipes, banged on gourds and drums, danced round camp fires, adorned the walls of caves with paintings of animals, painted Italian city princes and mayors of Ipswich, carved rocks, wrought bronze, built pyramids, triumphal arches, Georgian terraces and Victorian railway stations, and generally indulged in an unending orgy of artistic creativity. Why? Not because they have regarded it a noble thing to do; not because a few people have been specially talented; and certainly not because it has been an enjoyable optional extra after successfully killing a mammoth or two and heating the cave for the kids. Plainly, if evolutionary theory is not entirely mistaken, the countless hours spent by human beings of all colours, creeds and cultures in producing works of art must have done something far more important for them than adding a little cultural relish to the dull diet of their daily lives. So, once again, what have the arts done for us? To be dogmatic for lack of space to be otherwise, the answer is that they have provided us with the most profound kinds of language at our disposal: or perhaps I should say, they have provided us with a series of languages capable of great profundity, greater indeed than that of everyday speech. "Art is the most certain mode of expression which mankind has achieved," wrote Herbert Read in the thirties of this century; "we are nowhere near an understanding of mankind, until we admit the significance and indeed the superiority of the knowledge embodied in art... In all its essentials art is trying to tell us something: something about the universe, something about the nature, about man, or about the artist himself. Art is a mode of knowledge, and the world of art is a system of knowledge as valuable to man as the world of philosophy or the world of science."

He is right. Works of art "speak" by embodying, expressing and communicating to those with eyes to see and/or ears to hear some of people's most profound ideas about their own existence, nature, significance and place in the totality of things; and as these ideas have varied from age to age and society to society, so have the works of art produced by the various civilizations and cultures of the world down the ages. Thus, if we want to know what the people of some ancient society, newly discovered by archeologists, believed about themselves, their gods and their world, it is to their works of art that we turn for enlightenment. Each school of art — Paleolithic cave painting, Hindu sculpture, Renaissance painting, art deco —

uses a pictorial language of its own, complete with its own distinctive images, and the artists who invent them are the spokespeople of their parent societies, embodying in their works that society's ideas about itself and its significance: its self-understanding.

It is a tribute to the extraordinary profundity and vitality of these artistic languages that, unlike the various verbal languages, which so often die as their parent societies wither and change, the arts of ancient societies remain lively and intelligible virtually for ever, even if they probably do not speak to us so vividly or immediately as they must have done to the members of their parent societies. For instance, one would have to be both blind and artistically deaf not to "hear" the art of Pharaonic Egypt speaking about what it was like to be alive in that ancient and seemingly eternal civilization of the Nile valley: of what it must have been like to be a dusty little mortal under the colossal shadows of those demi-gods, the Pharaohs, as one approaches their images at Karnak, flanked by the huge avenue of those goat-headed sphinxes, which leads to the temple there. Similarly, it is difficult to imagine anyone insensitive enough not to feel a "frisson" of dread before the image of Sekhmet, the lion-headed goddess and destroyer of human-kind, in whom it was believed that the evil powers of the sun were incarnate, as she sits in her dark little chapel in the small temple of her consort, Ptah, also at Karnak. But if it is difficult to imagine such a person, it is far more difficult to imagine anyone so blind to the arts as not to notice how different the art of classical Greece is from that of Pharaonic Egypt. The whole ethos of Greek art is different, the artists speaking a radically different language. At Dodona, Delphi, Olympia, Epidauros, Brauron or wherever one is no longer made to feel a worm and no person, as one is at Karnak, Abu Simbel and Gizeh. The Greeks and their gods were ultimately derived from the same earth mother, Gaia, and people stood to pray; they were not abased by their gods, and this comes through in the divine humanism of Greek art, which speaks of a world, not of awful and terrifying force and mystery, but — as Erich Auerbach has remarked in his book, *Mimesis* — one in which, "clearly outlined, brightly and uniformly illuminated, men and things stand out in a realm where everything is visible".

Examples of this kind of thing could be multiplied; the arts of Aztec Mexico, the Congo in pre-colonial days, China during the Tang dynasty, and many others are so obviously speaking languages even more different from one another than those of Egypt and Greece that the point needs no elaboration. Instead it is worth asking what happens when a new culture, informed by a new self-understanding, is born. Initially, it will have no artistic language in which to express its deepest ideas, and this is precisely what happened when the Christian faith was born into the world. Moreover, the earliest Christian inherited from the Jews a profound mistrust of visual images of any kind; they were equated with idols and their use in worship with idolatry; but when the Greek world began to adopt Christianity as its faith, an urgent need arose for an artistic language in which that faith could be adequately expressed and communicated. Meeting that need was not easy, for the earliest Christian iconographers possessed an uninspiring and unpropitious stock-in-trade, out of which to forge a new language. Not only were the arts of the Greco-Roman world of the 2nd and 3rd centuries of our era languishing in the heat of the same syncretism which was enervating the pagan religions of the day, but the world was dominated by Rome which, unlike classical Greece, had no great artistic tradition of its own, though it is easy to underestimate the Romans artistically by thus comparing them with the Greeks whom they so much admired.

There was, however, a vigorous school of painting at work in Alexandria, which produced some lovely and lively things, of which the portraits on the lids of mummy cases are probably the best known; there was a well-developed iconography of the Old Testament spread throughout the synagogues of the diaspora, which seems to have sprung originally from some illustrations done for the Septuagint, and which is exemplified by the wall paintings in the synagogue at Doura on the upper Euphrates, and of course there was also the kind of wall painting still to be seen in many of the houses at Pompeii and elsewhere in the Roman world.

From these and other local styles, early Christian painters had "faute de mieux" to forge a Christian language or style: that is to say, a pictorial means of realizing, embodying and expressing the leading ideas and self-understanding of the Christian community.

It is not surprising that their first attempts met with little success; as David Talbot-Rice remarked of their works in his book, *The Beginnings of Christian Art*, "iconographically the fact that they are Christian is not always easy to distinguish. The Evangelists resemble pagan philosophers, while our Lord takes on the character of a classical divinity. He was usually shown with long hair and youthful appearance, like an Apollo." More often than not, he was beardless; sometimes he was plump, unprepossessing and undistinguished while in scenes depicting the Good Shepherd he looked like Hermes, as he does in the mausoleum of Galla Placidia, who died in AD 450. Meanwhile in a carved panel on the mid-4th-century sarcophagus of Junius Bassius in the crypt of St Peter's in Rome, he might easily be mistaken for a dissolute young emperor or patrician. But this state of affairs was not destined to last, and as the years passed Christian artists fumbled and felt their creative way towards a truly Christian pictorial language: the art of Byzantium.

"A truly Christian pictorial language" is an innocent phrase, but what does it mean? Christianity is based on a belief that the transcendent God, of whom St John the Evangelist said at the very beginning of his Gospel that "no man hath seen him at any time", was revealed in and through a number of events in history: that is to say, that the transcendent and eternal was made known in and through certain temporal and material phenomena. Plainly, this belief could not (and cannot) be represented by a totally abstract art, which is suitable only as an expression of some totally transcendent religious beliefs or, indeed, of some typically modern beliefs which claim that the universe and all that is in it is governed by such abstract scientific forces as those of thermo-dynamic and quantum physics; nor could it be represented by a purely naturalistic artistic style, which is suitable, for instance, as an expression of the humanist idea that "homo naturalis" is the crown of creation, but wholly unsuitable as an expression of the belief that the human being is the image of the transcendent God: a material being expressive of a divine mystery. Somehow, Christian artists had to concentrate on the "point" at which the Incarnation was believed to have taken place: the point of meeting and union between God and man, eternity and time, spirit and stuff; and thereafter they had to forge a pictorial language, which made that point of meeting visible. That they succeeded triumphantly in doing so should be abundantly clear to anyone beholding, say, the great Christ Pantocrator at Daphni in Greece or indeed any one of a thousand similar mosaics or icons in churches and monasteries throughout the Orthodox world which, though plainly depicting people and events in this world, cast the mind of the beholder beyond themselves — beyond the material images — to contemplate the transcendent reality they make present symbolically. Indeed, their success is perhaps even plainer in some of their icons than anywhere else. A favourite subject, such as the entry of Christ to Jerusalem on the first Palm Sunday, illustrates well how they solved their problem; for while it is obviously a picture of an actual event — that is to say, of a man on a donkey riding towards the city, while children strew palm branches in his path — it is equally obviously an event concerned not merely with ordinary historical men and women and children moving in a landscape, which is not subject to the mundane dictates of perspective, under a golden sky against which is outlined an ideal city rather than a squalid, crumbling, litter-filled Middle-Eastern city of material and geographical reality; and much the same is true of the whole of Byzantine art. It is the art of the irruption of God into this world and its consequent transformation: the art of the material man Christ transfigured and seen to be the image of God.

Superficially, all this may seem to have little relevance to the faith and worship of Christians in the West including members of the Church of England, but that would be to ignore the fact that the pictorial language of the Christian faith forged by Byzantine artists spread outwards from Byzantium over the whole of Christendom as the basis of a universal Christian school of art. First, it spread over eastern Europe and northwards to Russia, where some of the things produced in such places as Moscow, Kiev and Novgorod long after the Byzantine Empire had fallen to the Ottoman Turks were quite as splendid as anything which had preceded them; and it spread, too, to western Europe where Romanesque painting, Gothic sculpture, early medieval illuminated manuscripts and above all the art of such men as Cimabue, Duccio and Giotto — to mention only the most illustrious of the early Italian masters — would have been quite impossible without the art of Byzantium, out of which they sprang. Of course, over the years the artists of western Christendom developed the style they had inherited from their Byzantine mentors and made it their own; indeed it could be said that, while the Byzantines created the basic pictorial language of Christian theology and mysticism, the Italian and the Gothic artists of the West transformed it into the language of Christian humanism.

Like all generalizations, it would be only partly true, but there is truth in it; and the resulting tradition, further developed by such men as Simone Martini, Lorenzetti, Fra Angelico, Masaccio, Ucello, Piero della Francesca, and Botticelli, culminating in the work of such masters as Raphael, Michelangelo and Leonardo da Vinci, has shaped and formed, not only our places of worship and the images in them, but also the images we carry about in our heads of the characters, events and truths upon which the Christian faith is founded. Thus Byzantine art — the art of the icon — has indirectly had an incalculably great influence upon Christians in the West and upon their faith and worship; and that influence has been both rich and good.

It would be nice to end there, but that is not quite the end of the story. The process which transformed the art of Byzantium into the art of Christian humanism was an expression of the gradual transformation of Christian ideas at work in Western society over the centuries, and this slow evolution of Europeans' self-understanding did not suddenly stop. It continued, and as it did so, the art of

145

Christian humanism in its turn was itself gradually transformed into the art of secular humanism, as that belief — or non-belief — became predominant in post-Christian Europe. Thus there is a sense in which the wheel of history has turned full circle, and the church once again finds itself composed of a minority of Christians in a generally pagan world, the arts of which are speaking languages unsuitable to the expression of Christian faith. So, once again, artists wishing to tackle Christian subject are forced to do what the first Christian artists did, namely to fumble their way towards the invention of a new pictorial language capable of embodying and expressing the faith today. It is interesting to note that most of them put their roots down for nourishment behind and below the corpse of Western humanist art into Byzantine, Gothic or even Coptic soil. Let us hope that one day they will succeed in producing once again a living Christian art form.

The Veneration of Icons
Seen by a Woman Iconographer

JEANNE DE LA FERRIÈRES

We call an icon a painting representing Christ, the Mother of God or the saints. The icon painter, standing in a long tradition, tries to remain in the background when representing the model. Icons are generally paintings made with egg and natural pigments on wood, but there are also frescoes, wood carvings or embroideries which follow the iconographic tradition.

In Greek the word "icon" means "image" and this term designates Christ as the only true Image of the Father. Every one of us has been created in the image of God. We have been called to become with Christ images and true icons, like the saints whom we paint. They have become "images" of God in Christ. They are models, guiding us towards true "light", windows opening out on to the Kingdom of God — and the Holy Spirit, the true iconographer, makes the image grow in us towards "resemblance".

In the icon light is important. The painter starts with dark colours and ends with light colours. Little by little he or she works up to the light. There are no shadows. The perspective is reversed. The vanishing point is not in the icon: it is in the gaze of the one who contemplates and is in this way introduced into the icon.

The first icons date from the 4th century, the time of the triumph of Christianity under Emperor Constantine. Before then the representation of Christ and the saints was symbolic (art of the catacombs). It seems probable that the "Holy Face" of our Lord has been transposed from the shroud of Turin which was discovered in the 12th century in Constantinople. The Mother of God already appears in the art of the catacombs and tradition has it that St Luke was the first to have painted the Mother of God.

The Orthodox venerate icons in prayer and the icon portrays the one to whom a person prays. "We Christians", wrote Leonce, Bishop of Naples, in the 6th century, "possess images of Christ or of the apostles or of martys, and while embracing them, it is Christ and the martyrs whom we inwardly embrace."

After a long struggle in the 8th century for the defence of holy icons which ended with the "triumph of Orthodoxy" in 843, a theology of the icon has gradually been developed, particularly by St John of Damascus, a monk in Palestine, who wrote a dissertation "on the defence of the holy icons". It shows the true foundation of iconography: the Incarnation of God. The Son of God,

---

● This article was published in the newsletter of the WCC Youth Sub-unit, Vol. 11/2, 1987, p. 3.

becoming incarnate and carrying our human condition, has allowed creation to be worthy of God. Christ is the smile of God.

We can truly speak of the sacramental approach of the icon because it introduces us to divine mysteries. In the church, the icon has a well-determined place: it is an integral part of worship, and is venerated by the people. At home the family prays before the icons, in front of which a light burns permanently. Everyone has the icon of one's saint. Usually an icon is offered for baptism and marriage.

I would like to conclude by saying that icons are painted in prayer and in obedience to the disciplines of the Church; the faces of Christ, of the Mother of God or the saints, when surrounded by radiating light, are peaceful. The icon mediates between the one who prays and the one to whom one prays.

Iconography and Icon

VLADIMIR IVANOV

In the 19th century, it was very difficult to find any research into iconography which could clarify the spiritual laws of church art. Along with the awakening of interest in the old Russian icons in the 40s and 50s of the last century, and with data collected in a haphazard way, it became clear that there was obviously no established tradition in this field. Sakharov in his *Studies on Russian Icon-Painting* referred to the last traces of the ancient traditions in church art and noted how difficult it was to do research in the history of early Russian icon-painting. He admitted that he

> borrowed my list of the schools of icon-painting from the Russian people and from the opinions of experts and lovers of our antiquities, but is this classification correct? Does it conform to its true meaning? Is it based on historical and archeological data? This is another matter which should be settled by historical critique. I accepted the prevailing opinion of our people since I did not see any other as more probable.[1]

Kondakov admitted that the study of iconography remained "in embryo"[2] until the end of the 19th century: "People were interested in iconography, looked into the works of the 18th century, ascribed 16th-century icons to the Novgorodian school, but early icon-painting seemed a mystery to the collectors and expert icon-painters." Moreover, Kondakov openly admitted that "except for the 17th century, the whole history of Russian icon-painting is based on surmise by collectors and antiquaries". The word "surmise" is apt and perfectly describes the uncertainty about origins and traditions. This was not enough, and by the middle of the 19th century scientific research began to take a certain direction: the significance of the icon originals was understood, research into miniatures took on greater import-ance, and the problems of spiritual and cultural relations with Byzantium and the West gradually received attention.

But there were many difficulties in penetrating the mystery of a medieval icon. A major obstacle for the researchers was the need to overcome a system of vision which had been artificially nurtured by Russian educated society since the beginning of the 18th century. Very few were aware of the fact that since that time other kinds of knowledge had been acquired, life had been structured otherwise and another view had come into being. This vision was encouraged by Western

---

● This article has been translated from Russian by the Moscow Patriarchate.

European modern art with its requirements of linear perspective, anatomical precision, chiaroscuro modelling, etc. Increasing interest in Russian "antiquity" and in the pre-Petrine period led some people to believe that the renowned and authoritative aesthetical ideals were not totally correct. Buslaev admitted that the "excessive development of Western art was detrimental to its religious dimension".[3] Paradoxically, he saw "heathen" trends in Renaissance art, but at the same time reproached the old Russian icon-painting for its lack of "correct outline", "perspective", "colouring and the meaning given to it by chiaroscuro".[4] He also saw a basic artistic shortcoming of the icon in its "fear of reality"; in other words, an unwillingness to take lessons from reality "in correct outline of hands and feet, in the natural posture of figures and their movements which corresponded to the laws of nature and the disposition of the soul". All this was combined with a recognition of the high religious merit of the old Russian icon. Thus, there was a split between a clear awareness of the spirituality of icon-painting, and a recognition of its artistic imperfection. To understand iconology further, we need to take into consideration this psychological difficulty. Iconology began to deal exclusively with the subject and thematic aspect of an icon. In such a separation of the sacred image into a subject and a form, we can see signs of an epoch which treated the studies of the past mainly from a "literary" point of view. This was characteristic of all European science at that time and led to the definition of iconography "as a branch of the history of arts dealing with the subject, or meaning, of a product of art by contrast to its form".[5]

The notion of a hieratic image-symbol was replaced by an understanding of icon-painting as illustrative. For Buslaev, the founder of the iconographic school, it was a typical view of medieval art as an "immense illustration of the Holy Scriptures and the ecclesiastical books".[6] Such an approach required an icon to be a pictorial representation of a sacred text. This led to a certain extent to the origin of a picture with religious content, which by its style inevitably tended to be more natural. From this point of view, an illustrative didacticism constitutes a positive feature of Church art. According to Künstle, iconography "studies the products of art exclusively by the content of their conceptions". Art merely expresses ideas and concepts. The idea was understood not in Plato's sense of the *eidos* (subject), but in a nominalistic sense, whereas art was mainly understood as showing a certain didactic tendency. "The fine art of the old Christian times and the Middle Ages", wrote Künstle, "differs from the profane art of antiquity and modern times by the fact that its products have never been a goal in itself, but have sought to transmit religious ideas."[7] This didactic tendency had existed since the time of the Holy Fathers. Thus, Künstle corroborates his vision (not a subjective one, but one which expressed a certain theological tradition) of the prevailing didactic nature of Church art by referring to St Basil the Great, St Gregory of Nyssa, St Nilus, St Gregory the Great and St Paulinus of Nola. All this is summarized in a 9th-century dictum: *"Pictura est quaedam litteratura illiterato";* in other words, Church art is the equivalent of the Bible and spiritual literature for the illiterate.

Indeed, at first glance, many texts by church people leave no doubt that their aesthetic ideal was clearly mimetic: art should interpret religious subjects in such a way that the images strike us as authentically faithful to a particular event, be it a scene from the Bible or an episode from the life of a saint. In the letter from St

Nilus to Olympiodoros which was read at the Seventh Ecumenical Council as a testimony against the iconoclasts, a didactic programme is outlined:

> Let the hand of a skilful painter fill the holy churches everywhere with the stories from the Old and New Testaments so that those who cannot write or read the Holy Scriptures may recall, while looking at the pictures, the steadfast deeds of those who sincerely served the true God, and were encouraged to glorious and memorable courage through which the earth was replaced by heaven and the invisible was preferred to the visible.[8]

It is obvious that art was intended to encourage one to lead a righteous and holy life. And if such art addressed primarily the uneducated, its language should be extremely clear and intelligible and it should avoid sophisticated allegories and designs. According to some descriptions in the literature of the 4th and 5th centuries, one can imagine what these images looked like and how Christians perceived them. An example is "The Tale of the Martyr Euthymia" by Bishop Asterius of Amaseia (d. 410). He saw the picture in church and was deeply impressed by it. His description allows the reader to understand how an image was perceived in the 4th century. His aesthetic ideal is close to that of antiquity. In a desire to attain the perfection of the picture, he compared it with the works of "old painters" "who brought the art of painting to perfection and presented their pictures in such a way that they appeared to be almost alive".[9] The bishop gave a detailed description of the picture itself. He stressed that the painter "presented very vividly the story of suffering" of the Martyr Euthymia. The onlooker is amazed by the truthfulness of the events depicted, the ability to show the disposition of a soul by means of art. Speaking about the judge in the picture, Bishop Asterius noted: "Fine arts can vividly present wrath even in an unliving thing."[10] While describing the martyr, he shared his astonishment at the skilfulness of a painter in combining characteristics quite contrary to each other: male intrepidity and female bashfulness. The art with which some details of martyrdom are portrayed also deserves attention: "A painter depicted the drops of blood so well and you think they are really pouring out of the maiden's mouth, and you cannot help being moved to tears." Naturalism is valuable for Asterius not because it vividly shows the world of outward perceptions, but because it has a certain moral, didactic meaning. The more realistically an event is depicted, the stronger the impression on those who look at it, and the more they desire to acquire those virtues which are so vividly illustrated before them. Such a vision of the spiritual and moral meaning of an event, so naturally portrayed, seemed imperfect both spiritually and artistically for an eye nurtured in medieval hieratism.

As naturalism reached its apex in the 19th century, Solovyev noted that modern artists who were largely "alien to former religious contents of art" "turn completely to modern reality and adopt a doubly servile attitude to it: in the first place they try to copy the event of this reality in a servile fashion; second, they seek to serve meekly the current topic in compliance with the mood of the day, and to preach current morals, hoping to make art useful in this way".[11] On the one hand, the weakness of such aesthetics is obvious for Solovyev, but on the other, in spite of the visible imperfection of such an approach, he discerns something which was obscure even for representatives of this trend, something with a great potential. He wrote:

Still, there are signs of divine greatness in this rough and ready modern art which is marked by a sign of double servility. However, the challenges of reality and the demands of the direct impact of art, lacking sense in its rough and unclear application of today, give a hint of an elevated and profound idea of artistic activity which was not attained by either representatives or interpreters of pure art. Modern artists, not content with the beauty of the form, more or less consciously want their art to become a real force which enlightens and transforms the whole world.[12]

These ideas, projected on to the 4th century, help to understand better the relationship between the didactic aspect expressed by the art of late antiquity and the Byzantine hieratics. The 19th-century artists, according to Solovyev, while outwardly opposing the religious tasks of art, have nevertheless contributed to bring out its transforming nature. Therefore one can understand that Christians of the 4th and 5th centuries who demanded that art should be didactic and expressed in naturalistic forms, did so not merely because of love of outer edification, but because of their hopes for transfiguration and for the Christianization of the world which they had been given and in which they lived. These hopes have gradually led to the transformation of naturalistic methods in fine arts and helped to bring about a new hieratical artistic language free of naturalism. Thus it is necessary to consider didacticism in a certain historical perspective. Quite justifiable in the 4th century when the ground was being prepared for a new qualitative step in the development of art, it cannot be accepted as a universal principle, with lasting significance for all periods in Christian art. While Byzantine art passed the dialectical way of a thesis becoming an antithesis, i.e. naturalism becoming hieratics, early Russian art immediately accepted church art in all its greatness of the sacramental hieratics.

It began with the things which actually had been completed in Byzantium. It gave a specific character to the process of developing early Russian art. While the Byzantine and, to a greater degree, West European artists had traditions of the didactic epoch in their blood, the masters of the early Rus' had quite a different heritage. That is why, in spite of the "mirror" principle in the school of the Kremlin Armoury in the second half of the 18th century and the complete transition to the language of Western European graphic systems in the 18th century, this hieratical heritage continued in the depths of Russian tradition. This also explains why Archpriest Habakkuk and his followers took the betrayal of the traditional hieratism in icon-painting as a catastrophe. Naturalism and didacticism have never been primordial ground for Russian religious art, and this fact helped its development. That is why, due to the very logic of the subject, iconography was turning into the theology of the icon (iconosophy). In the works of Paul Florensky, the icon is freed from the last layers of naturalism and didacticism. For him, art is not an expression of a particular abstract idea or concept; he speaks of presenting an idea in the ontological Christian-Platonic sense: "The art goes out from subjective isolation, breaks through the limits of a conditional world and, starting with images and using them, goes up to the archetypes."[13] He suggested removing from aesthetical terminology (when he speaks about Christian or church art) any traces of subjectivism and psychological characteristics of the 19th century.

Art is not psychological, it is ontological; indeed, it is the revelation of the archetype... An artist is not designing an image, but unveils a universally existing image; he does not put colours on to the canvas, but clears away alien coatings, "crusts" of spiritual reality. [14]

This is the definition of church art, in its innermost nature. This noble ideal has been realized in different epochs with various degrees of clarity. There were periods when it was completely forgotten, but the very fact that it existed meant that it re-emerged under favourable conditions in the history of church art as a force defining its style.

Such an understanding essentially changes the approach to iconography. It overcomes historical immanence, and recognizes the action of the transcendental beginning in the development of church art. The realm of divine archetypes is the source of iconography. It reveals itself as a true reality in an enlightened view. The Seventh Ecumenical Council expressed this truth by pointing out that the Holy Fathers were the real creators of Christian iconography, and it did not arise as a result of certain subjective ideas of a painter or his personal conjectures. And again, this definition expressed the law, while historical reality did not always correspond to it. This undoubtedly hampered the formation of a unified system of Christian iconography. There are already brilliant attempts to give some outline to the iconography of the Mother of God (Kondakov), of the Gospel (Pokrovsky), based on an idea of developing a particular iconography as a purely immanent, historical process. Thus, Kondakov sowed the seed of an iconographical process in "the ground of the history of arts". His task consisted "not only of considering all the monuments and their groups on the basis of their stylistic relations with each other in the historical order of succession, but also in defining their character and significance in a given epoch". [15] The meaning of "an artistic milieu" in which a certain iconographical type exists is always underlined: "It is very important to know the degree to which a selected type is affected by a new artistic movement or to what extent it has retained old manners and survived in this form under certain isolated conditions". [16] Such a method proved to be very valuable. As a matter of fact, we do not have in our literature anything comparable in volume and importance to the works of Kondakov on the iconography of the Mother of God. However, one can see the narrowness of a purely iconographical method as understood by scientists focusing attention only on the historical processes in art. In the works of Florensky we find a new approach which overcomes an immanent method in the study of iconography.

Following his argument, we can speak of four categories of Orthodox iconography according to origin. First, the iconography of sacred biblical events. From ancient times it has been considered an equivalent of the Holy Scriptures with great didactic significance. St Gregory the Great wrote in the 6th century on the portrayal of the events from the Holy Bible: "We... depict the events of the sacred history in our churches in order to inspire piety and edify the inexperienced." [17] For him such images were first of all a visual aid for ordinary believers: "Icons enable those who do not know the Scriptures to *read* the things they cannot take from books." However, the whole biblical iconography, in which a didactical and illustrative nature was originally clearly expressed, cannot be explained in this way. All opinions on "the Bible for the illiterate" should be taken in a spiritual historical context which is remote from the psychology of the 19th-20th centuries with its subjectivism and abstract intellectualism. Even when an illustrative meaning of an icon is mentioned directly, it implies that an icon-painter, guided by the conciliar mind of the Church, is elevated by his imagination. Historical authenticity of some (biblical) events, as well as persons, does not exclude their being in eternity and therefore a possibility to contemplate when consciousness ascends beyond time.[18] Analysis of biblical iconography shows that we are not dealing with illustrations in the contemporary sense, but with the results of increased conciliar consciousness of typical biblical events. It is clear in this field how all visual representations dating from late antiquity undergo hieratical transformation. The inevitable result of turning to the Holy Scriptures was to overcome the classic perspective, the complication of the time structure of the composition and the demand for a sensible symbolism of colours. Through this development Byzantine biblical iconography has acquired more sacramental liturgical forms, with the didactic element retreating into the background or being transformed into spiritual contemplation of the biblical archetype.

Within the second category of iconography can be included "portrait-painting" born out of the individual experience of an icon-painter or, more precisely, out of the church memory. It would be proper to study the second category together with the third which comprises, according to Florensky, "icons painted on the basis of the past spiritual experience of others passed on orally or in writing". In a certain sense, all iconography of the saints goes back to either graphic or written evidence of eye-witnesses. If in the field of biblical iconography we speak of an "illustra-tiveness", and it is understood in a certain sense, yet in this particular case it has "documentary credibility". It is important for the church to preserve the genuine features of the saints. Hence, the surprising consistency in portrait features of the saints, despite the stylistic diversity of various schools and periods. The traditional credibility, of course, does not hold true for all cases. Many images of the saints were painted long after their demise and bore no connection to contemporary documentary sources. In such cases we see the reconstruction of the images of the saints by spiritual means. Regarding the spiritual reconstruction of what is lost, one invariably proceeds from faith and the existence of eternal archetypes in the divine world.

Thus, the Second Book of Esdras, referring to the loss of the Law of Moses in the fire which destroyed the Jerusalem Temple, says:

> For thy law has been burned, and so no one knows the things which have been done or will be done by thee. If then I have found favour before thee, send the Holy Spirit into me, and I will write everything that has happened in the world from the beginning, the things which were written in thy law, that men may be able to find the path, and that those who wish to live in the last days may live (2 Esdras 14:21-22).

Chapter 14 of the Second Book of Esdras witnesses to the problem of the archetype in a purely spiritual way. The archetype is eternal and unchanging. In its being it is taken out of the destructive flow of time. Even if its earthly reflection vanishes, it can always be seen by the spiritual eye. An interesting example of intertwining the two "memories of the Church" — material and spiritual — is given in a story from the *Lives of the Kievo-Pechersk Fathers* concerning an encounter of icon-painters from Constantinople with Hegumen Nikon. When they realized that they would have to do a bigger job than they had reckoned with, the painters said to Hegumen Nikon: "Bring those who have contracted us. We shall protest for they showed us a much smaller church than this one when negotiating with us — this can be witnessed by many. Take your gold back and let us return to Constantinople." The Hegumen asked: "Who negotiated with you?" The icon-painters named Anthony and Theodosius and described what they looked like. "My children," said the Hegumen, "we cannot bring them here. They departed this world over ten years ago. They are praying for us now, keeping this church, caring and interceding for this monastery and its inhabitants." On hearing this, the Greeks were horrified. They brought many merchants who came with them all the way from Constantinople and said: "Here are the witnesses to our bargain with the old men — they saw us taking gold from their hands. And now you do not want to bring them here. If they have passed away, show us their picture, and let the merchants see if they are the same old men." When the Hegumen brought the icons of the saints, the Greeks bowed saying: "Truly, these are them. And we believe that they stay alive after death and that they can help intercede and save those appealing to them."[19] This example speaks about the quality of pictorial evidence for the appearance of Saints Anthony and Theodosius, founders of the Kievo-Pechersk abode, on the basis of both a living memory and their purely spiritual image, contemplated by people who never saw the saints during their earthly life. The significance of the story is that people of the Middle Ages sought the true reflection of images of the saints in the icons and were not content with reproductions which did not conform to the archetype. The most ancient of the preserved Greek originals, "Ancient church history on the outward appearance of the God-bearing Fathers by Ulpicius the Roman", speaks of how tradition recorded the external features of the saints. The descriptions of the images of the saints are surprisingly realistic. Attention is affectionately focused on specific features of their appearance, which were often far from the ideal of late antiquity. For instance, St John Chrysostom was described as follows: "John of Antioch was rather a small man and very thin with a big head on his shoulders. The nose, with wide nostrils, was rather long in a pale yellowish face; the deeply-lined forehead was open and wide; the large hollow eyes were sometimes luminous with affability. He had large ears and a thin beard with traces of white."[20] If we compare this description with the saint's mosaic in the central apse of St Sophia Cathedral in Kiev, we will be surprised at how closely these two different portrayals correspond, though the painting was done about a hundred years after the writing. The mosaic preserves all the real features of the saint in such a way that the face, while reflecting every small detail with a true-to-life precision, becomes transformed into a hieratic image.

> Whatever is occasional or conditioned by outer circumstances, whatever does not belong to the true "face" is put aside by the energy of the image of God which, like a spring, has broken its way through the thickness of the material crust thus turning a face into the image. An image is a graphic reflection of the likeness of God on a human face.[21]

Here lies the principal difference between the icon and portrait, no matter how perfect the latter may be. The icon shows the image of a saint illumined with the divine energy which in an ordinary man is usually hidden under his subjective and sinful state. Thus, a true icon is somewhere between a realistic portrait and a hieratic sign. But it was not easy to maintain this balance in all historical epochs. It

155

was definitely upset, for example, in Russian church art of the 17th century. The demand grew for as natural a representation as possible. For Simon Ushakov, an icon was "the life of the memory of those who once lived in the past, a witness to bygone times, a propagation of virtues, an expression of power, an animation of the dead, the immortality of praise and glory, an encouragement for imitation to the living, a reminder of past exploits".[22] Understood in the context of the epoch, such a demand inevitably led to gradual replacement of the icon by a portrait. On the other hand, the icon-painted originals, both the painted and the interpreted, acquired more conditional features, a sketchiness and a more pragmatic nature.

Among the fourth category of icons are the so-called "apparitional" icons, those which were made under exceptional circumstances and therefore are more difficult to assess intellectually. The "apparitional" icon is the most mysterious in origin. While every icon is a sacred object, the apparitional icon is perceived as an infinite source of miracles and of breaking the "rules of nature". It is not without reason that most of the apparitional icons depict the Mother of God, since the worship of the Mother of God combines all visions of the mystery of the Incarnation, which surpasses any natural order of things by binding the divine and the human together.

The main objection of the Byzantine iconoclasts of the 8th century consisted in their denial of the icon as a source of sanctification. They referred to the absence of a prayer of consecration for an icon:

> The impious foundation of the falsely named icons has no ground either in the teaching of Christ or in the Apostolic tradition, nor in the tradition of the Holy Fathers; there is no special prayer to consecrate them in order to make them holy objects, and they remain common things without any particular meaning besides that which was given to them by a painter.[23]

The Seventh Ecumenical Council which restored the veneration of icons responded by confessing the sacramental meaning of an icon as a main source of sanctification. The icon itself is sanctified through the name of Christ, it receives the name of the Lord, and through this is in communion with Him; therefore it is venerable and holy... The icon receives the name of God and thereby enters into communion with the Prototype, this being sanctified without any need of a special rite, a sacramental deed or prayer: sanctification and communication with the Prototype come through the Name. Hence, if an image is named it becomes an icon, a holy image. The name of God is the sanctifying force. The Seventh Ecumenical Council affirmed:

> There are many objects which we consider holy without reading the sanctification prayer because they are full of holiness and grace by their very name... Therefore, we worship these objects as worthy of veneration and kiss them. Thus, the very image of the life-giving cross, though there is no special prayer for its sanctification, is considered worthy of veneration and is a sufficient means for our sanctification. The same holds true in regard to the icon: when naming it we ascribe its honour to the archetype; when kissing it with veneration and bowing down before it, we receive sanctification. In the same manner, when we kiss and embrace various sacred vessels, we hope to receive some sanctification through them. Otherwise, they should treat the cross and the sacred vessels as common objects unworthy of veneration, as things made by a carpenter, a painter, or a weaver without the sanctification prayer.[24]

Thus, the Seventh Ecumenical Council elucidated the difference between a production of human hands — of a craftsman or a painter — and sacramental church art with its power of sanctification. Therefore the principle of the "apparition" expressed the very essence of the veneration of icons and explained its genuine meaning. The icon is created by means which are of God-manhood. It is not the result of human creativity alone. Therefore, it is in the realm of divine archetypes where the iconography originates, rather than in a subjective fantasy of a painter. It is a characteristic of Russian church art that it has perceived such a notion of the nature of iconography from the very beginning. This is confirmed by the life of St Alimpius, the first Russian icon-painter. His life story tells us how he experienced an initiation into the true nature of icon-painting very early in his life:

> An awesome miracle was shown by God in this church. When the craftsmen were inside the sanctuary decorating it, and Alimpiy helped them and learned from them, an icon of the Most Pure Mother of God and Ever-Virgin Mary represented itself, and all those present saw a wondrous and awesome miracle: as they were looking at the icon, the image of our Lady became brighter than the Sun, and they could not look at it and fell down. [25]

Here the true spiritual and illuminative nature of an icon is revealed. Mysticism of the Divine Light is the very essence of the Orthodox spiritual experience, and the veneration of icons is its integral part. It is possible to recognize God "only through His energy and through the seeing of the light which He sends down". St Simeon said:

> There is no other way to know God but through the contemplation of the light emitted from Him... no one can say anything about the invisible God, the inaccessible glory of His face, and about the energy and power of His Holy Spirit until he sees this light with the eyes of his own soul and recognizes His radiance and energy in himself. [26]

It is impossible to come nearer to an understanding of the nature of the "apparitional" icons without comprehending the above. The icon is being gradually recognized through the prayerful and liturgical experience "as a certain fact of the Divine reality... based essentially on a genuine perception of the other world and a genuine spiritual experience."[27] The further success of iconography as a science depends on the degree to which this truth is realized; there are inexhaustible opportunities to pass from dry and superficial descriptions to the depths of spiritual life in Christ.

NOTES

[1] I. Sakharov, *Studies in Russian Icon-Painting*, Vol. 1, St Petersburg, 1850, p.8 (in Russian).
[2] N.P. Kondakov, *The Russian Icon*, Part I, Prague, 1931, p.6.
[3] F.I. Buslaev, *Works on Archeology and History of Arts*, Vol. I, St Petersburg, 1908, p.31 (in Russian).
[4] *Ibid.*, p.23.
[5] E. Panofsky, *Ikonographie und Ikonologie: "Bildende Kunst als Zeichensystem"*, Band I, Köln, 1984, p.207.
[6] F.I. Buslaev, *My Leisures*, Part II, Moscow, 1886, p.75 (in Russian).

[7] Karl Künstle, *Symbolik und Ikonographie der christlichen Kunst: "Bildende Kunst als Zeichensystem"*, Band I, Köln, 1984, p.66.

[8] *Acts of the Ecumenical Councils*, Vol. VII, Kazan, 1891, p.126 (in Russian).

[9] *Ibid.*, p.33.

[10] *Ibid.*, pp.117,118.

[11] V.S. Solovyev, *Collected Works*, Vol. III, St Petersburg, p.172 (in Russian).

[12] *Ibid.*, p.173.

[13] P. Florensky, *Articles on Art*, Paris, 1985, p.85 (in French).

[14] *Ibid.*, p.86.

[15] N.N. Kondakov, *Iconography of the Mother of God*, Vol. I, St Petersburg, 1914, p.6.

[16] *Ibid.*, p.8.

[17] *Acts, op. cit.*, p.67.

[18] Florensky, *op. cit.*, p.232.

[19] *Belles-Lettres of the Kievan Rus'*, Moscow, 1957, p.178.

[20] Cf. A.P. Golubtsov, *From Readings on Church Archeology and Liturgics*, Sergiev Posad, 1918, p.313 (in Russian).

[21] Florensky, *op. cit.*, p.211.

[22] *Masters of Arts about Arts*, Moscow, 1969, p.49.

[23] *Acts, op. cit.*, p.234.

[24] *Ibid.*, p.235.

[25] *Belles-Lettres, op. cit.*, p.217.

[26] Archbishop Basil (Krivoshein), *St. Simeon, le nouveau théologien*, Paris, 1980, p.203 (in French).

[27] Florensky, *op. cit.*, p.230.

A Prayer Recited
Before Painting an Icon

GENNADIOS LIMOURIS

O Divine Lord of all that exists,
thou hast illumined the Apostle and Evangelist Luke
with thy Holy Spirit,
thereby enabling him to represent thy most Holy Mother, the Theotokos
the one who held thee in her arms and said:
"The grace of him who has been born of me
is spread throughout the world."

Enlighten and direct my soul, my heart and my spirit.
Guide the hands of thine unworthy servant
so that I may worthily and perfectly portray thine icon,
that of thy Mother and all the saints,
for the glory, joy and adornment of thy Holy Church.

Forgive my sins
and the sins of those who will venerate these icons
and who, kneeling devoutly before them,
give homage to those they represent.
Protect them from all evil
and instruct them with good counsel.

This I ask,
through the intercessions of thy most Holy Mother,
the Apostle Luke
and all the saints.

Amen

Icons: Lines, Language, Colours, and History

GEORGES DROBOT

There is no difficulty for art historians in defining the role of icons and their place in the general history of the arts. They will begin with the customary scholarly data: period, style, influences; and they will define the icon as a form of religious art or, if they are believers, they will speak of sacred Christian art.

As Orthodox Christians we accept these definitions in general terms. But no approach, however well-disposed and positive it may be, can indicate all the depths of meaning in the icon, if it remains purely archaeological and aesthetic. To us who are members of the Church that produced the icon and continues to make the centuries-old tradition of the sacred in art part of its life, those who define the icon simply in terms of religious art in general are in fact ignorant of the role of the icon in church life. For while it has all the material characteristics of any work of art, if we look at the icon from the standpoint of its "message" we can see that it is as different from a picture — even one with religious content — as the heavens are from the earth. Thus if we take account of the most important element in an icon, i.e. its contents, we cannot simply place it in the general line of development and philosophy of art. It is not simply one way in which these have developed but a mutation in this field — a leap towards a genuine spirituality.

Any form of art, in fact, insofar as it is an attempt to translate the Beautiful and to serve it, turns us towards beauty and so towards one kind of spirituality. The mutation of art represented by the icon, while preserving all the specific qualities of art — which is an expression of how the artist sees things and living beings — concentrates its creative human effort on the Creator Himself: on the Creator not only of human beings but of beauty too.

As heir to the Old Testament tradition, the Church took over the idea of a God beyond our imagining and description. The first Christians, frequently of Jewish origin, kept the Ten Commandments strictly, fearing that idolatry might be provoked by pictorial representation; that is, they feared the application of religious feeling to created things or beings, to the detriment of worship of the true God. This attitude was natural in people characterized by a thousand-year-old tradition prohibiting any images of God, even mental ones, and not even daring to utter God's Name.

● This paper was translated from French by the WCC Language Service.

Icons developed and increased in scope together with Orthodox liturgy and dogmas, for they are a function of the eternal course of the Church's life. As the icon is always an affirmation of the Incarnation of God and the revelation of humanity's salvation, it is not surprising to see the emergence of "real" icons (i.e. pictures before which we do not hesitate to pray even today) in the 5th and 6th centuries: that is, after the first four Ecumenical Councils, which had defined and formulated the fundamental dogmas of the catholic and apostolic Orthodox church.

How are the growth and formation of the primitive Church reflected in art?

As the remaining traces of the first centuries of Christianity show us, what we may call Christian "hieroglyphs" were the first to appear. These are signs, rich in meaning for the baptized — for the initiates — and meaningless or hermetic to others. They include the Christ monogram, various forms of cross, and the fish; the initial symbolic representations were references to the New Testament, such as the branches of the vine, the Lamb and the loaves — and many others too. In the 3rd century, pictures appear which show scenes from Holy Scripture. These are preserved mainly in the catacombs in Rome. Thus early they were telling those Christians who contemplated them of the economy of salvation which concerns each believer. The Old Testament is represented there by the three young men in the fiery furnace: they had refused to worship an idol and confessed their faith in one true God alone — as the Christians were doing; we find Noah in his ark as an image of the believer saved by baptism; Jonah swallowed up by the sea monster and then resting under his gourd — a symbol of salvation by baptism, but also a prophetic image of the death and resurrection of Christ. There are also illustrations from the New Testament, usually referring metaphorically to the virtues of baptism and the Eucharist: for instance, Christ's conversation with the Samaritan woman at the well — the living water He promises her is Christianity, into which one comes by the water of baptism; healing scenes reflecting the healing from original sin by baptism; the multiplication of the loaves — a symbol of the Eucharist; and so on. Thus we see that these pictures which have come down to us from the first three centuries of Christianity had a didactic purpose: they told new Christians of the essential mysteries of the Church, but they certainly did not serve for prayer as the icons were to do.

The first two Ecumenical Councils belong to the 4th century and provided a creed for Christians, who were from then on protected by the emperors (except during the reign of Julian the Apostate). Thanks to the great Cappadocians — St Basil of Caesaraea, St Gregory of Nazianzus and St Gregory of Nyssa — and to St John Chrysostom, liturgy and theology assumed the form which still gives us spiritual food today. Once that Orthodoxy was affirmed, and after the Sixth Great Council put an end to the main Christological heresies, the icon was to appear as a confirmation and affirmation of Orthodoxy. As the history of the Church was to demonstrate on several occasions, the living and authentic art of the icon was indeed only possible within the true faith. Suppression of icons in the Byzantine iconoclastic period resulted from the heterodox views of those hostile to them, who were unable to grasp in its full depth the teaching of the Church on the person of our Saviour Jesus Christ, God and Man, and for whom spirit and matter remained wholly alien to each other.[1] The Church knew this very well, since it was to give the name "the triumph of Orthodoxy" to the Seventh Ecumenical

Council, which re-established the veneration of icons and provided an initial foundation for the theology of the icon.

Because of the iconoclastic period, very few icons dating from the 5th and 6th centuries have come down to us, but those we do know are of consummate beauty. These are first and foremost the icons of Christ giving a blessing and holding a closed evangelistary (gospel-book); there are some of the Mother of God, enthroned, with the Holy Child on her knees, and surrounded by angels and saints; and there are icons of the saints — the holy Apostles Peter and Paul, St George, St Theodore, etc. The icons of this period are characterized by their technique — they are painted with encaustic (colours mixed with wax) — and by the faces, with their noble features and intense expressions. On the other hand, the iconographic mosaics decorating the great basilicas are much more hieratic, but this is where we find the first works that are the basis for the icons of the great festivals of the liturgical year: we may instance the baptism of Christ in the baptistery of the Orthodox (San Giovanni in Fonte), the Ravenna (second half of the 5th century), or the Transfiguration in the basilica of St Catherine on Mount Sinaï (second half of the 6th century). The true icons of the great festivals were produced in parallel to the liturgy for these days, for now they were not testifying so much to the Incarnation of God for the salvation of humanity, as the first icons had done, but rather indicating visually the content and meaning of the festival — as did the singing and readings in the relevant liturgical material, using the human voice.

While in Byzantium, in the struggle with iconoclasm, the theology of the icon was coming into being, the Western Church had to reckon with the power of the "barbarians" — Franks or Germani — who paid no heed to such things. Their pragmatic Christianity did not enable them to grasp the subtleties of Byzantine theological language, and they found even the way in which it was justified futile. Thus the Frankish theologians of the age of Charlemagne were to declare that pictures did not deserve to be destroyed, for they were not idols, or worshipped or venerated; their presence or absence was immaterial as regards the true faith. In the end, lack of interest in the Christological side of the veneration of icons took Western sacred art into a decline: for though the West produced masterpieces of religious art, it had forgotten the icon.

We know that the decisions and the work of the Second Council of Nicea did not at once succeed in convincing the authorities of their heresy; it was necessary, in fact, to await the rule of a new dynasty, the Macedonians, for a revival of iconographic art in Byzantium. After the long "silence" of Byzantine sacred art during the years of iconoclasm (a few rare monastic icons painted in Syria during this period have been preserved for us in the collection of pictures in the Monastery of St Catherine on Mount Sinaï), resumption of artistic work in this field was initially quite slow. Our knowledge is primarily of mosaics belonging to this period — those of the church of St Sophia at Salonika (Greece) or the first mosaics of St Sophia at Constantinople. These compositions are just as hieratic as those in the basilicas of the 5th or 6th centuries in the West, but they already correspond to the iconographic patterns that are familiar to us. Thus, for instance, the ascension in the dome of St Sophia of Salonika (around 885) has all the elements of the icon for this festival: Christ, borne by the angels, is in the centre of the dome; the Mother of God, orant, is flanked by two angels who are showing the gathered Apostles their Lord who "will come in the same way as they have seen him go into heaven" (Acts 1:11). Finally, of this dual aspect of Christ — the glorified Master leaving his disciples, or the Judge of the end of the ages — it is the latter who was to predominate in the classical programme for the grouping of images in churches; according to some authors,[2] this was under the influence of Photius I, Patriarch of Constantinople.

Two leaves joined together as a diptych and preserved in the picture collection in the monastery of St Catherine on Mount Sinaï, dating from the 10th century, give us twelve small icons of the great festivals of the liturgical year. This series does not wholly correspond to the twelve great festivals of the year which we now celebrate: three Marian festivals are missing — the Nativity of the Mother of God, her Presentation in the Temple and her Dormition. On the other hand, they do include the resurrection of Lazarus and two Easter icons: the Descent into Limbo and the Appearance of Christ to the two Marys. This diptych is of great interest for us, for it seems to be the only monument of the age preserved for us and already showing "canonical" iconographical patterns.[3] The painting technique used is also the one familiar to us, and is a traditional survival. It is in egg tempera.

Let us pause for a moment over this diptych. The series of icons is "read" from left to right, and the two leaves on the diptych constitute a whole. The series begins with the Annunciation icon, simplified to two standing figures: the Archangel Gabriel, with his right arm stretched towards the Mother of God, who is also standing. Then comes the Nativity of Christ: a mountain fills the centre of the icon completely; in the cave which opens at the side we see the stone manger with the child wrapped in swaddling clothes and his Mother, half seated at his head, on the left; a ray coming from a star illumines the new-born Child's head, which has a (cruciferous) nimbus. On the left slope of the mountain three half-length angels can be seen; on the right slope there is a single herald angel turned to the right, where at the foot of the mountain two shepherds are standing; a young man, and an old man clad in sheepskin. Joseph is seated on a stone, in the left hand lower corner of the icon; his figure is bent, and his head rests on an arm, so that he seems to be asleep. At the bottom, in the middle, directly below the cave, the Child is being bathed: he has half his body in a basin filled with water and is tended by two women. In the right lower corner of the icon several sheep can be seen.

The series continues on the other leaf with the presentation of Christ in the temple (Hypapanté) and the baptism of Christ, of which practically nothing remains. The second group begins with the Transfiguration: Mount Tabor is symbolized by three small hills at the foot of which the three disciples have settled; almost the entire upper part of the icon is missing, but it is possible to distinguish the left side of the figure of Christ in light-coloured clothing and the fine, young face of Moses on the right. Then comes the resurrection of Lazarus. On the left, in an open sarcophagus, Lazarus is standing, wrapped in graveclothes; his face is young, he has no beard, and his head has a nimbus. An old man, and a young man who is holding his nose, are about to take off the graveclothes. In the centre of the icon, Martha and Mary are kneeling; one is turning towards her brother, while the other, bowed down, is kissing the hem of Christ's cloak — he is standing further over towards the right. He is stretching out his hand towards Lazarus and holding a rolled-up scroll in his left hand. On the far right there is a group of Apostles. This icon is followed by that of the entry into Jerusalem. As on all the icons for this festival that we know, in the centre of the composition is Christ riding on the ass.

163

But the originality of this icon is constituted by the fact that we see in it a profile of the Saviour, for he is so seated on his mount that his back is turned to the onlooker. The Apostle Peter, with characteristic white hair and beard, seems to be leading the ass, which is moving towards the group of "inhabitants of Jerusalem", to the right on the icon. On the left-hand side, the group of Apostles is following Christ. At the bottom, two children are spreading out garments under the ass's hooves. The landscape is indicated by a high mountain on the right, while a sketchy tree and buildings are to the right of it. The next icon is that of the Crucifixion. Its composition is very simple: in the centre, the Crucified is on a cross of the so-called "Byzantine" type, with eight arms; on the left is the Mother of God in an attitude of prayer but with her hands covered by her cloak; on the right there is the young Apostle, John the Divine ("the Theologian"). Of the icon of the Descent into Limbo, only the central part remains: a luminous figure of Christ, moving vigorously and pulling Adam (or Eve — for one can only see the right hand of the person on the right, held firmly by Jesus) from the grave. In contrast, the next picture is very static: Christ stands full face in the centre, and on either side of him two women are bowing low, with their hands covered by their cloaks. The design of the Ascension icon, too, is classical: at the top and in the middle Christ is seated giving a blessing with his right hand, and with a sealed scroll supported on his knee in his left hand. He is in a mandorla[4] carried by two angels in flight; immediately above him is the Mother of God with her hands open in a gesture of witness, flanked by two angels; to the left and right, two groups of Apostles, led respectively by St Peter and St Paul, have very typical heads: so the iconographer wanted to show here not the historical event of Christ's Ascension as described in Acts, but rather the moment of the return of the Son of Man to judge, or the icon of this event in its non-temporal, eternal significance. The series of icons ends with the Descent of the Holy Spirit. Though at first sight familiar, this icon is not really an illustration of Acts 2:1-4. In fact, the gathering of the Apostles, twelve in number, is in a semi-circle, presided over by the Apostles Peter and Paul, and includes the four evangelists, as indicated by the richly decorated evangelistaries held on the knees of four personages. Thus the iconographer has chosen to paint the Apostles who to him seemed especially appropriate as an image of the Church which is called to bring the Good News to all the nations. Also, two figures representing the nations are at the bottom centre of the icon, in an expectant attitude, turned towards the holy gathering.

With a detailed description of these icons, we wanted to show first of all that the iconographic tradition governing the "canon" of the icon had already been established in the 10th century, scarcely a hundred years after the veneration of icons was re-established (in 843); then to point out what liberties an iconographer could take within these limits, which to the superficial observer seem so rigid. It is also possible to see the will of God in the very existence of a definite iconographic programme at this point in history, for by evangelizing the Slavs Byzantium was to pass on to them the fullness of Orthodoxy.

There is no doubt whatever that the iconographic programme in the churches was established at the same period, for during the 11th century there was a great flowering of sanctuaries magnificently decorated with mosaics and frescoes, all of them faithful to the same spirit, and lavishly bestowing the same teaching on believers from every corner of the Orthodox world. In chronological order, these are: the mosaics and frescoes of Hosios Lukas (St Luke) at Phocis (Greece), the frescoes of St Sophia at Ohrid (Yugoslavia), the frescoes of St Sophia at Salonika, the mosaics and frescoes of St Sophia at Kiev (Russia), the mosaics of Nea Moni at Chios (Greece), the mosaics of St Mark at Venice, the mosaics at Daphne (Greece) and the frescoes at Vatopedi monastery at Mount Athos. This was a real explosion of masterpieces of Byzantine sacred art — the "triumph of Orthodoxy" displayed in colours on church walls. The arrangement of the pictures in the church is more or less the same everywhere. It underlines the importance of the sanctuary (in the apse or eastern part of the building) and shows the meaning by the more or less significant grouping of the great Fathers of the Church around the altar: St Basil of Caesaraea and St John Chrysostom occupy the central position. Immediately above is the picture of the Communion of the Apostles, not to be confused with the icon of the Lord's Supper:[5] Christ, standing behind the altar, is surrounded by two angels, and distributes the eucharistic bread and wine to twelve Apostles who come forward from both sides. There again we have a communion icon, for the line of Apostles on the right is generally led by Paul and the four evangelists are there. Finally in the conch of the apse we find the Mother of God, usually addressing her prayers to her Son whose image is in the dome. Thus, this grouping of images passes before the eyes of the assembled believers as an icon of the eternal liturgy: in the presence of the holy bishops, the Eucharist is celebrated by Christ himself, while his Mother, an image of the Church, is present, deep in watchful and constant prayer. And finally, the icon of the Annunciation, which is on the triumphal arch,[6] reminds us of the Good News of the Gospel: the Incarnation for our salvation of the Son of God who has given us access to the Kingdom, which is reflected in these sparkling mosaics. The other church walls show icons of the great festivals and of the events in the life of Jesus Christ, and figures of holy men — prophets, monks and martyrs.

The 12th century is just as dazzling as regards the spirituality and beauty of Byzantine sacred art and has left us even more priceless monuments. Whether it is the frescoes from Novgorod, on the northern frontier of Orthodox Christianity, or those of Cyprus (St Neophytos, Laghoudera) in the east, or the Sicilian mosaics (Cefalù and Palermo) in the west, and in the south the frescoes of Kourbinovo (Yugoslavia) or of the St Anargyri (Holy Mendicants) at Kastoria (Greece), to mention only the best known — all are incontestably related, for they are all nourished by the same mystical theology, the most notable representative of which for the period is St Symeon the New Theologian (950-1022).

Again it is the monastery of St Catherine on Mount Sinaï which has preserved a series of festival icons from the 12th century, with wonderful, pure, luminous colourings. To witness better to the undying light of the Kingdom of heaven, the icons, like the mosaics, are painted on a golden background. This surface, which seems to irradiate a gentle light, leaves no impression of depth: the iconographic message unfolds on one plane, here and now, but really in eternity. For the absence of depth, i.e. of any indication of distance in space, likewise indicates absence of the period of time that would have been necessary to cover that distance, and such absence implies eternity. The colours used at that period in the mosaics and frescoes and on the icons, were to continue to be part of the iconographic tradition and to be recorded finally in the manuals. But there also, in fact, a great deal of creative liberty is still left to the painter. An example of this would be the garments of Christ and of the Mother of God — the two personages most often represented and therefore inevitably well "typecast". Christ's garments consist of a brownish red tunic decorated with clavi[7] of gold and a dark blue cloak; now it can be seen that the shades of the first may vary on various icons from a quite vivid red to a purplish red (sometimes the tunic is blue) going through various shades of red. The cloak may be dark blue, royal blue or a greenish blue and any of the intermediate shades between these. The garments of the Mother of God are basically in the opposite colours: blue dress, red cloak. According to iconographic tradition she has to wear the garments of the Queen of Heaven (Platytera) — the imperial purple. It is true that the shades of purple reserved for those born to the purple (members of the imperial family) could vary; their pictorial representation, exaggerating just a little this or that shade, was to give the deep blue of the garments of the Mother of God in the mosaics. This blue could move almost towards black or towards a purplish violet. On the frescoes and icons, her cloak is often of a fine garnet red, becoming a brick colour or even chestnut in north Russia (10th-16th centuries), for the Russians did not know purple. Just like Christ's cloak, the Mother of God's blue robe could take on a green shade, sometimes even a vivid blue, almost azure. But the imperial red shoes remain an invariable attribute of the Mother of God in all the icons showing her feet, just like the three golden stars (one on her brow and one on each shoulder) decorating her cloak and indicating her triple virginity: before, during and after the birth of the Saviour. The colours of the garments of other holy personages are often subject to variations, despite the instructions (quite brief) in the iconographic manuals.[8]

In the 13th century the Byzantine empire was dismantled by the crusaders and the tremendous artistic upsurge of the so-called "classical" period was cut short. Because of political events, the influence of Byzantium in the neighbouring Orthodox states dwindled and the various nationalisms of the Slav nations awoke. But Russia hardly had time to create a large number of original iconographic works, for in 1233 it was invaded by the Tartar hordes and had to struggle for physical survival and to safeguard the Orthodox faith for a century and a half. In contrast, the Serbian kingdom stood guard for Byzantium. The fervent piety of the great Serbian kings and a great Orthodox culture gave shape to Serbian sacred art, which was at its most magnificent during the 13th and 14th centuries. Numerous churches completely covered with frescoes were built in Serbia. These murals remained true to the Orthodox liturgical vision of the world; their vigorous, deeply spiritual style testifies to the intense religious life of the people from which they sprang. In fact, while following the tradition and so remaining immediately recognizable, the holy personages on the Serbian frescoes often have the vigorous features characteristic of that people. For example, some faces of martyred saints in the church of Sopocani, with handsome, inspired countenances and intense eyes, seem to be portraits taken from life, while remaining extremely "iconic", thanks to their serenity and spirituality. Serbian icons of the 13th and 14th centuries are characterized by fairly dull colours but have some strong coloured highlights, blue or green accidentals and details in vermilion red. The relief of the faces is more contrasting, more bold, than that of the Byzantine icons of the previous century, and this makes them very expressive. When national cohesion was weakened, the development of Serbian sacred art seems to have been cut short. After the tragic battle of Kosovo (1389), only a small part of the kingdom was not wholly dominated by the Turks, and several churches decorated with frescoes were still being built there at the beginning of the 15th century. But their style is more academic — less original and dynamic but tending more to the contemplative. From the second half of the 15th century Serbia fell wholly under Turkish domination and its sacred art withered away.

The Bulgarian kingdom developed its own iconographic style before the Serbians; rare examples which have come down to us of its sacred art testify to a contemplative approach to the divine mystery in humanity, as is shown by the fine faces in the frescoes of Boïana (13th century), but they likewise testify to the hot-blooded temperament of those who were prepared to "take the kingdom of heaven by force" (cf. Matt. 11:12). Bulgaria fell to the Turks a century before Serbia; almost all the monuments of Bulgarian sacred art such as frescoes and icons were to perish before the flood of the Ottoman hordes.

In the same period, Byzantium also found itself under Ottoman sovereignty. Theologically the 14th century is that of the Hesychast controversies and also of St Gregory Palamas. Thus it is a spiritually intense and fruitful period, and it is not surprising to see this inward experience coming through on meditative icons in a great many faces, listening, it would seem, for "ineffable words". Hesychast teaching was to evoke great interest in Russia and also to be reflected in Russian icons.

As we have seen, Russia was given very little time to assimilate the Christian faith: two and a half centuries after her baptism into the faith (in 988), Russia was invaded by the Tartars, who were first pagans and then became Muslims. Only the north of the country remained free, though still under threat from those "crusaders of the north" whom we know as the Teutonic and the Swedish knights. Until the 13th century, Russia drew on Byzantine contributions: not only did Greek master iconographers work in Russia and teach their art to their Russian pupils, but also Russian spirituality needed to mature before it could be reflected in icons. Its first original expression appeared in the icons of Novgorod of the 14th century and in the frescoes of its churches of the same period. The most interesting of these were unfortunately destroyed during the last world war. The brilliant colours and simple lines of the Novgorod icons reveal a happy and secure popular faith. Often instead of gold leaf a vermilion which glows like embers covers the background of the icons; the faces in the icons, which in the 13th century were relatively primitively executed, acquire an expression of serene goodness in the 15th century. This is one of the characteristics of Russian iconography at its best. Russian sacred art has several schools, or rather regional styles, most of them coming together in what is known as the "Moscow school". Who today does not know those masterpieces of the Moscow school such as the Don Mother of God by Theophan the Greek — an icon in which the northern light has toned down the contrasts of the south; the Crucifixion by Master Dionysius in pure and delicate colours, with extended lines, as if bending under a burden freely accepted; and the Holy Trinity by Andrei Rublev, that perfect symbol of divine love. Above all it is the harmonious radiance of the pure and fresh colours which characterizes Russian icons: in this they resemble the Byzantine icons of the 12th century, but the colour composition of the Russian iconographers is even bolder. The faces in these icons have a very fine relief with little contrast; they do not belong to any special ethnic type. Their gentle luminosity and serenity speak of that kingdom of light and of the possible transfiguration of humanity and all creation which St Seraphin of Sarov had shown to his interrogator.

The crisis in Russian sacred art was not to be the result of external causes such as invasions, from which the Balkans and Greece had to suffer, but of subtle secularization and Westernization imposed on the country by the imperial authorities. As everything from abroad was fashionable and looked on with a well-disposed eye by the civil authorities, who from the 18th century onwards also controlled the Church's life, the icons became pictures with a religious content, or pious images. Happily, deep in the vastnesses of that great country, the Orthodox iconographic tradition was passed on from master to pupil. It was restored to honour at the beginning of this century, first by lovers of traditional art and then through rediscovery of the theological and liturgical meaning of the icons.

In Greece as in all countries where the rulers had to yield to powerful invaders who bring with them a spirituality or an ideology hostile to the traditional faith, the art of the icons was perpetuated far from the old political centres, and flourished again in Crete,[9] whence it spread widely to the continent — both on Mount Athos (frescoes of Theophan of Crete, 1522) and on Meteora (cliffs with monasteries in Thessaly, Greece) — and produced icon painters of great talent. Once again we have here icons reflecting the spirituality but also the temperament of the people who produced them. They show us faces which are energetic and full of life, resolute faces of Christians ready to defend their faith. The powerful contrasts of shade and light, of colours dull and bright, are as it were a reflection of the southern landscape. This was the final incandescence of Orthodox sacred art before this sphere of church life was Westernized, and like the other Orthodox countries Greece had to await the iconographic renewal of the 20th century to rediscover this treasure of the Orthodox church — which true icons are, since, if we may use a expression of the Fathers and of the great Ecumenical Councils, they have been created because "thus it seemed good to the Holy Spirit".

NOTES

[1] G. Ostrogorsky, the Byzantine scholar, was the first to emphasize the gnoseological side of the iconoclastic problem. Initially the iconoclasts used to denounce the "idolatry" of things made by human hands, on the basis of Exodus 20:4f.; later what they said was: "May those be anathema who would like to represent God the Word with the help of material colours on the pretext that he took the form of a servant, as if he had been an ordinary man, and to separate the Divinity which is inseparable from him by thus introducing a quaternity into the Holy Trinity" (Acts of the Seventh Council, Mansi, XIII, 205-363). The Orthodox reply to this was: "The icon is made in the likeness of the archetype…, or is an imitation and reflection of it, but differs from it in its essence" (Patriarch Nicephorus, in *P.G.*, 100, 277 A). According to Ostrogorsky's formula, the Orthodox approach to icons makes it possible to grasp "the difference in the hypostases at the same time as the essential difference (the icon)" (Ostrogorsky, "The Gnoseological Basis of the Byzantine Iconoclastic Controversy" in *Seminarium Kondakovianum*, II, 1228, p.49 in Russian).

[2] M. Chazidakis and A. Grabar, *La peinture byzantine et du haut Moyen Age*, Paris, 1965, p.22.

[3] In fact there is no iconographic "canon", i.e. no collection of laws or rules governing iconographic composition or technique, apart from a few late iconographic manuals. The canon of the iconographers is the tradition passed on from master to pupil, the bases for which

are given in the doctrine of the Orthodox church and the recommendations of certain Councils (Council "in Trullo" of 691-692; the Seventh Ecumenical Council of 787; the Council of the Hundred Chapters, 1551, Moscow).

[4] Mandorla: a halo around the whole body.

[5] The traditional icon of the Lord's Supper is that which corresponds to the liturgy for Holy Thursday. It is based on the Gospel story (Matt. 25:20-23; Mark 14:17-20; Luke 22:14; John 13:21-27) and shows Jesus and the twelve Apostles including Judas, seated round a circular or semi-circular table; on the table are generally dishes and knives, loaves, often vegetables, and a goblet of wine. Frequently St John has his head leaning on Jesus' shoulder while Judas takes something from a dish. The gestures and attitudes of the Apostles indicate a lively discussion.

[6] "Triumphal arch" is the name given to the two columns connected by a semi-circular arch and marking the boundaries of the sanctuary in the Byzantine churches and basilicas.

[7] The *clavus* (plural, *clavi*) is a purple strip decorating the tunic of dignitaries in the Roman Empire. Clavi started at the shoulders and went down to the hem of the garment. This strip can be seen on icons where Christ and the Apostles are in Roman attire.

[8] The best known of the iconographic manuals is that of Dionysius of Fourna (or Dionysius the Fournaghiote), based on the example of paintings by Manuel Panselinos made at the beginning of the 14th century at Mount Athos. Dionysius of Fourna's manual was translated into French and published by M. Didron in 1845 (*Manuel d'iconographie chrétienne, grecque et latine, avec une introduction et des notes*, Paris, 1845).

[9] Chazidakis links the Cretan school with the art of the Palaeologi dynasty and the Macedonian school (cf. M. Chazidakis, *La peinture post-byzantine*, Athens, 1953). It is in fact quite possible that painters who fled from Constantinople when it was threatened by the Turks had trained pupils of great talent in Crete.

The Moldavian Monasteries and their External Wall Paintings
Summary Notes

RENATE SBEGHEN

It would be strange to have such a rich collection of essays on icons and not to mention the amazing art of external wall paintings in the Orthodox monasteries of the Moldavian region of Romania (Plate 14). Most of them date back to the 15th and 16th centuries and were built during the reign of Stephen the Great and his descendants; they are evidence of the astounding arts of construction and painting in medieval Romania. The majority of them, still used today, have coloured outdoor frescoes and their colours are as fresh as 400 years ago. The colour of these frescoes has resisted the effects of the weather, and nobody has yet been able to solve the mystery of how the colour mixtures were prepared and the plasterwork done. Due to the competent use of lines, of combining colours, of outlining light and shade, the Moldavian artists created inside and outside wall paintings of great value.

This chain of Moldavian churches/monasteries has its very own Romanian style which has remained unspoilt until today; however, it can clearly be seen that many Gothic and Byzantine elements have influenced the style. It is said that in medieval times the custom on festival days was for the whole population of the area to assemble around the princes or feudal landlords; as the churches were small, the majority of the peasants had to stay outside and so the outer walls of these churches were adorned with icons and other holy paintings, thus giving the faithful the possibility of at least seeing and experiencing salvation from afar. In the iconography of these frescoes religious motifs and biblical scenes (e.g. the Last Judgment, Genesis or the "ladder of virtues") were combined with events of that time.

The architecture and art bear the seal of Stephen the Great (1457-1504). After each victory over the Turks he ordered a monastery to be built. During his long and glorious reign 44 monasteries were erected, but most of the names of the Moldavian artists working on them remain unknown. These buildings house an enormous wealth of religious treasures and radiate simple Christian faith and Romanian Orthodox spirituality. Therefore, they can be considered a chronicle of the Moldavian state. Their architecture is one of the most original and artistic in the world.

Monumente Istorice Bisericesti din Mitropolia Moldovei ci Sucevi, Iasi, Editura Mitropoliei Moldovei ci Sucevi, 1974.

The History of Painting in the Armenian Church

VIKEN AYKAZIAN

> In times of war and invasion carry the manuscripts to the cities and bury them, but in times of peace take them out and read them for closed books are like idols.[1]

For the people of western Asia religion permeates every aspect of life. Therefore, artistic expression most commonly relates to religious observance. As with the religious carving and church architecture upon which the Armenians focused their attention, so it is with painting. In Armenia, painting became very highly developed in the monumental art form of church frescoes and miniature paintings for religious manuscripts. It was another form of decoration used in Armenian churches. Usually the interior of the church was decorated with paintings and mosaics, and the exterior or the walls with rich ornaments or figures. In several 7th-century churches the remains of paintings exist, like the churches of Mren, Tekor and Talin. But due to the method employed, very few examples of fresco paintings remain. Therefore, the history of painting in Armenia can best be traced in the pages of illustrated religious manuscripts. Unfortunately, from pre-Christian times, there is only one existing example of pictorial art, a mosaic from the temple of Garni which shows the Ocean and the Sea as personified deities.

Manuscripts

The real history of Armenian religious painting is to be found in the study of the numerous illuminated manuscripts of the Gospel. Before the invention of printing, the Bible was painstakingly copied by hand, in exquisitely stylized penmanship. It was a tedious operation. From a very early date painters collaborated with scribes in the production of manuscripts, especially in the copying of liturgical manuscripts in which the illustrations were held to be almost as important as the sacred text itself. We also have descriptions of the problems of the monks who, fleeing their monasteries in times of foreign invasion, would carry with them the manuscript they were working on. In spite of difficulties a large number of manuscripts were produced over the centuries. Armenians attached great importance to them, regarding them as treasures from God. The copying of a manuscript merited almost as much praise as erecting a church.

The illumination of manuscripts in Armenia must have started soon after the invention of the Armenian alphabet in the 5th century, but the first stages of its history, from the 5th to the 6th centuries, remain obscure because no illuminated

171

manuscripts have survived. However, from the second half of the 9th century up to the 18th, we can follow its development almost without interruption.

The 7th-century treatise on the iconoclasts by Vrtanes Kertol is the first written document preserved in the defence of the veneration of images in the Armenian church. Vrtanes Kertol was a prominent figure in Armenian church history, the assistant of the Catholicos Moses. He directed his treatise against an Armenian sect opposing the use of images in churches. He defended the practices of Armenian churches and the use of images such as the Holy Virgin with the Infant Jesus, St Gregory the Illuminator and St Stephen the first Christian martyr, St Gayane and Herepsimé with all of their forty companions. In addition, he also mentioned briefly scenes inspired by the life and miracles of Jesus Christ: "All the wonders of Christ that are related in scriptures we see painted in the churches of God; the Nativity, Baptism, Passion, Crucifixion, Entombment, Resurrection and Ascension into Heaven." Though the authorship of Vrtanes has been questioned by some scholars, Der Nersessian believes that the treatise must date from before the 8th century. While we do not have enough historical evidence of 7th-century paintings, the treatise of Vrtanes is more or less sufficient to prove the existence of paintings in 7th-century Armenian churches. No surviving monument from this period has preserved the whole or even part of this cycle of scenes described by Vrtanes. Remnants of compositions in the churches of Lmbat, Talin, Mren and Gosh, as well as archeological remains and literary testimonies like the above, bear out the idea that Armenian artists had opportunities to use monumental images as models for manuscript illumination.

John Odsnetsi, another prominent figure in Armenian church history, also defends the worship of the image of Christ and the cross. He writes: "We worship the image of the only-begotten and the sign of His Triumph."

The historians Ghevond and Stephan Orberian also speak of the existence of paintings in the 8th and 10th centuries. Orberian tells us about the richness of paintings in Siunik around the 10th century.

Armenian manuscript paintings can be described as having two contrasting trends: an earlier, more oriental style, a product of the indigenous Armenian artists' evolution; and the later Cilician style, much more subject to Western or Byzantine artistic influences. The earlier style, close to purely Armenian origin, was followed in the remote regions of the country where people were least subject to outside influences. In these outlying monasteries the painters were generally monks, who created an expressive intensity in their work by emphasizing stylized linear qualities in their compositions. They simplified human figures, playing down the aspects of shading or contouring. These works were commissioned by villagers who appreciated this style of painting. In the earlier style no emotions are portrayed and the "clothing that the figures wear falls stiffly, not revealing the contours of their bodies".[2] The interior of the church of Aghtamar, which is the only one where painted decoration has been preserved, has the style of original Armenian paintings.

In the 9th and 10th centuries many monasteries existed in Armenia, among them the monastery of Tatew which was a centre of learning. About five hundred priests and scholars lived there. They were "skilled painters and incomparable scribes".

In contrast to these trends, the Cilician style of painting was developed by artists often schooled in the traditions of Western art. During the 9th and 10th centuries in particular, Byzantine art influenced Armenian painters who combined its style with their own innovations; this gave rise to the development of the Cilician school, named for the kingdom, where the nobility supported the artists. If the Armenians used Byzantine art as a model for their manuscripts, which undoubtedly they did, they nevertheless added features of their own. "By the 11th century, for example, canon tables were being framed by drawing of trees, something which does not appear in Byzantine art."[3]

The ornamental elements in Cilician manuscript paintings later included birds or imaginary creatures painted with precision and perched on the first initial of the words. The artists used an expanded range of colours, applying the paint generously. In contrast to Armenian artistic conventions, these artists stressed detail, made human forms more life-like and placed more importance on background landscapes.

The Cilicians did beautiful work, rich in colour and varied in motif. "The Armenian ornamental repertory is more varied than that of the Byzantine manuscript; at the same time the compositions avoid heavy profusion of Muslim decoration."[4] Some of the decoration is very whimsical, with imaginary creatures, and human or animal heads replacing the leaves in floral scrolls. Such originality is most evident in the work of Toros Roslin, who was the leading painter of the 13th century. The formal severity of the earlier style gives way, in his work, to liveliness. His figures are graceful and often emotional, while his interpretations of Gospel passages are frequently personal.

By the 14th century, the style of manuscripts had reverted to the original simplicity and formality of the earlier centuries. The painters abandoned the rich and delicate ornaments of the preceding period, the elegant style of Toros Roslin, and found a more severe and simple form, which we see in the work of Sargis Pidzak. He foregoes ornate floral decoration in favour of simple geometric designs, his figures are rather short and heavy, and he prefers eastern motifs to classical art. In his style the drawings of birds and animals have disappeared. His work was harmonious and closer to the works of Greater Armenia and national tradition, and were imitated in Cilicia and Greater Armenia.

The Mameluke conquest of Cilicia ended artistic activity there, but in Greater Armenia it continued into the 17th century, and the manuscripts produced there show the influence of the Cilicians, with rich colours and vivid ornamental compositions. The oldest surviving Armenian illuminations, the final four miniatures of the Etchmiadzin Gospel, two leaves painted on each side stitched on a pair of stubs at the end of the text before the colophon, originated from an older manuscript. On the basis of style, Der Nersessian has argued that the miniatures belong to the "sphere of Armenian painting prior to the Arab invasion that began in 640".[5]

These four precious New Testament miniatures — Annunciation to Zachariah, Annunciation to the Virgin Mary, Adoration of the Magi, and Christ's Baptism — all expound pictorially the theme of the New Testament revelation. The unifying theme of the four miniatures is obviously the Feast of the Epiphany, the celebration of which, on 6 January, opens the Armenian church calendar and embraces the Nativity and Baptism of Christ as told in the Gospel readings for the occasion (Matt. 1:18-25). The selected scenes from the life of Christ, which artists of the late 10th and early 11th centuries had grouped at the beginning of the Gospel in the school of Greater Armenia, reappear frequently in manuscripts copied from the conservative "Van" school of paintings. Der Nersessian divides this school into two groups. The first comprises manuscripts copied at Van, Vaspurakan, Aghtamar, or in the monasteries along the northern and eastern shores of Lake Van. The second, which is called the "Khizan school", comprises manuscripts copied in Khizan (Hizan), south of Lake Van, and in the region of Mok (Müküs).

Manuscripts continued to be produced and illustrated even after the introduction of printing in 1512. The most active centres were among the Armenian communities in Constantinople, the Crimea and Isfahan. A manuscript of four Gospels copied by the artist Nikolayo in the Crimea in 1658 merits special attention. The two miniatures represent the Ascension of Christ and the Pentecost. The latter is an important one. The main feature is the figure with a human body and animal head among the "pious men of all nations" who were sojourning in Jerusalem. This figure, which appears in most Armenian miniatures of the Pentecost from the 13th century onwards, was traditionally placed under the arc below the feet of the twelve Apostles seated in a semi-circle. The semi-naked figure, demoniac in appearance, has a human head, from the right of which protrudes an animal head. The figure, which is virtually unique to the Armenian Pentecost with the exception of three Syriac examples from the 13th century on, continues in Armenian manuscripts well into the 17th century. The animal figures represented are of pagan people from a distant land.

Though the Armenian illuminated manuscripts are indebted to Byzantine, Syriac and Persian art, they have their national character as well. They not only occupy an important place in Christian art of the East, with their artistic quality and number of surviving examples, but also bring their contribution to Christian art as a whole.

Manuscripts are the centre, the core of the Armenian church art. A copy of the scripture was considered to be an inestimable treasure sent by heaven, a belief best expressed by the scribes' repeated quotation of the words of the prophet Isaiah: "Blessed is he who has children in Sion and a family in Jerusalem."

The khatchkar — stone cross

The "khatchkar", literally stone cross (Plate 12), represents an important and original aspect of the cultural life of Armenians throughout many centuries. Armenians who belong to the Eastern Christians have carved their faith in stones, as devout believers and followers of Christ.

The carving of a khatchkar is an artistic tradition unique to Armenians. Khatchkars are upright stone slabs carved with inscriptions and designs. The cross, the Christian symbol of faith, the vehicle of the new doctrine which is the holy sign, witness of the new faith, is the central motif.

From primitive times we find traces of Armenian culture, like "vishabs", with religious connotations. Vishabs are the first traces of engraving in Armenia, erected near sources of lakes and streams suggesting their link with worship in the pre-Christian period of Armenia. The khatchkar is a more advanced version of a vishab, the latter being carved first in wood and later in stone.

The true khatchkar appeared in Armenia between the 9th and 10th centuries, after liberation from Arab domination. These monuments are huge stone slabs, fixed on rectangular bases, and may be anywhere between two to ten feet high.

Khatchkars were decorated with bas-reliefs on all sides, symbolizing the triumph of Christianity in Armenia. First they were carved and set in the walls of churches and holy places; later they were placed more randomly.

With the Christianization of Armenia, the Church Fathers converted certain pagan sanctuaries for Christian use by erecting a cross, the symbol of Christianity, or building a new church on the site of the destroyed pagodas.

From historical documents we believe that khatchkars also have a pagan origin and are the vishabs of the new religion. From the very beginning of Christianity the Armenians adopted the cross and started to erect it in churches or on the exterior walls, as St Gregory the Illuminator did at Vagharshabad on the site of the martyrdom of the Hripsimiants Virgins.

The khatchkars have a different symbolic significance; they were erected to protect fields against natural disasters such as drought, hail, earthquakes and other calamities. They were also erected as funeral monuments, gravestones, to commemorate unrequited love, military victories, completion of churches, fountains, bridges, and on such occasions as the restoration of churches or monasteries. They have various functions, placed by the entrance of churches in the porch, along roads or at crossroads, on hills, integrated into church architecture, carved on rocks. The oldest known khatchkar dates from the 9th century. It was erected in Garni by Queen Katranide (879), wife of King Ashot I Bagratouni. It is an example of a stellar with quadrangular sections, standing directly on the ground with a cross taking one entire side.

In the 9th and 10th centuries spirituality reached its highest level and many monasteries were built. The khatchkars began reflecting a new artistic expression, thus developing the Armenian national culture to its highest manifestation. Cultural life flourished in many ways, with a new spirit reflecting the liberation from the Arab domination. Hence, the main purpose of the 9th-century monuments, specially the khatchkars, was the salvation of the soul. It is in this context that khatchkars represent the symbolic image of the Crucifixion and the Redemption.

According to Levon Azarian, the idea of liberation and national independence has links with the Crucifixion and Redemption of the Son of God, martyred for the salvation of humankind. He says: "In Armenia, the struggle for liberation from Arab domination and re-establishment of national independence during the 8th and 9th centuries was linked to the idea of the Crucifixion and Redemption of the Son of God, who was martyred for the salvation of humankind."[6]

In the 11th and 12th centuries new themes were sought for greater unity of composition. The 12th and 13th centuries were periods of final improvement and perfection. The development and stylistic changes that took place during this period finally achieved a unified form in khatchkars. In the 10th and 11th centuries images were often carved in the upper sections of the khatchkars, representing the Almighty, the Mother of God, the Christ crucified, baptism, the Apostles, saints, sometimes the figure of the varped (teacher) and in rare cases we even come across the picture of the donator.

A group of khatchkars called "Amenaprkich" (of the Saviour) differs from others. They are richly carved with figures and both their shapes and iconographic concept are more original. This group derives its name from iconographic themes: the Crucifixion and the Resurrection of Christ. They have power to heal the sick and they are still visited by pilgrims. According to Azarian, "they were endowed by the people with significance as nature's elements, symbols of power to restrain exiles".[7] Another striking point about some of these khatchkars is that there is no starting or ending point in the linear network, this being the expression of infinity and eternity.

After liberation from Arab domination there was a period of calm in the historical and cultural life of the Armenians. But this did not last long, and was followed by the Seljuk invasion. The presence in Armenia of these two alien cultures interrupted the process of cultural and artistic development in building activities.

In the 16th and 17th centuries, when Armenia was dominated by the Turks and Persians, khatchkars were again erected in the eastern part of the country; however, after the loss of political, economic and cultural independence, they were generally relegated to cemeteries. In this same period, when Armenia was finally divided between Turkey and Persia, there was a revival of the tradition of erecting khatchkars, although from an artistic point of view it never reached the standards of the Middle Ages because of the political and economic situation. The khatchkars of the cemetery of Djoogha are examples of the final phase of development of the art. This was also the period when they were known for their simplicity. Here we notice the influence of Iranian art too. The decoration changed and became a "narrow, slender, massive pillar". The historical course of this national and original Armenian art comes to an end with the khatchkars of Djoogha.

Thus, in certain cultures stones have been considered sacred. Human beings have seen through and in them more than simple objects. "An object, in fact, becomes sacred insofar as it incorporates (that is, reveals) something other than itself, no matter if this is due to its particular form, its effectiveness or its strength, or if it derives from participation in some form of symbolism through consecration, or only because it is placed in a sacred area" (Eliade).

If the iconic sign is in relationship with the object symbolized, then it has certain parallels with khatchkars, which are not only a representation but an existential structure which we may say is a true icon of the cross. Khatchkars do not belong to the past but to the present and they attest to the presence of the original, before which "we cannot be purely spectators, but must prostrate ourselves in an act of adoration and prayer".[8]

BIBLIOGRAPHY

J. Paul Alexander, "An Ascetic Sect of Iconoclasts in 17th Century Armenia", in *Late Classical and Medieval Studies in Honor of A.M. Friend*, Princeton, 1955.

P. Evdokimov, "L'Orthodoxie", Neuchâtel-Paris, 1956.

André Graber, "Etudes sur la tradition arménienne dans l'art médiéval", Revue des études arméniennes III, 1966, pp.31-37.

Arch. Garegin Hovsepian, "Articles and Studies in the History of Armenian Art and Culture", V.VI, New York, 1949, pp.46-127, also 66 (in Armenian).

A. Khatchatrian, "L'Architecture arménienne", Paris, 1948.

F. Thomas Mathews, "The Early Armenian Iconographic Programme of Ejmialin Gospel", in *East of Byzantium, Syria and Armenia in the Formative Period*, N.G. Garzoïan, T.F. Mathews & R.W. Thomson eds, Dumbarton Oaks Symposium, 1980, Washington, 1982, pp.199-215.

Sirarpie Der Nersessian, "The Armenians", New York, 1969, ch. IX; "The Medieval Art", Erevan, 1973 (in Armenian); "Armenia and the Byzantine Empire", Cambridge, Mass, 1947.

N. Thierry, "La peinture médiévale arménienne", XX Corsi di Culture sull'Arte Ravannate e Byzante, 1973, pp.397-407, figs 1-3.

Levon Azarian, "Armenian Khatchkars", Etchmiadzin, 1973; "Khatchkar — Documents of Armenian Architecture", Venice, 1977.

NOTES

[1] From the Armenian Colophon quoted by S. Der Nersessian, in *The Chester Beatty Library: a Catalogue of the Armenian Manuscripts*, Dublin, Hodges Figgis & Co., 1958.
[2] S. Der Nersessian, *The Armenians*, New York, 1969, p.126.
[3] S. Der Nersessian, *Armenia and Byzantine Empire*, Cambridge, Mass., 1947, p.123.
[4] Der Nersessian, *The Armenians*, *op. cit.*, p.149.
[5] Der Nersessian, *Armenia and Byzantine Empire*, *op. cit.*, p.149.
[6] Levon Azarian, *Armenian Khatchkars*, Erevan, 1973, p.28.
[7] *Ibid.*, p.28.
[8] P. Evdokimov, *L'Orthodoxie*, Neuchâtel-Paris, 1956.

The Christian Coptic World and Icons

ATHANASIOS

The ancient Egyptians used to decorate their buildings with paintings and many other artistic works. In some tombs in the Valley of the Kings on the west bank of the Nile at Luxor — Ancient Thebes — are some beautiful and well-preserved paintings. They are about the great events of the people: their life, their friends and deeds, as well as their aspirations for life after death and life after resurrection. The paints used are of pure vegetal sources and the figures are lively.

In the early centuries of the Christian era there were universal symbols. Coptic art made use of the fish, the grape leaf, the cluster of grapes as well as the ancient Egyptian "onkh" — a cross with a hollow oval head symbolizing the key of heaven — and the palm leaf.

Coptic icons are characterized by realism, simplicity and peace. St George or St Theodoros, depicted killing the dragon, does not show any fierceness. The martyrs express no fear, the ascetics are not pale, the children watching their parents being tortured are not horrified. There is simplicity and peace in all faces. This quality prevails up to the beginning of the 19th century.

In that century the Copts adopted some of the elaborateness of Byzantine art. Saints appear in glorious church vestments, and the mitre and the panagia were used in the services and depicted in the icons. The iconostasis of the cathedral in Cairo centre which was built in the 19th century is no different from those of the Greek churches of the time. The icons are almost the same. Both iconostasis and icons were imitated in many churches of that period. Then the 20th century witnessed a move back to the Coptic shapes.

Throughout the ages, religious images were painted on wooden frames, canvas, walls, manuscripts, bone, ivory, bronze, pottery, ceramics, and home utensils. On church walls, frescoes seem to have been earlier than ceramics. There are remains from the 4th century of beautiful paintings on plaster, which can still be seen in the tombs of the oasis of Kharga, Bagawat, St Shenouda Monastery at Sohag and the monasteries of Sts Paul, Anthony or Macarius in the Coptic museum in Cairo. "Painters continued to practise this art on plaster on the walls with water colours up to the 11th century or a little later. Then they changed their method and drew on wooden panels."[1] The sanctuary of St Tekla Haymanout the Ethiopian and the Hanging Church in Old Paris still retain signs of such frescoes. In most cases the painter used the white of egg instead of oil in creating icons. In later periods the wooden panels were covered with a soft layer of gypsum. The gold colour used in

178

part of the icon might have been added later. The gold background of the whole icon was applied in the very late centuries. In some early icons the faces were large in proportion to the bodies to indicate the greatness of the spirit.

These are the main characteristics of Coptic icons. Undoubtedly some painters in various ages were affected by foreign elements: Greek, Roman, Russian or Ethiopian. Some icons were brought by pilgrims from the Holy Land and their beauty influenced painters.

The features of the Copts are not slim as in some Byzantine icons, the faces are not round and radiant as in the Russian ones, and the eyes are not very sharp as in the Ethiopian icons. Features are average, faces are plain and peaceful, and clothes are simple.

Icons are held in reverence among the Copts. Some are wiped with myron (holy oil) to be consecrated for worship services. All those which are in church buildings are consecrated in the same way as all parts of the building. Yet icons are not often found in private homes as is the case with other Orthodox peoples.

NOTE

[1] R. Habib, *The Coptic Icons*, Cairo, Mahabba Bookshop, p.5 (English and Arabic).

Iconography in non-European Christianity

PAULOS MAR GREGORIOS

Most people associate icons with Byzantine or Slavonic Orthodox Christianity. There are those non-Orthodox like Ernst Benz who argue that an understanding of Byzantine or Slavonic iconography is the best entry point to the understanding of Eastern Orthodox Christianity.

But few are aware of the fact that Christian iconography began on Asian-African soil and that Byzantine iconography developed out of Syro-Palestinian and Egyptian iconography, which in turn came under heavy Hellenistic influence. The Russian professor Leonid Ouspensky, one of the leading authorities on Christian iconography, once told the present writer that Eastern iconography was basically of Syro-Palestinian origin, and he wondered why it had not flourished there as in the Byzantine, Slavonic, and Romanian traditions of Orthodoxy.

We will not here go into the question of Syro-Palestinian and Egyptian influences in the Christian art of the Roman catacombs of the 3rd century. We should not forget, however, that the leading philosopher of 3rd-century Rome, Plotinus, was himself trained in Syria, Persia and Egypt. And Plotinus substantially altered the classical conception of art as *mimesis*, or imitation of what is outside. He developed the philosophical notion, characteristic of late-antique Christianity, that art is form, and also that form is basically colour and light, and not geometrical designs. Late-antique Christianity accepted this Plotinian notion of art as an action of the mind in apprehending beauty through colour and light.

The Syrian tradition

The artistic tradition of Syria and Mesopotamia first took shape in illuminated codices and decorated cultic vessels, rather than in paintings with a definite cultic purpose. We have very few pieces of this once vast production of ancient Christian symbols in illuminated manuscripts and richly decorated sacred vessels.

The *acheiropoietos* (non hand-made) in Edessa and the adoration accorded to it in that Syrian city-state clearly attest to the prevalence of the practice of veneration of images there from the beginning of the Christian era. The origin of the "acheiropoietos" (not-made-with-hands) face of Christ is lost in legend, but its antiquity is not. One version of the legend attributes its painting to King Abgar of Osrohene (AD 179-216), while another, more credible version sees its origin in connection with the present Turin shroud, on which the face and figure of Christ have been inscribed in a manner and technique that is difficult to explain. The legend which says that this 14-foot long white linen cloth was the shroud in which Christ was buried and inside which the resurrection took place is easier for Christians to accept than for many modern rational minds.

The fact that this shroud and the representation of Christ's visage on it were objects of high veneration for Christians seems fairly well attested. John of Damascus (8th century) states that Emperor Constantine ordered the reproduction of the Edessa image as standard for paintings and mosaics of Christ.[1] Andrew of Crete (ca. 660-740) repeats the features of Christ described by John of Damascus.[2]

Until Byzantine conquerors took it away from Edessa, the Syrian city, to Constantinople, the Byzantine capital, in 944, this Edessa "acheiropoieton" was not only venerated by Christian pilgrims from far and near, but became the model for later Byzantine and Slavonic developments. The West stole it from Byzantium during the Fourth Crusade (1204), and Baudouin II is believed to have sold it to Louis IX of France in 1247. Many reproductions then appeared in the West, beginning with the 14th century or earlier, and thus the Syrian icon also inspired iconographic developments in the West. The veil of Veronica with the face of Christ became very popular in the West. The name Veronica itself, according to some scholars, is a corruption of *vera icone*, the true icon or not-man-made representation of Christ's face on the Turin shroud. Whether this is true or not, it is reasonable to assume that long before the Byzantine iconographic tradition developed, the veneration of icons had become popular in many Asian-African churches, including those of Syro-Palestinian, Edessan, Egyptian and Asia Minor origin.

The roots of Syrian art go back to Ugaritic civilization (ca. 5000 BC). It took in Sumerian, Mesopotamian and Egyptian influences already in the pre-Christian period. During the Greco-Roman period Syria was heavily Hellenized and Romanized. Antakia (Antioch), Latakia (Laodicea), Beroea (Aleppo) and Apamea, Palmyra and Damascus became centres of a Syrian culture which had drunk deep at Roman and Hellenistic sources.

Along with Edessa, Doura-Europos became a centre of this Syrian culture, conscious of its identity and resisting assimilation into Greek or Roman identities. Doura-Europos already had a Christian church when it was destroyed in AD 256. In 379 Emperor Theodosius constructed a basilica on the ruins of the old church. By that time the Syrian and Byzantine styles began to be integrated both in Syria and around Constantinople.

As the Arabs conquered and occupied Syria, many mosques were built. But the architecture of the mosques was inspired by the Christian Church of St Sophia in Constantinople. Muslim orthodoxy, however, abjured painting and sculpture, and Syrian Christian iconography therefore had nothing to receive from the paintings of the Arabs. The Syrian Islamic debt to the Arab was mostly in the realm of architecture.

Eusebius, the church historian (ca. 260-ca. 340), tells us that painted icons of Christ and of the Apostles Peter and Paul were widely prevalent in Syria and Palestine in the early 4th century.[3] He also gives us a first-hand report of a bronze relief representation of Christ healing the woman with an issue of blood. According to legend, the healed woman herself had commissioned this statue as a thank-offering and it was still there in Caesarea Philippi when Eusebius wrote.

181

This was probably not an icon in the later traditional sense, but it seems to have been venerated by Christians.

Syrian iconography soon spread throughout the Greek lands (Asia Minor, Cyprus) and also to the monasteries of Mount Sinai and Egypt as well as to Nubia and Ethiopia, Iberia (Georgia) and Armenia, possibly also to Persia and India, Bactria and Parthia.

The Syrian Orthodox Church in Jerusalem claims to have the original painting of our Lord by St Luke the Evangelist, but what is seen there today cannot be that old.

The Egyptian or Coptic tradition

The Coptic tradition of iconography was certainly not derived from the Byzantine, but antedates it by many centuries. Though it reached full maturity only in the 5th and 6th centuries, primarily in the monastic centres, its origins go back to the beginning of Christianity itself.

While late Hellenistic culture dominated Alexandria, the countryside, especially Upper Egypt, received its inspiration from the Pharaonic culture, and rejected the cosmopolitan elitist trends of Hellenism in the cities. And it is from the countryside and the lower economic classes that the Egyptian monks came. The great monastic organizers like Amba Shenuda and Amba Pachomius, who were mainly responsible for transforming the anchorite settlements into cenobitic communities, were themselves rather vehemently anti-Hellenistic and anti-aristocratic. In the beginning the monastic cells seem to have been centred on the veneration of the cross alone with decorative motifs like flowers, plants, animals, but no icons.

Long before the Chalcedonian Schism (325), however, an authentic Coptic tradition of iconography had developed not only in the monasteries, but also in many town and country churches where Hellenism had not come to dominate. Coptic art borrowed freely from Persians, Greeks, Byzantines, and later on from the Arabs. Our evidence for Coptic icons comes largely from the 6th to the 7th centuries, when the Coptic tradition finally broke with the Byzantine. By that time Coptic iconography had developed its own distinctive style which assimilated all these influences.

The Arab invasions of 640 and 642 brought in a measure of Islamic influence, which can be seen in the art of the monasteries and churches of that period. After the iconoclastic controversy and the renaissance of iconography in the Constantinople church, Byzantine influences also came to Egypt, but most of the Coptic development had come to an end by the 8th century when the iconoclastic controversy was settled in favour of icons.

The Islamic invasions led to the destruction of many Coptic churches. Very few Coptic painted icons of this period have come down to us. But we do have significant evidence from the Deir-es-Suriyani, Deir-Abu-Hennis near Antinoë, Abu Girgis near Alexandria and St Simeon near Aswan. If there is any outside influence in these, it is predominantly Syrian, but the main lines come from Pharaonic art. Persons are presented frontally, in clear and pure colours, linear and two-dimensional.

By the 12th century Egypt was fully open to other neighbour traditions, particularly the Syrian and Armenian, as well as the Byzantine. The Coptic

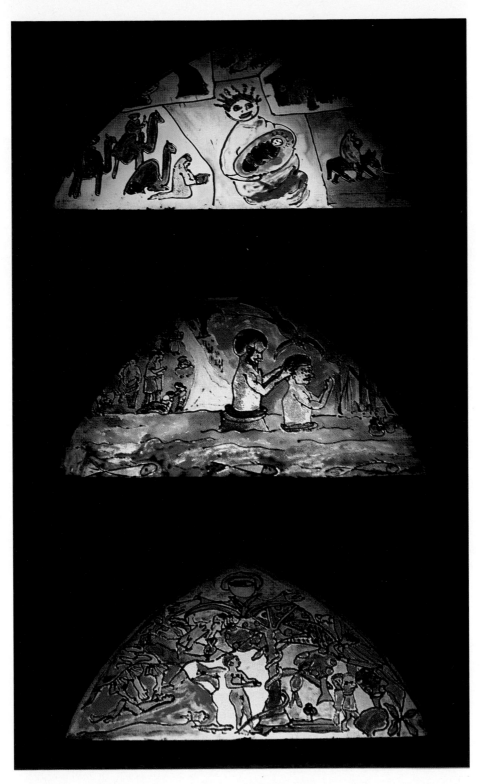

Plate 13: *Nativity of Jesus, baptism of Jesus, Adam and Eve in paradise:*
stained-glass windows, modern,
First Missionary Methodist Church, Kinshasa, Zaire

Plate 14: *Wall painting, 15th century, Monastery of Neamt, Moldavia, Romania*

Plate 15: *Monk iconographers, Holy Mount Athos, Greece*

Plate 16: *Coptic icon of Jesus Christ, contemporary,*
Ecumenical Centre, Geneva, Switzerland

tradition has had many revivals, the most recent having begun in the sixties of our century, helped by the great Russian iconographer Leonid Ouspensky in Paris.

There can be little doubt that in Egypt, the tradition of reverence to icons is as old as the Church itself.[4]

The Nubian frescoes of Faras

It was only in the 1960s that a Polish expedition headed by Kazimierz Michalowski completed the excavation of the site of Faras, an ancient Nubian city.[5] This great ancient African Orthodox church, located between Egypt and Ethiopia in what is now Sudan, has completely disappeared. The frescoes in the excavated cathedral of Faras are rich and magnificent, and date from the second half of the 8th to the late 12th century.

The Arab invasions of around 1175 put an end to the Nubian church, while the Ethiopian church survived those invasions. The Nubian style is distinctly local, with heavy influence of Palestinian, Byzantine and Coptic styles.

It is only in the 11th and 12th centuries that native creativity in the Syro-Palestinian and Egyptian Coptic iconographic traditions begins to weaken and borrowings from the Constantinople tradition tend to become heavier. Earlier, in the late 9th and 10th centuries, Syro-Palestinian iconography was exceptionally strong and had a vital influence in the development of Coptic as well as Nubian iconography. It seems clear again that the independent Asian-African traditions of Syria, Palestine, Egypt, Ethiopia and Nubia were indigenous traditions, not uninfluenced by Hellenic and Byzantine traditions but also not directly shaped by them.

It is also clear that the veneration of icons was rather universal in the ancient Christian Church, and long antedates the iconoclastic controversy in the Byzantine tradition. In the case of Nubia early evidence of iconography is rather scanty, but the tradition of *iconodouleia* seems as old as the Christian Church.

Ethiopian iconography

Very few specimens of ancient Ethiopian iconography have come down to us. But a strong Ethiopian iconographic tradition had already developed by the 11th century, and the noticeable influences are more Syro-Palestinian and Mesopotamian than Egyptian or Byzantine. Some Armenian and Greek influences are also noticeable, Armenian and Byzantine settlers having come to Ethiopia rather early.

No adequate study of Ethiopian iconographic development has yet been made. The present author can say from personal experience that a distinct and devout iconographic tradition is still alive in Ethiopia today — which cannot be accounted for by Egyptian or Byzantine influence. The iconodulic tradition in Ethiopia seems to be as old as that church (4th century).

The traditional Ethiopian churches and monasteries have today rich and colourful religious paintings. These are largely two-dimensional, in simple colours (mostly blue, green and red), and of a style that bears a close resemblance to 6th- and 7th-century European icons, but basically of independent origin.

The Armenian tradition

In the Armenian tradition iconographic tradition had rather restricted development. While the Armenian Christians were extremely creative in church music and church architecture, their contributions in the field of painting are largely in the field of illuminated manuscripts. Where icons do appear in the churches a heavy Byzantine influence is often noticeable. But the practice of venerating icons seems to have been prevalent throughout its history.

The Indian tradition

The ancient tradition of the St Thomas Christians in India, as far as iconography is concerned, seems completely lost today. What we can find are church paintings hardly 300 years old, and these witness to a dynamic and living iconographic tradition. Very little of Byzantine influence came to India. The Spaniards and Portuguese brought their iconographic tradition in the 16th and subsequent centuries, but this did not take root. Now a decadent late Italian tradition dominates. Here again, "iconodouleia" is completely accepted by the tradition of the Malabar Christians, but the iconographic tradition shows no signs of vitality.

The political background of the iconoclastic controversy

Long before the Byzantine tradition took the decisive step in iconographic development following the iconoclastic controversy, the Asian-African tradition developed along with the construction of new and magnificent churches like the Church of the Holy Sepulchre built by Empress Helena in the 4th century, and the great cathedral in Edessa from about the same time.

The iconoclastic controversy of the 7th and 8th centuries was partly a consequence of the clash between Byzantine and Islamic cultures. Long before that the post-Chalcedonian rupture between Greco-Latin European churches on the one hand and the Asian-African churches of Syria, Egypt, Armenia and Ethiopia had already taken place.

During the 7th and subsequent centuries, the ante-Chalcedonian Asian-African churches watched the conflict between the Byzantine and Persian nations with uncertain minds. On the one hand they rejoiced that Persia had conquered Egypt (611-619). On the other, they were grieved by the Persian rape of Jerusalem and the removal of the Relic of the True Cross from Jerusalem to Persia.

While the Byzantines regarded the war with the Persians as a holy war, the Asian-African Christians were less moved by it. They were less than happy when Byzantine Emperor Heraclius (610-641) managed to recover Byzantium and the imperial provinces of Asia and Africa (622-628) from the Persians. But soon after the death of Heraclius in 641 the Arabs reconquered the Byzantine provinces of Syria, Mesopotamia, Armenia and Egypt.

In the two big trials of strength between the Byzantine state and the Ummayyad Caliphate (678 and 718), Asian-African Christians were ambivalent in their loyalty to Byzantine rule and were often persecuted for that reason (rather than on account of doctrinal differences).

By the middle of the 7th century the three patriarchal Sees of Alexandria, Antioch and Jerusalem were in Arab hands. The attitude of the Syrian one-united-nature Christians (maliciously mis-named Monophysites) is reflected in the writings of Bar Hebraeus several centuries later:

> The God of Vengeance delivered us out of the hands of the Romans (i.e. Byzantines) by means of the Arabs... It profited us not a little to be saved from the cruelty of the Romans and their bitter hatred against us.[6]

The same sentiments were expressed by Coptic Patriarch Benjamin (623-662), as recounted by a 10th-century writer:

> I was in my city of Alexandria and found a time of peace and safety after the troubles and persecutions caused by the Melkite (i.e. Byzantine) heretics. [7]

Emperor Heraclius desperately tried to maintain the unity of the Byzantine empire by abandoning the Chalcedonian position and espousing a pre-Chalcedonian Christology. He imposed that Christology on the Chalcedonians through the "Exposition" (638), but neither side was willing to accept the compromise.

The pervasive misuse of icons and the Semitic opposition to engraved images, as well as the iconoclastic controversy which resulted, have to be seen in this context of the conflict between the Byzantine and the Arab empires.

Emperor Constantine IV had triumphed over the Arabs in 678 when the Arabs were forced to lift the siege of Constantinople. It was this triumph that enabled him to convene the Sixth Ecumenical Council of Constantinople which condemned Monothelitism. But the major Monotheletes condemned were not one-united-nature Christians in Egypt, Syria, Armenia and Ethiopia, but rather Pope Honorius of Rome and Patriarch Sergius of Constantinople. The rupture between Byzantine two-united-natures (Chalcedonian) Christians and the Asian-Africans was fairly complete by this time. The patriarchate of Constantinople became very powerful, not only because of the major role (including large financial contributions to the Arab war) in repelling the Arab conquest of Byzantium, but also because the rival sees of Alexandria and Antioch had passed into Arab hands and no longer offered any competition to Constantinople. The Byzantine patriarch was free to take on the title "ecumenical", though neither the one-united-nature Christians nor the Western Church of Rome acknowledged him as such. The Hellenic culture could now be imposed on an empire devoid of Syrian and Egyptian power of the major resisters of that culture.

It is in this context that Byzantium experienced a revival of its culture. One aspect of that revival was the replacement of Latin by Greek as the official language of the empire. By the end of the 7th century the Eastern European empire of the Rhomaioi or Rumi was fully Greek in language, culture and theology. The Byzantine liturgy developed as an expression of this new identity, with tremendous developments in hymnography (St Andrew of Crete, ca. 660-740) and hagiography. [8]

It is this revival of piety in an isolated Byzantium that gave rise to the notorious misuse of icons in a superstitious manner and to the iconoclastic controversy arising out of it. Opposed to the misuse of icons was a mixture of Greek rationality and Semitic "aniconism" or the forbidding of graven images.

The iconographic-hymnographic-hagiographic expression of a distinctly Byzantine Christianity became thus an expression also of the specific identity of Byzantine culture. Hence the triumph of the iconodule faction over the iconoclasts in the Seventh Ecumenical Council was a triumph of this Byzantine culture and identity. The "triumph of Orthodoxy", as Byzantine Christians called it, did not affect the Syrians and Egyptians, and neither did the iconoclastic controversy.

The Syrians, Egyptians, Armenians and Ethiopians had an unbroken iconographic and iconodulic (veneration of icons) tradition. The Seventh Ecumenical Council led to a magnificent flourishing of the Byzantine iconographic tradition in and around Constantinople. We see signs of this tradition extending as far as the Monastery of St Catherine in Mount Sinai.

But the Sinai icons we can see today depict, according to Kurt Weitzmann of Princeton, icons from the 7th, 8th and 9th centuries, an unbroken development from the 6th to the 10th centuries to which not only Byzantine artists contributed, but also Palestinian, Syrian and Egyptian painters.[9] Sinai was part of Palestine, Palestina Tertia, and Weitzmann thinks that the Palestinian tradition is the main element in the Sinai icons, with substantial contributions from Constantinople artists.[10] The monastery of St Catherine also had a large Syrian contingent of monks, and still retains a collection of more than 250 ancient Syriac codices. In that Sinai library, there is a room with more than 1000 old icons stored, some of which antedate the iconoclastic controversy.[11] The "Grado Chair ivories" of the monastery show strong signs of Syrian, Palestinian and Egyptian, as well as classical Hellenistic, influence.[12] At least in the icons of St Catherine's, it is difficult to see just one tradition — whether it be Byzantine or Egyptian or Syro-Palestinian.

Conclusion

On the basis of available information, the following affirmations can be made:

1. A distinction has to be made between *iconodouleia*, or the veneration of icons, and *iconography*, or the tradition of painting icons in a particular style.

2. *Iconodouleia* is a fairly universal characteristic of all Christian churches right up to the Protestant Reformation of the 16th century.

3. The iconographic tradition first developed in the Syro-Palestinian or Asian geographical-cultural context, since that was where the Christian Church was born and brought up.

4. The Byzantine iconographic tradition was one among many prevailing in the ancient Church, some of the others being Egyptian, Nubian, Ethiopian, Syrian, Armenian, Roman and Georgian.

5. The iconoclastic controversy of the 8th century was an internal affair of the patriarchate of Constantinople, a regional church. That controversy led to the so-called "triumph of Orthodoxy" in which the iconoclastic group was defeated. This defeat, in the eyes of other Eastern churches, was quite normal, since "iconodouleia" was a universally accepted element in the Christian tradition and iconoclasm was a deviation — however serious the misuse of icons may have been.

6. The peculiar experience of the Constantinople church in the iconoclastic controversy led to a doubly forceful renewal of iconography and "iconodouleia" in the Byzantine church; neither this experience nor its consequence was shared by the other churches of Christendom. Hence iconography and "iconodouleia" are less central in the churches not following the Byzantine tradition.

7. The particular stress on "iconodouleia" in the Byzantine tradition is reflected in the iconostasis. The iconostasis did not belong to the pre-iconoclastic period, and does not obtain in Syrian, Egyptian, Indian, Armenian or Ethiopian churches. It remains a peculiarity of those who follow the Constantinople tradition, like the Georgians, the Slavic Orthodox and the Romanians, as well as the Greeks.

8. Because of this particular post-iconoclastic double stress on "iconodouleia", the iconographic tradition flourishes much more in the churches which follow the Constantinople tradition. But both the "iconodoulic" and the iconographic tradi-

tions are alive also in all the other pre-Reformation churches. The difference is mainly one of accent, style and degree of centrality.

NOTES

1 *Epistula ad Theophilum*, in PG 3.
2 J.F. Boissonade, *Anecdota graeca*, IV, Paris, 1829-33, p.473.
3 *Hist. Eccl.*, VII:18.
4 The Swissair Gazette of December 1985 has very good articles on Coptic art.
5 Cf. K. Michalowski, *Faras, die Kathedrale aus dem Wüstensand*, Einsiedeln/Zürich/Köln, 1967.
6 A.J. Butler, *The Arab Conquest of Egypt and the Last Thirty Years of Roman Dominion*, Oxford, 1902, p.158.
7 *Ibid.*, p.445.
8 The *Patrum Spirituale* is full of pious stories of monks and hermits, mostly from Palestine and Egypt, not from Byzantium proper (for text see edition by N.H. Baynes, in *Orientalia Christiana Periodica*, 13, 1947, pp.404-414). *The Life of St. John the Almsgiver* recounted the life of the patriarch of Alexandria in early 7th century, renowned for his love of the poor and championship of the oppressed. See in *Analecta Bollandiana*, 45, 1927, pp.5-74; see E. Dawes and N.H. Baynes trans., *Three Byzantine Saints*, Oxford, 1948, pp.193-270.
9 Kurt W. Weitzmann, *Studies in the Arts at Sinai*, Princeton, NJ, Princeton University Press, 1982, pp.49ff.
10 *Ibid.*, p.74.
11 *Ibid.*, p.105.
12 *Ibid.*, p.159.

Icons "Coming to Life"

SISTERS MINKE, ALBERTINE AND OLGA

Sister Minke

Since the beginning of the ministry of the Grandchamp community, religious images have played a particular role in accompanying meditation on the Word of God and in welcoming our guests to their rooms. Our community is founded on the rediscovery of silent meditation on the Word and of the call to welcome people in the silence of a retreat.

When I arrived in 1958, there were mainly reproductions of paintings from medieval times (Fra Angelico, etc.), sculptures from Chartres, and so on. Already at the beginning of the sixties, the first reproductions of icons began to make their appearance, at about the same time as Sister Silvia, together with a Roman Catholic nun, was called upon to paint the iconostasis of a new convent for Orthodox nuns at Mer Yaoub in the Lebanon.

I still remember very well how impressed I was on my first visit to the Russian church of St Serge in Paris in 1959 when I saw the iconostasis from the entrance... at that time I was with our working fraternity at St Onen. Soon afterwards I was able, like many other sisters, to see the icons "come to life" in the Orthodox churches of Lebanon and Jerusalem.

The bond which united our founder, Mother Geneviève, and Paul Evdokimov has most certainly helped us to understand better how icons express the interior life and prayer of the Orthodox churches.

We have come to use icons to illustrate the various stages of the liturgical year. First of all we introduced them very timidly in our chapels, and then more freely. For more than fifteen years the "philoxenia" has been at the centre of our prayers wherever we are. The icons are of great help in developing the spiritual and prayer life of many of our sisters, especially the young ones.

Icons are in fact open windows towards the invisible world. Particularly the face of Christ on his descent into hell is a force which catches hold of the love and compassion of the Father, made visible in the face of Christ. Icons are very often a remedy for all kinds of internal images which can encumber or tempt us,

---

● The three sisters made these comments to the editor. Grandchamp is a Swiss Reformed community of sisters founded during the second world war. Ecumenically oriented, it uses different liturgical forms of prayer and spirituality. This text was translated from French by Renate Sbeghen.

so that all our inner being is illuminated by the Lord's presence and our vision is simplified.

We have three sisters who paint icons. Their work is one of prayer and represents a genuine spiritual undertaking, often involving an inner battle. Other sisters are learning how to paint icons in their spare time or at retreats; for them also this is much more of an inward task than an artistic apprenticeship. The Mother of our Lord is thus gradually finding a more central place than before in the spiritual life of the community.

It is significant that at Easter last year a small cemetery chapel in a village in German-speaking Switzerland received an icon of the Resurrection, of the empty tomb, painted by Sister Silvia. Are our Reformation churches being decorated — even in an area marked by Zwingli's Reformation — or is this simply the influence, the outreach of our community — we have a retreat centre in this very area?

I think it is true to say that we can no longer imagine our lives without icons.

Sister Albertine

> Thou hast said, "Seek ye my face."
> My heart says to thee,
> "Thy face, Lord, do I seek" (Ps. 27:8)

The community of Grandchamp, whose mother house is in Switzerland, developed out of the Reformation churches. It is marked by Christ's prayer "that all may be one so that the world may believe" and has, therefore, right from the beginning been open to the spiritual treasures of the universal Church as well as to the riches and sufferings of women and men all over the world. Its spirituality is that of Taizé (France) whose rules have been adapted to the particular conditions of the Grandchamp sisters.

The sisters live their vocation of prayer and reconciliation between Christians and with all human beings in different parts of the world through their welcome to visitors, the presence of small communities, and by participating in the explorations and questionings of our times.

"Thy face, Lord, do I seek." Here is the place of the icon in our prayers. Word and icon together guide our inner gaze towards the face of God. An icon evokes the realities of the Kingdom which the Word reveals to us. Iconography is a contemplative art. It derives quite "naturally" from our vocation to pray and listen to the Word of God.

In the centre of our chapels you will always find the icon of the Trinity. Other icons can be seen on feast days during the liturgical year.

Because of its simplicity and its theological truth, an icon can be likened to a window open on invisible reality. Far from being considered as an element alien to our tradition, it is for many of us an invaluable artistic expression of our faith. It sustains our prayers, averts our gaze from ourselves and purifies our thoughts and inner images.

"Thy face, Lord, do I seek." I seek the face of the Lord in his Word so that I can recognize him among his friends, among the smallest of his brothers and sisters. Therefore, it is always his face, the face of Christ, that I am seeking in the people depicted in icons. These persons, already transfigured, draw me towards my inner self so that I may listen to the Lord and allow my gaze to become transformed.

At certain retreats we try to open up for our guests the complementarity of the Word of God to an icon, towards a spiritual understanding of the theology of the icon meditating on the Incarnation — "It is the image of the invisible God" — and on the Transfiguration.

I should mention that we do not have our own interpretation of the Orthodox theology of the icon in general — nor of the one of the face of Christ in particular. But perhaps I can say that we receive the tradition of the Church and the witness to the faith by our Orthodox brothers and sisters in relation to this subject by trying to understand its scriptural roots. Our approach is above all one of biblical meditation, but a meditation illuminated by certain patristics and liturgical texts.

The icon thus finds its place in our prayer life and our common and personal meditations; in no sense is it image worship. It is at the level of prayer and faith lived out that Christians of various confessions can meet each other in a more profound way. For many Christians in the West icons have opened the way to an understanding of Orthodoxy.

I think that this art represents one of the privileged places where Christians of different confessions can find "access in one Spirit to the Father".

Sister Olga

The icon becomes integrated into the common praise, "what the ear hears, the eyes are contemplating". An icon helps me to concentrate more on my prayer by reminding me of the presence of Christ among his people.

It is an expression of our faith in the mystery of the Incarnation. For many it is often a new element, but we meet a lot of openness towards this mystery, and we are ready to answer questions which might be asked by guests who are particularly sensitive to shapes and colours.

Meditation on the scriptures helps us to recognize the presence of Christ in holy history and in each of his friends. The liturgy teaches us how to understand them better.

By trying to understand an icon and meditating on it, my comprehension of God's infinite love is deepening. The prayer of Jesus provides the atmosphere in which I can paint best. Evagrius the Pontic said: "Everybody who prays is a theologian."

The painting of icons represents a witness to their faith on the part of the iconographic sisters. "The icon is the knowledge of my Lord" (Mother Ludgarde).

One Stage on
a Spiritual Pilgrimage

FRANÇOIS SEJOURNÉ

In the monastery of Chevetogne (Belgium) the icon has an important place in the liturgical life of the community. Though produced by an individual it expresses a people's faith.

At Chevetogne the Benedictine tradition is not epitomized by the monastery building or the pure lines of a Norman arch, but by the welcome and the openness given to theological research.

Orthodox Christians say that "to understand us you have to pray with us", and the monks of Chevetogne have followed this advice to the letter. From the start two groups have coexisted within the unity of a single family, and under the authority of a single prior: a Byzantine group prays in Greek or Slavonic, and sometimes in French also; a Latin group has adopted French, though it leaves room for Gregorian chants. Three times a week a Eucharist for the monks brings the two groups together. For the rest of the time the visitor can pray in the Latin chapel or the Eastern church. Each monk remains in the group of his choice till the evening of his days: the Greek or Latin cross in the cemetery will be the evidence of this loyalty.

Not a museum

Thus in this monastery, where there are monks of all ages (average age: 40), the Eastern church is not a museum. What matters here is not the preservation or readoption of one tradition rather than another, but participation in prayer which involves the whole person, not just the spirit but also the body and the senses. Icons cover the walls completely and are so many invitations to set out on the exodus to which God never ceases to call his people.

In the narthex (or vestibule) the icons represent Old Testament scenes. The nave, where the monks stand to worship, suggests the meeting of heaven and earth (the first symbolized by the dome and the second given material form by the rectangular space). Christ is represented at the top in the gallery — the omnipotent Christ (Pantokrator) leading creation towards its final destination. Finally the sanctuary where the altar is situated is separated from the nave by a partition covered with icons, the iconostasis. Paradise is there, still veiled from our sight. The doors of the iconostasis are opened on Easter eve to indicate that through

---

● This text was translated from French by the WCC Language Service.

Christ we have access to the Father. But we are still on earth. And except during the services, these doors remain closed "as an invitation to the faithful", says Father Theodore, "to contemplate more deeply, with the eyes of faith".

As the entire Eastern church of Chevetogne shows, the icon is there to awaken us to a reality we cannot as yet see.

"As I paint I pray"

One of the monks in his workroom says to me: "We go from darkness into light, from dull shades to bright, through imperceptible nuances of colour. Never except for the final touches do we use white, which is opaque. On the other hand, yellow ochre keeps a certain transparency and this gives an inner light to icons."

When you paint an icon are you just copying?: "My reproduction will be very different from the original although my intention will always be to reproduce it. Why? Because some restraint is needed — we must acknowledge an icon for what it is. What we create will be all the more original because of that."

How do you set about this task in your workroom?: "As I paint, I pray. I use the Jesus prayer. I try to keep a calm, prayerful atmosphere. My work is an endeavour to cooperate with God, to try to paint his face. For even in painting a saint we are painting the face of Christ: a saint is another Christ. Each icon is one stage on a spiritual pilgrimage."

The community's vision

Father Michel, the prior of Chevetogne, stresses that the icon communicates the faith of the people of God. It expresses not a subjective vision but one of the community. "The icon is a vision of faith and undergirds prayer."

The monks of Chevetogne have not opened up any of their several workrooms to others wishing to paint icons. But in their church and liturgy the icon finds its full meaning: it calls on us to set out on a journey with a whole people whose faith it expresses.

Images, Signs and Symbols

TENY PIRRI-SIMONIAN

Images, signs and symbols have played an important role in Orthodoxy. This heritage, coming from our Lord Jesus Christ, has deepened the faith of all Orthodox peoples. Signs, images and symbols have also been an integral part of the *cultural* ethos of the Armenian nation; some of them go back to pagan times, and have since been Christianized. Forced into exile by massacres and deportations, Armenians carried their signs and symbols (expressing their faith and representing their homeland, as transmitted through their ancestors) wherever they went. They organized their lives in the host communities around these signs and symbols.

Today, in Switzerland, the fourth "home" in my own life, the only way I can bring up my child as an Armenian is by following and living the tradition of my ancestors: by teaching the essence of Christian faith, language, history, and cultural heritage through the living reality of the images, signs and symbols that I inherited. He will learn that the two Apostles, Thadeus and Bartholomew, brought Christianity into Armenia; that St Gregory the Illuminator is the patron saint of the nation, and that his relics are placed on the head of the new Catholicos during the ceremony of enthronement according to ancient tradition, a ceremony which marks the continuity of the Armenian church in history. My son, Nareg, will also learn that the holy oil — the myron — used in the sacraments and particularly in chrismation or confirmation, is blessed and consecrated with the relics in the church. The holy oil is the continuity of the holy oil which Jesus Christ gave to the Apostles when he sent them out to evangelize and preach the Good News to the nations, as St Matthew says. Nareg will learn that sanctuaries, chapels, churches, schools and other institutions are given the names of saints, martyrs and national heroes.

In addition to performing social or religious functions, images, signs and symbols remind us of our roots, of our history. They also strengthen us in our present struggle and make us look to our future with hope and faith; they are dynamic realities, and in the diaspora situation they are crucial to our keeping our identity intact and strong. They become "church" when we don't have one; they serve as "homeland" to a homeless nation. They are "fences" to protect our faith

---

• This was a meditation delivered during the Week of Meetings, 2-6 November 1987, at the Ecumenical Centre, Geneva.

against the de-Christianizing trends of our times. These symbols promote solidarity. Around them religious and national activities are organized, processions take place, speeches are made reminding the Armenian people of their past, national songs are sung and poetry read. In other words, around these signs and symbols a new life is re-created, reminding the people of their history, homeland and heritage.

I want to be certain that Nareg learns how Armenian women revere the image of the first woman martyr, St Herepsimé, the sister of the pagan king of the time. St Herepsimé and forty other young women started the diakonia among the poor and the sick. The king ordered the killing of his sister and her companions and imprisoned St Gregory the Illuminator in a dungeon for eighteen years until the king repented and declared Christianity as the national religion. In 1979 the relics of St Herepsimé and her companions were discovered in Etchmiadzin. A few months ago, some of these relics were brought to Lebanon. A special annual feast day has been dedicated when these relics will be exposed and women's activities will be organized. These activities are intended to make Armenian women aware of their place and responsibility in keeping the Armenian identity alive. The relics, which symbolize attachment to the Mother Church and motherland, will evoke prayer and spirituality, and redefine the place of women in the ecclesial community. In the tradition of St Herepsimé, the women are called to serve their people, to become the new Herepsimé in a new world, offering, receiving, but also sacrificing. In war-ravaged Lebanon, one of the important centres of the Armenian community, Herepsimé is an ideal symbol to serve as the mobilizing force for women to rediscover themselves.

Nareg will know that relics, as images, signs and symbols of our history, affirm our Christian faith and tradition; that they make us existentially aware of our past and open new horizons for dialogue with our present; that they help continually to bring and to bind us together. He will also know that, far from being objects of idolatry and veneration, they create new forms of spirituality, of belonging. We venerate the content, not the physical appearance of these images, signs and symbols; they transcend what they are in actuality, thus guiding the future. They contribute to the process of the renewal and transfiguration of the world, towards a new creation which is sanctified by the Incarnation of our Lord.

Finally, when Nareg starts reading in Armenian, he will discover that his name is the title of the most powerful prayer book produced in the 10th century, that written by St Gregory of Nareg.

Icon: an Expression of Prayer and Sacrament

The following text is an extract from a letter written by an iconographer of Moscow to a priest friend of his in 1930. This text is of interest to us today because it indicates the approach to icons at that period and shows the problems raised by the revival of the art.

It is absolutely essential to have a clear idea of the aims of Iconography (I spell it deliberately with a capital "I"), of how it affects a sincere beholder and of the media used for it, i.e. the plastic laws which govern it.

As to the purpose of iconography, it is clearly the same as that of the entire life of the Church, and reveals itself accordingly. We might say that it is dual. First and foremost, Iconography has its own intrinsic existence and meaning; it ascends towards the sublimest heavenly images and merges with them. But it also has an active, instructive meaning, for it teaches mystery. These two aspects are not separate, of course, but constitute a whole. However, for greater convenience we may treat them as distinct from each other.

What does an icon as such — i.e. a picture expressed, or more exactly, revealed, in a plastic form — do? It does the same as a prayer and, in its highest modes of expression, a sacrament.

A prayer is authentic insofar as it is a real bond with the prototype whose action impresses its character on that prayer. Like a prayer, an icon, when it reaches certain high levels, has within it the grace of its prototype which acts through the icon and performs miracles.

But it can happen that certain states of prayer are false — when prayer is thought of as an end in itself and the activity of the prototype is replaced by imagination. The soul is then transported into a world of dreams and of spatial infinity. The action of this dream on the soul is taken for the action of the prototype — blood stirring in the body is confused with communion in the life of that prototype.

Just as much as genuineness in one's attitude is important in prayer, to keep the faithful from being led astray, so too the laws of iconographic painting are linked with the final purpose of that art; in fact the actual form of a genuine icon, like the essence of true prayer, has in itself something of the prototype.

● This text appeared in the *Messager de l'Exarchat russe en Europe occidentale*, 101/104, January-December 1979, Paris, pp.85-93. It was translated from French by the WCC Language Service.

What are the laws that protect and govern Iconography? This can best be explained by a comparison. The icon and its art are in many points contrary to secular painting (understood as an art which has worked out its own laws, has developed through study of *what we call* the actual object, and uses the media at its disposal to the full). Secular painting (when its laws are fully developed) aims to provoke in the soul and imagination of those contemplating it an unquenchable desire to fill themselves to infinity with the images of this world. Its fullest expression — making best use of the media at its disposal — is naturalist painting. All other kinds, even if hardly differing in aim from naturalism, often find expression despite themselves by triumphing over the media available for painting and transcending them. But naturalism exploits them to the full.

In talking about painting, then, I am referring to naturalist painting. And it is this kind of painting which aims to fill the soul with images that lead into (a purely material) infinity. This is what the holy Fathers call "wandering of the mind". The media used in painting and the sense of its technical possibilities are wholly in keeping with this purpose.

Every picture is a dream-window in a material world; every image has an existence in the imagination beyond the plane or surface of that window, and extends — a metre, kilometre or infinity as the case may be. The thought-content in that space, i.e. everything filling it, moving, thinking and living in it, represents as it were a small part of that spatial infinity, for it is in no way totally realized.

In these circumstances, therefore, the beautiful is, in essence, not measured by a beautiful form (as being something immutable and complete in itself), but by the extent to which the image is filled with that spatiality. Accordingly, the media that can be used for painting take on a specific significance. To start with, a frame is needed — as a kind of gateway into this imaginary world. Beyond the frame there is an open space: there is no surface and none is needed. The colour as such, the actual shade, exists only insofar as it does not hinder the expression of that spatial quality. Form and line, too, have a solely subsidiary part to play. Likewise, any "body" (not in the sense of human flesh but of an object in general) is purely imaginary. As the painting in question evolves, it loses all concreteness and changes for the worse, dislimning into something of unadulterated conventionality.

Western painting has its origins in Byzantine ontological art, too. Initially spatial characteristics were felt to be merely a subsidiary element, but in time this has come to play an increasingly active role and gradually become a rule for painting.

The Renaissance affirmed this principle of an imaginary spatial element as an absolute and worked out laws for perceiving that imagined space: perspective. In its subjects, nevertheless, it kept a link with ontological art. Subsequent logical development gave rise to the need for "immediate" (naturalist) perception of the world or, in other words, for human beings to have knowledge of a fallen world. Those subjects which by their nature are ontological and essential become contingent; and in the end the naturalist perception of an imaginary material infinitude removes all traces of ontologism. Thus the material world becomes fully aware of itself through imaginary forms.

Contrary to secular painting, Iconography focuses mind and soul on a space which is materially limited. Great works do not require spatiality. In their very circumscription, they contain in themselves the infinite; but a real and not an imaginary infinite. As the spiritual world is the supreme reality, it has nothing of spatial infinity — that infinity which is a result of the world's sin and of our fallen understanding. The spiritual world is authentic and simple; its infinity is real. Thus the images of that real infinity are incarnated and live only in the simplest, most concrete and non-imaginary form. For this reason all the media available to artists for the creation of a plastic image are part and parcel of that image in a material and non-abstract way. The surface of the panel is the material datum, the limited space in which the image incises itself. Materially and authentically, line has a share in this fashioning of the icon; and while remaining *what it is in itself*, colour is the fabric of this image, with a certain wholly concrete, material substantiality. This, then, is the body of the icon, the unique plastic expression of the spiritual-ized human body.

This material body, really existing and capable of being known only creatively, can in fact be spiritualized. In other words, this iconographic body created through the medium of panel and line, of colour and surfaces, is the only form which in its concrete simplicity can be indwelt by grace.

We all know, however, that there are naturalist, miraculous icons. This merely means that "the Spirit blows where it wills", and it in no way refutes the fact that the supreme vehicle of the Spirit is the simplest body, the iconographic body, which is created not by the imagination but from material elements. Over a number of centuries, the Church created that body and the laws, conditions and methods that made it possible for it to attain to fullness of expression. Reversed perspective, a complementary surface, the way the ochres and lights on the faces were placed and so on — all these things give this body its form to perfection, but are also all organically bound up with it as a unity. As all these processes are indispensable parts of this body to such a degree, and since the whole has an integrity of its own, that integrity is grace, and is artistic creation.

All Rublev's icons were regarded as miraculous, doubtless not just because of the painter's saintliness but also because the integrity and harmony of all the elements of his creations reached a sublimity appropriate to the divine.

We have said that the panel itself and its surface is the world from which the body of the image is formed. The action of the image, however, is not wholly limited by the plane surface, but has a certain "shallow depth". Beyond that surface in which the main action evolves there is another plane, and there can be a third which can complement the first but which is also a plane surface with the same processes — reversed perspective, additional surface, touches of light — giving fullness to the image. But each image, whether part of the first or of the second surface, is subject first of all to the general laws governing its full expression and then to the coordination of all the parts of the icon considered independently of the plane in which they belong, as if on a single surface.

The inter-relationship of several surfaces (in strict horizontal arrangement), and their harmony, which is linked to the above processes and produces the effect of a single surface, makes possible an extremely rich content which fills the soul.

The planes represented are not imaginary. However, their depth is so insignific-ant that thought is not diverted from the plane surface, and the processes of complementary surfaces and reversed perspective give the image its necessary fullness.

The additional surfaces bring into the image those parts of the material body which the eye cannot see by the laws of visual perception (or in terms of perspective). For instance, when a face is depicted front on, a surface is added which is simply the back of the head; or again, in a three-quarters portrait we see the missing quarter.

Reversed perspective serves the same purpose. It prevents the viewer imagining a figure in depth and, to give greater fullness of impression, moves the object round by a law contrary to optical perspective.

The actual fabric of this iconographic body — with the colour and shade expressing only themselves — is also part of the general harmony. It is integral to the materially constituted image (the relations and harmonies of the colours are a highly creative and mysterious element; there is a multifariousness in this, a great wealth of content). In brief, in conformity with the general, essentially ontological principle, each specific element of the icon remains what it is in itself and does not play any subordinate role.

All the elements mutually complement each other and retain their material participation and specific character, and one might say that this reconstructs the primitive beauty and purity of the material which sings the praise of God, and creates an image which with peace and assurance imparts to the soul the real and infinite integrity of true life, the mystery of another, heavenly world.

Here we must also look at something fundamental: How is the image produced in creative contemplation, and how does it attain a creative incarnation? Contemplation is distinguished on the one hand by its strength and depth, and on the other by the elevated nature of what is contemplated... Each one of life's phenomena — as the object of creative contemplation — has its place in this framework and the gift each person has corresponds more or less to a place in this system. The Fathers of the Church use the word *diataxis* (order) to describe this faculty that characterizes the degree of depth in contemplation and the level of what is contemplated.[1]

We may therefore say of each creative phenomenon that it belongs to such a *diataxis*. For example, a particular picture will be a surface contemplation of a very sublime image, or again this or that order of contemplation will be appropriate to a particular writer, painter or iconographer, who belongs to one or other *diataxis*.

How does deep contemplation differ from surface — superficial — contemplation? In it the creative energy penetrates *beyond* the surface and enters into the depth of the image, seeing the prototype in that depth and returning (or ascending) towards it. The energy, in creatively contemplating that prototype, becomes as it were a ladder or guide towards the prototype, which by this very means is mysteriously incarnated. The image created does not merely tell us about the prototype contemplated; here, both the object of contemplation and the image are genuine reflections of the prototype. This is what we find in the images of true Iconography.

It is beyond question that only a creative "ascent" towards the prototype bestows on creative energy the power which allows the iconographic image to evolve from within. The very material from which the image is made, its material substantiality, gives its form to everything — to persons, to the earth, to architecture. As the icon is ontological (i.e. not just symbolical) this very substantiality has within itself something bestowed upon it by the world above; depending on the degree of elevation towards the prototype, this *body* possesses in itself various degrees of spiritualization and subtlety.

As every prototype is part of the Word of God, this is the only kind of contemplation that is churchly. However, even within the order of "surface" contemplation, the actual sublimity of what is contemplated sets a seal of the Church on everything which is the *object* of contemplation and which is translated into an image; and, through the mercy of God, such an image is the bearer of grace.

Thus Iconography is part of the first order of creative phenomena: it is the product of a deep contemplation of the prototype.

Each icon, everything we call an "original" or a "replica", has as its starting point an immediate vision of the prototype. But iconographers do not limit themselves to borrowing from their predecessors; as they contemplate what they have produced, they too return towards the prototype.

Even the most unsophisticated icons from the period when iconography flourished bear the marks of this deep contemplation. Later, iconography gradually lost its special features; though it remained an art, it lost its ontological characteristics. Purely symbolical elements appear in it and these in the end were to deprive the icon of its essential character. Iconographical processes became a matter of chance, or even pointless. Then came the final step: from the moment when contemplation was no longer deep, and no longer returned to the prototype, forms were needed which would undisguisedly express surface contemplation. This gave rise to what are called "friaz" and then to secular painting. These are the appropriate expressions of second order *diataxis*, proper to the age.

But then another period dawns: an intense need to know the prototype makes itself felt. The old-style icon stands like an inaccessible beauty, a fullness of churchliness. We dream of an art that shows us the prototype of which we have been deprived. The growing interest in icons and the quest for ways of coming back to Iconography encourage recourse to iconographic craftsmanship, a craftsmanship which has preserved the technical processes — all that remained of iconographic art.

But what does this iconographic craftsmanship represent? Can we start from here and find life? Is the knowledge possessed by iconographers sufficient to prepare the material frame that can contain the order *(diataxis)* of creative iconographic art? That frame *must* be prepared; but the doors are still closed. However, the conscious need for a contemplation that is not superficial has gone so far that it may point the way to their opening. Everything depends on the will of God. But what, then, does iconographic craftsmanship offer? It provides a knowledge of the purely mechanical processes which are absolutely indispensable. It is necessary to know how to prepare a panel, and the coating, how to cover an icon with olipha (boiled linseed oil), how to mix the egg emulsion (tempera) — in short, everything that constitutes part of iconographical technology. However, those who practise this craft are still uninitiated as to the laws on which icons are based.

Iconographers, who are excellent restorers, have adapted themselves over a number of centuries to the needs of the early ritualists and have attained perfection in the art of copying. In exceptional instances, when they are very gifted, they can be good copyists. But even armed with their knowledge and gifted with good artistic taste and talent, one still cannot create an icon or even a valid iconic structure — the one essential aim of someone who aspires to the rebirth of the icon. An icon, even if painted with perfect knowledge of all the iconographic processes, with taste but without a creative appropriation of the laws of iconography, becomes counter-productive. Instead of gathering together the forces of the soul it dissipates them and is disturbing. Whatever resemblance there may be to an early icon in the grand style, it is false and all the more so because some elements in it resemble early elements. And if its *diataxis* extends no further than secular religious painting, what is the use of this grand style, and is not secular painting more honest?

This is my impression of the icon of St Theodore the Studite executed by a contemporary painter, despite all his mastery and his taste. This artist is on the wrong track, like so many others who have learned mechanically the processes of the grand style but know neither what its real mode of expression is, nor the significance of an iconic creation — or of the processes which constitute a living part of it. In what they are doing there is no realization of the spatial plane: the groups of persons are not incised in the plane surface and the daubs of colour follow no plan; their position is a product of chance and they are distributed haphazardly over the surface; while the image as a whole does not have a calming effect. Everything seems to be there, but nothing has the same meaning as in the works of the ancient iconographers. For them all these processes were a living necessity and proceeded from the inwardness of their lives. Thus everything that imitates the ancient processes and the Novgorod colours is not merely unjustified: it is an accusation of falsehood, for it is the fruit of superficial contemplation of ancient icons without any creative ascent towards their prototype. I stress the word "creative" for while the moral element may very well be discernible it cannot be decisive. A *creative gift* is necessary if an icon is to be a door opening on the prototype.

So what should we do? Are we to give up trying to paint icons?... To me that too seems wrong. The knowledge provided by iconographic craftsmanship is necessary and useful, but we should not let ourselves be deceived into entertaining the hope that this is enough for painting icons. There is something great too in making good copies of early icons and one may apply one's gifts and one's taste to this, which craftsmen at present do not have; a good copy of an early icon is worth more than a false one. But to prepare the way for creative painting of icons something else is needed: we must become aware of the laws which govern the plastic form of iconography.

It is almost impossible to learn these laws: to become aware of them is the only course, and such knowledge is the minimum essential.

All in all, there seems to be no way out of the difficulty. But is not the work to which we are aspiring itself almost a miracle? Every effort towards its achievement has its value and is indispensable. Only substitutes which give the illusion of the grand style are hypocritical and harmful. If the Iconography is poor, at least let it be faithful.

But we cannot fail to strive for a return to iconographic form, any more than we can give up striving for knowledge of the prototype.

NOTE

[1] *Diataxis* (literally "arrangement" and hence "order") is the way one tackles creative activity, and is first and foremost something immutable, a kind of *order* in creation and contemplation. That order appertains to every phenomenon of contemplation and creation. Thus *diataxis* does not relate directly to the moral level of human beings, so deep contemplation of sublime images does not necessarily mean great spiritual or moral elevation. Moreover there may even be saints who are in the order of surface contemplation. At all stages of moral and spiritual development an individual expands within the order that is appropriate to him or her. Thus *diataxis* does not coincide with ideas of good and evil. It is, however, certain that the possibilities at the highest level are greater than those at the lowest: the possibility of contemplating the sublimest images permits someone of great spirituality to be marked by the influence of these sublime images.

The Triune God:
the Supreme Source of Life

Thoughts Inspired by Rublev's Icon of the Trinity

DAN-ILIE CIOBOTEA and WILLIAM H. LAZARETH

How can the divine nature of God be conveyed in human form? Or the invisible God apprehended through human senses? Nevertheless, the Church worships, confesses and glorifies God precisely because God speaks and reveals Himself to us (Heb. 1:1-4). But the image which the Living God reveals to us is not one of eternal solitude but one of eternal communion. God is Love because God is Triune. The mystery of the Triune God is the supreme mystery of unity and communion together.

The icon, or image, of the Holy Trinity is an expression of the Orthodox Church's adoration of the Living God. Andrei Rublev, the Russian Orthodox monk who painted the icon of the Trinity (c.1422, Plate 8), intended it as an affirmation of life amid all the daily forces of death during the Tartar domination. In the Orthodox tradition, icons are a kind of spiritual window between earth and heaven. Through the icons, the worshipping congregation contemplates the heavenly beings and establishes a spiritual link with them.

So the golden background of the icon represents the heavenly aura that surrounds God and the saints of God. To look through the window of the icon with the eyes of faith is to look into the heavens beyond.

In faithfulness to this profound devotional piety, the theologians of the early Church, meditating on the mystery of the Incarnation of God, found even in the Old Testament texts which speak about prefigurations of the Holy Trinity. They settled on a passage in Genesis, chapter 18, that deals with a mysterious visit of three angels to Abraham in the grove of Mamre. This visit was taken to signify a manifestation of the Holy Trinity. The Orthodox liturgical commentary says: "Blessed Abraham, thou hast seen and received the One and Triune Godhead."

Through lines and colours, the icon of the Trinity conveys the glory of the living God who revealed Himself by the oaks of Mamre. The blue symbolizes the divinity of all Three. The gold of their halos symbolizes their holiness; the royal sceptres, the Lordship of all Three. At the same time, each Person is differentiated by attitude or by relationship to the two others and by the colours assigned to each. Similarity and difference, rest and movement, youth and maturity, joy and

---

● This text was prepared for the Sixth Assembly of the World Council of Churches in Vancouver, Canada, July-August 1983.

compassion, restraint and pity, eternity and history, these all come together. There is no separation or confusion or subordination of the Persons.

The figures of the Son and the Holy Spirit are turned towards the Father, who is the Source of their life and whom they call: "Abba!" or "Father" (Mark 14:36, Gal. 4:6). The Father exists to give life eternally to the Son and the Holy Spirit. The Son and the Holy Spirit exist from all eternity since the Father has given Himself to them throughout all eternity. The Son and the Holy Spirit are living because they give themselves in turn to the Father. Each Person lives only for the others. None can be thought of in isolation from the two others. Each lives the life of the others and gives Himself totally to the others in such a way that each of the persons of the Trinity is in the others (John 17:21).

That flow of love within the Trinity can also be seen in the history of salvation in which the process of salvation and sanctification of the world is accomplished in the flow of love. The faces of the three Persons whose eyes are centred on the cup of crucified love are expressive of infinite tenderness, compassion and pity.

The Father clothed in glazed gold is the Person taking the initiative. The position of the right hand is suggestive of an act of giving and sending. Burning with love, the Father gives the Son for the world (John 3:16). The Father sends the Son and the Holy Spirit into the created world in order to involve the world within the divine life. This is symbolized by the tree that is drawn into the movement of the response by the Son and the Spirit to the Father.

While the Father gives the Son for the life of the world, the Son having become human gives Himself to the Father as a sacrifice for the sin and life of the world. The garment of blood red symbolizes the Son's assumption of human form with His body and blood offered in the Eucharist. That is why He is for all eternity our High Priest bearing the golden stole as the sign of the glory of his sacrificial love. In Rublev's icon, the Person of the Son stands out because He came nearer to us, even becoming one of us.

The Father gives the cup, the Son blesses it and sanctifies it by the gift of Himself, and then the Holy Spirit transmits it to the world, being the personal Spirit of the communion (2 Cor. 13:3). The Spirit, clothed in translucent green, transmits to the world the life given by God which is divine life. Hence the Spirit is the giver of life or life-giving (Rom: 8:2).

Empowered by the Holy Spirit and touched by the love of the Father and the Son, we call Christ "Lord" and cry to the Father "Abba!" (Rom. 8:15). The indivisible Trinity is thereby the model and source of the Church's unity: "May they all be one, as we are one" (John 17:21-22), prayed the Incarnate Son about His disciples to the Father.

This image of the divine Trinity rules out all egotism — whether individual or collective — all life-destroying separation, any subordination or levelling of persons. It invites all humanity to make this world a permanent eucharist of love, a feast of life. Created in God's image (Gen. 1:26), humanity is called to live in the image of the divine life and to share its daily bread together.

In the midst of the Holy Trinity is the Word of Life made flesh, Christ crucified and raised for the life of the world. In confessing "Jesus Christ — the Life of the World", Christians affirm both the sovereignty of the Risen Lord and the universal scope of his reign.

There is a cosmic thrust in the New Testament which declares that "all of God's fullness" is revealed in Christ and that "all things" are to be reconciled through Christ (Eph. 1:9-10; Col. 1:15-20; Heb. 1:1-3).

The cup which he blesses and offers to the world signifies the life which has become "eucharist" (*eucharistia*, thanksgiving): the gift of oneself for others and in communion with others. The cup, which in the Orthodox tradition contains both the bread and the wine, is the central message of this icon for the life of the world. The lack of daily bread, for which Christ taught us to pray, brings hunger, starvation and death to a world that is now unjustly divided between the rich and the poor. Here is the meeting of ecumenics and economics. The Eucharistic cup calls for a daily sharing of bread and of material and spiritual resources with the millions of hungry people in this world. Through them God, the Trinity, comes on pilgrimage to us at every moment.

Perfect Unity in Community, supreme Source of Life, most blessed Holy Trinity, Glory be to You. Amen.

"Jesus Christ — the Life of the World" in Orthodox Iconography

AMBROSIUS

Word and image

To my monastery come about 100,000 visitors each year. The majority of them are Protestants, and the question that they ask most frequently is how we see the basic differences between the churches. This is how we answer: when a Protestant minister delivers a sermon, he may conclude it by saying: "The Lord is good, think about it." What should an Orthodox priest say, if he takes the trouble to deliver a sermon? He could well say: "Come and taste and see how good the Lord is!"

The Western Church has traditionally emphasized a certain individualism in the proclamation of the Word, employing scholastic categories and even logical or rationalist arguments in the debate over the existence of God. In the East, however, this has not been the case. During certain periods, the Western Church has also enjoyed a close relationship with pictorial art and literature, although the Eastern Church has traditionally laid greater emphasis on the pictorial image.

In the icons of the Orthodox church, the dynamic aspect of the Church's faith is visible. They are expressions of the continuous working of God in the Church, and its art and theology. The icon painter is not a copyist, merely a mechanistic hand of the Holy Spirit. His art is derived from the ancient practices and iconographical canon of the Church of the Councils.

Picture and word express the same reality in the proclamation of the Church. According to Basil the Great, "that which the word communicates by sound, the painting shows silently by representation". The spoken word, however, soon reveals its limitations. As the 20th-century philosopher Ludwig Wittgenstein wrote: "In my innermost self I am a painter, and often a very bad painter."

The art of icon painting is always related to other forms of art. One could say that all art is an attempt to articulate the objective structure of the cosmos. All art (not merely icons) has a tendency to the metaphysical and therefore is ultimately bound to go beyond the limits of present reality. For this reason and in this sense, art is necessarily in part eschatological. Icons are liturgical art, and as such are particularly significant expressions of Christological truths. The function of the icon is also to reflect the Christian world-view, upon which it depends for its intelligibility and great, even unique, significance. For the icon aims to open our

---

● This article appeared in *Jesus Christ the Life of the World*, ed. Ion Bria, Geneva, WCC, 1982, pp.76-84.

eyes to a deeper world beyond our grasp and to make it meaningful to our limited senses. As we, in a Protestant environment, say in the Orthodox Church of Finland: "The icon is a window to eternity."

Konrad Raiser has written:

> To confess Jesus Christ as the life of the world means speaking today about the mystery of Incarnation. The theme compels us to listen again to the testimony of the doctors of the Church... God became human that we might partake of what He is, that we might share His life. Life finds its fulfilment in the eternal vision, in the presence of God.

What other aspect of the witness of the church can show this in such concrete and universal terms as the icons, which break through the many limitations of the spoken word, especially today when much of Western society and even Christianity is tired of verbal communication?

Icons and the Incarnation

Iconography is based on the Incarnation of Christ. Because Christ became man, the incorporeal, invisible, immaterial and uncircumscribed God has become corporeal, visible, material and circumscribed in Christ. To the Church, the Incarnation is historical reality and the foundation of salvation. In defending icons and their veneration, the Fathers of the Councils drew upon the tradition of Christ's human nature in the Incarnation.

God is beyond description, but as Jesus says: "He who has seen me, has seen the Father" (John 14:9). For this reason we should be satisfied and happy with the image of Christ, because he has made the Father known to us. We describe and portray Christ and, by so doing, we adore him especially as the Triune God, not only as one part of the Trinity.

Many iconographic themes describe the events of the earthly life of Jesus. In the creed we have a more elaborate treatment of the Son than of the Father and the Holy Spirit. The clarification of the Christological issues played a prominent role in the work of the theologians in the Ecumenical Councils. It is the same interest which points strongly towards Christological themes in iconography. On the other hand, this centring of interest in the second person of the Trinity was natural for the reason that this person came into the world as a man.

Icons safeguard a full and proper doctrine of the Incarnation. Fr Dumitru Staniloae emphasizes how icons of Christ serve as a "support and solid guide" whilst pointing towards "the perfect image of God which is the humanity of Christ, that is, Christ as man", and the icons counterbalance the human tendency towards forming an image of Christ in human imagination. On the other hand, the icons serve as continuous reminders of the full humanity of Christ against much of contemporary theistic interpretation of Christian faith in modern European religion.

Icons as part of the Church's teaching

Those iconographic themes which describe Jesus are basically of two kinds. First, the descriptions of the events of the Gospel, where Jesus lives and works among men. These have no special doctrinal emphasis. Second, various icons which aim to transmit to us the central doctrinal elements of the Incarnation — Baptism, Transfiguration, Crucifixion, Resurrection and Ascension.

Within early Christian circles, Christ was often depicted symbolically as a fish, anchor or lamb. Gradually these were replaced by representations in human form, especially after the Synod of Trullo in 692, which expressed the conviction that the time for portraying Christ in symbolic form had passed. In the 4th century, images of Christ had been made showing him as teacher, preacher, shepherd, judge or king. Clarity was sought over the form in which Christ was to be depicted, particularly as such representations were used in the instruction of the unlettered. The movement towards the domination of the human representation coincided with the decline of persecution against the early church and flourished during the later establishment of Christianity as the imperial state religion.

The two dominant images of Christ at that time were based upon Old Testament prophecies and have repeatedly come down to us through the texts of the Church Fathers. One view drawn from Isaiah saw Christ as "a man of sorrows and acquainted with grief" (53:3). The other view, revealed in the Psalms of David, emphasized the beauty and nobility of the Messiah as the Son of Man: "You are the fairest of the sons of men, grace is poured upon your lips; therefore God has blessed you forever" (45:2).

In fact, the whole of icon painting with Christ as its theme can be placed between these two views which, when synthesized, reveal Christ as the God-Man, who combined in his Incarnation the likeness of the Transfiguration with that of the slave.

Although the style of icon painting can reflect the different ages and societies within which it has been practised (for example, contrast Byzantine with 19th-century Romantic forms), artists have usually taken great care to remain truthful in spirit to Scripture and Tradition. Take, for example, the common representations of Christ in icons as Pantokrator, which finds its inspiration already in the writings of prophets such as Ezekiel, Isaiah, Daniel and King David:

> Be exalted, O God, above the heavens! Let thy glory be over all the earth! (Ps. 108:5)

and

> The Lord reigns, He is clothed with majesty (Ps. 93:1).

The same theme is expressed repeatedly in the New Testament, for example in the Annunciation to the Virgin Mary by Archangel Gabriel:

> He will be great, and will be called the son of the most high; and the Lord God will give to him the throne of his father David, and he will reign over the house of Jacob for ever; and of his kingdom there will be no end (Luke 1:32-33).

On the other hand, in front of Pilate, Jesus replied to the question of whether he was the king of the Jews thus: "My kingdom is not of this world" (John 18:36). It is exactly this Christ who is described in much Orthodox iconography — this Christ whose kingdom transcends time and space, reaching through all the world. He is the Pantokrator, whose hand blesses all creation: "He is the image of the invisible God, the First-Born of all creation" (Col. 1:15).

Icons pointing towards contemplation

Icons serve also as permanent reminders to "one-dimensional man" of the contemporary Western world that the human being has been created in the image of God, and that one's vocation is to grow in the likeness of God. Icons of Christ and of many saints in the history of the Church serve as concrete examples and models in this process. This spiritual growth towards purification, illumination and theosis requires time, silence, solitude, self-examination, things which used to be practised during the many centuries of our Church life by many of the Fathers, in the deserts of the Mediterranean, and likewise in the wilderness of the northern European forests. Unfortunately our churches today are busy with so many things that contemporary people are not given enough models for this kind of life-style. Our image of Jesus tends to point towards another direction: he is the permanently active miracle-worker, always among the people, saving them, forgiving their sins, healing them, travelling continually with his disciples, preaching here and there.

In fact many icons describe Jesus this way, and for this reason he is often represented as busy and hard-working. What we easily forget is that Jesus was frequently in solitude, praying by himself or with his disciples, retiring from the crowds seeking words and signs from him. He was a man who prayed in solitude, who climbed a mountain to reflect on his vocation, and to reflect on the world he lived in, and to prepare for the most unique sacrifice that he gave for us and for the life of the world.

This meditative and retiring aspect of Jesus is recorded in the Gospels, but strangely enough, we do not much emphasize this aspect of him, even in the Orthodox church.

Icons and the history of salvation

In icons we describe Christ, the saints of the Old and New Testaments and the Church, and many great events from the vast drama of salvation history. In this history three phases can be recognized.

Firstly, there are the prophecies of the Old Covenant. Even the title of G. Barrois's book, *The Face of Christ in the Old Testament,* refers to this. In the patristic age the Fathers and the icon painters both knew the invisible form of God in the Old Testament as revealed and depicted for example in the three angels who visited Abraham. This Old Testament trinity has been best pictured in the icon of Andrei Rublev, and this very icon has become one of the most classical and splendid examples of later Byzantine iconography. Yet in the opinion of Fr Staniloae, in the Old Testament God only appeared in passing in a visible form in one or other of his energies. This can be seen for example in the cloud or the pillar of fire which led the Israelites in the desert (Ex. 13:21-22), or in the fire which consumed the sacrifice of Elijah, or in the still voice revealed to Elijah (1 Kings 18:38-39, 19:11-13).

Secondly, the New Testament reveals the human face of Christ, and the permanent humanity of Christ. This idea has been the subject of innumerable icons portraying Jesus' earthly life and mission. Yet these do not use the techniques of naturalistic portraiture; rather, they adopt the perspectives of the Gospel writers, setting forth his humanity, his personality, his whole being, in the perspective of the resurrection faith.

Thirdly, the Gospels take us to the era of the early Church, indeed they are a product of that Church. They reveal Christ transfigured and resurrected. He is the Pantokrator by whose hands heaven and earth, all that is visible and invisible, were created and are sustained. Not just Christ, but the whole history of salvation is depicted on icons. Icons of saints are icons of the icons of Christ, and they all point towards Christ. Icons are always present, acting as "a point of meeting between the living members of the church and those who have gone before", writes Kallistos Ware. They help us to look on the saints not as legendary figures of the past, but as contemporaries, personal friends and examples.

Icons and the Church

"The icons which fill the church serve as a point of meeting between heaven and earth," adds Father Kallistos. Whilst we pray in church, we are "surrounded by the figures of Christ, the angels and the saints". These visible images remind us of "the invisible presence of the whole company of heaven" at the liturgy and in every act of worship.

The right milieu for icon painting is the Church, and it is the Church which accepts and cherishes the icons, by blessing them and incorporating them in its liturgical cycle. Over and above his personal skill the individual icon painter must practise constant prayer and the ascetic life-style of the Church. As Paul Evdokimov writes: "The icon painter is a charismatic who contemplates liturgical mysteries and teaches theology." "Because the icon is a part of the Tradition, the icon painter is not free to adapt or innovate as he pleases; for his work must reflect, not his own aesthetic sentiments, but the mind of the Church," says Kallistos Ware. This does not exclude his artistic inspiration, but it should be exercised within prescribed rules. In the Orthodox church, the painter and likewise the hymn writer transmit to us through their art a vision of the spiritual world, the common faith of the Church.

An icon painter's work has close connection with the task of the Church as the eucharistic community. Icons express the same mystery of life in Christ as the sacraments. The human being uses the material world to describe the indescribable perfection of God's creation. Earth, clay, stone, wood, ivory and precious metals are all of equal value in the Creator's eyes when they are used to express his holiness and holy work. Similarly, the Church uses incense, wax, oil, water, and seeds as the means for expressing God's grace. Jesus himself said that even the dead stones are prepared to proclaim the glory of God (Luke 19:40).

The prayer of the prophet-king David, while blessing the material to be used in building the temple at Jerusalem: "for all things come from thee, and of thy own we have given thee" (1 Chron. 29:14), has great significance when we reflect on icons on which the image of God is painted. These words of David take on an even deeper meaning in the Holy Eucharist, as the priest elevates the elements and says: "We offer thee thine own, in all and for all." In the same way, what is offered as a gift to God in the form of an icon emphasizes the icon's liturgical meaning. By using the materials from nature in icons, the Orthodox repeatedly express their conviction that physical matter is equally part of God's creation and care, and as such good.

Creation

The icon is above all an object of veneration, to be used in churches, homes, cars and processions, representing in clear terms the doxological nature of the Christian faith, the vision and the praise of God. The Seventh Ecumenical Council declared icons as possessing "theopneystia", that is, the breath of the living God, and to be equal in status as objects of veneration with the cross of the Lord and the Holy Gospels. The Bible, particularly the Gospels, are the written icons of Christ, since both Scripture and icons are part of the same Tradition. This can already be seen at the beginning of the divine liturgy of St John Chrysostom when, during the service of preparation, the priest and the deacon go before an icon of Christ and say: "We venerate thy most pure icon, good Lord, seeking forgiveness of our sins."

The lighting of candles, making the sign of the cross, incense, kissing the gospel, venerating the icons and carrying them in processions, kneeling and prostration — these are all part of the adoration given to God and the Life-giver, Jesus Christ.

The liturgical function of icons is also to bring the believer into the milieu of eschatological expectation. This anticipation is described in the design of the icon which radiates the unceasing light of eternity. The aim of the icon painter is to express this in the icon by the methods of painting. In doing so he tries to paint the icon in such a way that the light seems to come through the back of the painting. In some of the best products of our icon heritage, light spreads through the whole painting, showing and pointing towards the divine light of the transfiguration, which the icon shows as shining through all creation.

The Orthodox doctrine of icons is bound up with the Orthodox belief that the whole of God's creation, material as well as spiritual, is to be redeemed and glorified. Nicholas Zernov says:

> (Icons are) dynamic manifestations of man's spiritual power to redeem creation through beauty and art. (By using definite colours and modes of expression) the artists aimed at demonstrating that men, animals, and plants, and the whole cosmos could be rescued from their present state of degradation and restored to their proper "image". The (icons) were pledges of the coming victory of a redeemed creation over the fallen one.

Yet, potentially, Orthodox icons include this aspect of inwardness and permanent values so much longed for by contemporary Western culture. The icons serve communicative and charismatic functions, but even more, they are definite corner-stones of the contemplative nature of man. They always point beyond the visible world, even beyond the images of the invisible world, to the depth of the mystery of God. It is exactly this kind of mystical search which is so common, especially among young people today, the young people who are eager to make journeys from Western Europe and America to the pilgrim centres of Asian religions, and to a certain extent also to the monasteries and retreat centres of our own church. This search, which is typical of our time, is a sign of the need for contemplative religion, and of a reaction against the materialistic world. Icons point to this mystery of man, which can be grasped in meditation and prayer, transfiguring and pointing beyond even much of the ritualistic religion so often over-emphasized in our Orthodox heritage.

The search was evident for a more contemplative and iconocentric religion in the West during the last decade, and on a certain level this can be interpreted as a reaction against the politically and socially oriented Christianity of the 1960s. Such Christianity cannot satisfy the spiritually open and thirsty young people who seek a permanent, profound basis for life in mystical religion, and a peaceful and just world, through non-violence and the rejection of the "haste and waste" life-style. It is ironic that even the Magnificat, that great hymn of humble acceptance of God's will and deep contemplation of his great mercies, has been made a kind of hymn for politically oriented Christians — a kind of "internationale", which over-emphasizes the social and political tasks and vocation of the Church.

The Orthodox Christian may, in an ideal sense, look also at his or her own time and contemporaries as an icon of God, and henceforth as an image of Christ. It is a pity for this reason that many puritanical representatives of iconographical art draw too strict borderlines between the art of the Church and other expressions of life. In and through icons we learn to see the hidden beauty of the world in time and history. "I shall not cease to venerate matter, for it was through matter that my salvation came to pass," writes St John of Damascus. The icons and various other symbols of humanity point in the same direction, to "the Heavenly King, the Paraclete, the Spirit of Truth, everywhere present and filling all things, the treasury of blessings and giver of life", whom we pray to "come and abide in us, cleanse us from every stain and of his goodness save our souls". For the sake of our humanity, we also need symbols of imperfection and protest and there are enough of these in each of us!

The Orthodox church emphasizes the overall significance of the victory of Christ over death as the eschatological event which inaugurates the metahistorical era. "The hour is coming, and now is, when the dead will hear the voice of the Son of God, and those who hear will live" (John 5:25). This same state where natural chronological time has lost its importance is also depicted in the icons, and iconography strongly emphasizes this eschatological time of the Church.

The icons point towards those holy Fathers and Mothers of the Church who have achieved this reality in Christ and already participate in the life of the world. Icons are eschatological signposts for the future where "God shall be in all". In this sense human history matures not only for judgment but also for consummation. By voluntary and active participation human beings become and are already part of this cosmic process towards maturity and apokatastasis which will be realized in the second coming of Christ. Of this future the Bible speaks in images and parables. In the parallel sense icons witness to us the unceasing life which has already been achieved by "the faithful departed, forefathers, fathers, patriarchs, prophets, apostles, preachers, evangelists, martyrs, confessors, ascetics and every righteous spirit made perfect in the faith". They also remind us of and point to the Church Triumphant against which "the gates of hell shall not prevail".

The Valamo Mother of God

ARCHBISHOP PAUL

Behold, from henceforth all generations shall call me blessed (Luke 1:48).

Although Valamo monastery had existed for hundreds of years, it did not have an icon bearing its own name until the last half of the 19th century.

The 19th century was a lively period of building at the monastery. At that time many subsidiary monasteries, or sketes, were built in the Valamo archipelago, and a new and larger church was constructed for the main monastery. Valamo had a group of distinguished masters and a large number of workers in its icon-painting workshop. The new main church was decorated with paintings executed in the style of the time, deviating from the traditional art of the icon. At the same time the monastery also acquired a new type of icon of the Virgin. Unlike traditional icons, it is painted in oils in the Western manner, and other features also display the Western influence — for instance, the fact that the Mother of God is represented standing on a cloud. This icon became Valamo's namesake. It bears the date on which it was finished, 17 October 1878, and the words "the work of Valamo monks". It is said that the icon was painted by the priest-monk Alipi.

The Valamo Mother of God has not become widely known, but for visitors to the monastery, at new Valamo as well, it is like a symbol of the monastery itself.

The Synod of the bishops of the Orthodox Church of Finland, in its session on 28 January 1987, resolved that the annual feast day for the veneration of the icon of Our Lady of Valamo is to be celebrated on 7 August.

Theotokos, Virgin,
we rejoice looking at your holy icon,
for in front of it, on the island of Valamo,
fervent prayers were fulfilled
and the exhausted strength of the ascetics renewed.
Hear, O most pure one, also our supplications,
strengthen us in faith and love
beseeching peace for the world
and great mercy for our souls.

A Great Iconographer and Theologian: Leonid Ouspensky (1902-1987)

CONSTANTINE SCOUTERIS

When the Grand Prince St Vladimir received holy baptism and the Russian people not merely became adherents of Orthodox Christianity but embraced it with their whole heart, with their whole mind and with their whole soul, a new chapter was opened in the life of the Body of Christ. Although the contributions of Russia to the common inheritance of the Orthodox over the past millenium are beyond number, it is perhaps most particularly for her iconography that she is warmly and lovingly remembered by the world at large. Therefore, I deem it appropriate to dedicate this brief paper to Leonid Ouspensky, one of the greatest contemporary masters of iconography and true son of Orthodox Russia and, more precisely, to the patristic foundation of his theology.

The theologian and iconographer, "the servant of God", Ouspensky passed away in Paris on the night of 11-12 December 1987. He was born into a peasant family in the city of Golosnovka in the province of Voronege. At the age of 25, he moved to Paris, where he devoted his entire life to the indefatigable and inspired work of iconography which he passionately loved. Not deeming it a mere technique, a craft, he carefully studied its patristic foundation, producing remark-able theological treatises and books.[1] His entire theological attitude was in complete harmony with the spirit and the ethos of Orthodox life. This vision he communicated to many students from all over the world, teaching them the theology of icons, the art of iconography and the restoration of icons. The man, Leonid Ouspensky, whom it was my very great honour to know personally, was the living embodiment of the Orthodox servant of God. Through his word and through his silence, through his iconography and through his simple, ascetic way of living, Ouspensky edified all who met him. Living in the midst of a society which valued above all worldly success and achievement, his quiet, gentle witness eloquently proclaimed the Orthodox *phronema*.

Ouspensky's catholic vision of Orthodox tradition

When we study the writings of Ouspensky, we are struck by his catholic and comprehensive vision of the Orthodox patristic tradition. His theological works are not simply filled with patristic references and quotations but are alive with the

---

● This paper was presented to the Third International Conference on Russian Orthodox Liturgical Life and Art, 31 January-5 February 1988, Leningrad, USSR.

spirit of the Fathers. His entire effort was not to amass citations to support his arguments but, rather, to grasp and to reveal clearly the power and depth of patristic thought. He uses material from the writings of the Fathers, from the hymnology of the Church and from the acts and definitions of the Ecumenical Councils, combining them with biblical data in a way which reveals his knowledge as well as his overall and extensive vision of the Orthodox inheritance. We may say without hesitation that Ouspensky's theology arises from within the Orthodox patristic tradition. For him tradition is not a mere hankering back to the past, but rather a voice with eternal significance. Tradition is not antiquarianism, esoteric archeology or even a simple reference to the past, but a reality ever-young and ever-relevant to the human condition. Fidelity to tradition does not mean for Ouspensky simply an acceptance and a recognition of the historic past but also a genuine and vital presentation of the inheritance of the Church in every historical age and to every cultural and all national circumstances. He puts it beautifully in one of his works when he says:

> The Church does not reject particularities connected with human nature or with time and place (for example national, personal or other features), but sanctifies their content, filling it with new meaning. In their turn, these particularities do not interfere with the unity of the Church, but bring into it new forms of expression, peculiar to them. In this way, it realizes that unity in multiplicity and richness in unity, which both in totality and in detail expresses the catholic principle of the Church. As applied to the language of art, it means not uniformity or a certain general, stereotyped manner, but the expression of a single truth in varied forms of art appropriate to every people, time and individual man, forms which allow us to distinguish between icons of differing nationalities and differing epochs, despite the similarity of their content. [2]

I think that passage of Ouspensky is very indicative of his theological approach as well as of his work as an iconographer. It demonstrates that his entire effort was to present the richness both of patristic theology and of Orthodox iconography, not in a sterile and stereotyped manner but in fresh ways, relevant to the needs of people today.

His ecclesiastical consciousness

It is self-evident from what has been pointed out above that Ouspensky was working from within the Church and in the service of the Church. His theology was never an exercise in subjective philosophizing, a speculation concerning doctrinal and aesthetic issues. He especially uses material from those Fathers who have written treatises defending the use and veneration of icons: St John of Damascus, St Theodore the Studite, Sts Germanus and Nicephorus of Constantinople, and, of course, from the Acts of the Seventh Ecumenical Council. However, he continually strives to present the Orthodox faith in fresh and vital ways. His work was indeed a diakonia within the body of the Church for the spiritual benefit of the people of God. Likewise, he never understood iconography to be a mere art, not even a "religious" art, but a way to proclaim the Gospel. His work as an artist is not an end in itself, but rather points beyond itself. "The fundamental principle of this art", he affirms, "is a pictorial expression of the teaching of the Church, by representing concrete events of sacred history and indicating their inner meaning."[3] Thus icons are not fundamentally intended to satisfy the inner human search for beauty but, rather, to arouse repentance and compunction.

The ecclesiastical basis of his theology of icons and iconography is well illustrated by the following passage:

> The Orthodox Church has preserved intact an immense wealth in the areas of liturgy and of patristic thought, as well as in that of sacred art. It is well known that the veneration of icons holds among the Orthodox a very important place. This is because the icon is not a simple image, neither a decoration nor even an illustration of Holy Scripture. It is something more: ... a cultic object which forms an integral part of her liturgical life; hence, the importance which the Church attributes to the image: not to religious images in general, but to a specific image which she herself has elaborated in the course of her history, especially in her fight against paganism and against heresy, an image for which she, during the iconoclastic period, has paid dearly through the blood of a great many martyrs and confessors, to the Orthodox icon. In the icon, the Church sees not merely one of the facets of Orthodox teaching, but the expression of Orthodoxy in its totality, of Orthodoxy itself. Thus, one can neither understand nor explain the sacred image from outside of the Church. The icon, sacred image, is one of the manifestations of the tradition of the Church, in the same sense as written and oral tradition.[4]

The doctrinal character of his theology

A true follower of the patristic tradition, Ouspensky firmly bases his investigation concerning the theology of icons upon the Church's teachings. Throughout the prolonged iconoclastic controversy, it was stressed in varying ways that the Church's use of icons forms an integral part of the doctrine of the Incarnation of the eternal Logos of God; thus, the teaching about it has a Christological dimension.

The main questions confronted by both Orthodox and iconoclasts during the iconoclastic controversy could be formulated as follows: Was God's incarnate Logos circumscribed or uncircumscribed? The iconoclasts declared that Christ was uncircumscribed as God-Man; thus the unity of divinity and humanity allowed no room for his depiction. According to the position of the iconoclastic theologians as expressed at the Council of Hieria (754), an iconographer painting an icon of Christ represents either his humanity, separating it from his divinity, or both the humanity and divinity of the incarnate Logos. In the first case, he is a follower of Nestorios; while in the second, he confuses divinity and humanity and thus falls into the Monophysite error. Even worse, he assumes that the uncircumscribed divine nature can be circumscribed by his humanity, which is of course blasphemy. Although at first glance these arguments may appear reasonable, it is evident that the iconoclasts did not understand clearly that an icon represents neither the one nor the two natures of Christ, but *His Person*, since an icon can only be a personal (hypostatic) representation. The Christological discussions between Orthodox and iconoclasts are preserved for us in the writings of the Fathers of the iconoclastic period as well as in the Acts of the Seventh Ecumenical Council.

Ouspensky is fully aware of this patristic perspective and presents it in a lucid way, often drawing upon the hymnology of the Church which he considers a concise summary of the Fathers' teachings. For example, he often cites the Kontakion for the Sunday of Orthodoxy, which he considers to be the most comprehensive statement of the Seventh Ecumenical Council's teaching concerning the icons:

> The uncircumscribed Word of the Father became circumscribed, taking flesh from thee, O Theotokos; and He has restored the sullied image to its ancient glory, filling it with the divine beauty. This our salvation we confess in deed and word, and we depict in the holy icons.[5]

The success and the enduring contribution of Ouspensky is that he helped the West, at both an academic and a popular level, to become aware of the Christological foundation of iconography. Having imbibed to the utmost the patristic heritage, he opened its treasures to modern Western people.

* * *

An appreciation for the depth and beauty of the Byzantine icon was not only unknown to the West but unfortunately forgotten in much of the Orthodox world. Leonid Ouspensky is one of the chief contributors to the contemporary revival of interest in Byzantine iconography. His writings in modern Western languages have been eagerly read by Orthodox and non-Orthodox alike. In fact, not a few men and women have been led to holy Orthodoxy thereby. This revival in Orthodox iconography has also borne fruit in the Greek-speaking world. Its chief proponent was Photios Kontoglou, himself an accomplished iconographer and author. It is significant that, in spite of a difference in culture and style, these two great pioneers were personal friends and collaborators. Thus, we see again the wonder of the communion in the Spirit which we share in the one Body of Christ.

NOTES

[1] Leonid Ouspensky and Vladimir Lossky, *The Meaning of Icons*, Boston, Boston Book and Art Shop, 1952, p.30; and Léonide Ouspensky, *La théologie de l'icône dans l'Eglise orthodoxe*, Paris, Les Editions du Cerf, 1980, p.9.
[2] *The Meaning of Icons, op. cit.*, p.30.
[3] *Ibid.*, p.29.
[4] *La théologie de l'icône dans l'Eglise orthodoxe, op. cit.*, p.9.
[5] *The Meaning of Icons, op. cit.*, p.33.

Bibliography

There is a rich bibliography in relation to the subjects dealt with in this publication, and the following is very selective and incomplete. However, our endeavour has been made to be ecumenical, and rather to cover the field by citing contributions related directly or indirectly to the Seventh Ecumenical Council and articles which have contributed to the understanding of the meaning of icons, their spirituality and art. We would like to apologize for any omissions.

Gennadios Limouris

P.J. Alexander, *The Patriarch Nicephorus of Constantinople, Ecclesiastical Policy and Image Worship in the Byzantine Empire*, Oxford, 1957.

P.J. Alexander, "Church, Councils and Patristic Authority: the Iconoclastic Councils of Hieria (754) and St Sophia (815)", in *Harvard Studies of Classical Philology*, 431, 1958, pp.493-505.

A.M. Allchin, "Anglicans and the Decisions of the Seventh Ecumenical Council", in *Sobornost*, 7, 1958, pp.588-594.

M.V. Alpatov, *Early Russian Icon Painting*, Moscow, 1978.

C. Argenti, "La signification des icônes dans la Tradition", in *SOEPI (Mensuel)*, 40, 1987, pp.15-16.

A.H. Armstrong, "Some Comments on the Development of the Theology of Images", in *Studia Patristica*, IX, TU t. 94, pp.117-129.

C. Aslanoff, "Icônes miraculeuses et apparitions de la Vierge", in *La vie spirituelle*, 140, 1986, pp.663-668.

J. Audebert, "L'icône, présence de Dieu", in *La vie spirituelle*, 140, 1986, pp.631-637.

J. Baggley, *Doors of Perception: Icons and their Spiritual Significance*, London & Oxford, Mowbray, 1987.

H.U. von Balthasar, *Kosmische Liturgie. Maximus der Bekenner: Höhe und Krise des griechischen Weltbildes*, Freiburg i.B., Herder, 1941.

R.B. Bandinelli, R.B., *Archeologia e Cultura*, Milan, 1961.

R. B. Bandinelli, "Rome and the Late Empire Art A.D. 200-400", in *The Arts of Mankind*, eds André Malraux and André Parrot, New York, George Brailler, 1971.

P. Batiffol, *L'Eglise naissante et le catholicisme*, Paris, 1911.

N.H. Baynes, "The Icons before Iconoclasm", in *Harvard Theological Review*, 44, 1951, pp.93-106.

H.G. Beck, *Kirche und theologische Literatur im byzantinischen Reich*, Munich, 1959.

217

J. Beckwith, *The Art of Constantinople*, London, Phaidon Ltd, 1980.

St. Beissel, *Vatikanische Miniaturen*, Freiburg i.B., 1893.

E. Benz, "Theologie der Ikone und des Ikonoklasmus", in *Kerygma und Mythos*, VI/2, 1964, Hamburg, pp.75-102.

S. Bettini, *Mosaici di San Marco*, Milan, 1968.

St. Bigham, "Death and Orthodox Iconography", in *St Vladimir's Theological Seminary Quarterly*, 4, 1985, pp.325-341.

O. Bihalyi-Merin, *Fresques et icônes*, Munich, 1958.

R. Blumenkranz, *Le juif médieval au miroir de l'art chrétien*, Paris, 1966.

B. Bobrinskoy, "The Icon: Sacrament of the Kingdom", in *St Vladimir's Theological Quarterly*, 4, 1987, pp.287-296.

F. Boespflug, *Dieu dans l'art*, Paris, Le Cerf, 1986.

F. Boespflug & N. Lossky, *Nicée II*, Paris, Le Cerf, 1987.

G. Bouini, *Ravenna*, transl. R.W. Wolf, New York, Harry N. Abrams, Inc., 1972.

L. Brehier, "Les caractères généraux et la portée de la réforme iconoclaste", in *Revue des cours et conférences*, 11/4, 1901, pp.226-235.

L. Brehier, *La querelle des images (VIIIe-IXe siècles)*, Paris, 1904.

L. Brehier, *L'art chrétien, son développement iconographique*, Paris, 1928.

B. Brenk, "Die Anfänge der byzantinischen Weltgerichtsdarstellung", in *Byzantinische Zeitschrift*, 57, 1964.

P. Brown, "A Dark Age Crisis: Aspect of the Iconoclastic Controversy", in *The English Historical Review*, 88, 1973, pp.1-34.

A. Bryer/J. Herrin eds, *Iconoclasm*, Birmingham, 1977.

E. de Bryne, *The Esthetics of the Middle Ages*, trans. Eileen B. Hennessy, New York, Frederick Ungar, 1969.

V.V. Bychkov, "Obraz kak kategoriya vizantiiskoi estetiki (The Image as a Category of Byzantine Aesthetics)", in *Vizantiiskii Vremennik*, 34, 1973 (in Russian).

V.V. Bychkov, *Iz istorii vizantiiskoi estetiki (From the History of Byzantine Aesthetics)*, 37, 1976 (in Russian).

R. Byron & D. Talbot Rice, *The Birth of Western Painting*, London, 1930.

P.Th. Camelot, *Le Concile et les Conciles*, Chevetogne, 1960.

P.Th. Camelot, "Jean de Damas, défenseur des Saintes Images", in *La vie spirituelle*, 140, 1986, pp.638-650.

R. Carpentier, *The Esthetic Basis of Greek Art*, Bloomington, IN, Indiana University Press, 1959.

C. Cavarnos, *Byzantine Sacred Art*, New York, 1957.

C. Cavarnos, *Byzantine Thought and Art*, Belmont, 1968 and 1974.

C. Cavarnos, *Orthodox Iconography*, Institute for Byzantine and Modern Greek Studies, 1977.

M.A. Charles, "Hagia Sophia and the Great Imperial Mosques", in *The Art Bulletin*, XII/4, 1930, pp.325ff.

O. Clément, *Le visage intérieur*, Paris, Ed. Stock, 1978.

O. Clément, "L'icône — visage tranfiguré", in *Espace*, 5, 1979, pp.15-22.

H. de la Croix and R.G. Ransey, *Gardiner's Art through the Ages*, New York, Harcourt, Brace & World, Inc., 1970.

A. Cutler, "The Problem of Realism in Byzantine Literature and Art", rev. of "The Art of the Byzantine Empire, 312-1453", by C. Mango, in *Byzantine Studies*, I/2, 1974, pp.190-193.

O. Dalton, *Byzantine Art and Archeology*, Oxford, 1981.

J. Darrouzes, "Listes épiscopales du Concile de Nicée (787)", in *Revue des études byzantines*, 33, 1975, pp.5-76.

M.-M. Davy, *Essai sur le symbolique romane*, Paris, 1955.

N. Demine, *La Trinité d'André Roublev*, Moscow, 1963 (in Russian).

O. Demus, *Byzantine Mosaic Decoration*, London, 1948.

Ch. Diehl, "La renaissance de l'art byzantin au XIVe siècle", in *Byzantion*, 2, 1925/1926, pp.220ff.

Ch. Diehl, *La peinture byzantine*, Paris, 1933.

G. Drobot, *Icône de la Nativité*, Ed. Abbaye de Bellefontaine, 1975.

G. Drobot, "Icône et pédagogie", in *Espace*, 5, 1979, pp.25-27.

D. Dukas, "The Technique of Byzantine Icon Painting", in *The Greek Orthodox Theological Review*, Vol. II/1, 1956.

G. Dumeige, *Nicée II*, Paris, 1978.

C.-J. Dupont, OP, "L'inspiration théologique d'André Roublev dans l'icône dite de Trinité", in *La vie spirituelle*, 140, 1986, pp.669-677.

F. Dvornik, "The Patriarch Photius and Iconoclasm", in *Dumbarton Oaks Papers*, 7, 1953, pp.67-97.

Encyclique Patriarchal and Synodical (Ecumenical Patriarchate), at the occasion of the 1200th Anniversary of the Seventh Ecumenical Council (787-1987), Athens, 1987 (in Greek).

R. Erni, *Das Christusbild in der Ostkirche*, Lucern, 1963.

M. Evdokimov, *Lumières d'Orient*, Limoges, Droguet et Ardant, 1981.

P. Evdokimov, *L'art de l'icône, théologie de la beauté*, Desclée de Brouwer, 1970.

A. Fabre, "L'iconographie de la Pentecôte", in *Gazette des Beaux Arts*, Vol. VIII, 1923, pp.33ff.

R. de Feraudy, *L'icône de la Transfiguration (La Transfiguration dans l'art chrétien)*, Ed. Abbaye de Bellefontaine, 1978.

J. de la Ferrieres, "The Veneration of Icons in the Orthodox Church", in *Youth* (Newsletter of the Youth Office/WCC), Vol. II/2, 1987, p.3.

B.D. Filow, *L'art ancien bulgare*, Sofia, 1924.

J. Fink, "Die Anfänge der Christusdarstellung", in *Theologische Revue*, 51, 1955, pp.241-252.

Firathy-Nezih, *Iznik (Nicea)*, Istanbul, 1959.

P. Florenski, "Ikona", in *Le messager de l'Exarchat Russe en Europe Occidentale*, 65, 1969, pp.39-64 (in Russian).

P. Florenski, "On the Icon", translated from Russian with an introduction and notes by J. Lindsay Opie, in *Eastern Churches Review*, 8/1, 1976, pp.11-37.

G. Florovsky, *Vizantiiskie Ottsy V-VIII (Byzantine Fathers of the Fifth to Eighth Centuries)*, Paris, 1933 (in Russian).

G. Florovsky, "Origen, Eusebius and the Iconoclastic Controversy", in *Church History*, 19, 1950, pp.77-96.

D. de Fourna, *Manuel d'iconographie chrétienne*, Paris, Ed. M. Didron, 1845; Saint Petersburg, Ed. A. Papadopoulos-Kerameus, 1909.

219

A. Gardner, "Some Theological Aspects of the Iconoclastic Controversy", in *The Hibbert Journal*, 1, 1904, pp.360-374.

H.P. Gerhard, *The World of Icons*, London, 1971.

S. Gero, "Byzantine Iconcoclasm during the Reign of Leo III", in *Corpus Scriptorum Christianorum Orientali, Subsidia*, t. 41, Louvain, 1973.

S. Gero, "The Libri Carolini and the Image Controversy", in *Greek Orthodox Theological Review*, 18, 1973, pp.7-34.

A. Geza, "The Crisis of the Third Century", in *Greek/Roman and Byzantine Studies*, XV/1, 1974, pp.89ff.

C. Gotsis, *The Mystical World of Byzantine Icons*, Vol. 1-2, ed. Apostoliki Diaconia of Church of Greece, Athens, 1973 (in Greek).

A. Grabar, *La décoration byzantine*, Paris-Brussels, 1928.

G.H. Hamilton, *The Art and Architecture of Russia* (The Pelican History of Art), Baltimore, 1954.

S. Harakas, "Icons and Ethics", in *One World*, 131, 1987, pp.12-14.

J.J. von Hefele/H. Leclercq, *Histoire des Conciles*, Paris, 1907.

A. Hohlweg, "Byzantinischer Bilderstreit und das 7. Oekumenische Konzil. Hintergründe und geschichtlicher Umriss", in *Orthodoxes Forum*, 2, 1987, pp.191-208.

T. Hopko, "The Human Icon", in *One World*, 131, 1987, pp.14-15.

N. Iorga, "Les origines de l'iconoclasme, Académie Roumaine", in *Bulletin de la section historique*, 11, 1924, pp.142-155.

B. Istavrides, *The Seventh Ecumenical Council of Nicea II (787)*, Thessaloniki, 1987 (in Greek).

I. Itten, *L'art de la couleur*, Desain et Tolra, 1975.

E. Ivanka, *Hellenisches und Christliches im frühbyzantinischen Geistesleben*, Vienna, 1948.

G. de Jerphanion, "L'image de Jésus-Christ dans l'art chrétien", in *Nouvelle Revue Théologique*, 65, 1938, pp.257-282.

E. Kaegi, "The Byzantine Armies and Iconoclasm", in *Byzantinoslavica*, 27, 1966, pp.48-70.

C. Kallinikos, *Le temple chrétien et tout ce qui s'y déroule*, Athens, 1969 (in Greek).

C. Kalokyris, *The Essence of Orthodox Iconography*, Brookline, MA, Holy Cross School of Theology, 1971.

C. Kalokyris, *Introduction à l'archéologie chrétienne et byzantine*, Thessaloniki, 1985 (in Greek).

V. Karayiannis, *Le concept de l'icône dans l'Eglise orthodoxe*, ed. Tertios, 1987.

M. Karger, *Novgorod — Architectural Monuments 11th-17th Centuries*, Leningrad, 1975.

E. Kitzinger, "The Cult of Images in the Age before Iconoclasm", in *Dumbarton Oaks Papers*, 8, 1954, pp.83-150.

L. Koch, *Die altchristliche Bilderfrage nach den literarischen Quellen*, Göttingen, 1917.

L. Koch, "Zur Theologie der Christusikone", in *Bened. Monatsschrift*, 19, 1937, pp.375-387; 20, 1938, pp.32-47; 168-175; 281-288; 437-452.

Ph. Koutoglou, *Exphrasis tis Orthodoxou Eikonographias (Explanation of Orthodox Iconography)*, Vols. I-II, Athens, 1960 (in Greek).

G. Kretschmar, "Die Entscheidungen des 7. Oekumenischen Konzils und die Stellung der aus der Reformation hervorgegangenen Kirchen", in *Orthodoxes Forum*, I/2, 1987, pp.237-252.

G.I. Krug, *Carnets d'un peintre d'icônes*, Lausanne, Editions l'Age d'Homme, 1983.

L. Kueppers, *Göttliche Ikonen*, Düsseldorf, 1949.

G.B. Ladner, "The Concept of the Image in the Greek Fathers and the Byzantine Iconcoclastic Controversy", in *Dumbarton Oaks Papers*, 7, 1957, pp.1-34.

L. Lamza, *Patriarch Germanus I von Konstantinopel (715-730)*, Würzburg, 1975.

V. Lasarev, *Icônes russes*, UNESCO, Le Grand Art et Livres de Poche, Flammarion, 1962.

V. Lasarev, *The Moscow School of Icon Painting*, Moscow, Isskustro, 1971 (in Russian).

J. Lassus, *The Early Christian and Byzantine World*, London, Paul Hamlyn, 1967.

V. Laurent, "Eiconomachia", in *Byzantion*, 5, 1964, pp.395-405.

W.B. Lethaby and H. Swainson, *The Church of Sancta Sophia*, Constantinople, London, McMillan & Co., 1894.

G. Limouris, "The Apocalyptic Character and Dimension of the Icon in the Life of the Orthodox Church", in *The Greek Orthodox Theological Review*, 1987.

N. Lossky, "Windows on Heaven", in *One World*, 131, 1987, pp.10-11.

V. Lossky, *In the Image and Likeness of God*, London, A.R. Mowbray & Co. Ltd, 1957.

V. Lossky, *The Mystical Theological of the Eastern Church*, London, James Clark & Co. Ltd., 1957.

V. Lossky, *The Vision of God*, The Faith Press, 1963.

G. Luciano, *Arts de Cappadoce*, Geneva, Nagel, 1971.

H. Luetzeler, *Icons of the Saviour*, Fribourg, 1944.

G. Mango, "Materials for the Study of the Mosaics of Saint Sophia", in *Dumbarton Oaks Papers*, 8, 1962, Washington.

Mansi, *Sacrorum Conciliorum nova et amplissima collectio*, ed. D. Mansi, Vols. I-XXXI, Florence and Venice, 1759-1798.

J.L. Marion, *L'idole et la distance*, Ed. Grasset, 1977.

E.J. Martin, *History of the Iconoclastic Controversy*, London, 1930.

E.J. Martin, *A History of the Iconoclastic Controversy*, London, SPCK, 1949.

L. von Matt, *The Councils*, London, 1961.

G. Mercier, *L'art abstrait dans l'art sacré*, Paris, 1964.

J. Meyendorff, *Le Christ dans la théologie byzantine*, Paris, 1968.

K. Miatev, *Les peintures murales de Boïana*, Dresden-Sofia, 1961.

P.-A. Michelis, *Esthétique de l'art byzantin*, Paris, 1959.

A. Milton, "The Ethical Theory of Images Formulated by the Iconoclasts in 757 and 815", in *Dumbarton Oaks Papers*, 8, 1954, pp.152-160.

A. Milton, "The Argument for the Iconoclasm as Presented by the Iconoclastic Council of 754. Late Classic and Medieval Studies", in *Honour of A.M. Friend Jr*, Princeton, 1955, pp.177-188.

G. Millet, *Monuments byzantins de Mistra*, Paris, 1910.

P. Miquel, "Théologie de l'icône", in *Dictionnaire de spiritualité ascétique et mystique*, t. VIII/2, Paris, 1971, pp.1229-1239.

C.R. Morey, *Medieval Art*, New York, W.W. Norton & Co., 1942.

C.B. Moss, *The Church of England and the Seventh Council*, London, 1957.

P. Mouratoff, *Les icônes russes*, Paris, 1927.

S. Der Nersessian, "Une apologie des images du septième siècle", in *Byzantion*, 17, 1944/45, pp.58-87.

S. Der Nersessian, "Image Worship in Armenia and its Opponents", in *Armenian Quarterly*, 1, 1946, pp.67-81.

221

Th. Nikolaou, "The Place of the Icon in the Liturgical Life of the Orthodox Church", in *The Theology of Icon*, Acts of 18th Meeting of the Clergy of the Greek Orthodox Archdiocese of Western Germany, Bonn, 1984, pp.31-44 (in Greek).

Th. Nikolaou, "Die Entscheidungen des 7. Oekumenischen Konzils und die Stellung der Orthodoxen Kirche zu den Bildern", in *Orthodoxes Forum*, I/2, 1987, pp.209-223.

C. Norberg-Schulz, *Meaning in Western Architecture*, New York, Praeger Publications, 1975.

H.J.M. Nouwen, *Behold the Beauty of the Lord: Praying with Icons*, Indiana, Ave Maria Press, 1987.

G.A. Ostrogosky, "The Connection between the Question of the Holy Icons and Christological Dogmatics in Works of Apologists for Orthodoxy in the Early Period of Iconoclasm", in *Seminarium kondakorianum*, Vol. I, Prague, 1927 (in Russian).

G.A. Ostrogosky, *Studien zur Geschichte des byzantinischen Bilderstreites*, Breslau, 1929.

L. Ouspensky, "Quelques considérations au sujet de l'iconographie de la Pentecôte", in *Le messager de l'Exarchat Russe en Europe Occidentale*, 33-34, 1960.

L. Ouspensky/V. Lossky, *The Meaning of Icons*, transl. by G.E.H. Palmer-E. Kadloubovsky, Olten, 1969.

L. Ouspensky, *Theology of the Icon*, New York, St Vladimir's Theological Seminary Press, 1978.

L. Ouspensky, *Théologie de l'icône dans l'Eglise orthodoxe*, Paris, Cerf, 1980.

L. Ouspensky, "Iconography of the Descent of the Holy Spirit", in *St Vladimir's Theological Quarterly*, 4, 1987, pp.309-347.

N. Ozoline, "The Theology of the Icon", in *St Vladimir's Theological Quarterly*, 4, 1987, pp.297-308.

E. Panofsky, *Idea: a Concept in Art Theory*, transl. Joseph J.S. Peake, Leipzig, B. Teuber Verlag, 1924; rept. Harper Icon Editions, 1968.

A. Papadakis, "Hagiography in Relation to Iconoclasm", in *The Greek Orthodox Theological Review*, 14, 1969, pp.159-180.

Ch. Papakonstantinou, "The Triumph of the Icon as Triumph of Orthodoxy. The Icon — Element of Identity of Orthodoxy", in *The Theology of Icon*, Acts of the 18th Meeting of the Clergy of the Greek Orthodox Metropolie of Western Germany, Bonn, 1984, pp.22-29 (in Greek).

Ch. Patrinellis, *Monastery of Stavronikita*, Athens, 1974 (in Greek).

Archbishop Paul of Finland, *The Faith We Hold*, New York, St Vladimir's Seminary Press, 1980.

P.G., *Patrologiae cursus completus. Series Graeca*, ed. J.P. Migne, Paris, 1857ff.

Vl. Pheidas, *The Border of Byzantine Painting*, Athens, 1982 (in Greek).

B. Photiades, *Iznik the Old Nicea*, Istanbul (mimeographed).

P.L., *Patrologiae cursus completus, Series Latina*, ed. J.P. Migne, Paris, 1844ff.

G. Poggi, *Michelangelo*, Firenze, 1951.

J.J. Politt, *The Ancient View of Greek Art: Criticism, History and Terminology*, New Haven, Yale University Press, 1974.

E. Ponsoye, *Saint Damascène. La foi orthodoxe suivie de défense des icônes*, Paris, 1966.

M. Quenot, *L'icône*, Paris, Cerf/Fides, 1987.

I. Reau, *World History of Art*, Athens, 1955.

P. Reina, *La prospettiva*, Milan, 1940.

I. Reznikov, "La transcendance, le corps et l'icône dans les fondements de l'art sacré et de la liturgie", in *Nicée II (787-1987), Colloque Paris 1986*, eds F. Boespflig and N. Lossky, Paris, 1987.

D. Rousseau, *L'icône splendeur de ton visage*, Desclée de Brouwer, 1981.

S. Runcimau, *Byzantine Style and Civilization*, Penguin Books Ltd, 1975.

S. Salaville, "L'iconographie de Sept Conciles Oecuméniques", in *Echos d'Orient*, 24, 1925, pp.445-470.

S. Scaglia, *Manuel d'archéologie chrétienne*, Turin, 1916.

E. Sendler, *L'icône: Image de l'invisible, élément de théologie esthétique et technique*, Collection Christus no. 54, Desclée de Brouwer, 1981.

G. Schiller, *Iconography of Christian Art*, London, 1971.

A. Schmemann, "Byzantium, Iconoclasm and the Monks", in *St Vladimir's Theological Quarterly*, 3, 1959, pp.18-34.

J.B. Schömann, "'Eikon' in den Schriften des Heiligen Athanasius", in *Scholastik*, 16, 1941, pp.335ff.

Ch. Schönborn, OP, *L'icône du Christ. Fondements théologiques élaborés entre le premier et deuxième Concile de Nicée (325-787)*, Fribourg, 1978.

Ch. Schönborn, "Les icônes qui ne sont pas faites de main d'homme", in *La vie spirituelle*, 140, 1986, pp.679-692.

Ch. Schug-Wille, "Art and the Byzantine Word", transl. E.M. Hatt, *Panorama of World Art*, New York, Harry N. Abrams Inc., 1969.

A. Soljenitsyne, *Des voix sous les décombres*, Ed. Les Seuil, 1974.

H. Stern, *L'art byzantin*, Paris, 1966.

P. Stockmeier, "Die Entscheidungen des 7. Oekumenischen Konzils und die Stellung der Römisch-Katholischen Kirche zu den Bildern", in *Orthodoxes Forum*, I/2, 1987.

J. Stuart, *Icons*, Faber & Faber, 1975.

A. Stylianou and J. Stylianou, *The Painted Churches of Cyprus*, London, 1985.

A. Tarkowsky, *André Roublev*, Editeurs Réunis, 1970.

M. Torelli, "Il monumento teatino di C. Lucius Storax al Museo di Chieti", in *Studi Miscellanei*, 10, 1966, pp.61-84.

E.N. Trabetskoi, *Icons: Theology in Color*, St Vladimir's Seminary Press, New York, 1973.

J. Travis, *In Defense of the Faith: the Theology of Patriarch Nicephorus of Constantinople*, Greek Orthodox School of Theology, Brookline, MA, 1984.

E.W. Tristram, *English Medieval Wall Paintings*, Oxford, 1944.

J. Tyriak, *Jahreskranz der Güte. Das Jahr der Kirche*, Mainz, 1953.

P. Underwood, *The Kariye Djami*, Vols I-III, Pantheon Books, 1966.

A. Vyse, *The Art and Architecture of Medieval Russia*, Norman, OK, University of Oklahoma Press, 1967.

C. Walter, "L'iconographie des Conciles dans la tradition byzantine", in *Archives de l'Orient Chrétien*, 13, 1970, Paris.

C. Walter, "Death in Byzantine Iconography", in *Eastern Churches Review*, 8/2, 1976, pp.113-127.

C. Walter, "Church Appointments in Byzantine Iconography", in *Eastern Churches Review*, 10/1-2, 1978, pp.108-125.

T. Ware, "The Theology of the Icon: a Short Anthology", in *Eastern Churches Review*, 8/1, 1976, pp.3-10.

X. Weidle, *Les icônes byzantines et russes*, Florence, 1950.

K. Weitzmann, *The Icon*, Chatto & Windus, 1978.

K. Weitzmann, *The Icon*, Evans Brothers Ltd., 1982.

E. Wellesz, *The Vienna Genesis*, London, 1960.

Th. Whittemore, *The Mosaics of St Sophia at Istanbul: the Mosaics of the Narthex*, Oxford, 1933.

R. Williams, "Christian Art and Cultural Pluralism: Reflections on 'L'art de l'icône' by Paul Evdokimov", in *Eastern Churches Review*, 8/1, 1976, pp.38-44.

J. Wilpert, *Pitture delle catacombe*, Rome, 1903.

J. Wilpert, *I sarcofagi cristiani antichi*, Rome, 1929.

O. Wulff, *Altchristliche und Byzantinische Kunst*, I, Berlin, 1914.

A. Xyngopoulos, *"Icons" in Byzantine Art*, Athens, 1954.

B. Zevi, *Architecture as Space*, transl. Milton Gendel, ed. Joseph A. Barry, New York, Horizon Press, 1957.

V.M. Zhivov, "The Mystagogia of Maximus the Confessor and the Development of the Byzantine Theology of the Image", in *St Vladimir's Theological Quarterly*, 4, 1987, pp.349-376.

Contributors

Bishop Ambrosius of Joensuu (Orthodox Church in Finland) is a member of WCC Faith and Order Commission, professor at the Theological Seminary, Kuopio, Finland, and member of many international bilateral dialogues.

Archbishop Athanasios (Coptic Orthodox Chuurch) is a member of the Executive and Central Committees of the World Council of Churches.

Rev. Viken Aykazian (Armenian Apostolic Church, Catholicosate of Etchmiadzin) is Rector of the Armenian Church in Geneva and All Switzerland, a member of the Orthodox Advisory Group of the Commission on World Mission and Evangelism, and a member of the WCC Central Committee.

Rev. Dr Alain Blancy (Reformed Church in France), former lecturer at the Ecumenical Institute Bossey, is now a pastor in Lyons, France.

Rev. Canon Anthony C. Bridge (Church of England) is Dean of Guildford Cathedral, England.

Rev. Dr Emilio Castro (Methodist Church, Uruguay) has been general secretary of the World Council of Churches since 1984.

Metropolitan Chrysostomos of Myra (Konstantinidis) (Ecumenical Patriarchate) is a member of the Holy Synod of the Ecumenical Patriarchate, professor of systematic theology at the Theological School of Halki, and vice-moderator of the WCC Central Committee. He is also a former vice-moderator of the Faith and Order Commission.

Rev. Dr Dan-Ilie Ciobotea (Romanian Orthodox Church), formerly lecturer at the Ecumenical Institute Bossey, is now counsellor to the Patriarch of Romania.

Very Rev. Prof. Dr George Dragas (Greek Orthodox Archdiocese of Thyateira and Great Britain/Ecumenical Patriarchate) is an Orthodox priest and professor of patristics at the University of Durham, England, and member of the Reformed/Orthodox and Anglican/Orthodox international dialogues as well as of the WCC Commission on Faith and Order.

Archpriest Dr Georges Drobot (Archdiocese of Russian parishes in Western Europe/ Ecumenical Patriarchate) is an Orthodox priest and iconographer in Paris, France.

225

Ms Jeanne de la Ferrières (Archdiocese of Russian parishes in Western Europe/ Ecumenical Patriarchate) is a young Orthodox theologian, graduated from the Orthodox Theological Institute St Sergius, Paris, France, and an iconographer.

Mgr Eleuterio Fortino (Roman Catholic Church) is under-secretary in the Pontifical Council for Promoting Christian Unity and a member of the Roman Catholic/Orthodox international dialogue.

Metropolitan Paulos Mar Gregorios (Malankara Syrian Orthodox Church) is head of the Delhi Orthodox Centre, India, and a WCC president since 1983.

Archpriest Prof. Vladimir Ivanov (Russian Orthodox Church) is an Orthodox priest and professor at the Moscow Theological Academy, USSR.

Rev. Dr Irmgard Kindt-Siegwalt (Evangelical Church in Germany: Lutheran) is an ordained pastor and an executive secretary in the Secretariat of the WCC Commission on Faith and Order.

Prof. Dr Georg Kretschmar (Evangelical Church in Germany: Lutheran) is professor of Church history and New Testament at the Faculty of Protestant Theology, University of Munich, and secretary of the international Lutheran/Orthodox dialogue.

Bishop Dr William H. Lazareth (Evangelical Lutheran Church in America) is Bishop of the Metropolitan New York Synod and former director of the Secretariat of the WCC Faith and Order Commission.

Very Rev. Prof. Dr Gennadios Limouris (Ecumenical Patriarchate) is an Orthodox priest on the staff of the Secretariat of the WCC Commission on Faith and Order, and professor at the University of Strasbourg, France.

Sister Minke (Community of Grandchamp) is the mother superior of the Reformed Community in Grandchamp, Switzerland; *Sisters Albertine* and *Olga* belong to the same Community.

Archpriest Dr Nicolas Ozoline (Archdiocese of Russian parishes in Western Europe/ Ecumenical Patriarchate) is an Orthodox priest, professor at the Orthodox Theological Institute St Sergius in Paris, France, and responsible for the Orthodox programmes of the French television.

Archbishop Paul of Karelia and All Finland (Orthodox Church in Finland) was formerly head of the Orthodox Church in Finland. He died in 1987.

Prof. Vittorio Peri (Roman Catholic Church) is director of the Biblioteca Vaticana, Vatican City, Vatican.

Prof. Vlassios Pheidas (Church of Greece), is professor of Church history at the Faculty of Theology, University of Athens, a member of the Faith and Order Commission, of the Working Group of the Programme to Combat Racism (WCC), and of the joint Lutheran-Orthodox dialogue.

Ms Teny Pirri-Simonian (Armenian Apostolic Church, Cilicia) is a sociologist, former executive secretary of the department of interchurch aid and development services of the Middle East Council of Churches, and now responsible for development education in the WCC's Sub-unit on Education.

Prof. Dr Todor Sabev (Bulgarian Orthodox Church) is professor of Church history at the Theological Academy of St Clement of Ochrid in Sofia, Bulgaria, and deputy general secretary of the WCC, Geneva.

Ms Renate Sbeghen (Evangelical Church of Germany: Lutheran) is administrative assistant in the Secretariat of the WCC Commission on Faith and Order.

Fr Christoph Schönborn OP (Roman Catholic Church) is a Dominican priest and professor of patristics at the Faculty of Theology, University of Fribourg, Switzerland.

Prof. Constantine Scouteris (Church of Greece) is professor of patristics at the Faculty of Theology, University of Athens, and a member of the international Anglican/Orthodox dialogue.

Mr François Sejourné (Roman Catholic Church) is a lay person working at the Benedictine Monastery, Chevetogne, Belgium.

List of Plates

Plate 1: Baptism of Jesus, mosaic, 15th century, monastery of Daphni, Greece, copy presented to the WCC by Ecumenical Patriarch Athenagoras in 1967

Plate 2: Icon of the resurrection, mosaic, 14th century, Chora monastery (now the Kariye museum), Istanbul

Plate 3: Icon of Pentecost, 1988, by Vassiliki Papantoniou, Greece

Plate 4: Icon of St Paul's vision at Troas (Acts 16:9), 1975, by Rallis Kopsidis, St Paul's Church, Orthodox Centre of the Ecumenical Patriarchate, Chambésy, Geneva, Switzerland

Plate 5: Icon of the nativity, 16th century, monastery of Meteoras, Greece

Plate 6: Icon of the prophet Elias, first half of the 13th century, monastery of St John the Labadistos, Kalopanaghiotis, Cyprus

Plate 7: Icon of St Sergius the Radonez, 15th century, St Sergius Lavra, Zagorsk, USSR

Plate 8: Icon of the Holy Trinity, 15th century, Andrei Rublev, Hermitage National Museum, Leningrad, USSR

Plate 9: Icon of St Herman of Alaska, contemporary, Valamo monastery, Finland

Plate 10: "Law and Grace", c. 1535, Lukas Cranach, Germanisches Nationalmuseum, Nürnberg, Federal Republic of Germany

Plate 11: The burning bush, 1970, children's painting, France

Plate 12: Stone cross or khatchkar, 12th century, Holy See of Etchmiadzin, Armenia, USSR

Plate 13: Nativity of Jesus, baptism of Jesus, Adam and Eve in paradise: stained-glass windows, modern, First Missionary Methodist Church, Kinshasa, Zaire

Plate 14: Wall painting, 15th century, Monastery of Neamt, Moldavia, Romania

Plate 15: Monk iconographers, Holy Mount Athos, Greece

Plate 16: Coptic icon of Jesus Christ, contemporary, Ecumenical Centre, Geneva, Switzerland